David Hume

The History of England from the Invasion of Julius Caesar to the Revolution in 1688

Volume III.

David Hume

The History of England from the Invasion of Julius Caesar to the Revolution in 1688
Volume III.

ISBN/EAN: 9783742816405

Manufactured in Europe, USA, Canada, Australia, Japa

Cover: Foto ©ninafisch / pixelio.de

Manufactured and distributed by brebook publishing software (www.brebook.com)

David Hume

The History of England from the Invasion of Julius Caesar to the Revolution in 1688

THE
HISTORY
OF
ENGLAND,

FROM THE

INVASION OF JULIUS CÆSAR

TO

The REVOLUTION in 1688.

In EIGHT VOLUMES.

By DAVID HUME, Esq;

VOL. III.

A NEW EDITION, with the AUTHOR's last
CORRECTIONS and IMPROVEMENTS.

To which is prefixed,
A short ACCOUNT of his LIFE, written by himself.

LONDON:
Printed for T. CADELL, in the Strand.
MDCCLXXXVI.

CONTENTS

OF THE

THIRD VOLUME

CHAP. XVII.

RICHARD II.

Government during the minority——Insurrection of the common people——Discontents of the barons——Civil commotions——Expulsion or execution of the king's ministers——Cabals of the duke of Glocester——Murder of the duke of Glocester——Banishment of Henry duke of Hereford——Return of Henry——General insurrection——Deposition of the king——His murder——His character——Miscellaneous transactions during this reign.
Page 1

CHAP. XVIII.

HENRY IV.

Title of the king——An insurrection——An insurrection in Wales——The earl of Northumberland rebels——Battle of Shrewsbury——State of Scotland——Parliamentary transactions——Death and character of the king. 61

CONTENTS.

CHAP. XIX.

HENRY V.

The king's former disorders —— His reformation —— The Lollards —— Punishment of Lord Cobham —— State of France —— Invasion of that kingdom —— Battle of Azincour —— State of France —— New invasion of France —— Assassination of the duke of Burgundy —— Treaty of Troye —— Marriage of the king —— His death —— and character —— Miscellaneous transactions during this reign. Page 15

CHAP. XX.

HENRY VI.

Government during the minority —— State of France —— Military operations —— Battle of Verneüil —— Siege of Orleans —— The maid of Orleans —— The siege of Orleans raised —— The king of France crowned at Rheims —— Prudence of the duke of Bedford —— Execution of the maid of Orleans —— Defection of the duke of Burgundy —— Death of the duke of Bedford —— Decline of the English in France —— Truce with France —— Marriage of the king with Margaret of Anjou —— Murder of the duke of Glocester —— State of France —— Renewal of the war with France —— The English expelled France. 123

CHAP.

CONTENTS.

CHAP. XXI.

Claim of the duke of York to the crown——The earl of Warwic——Impeachment of the duke of Suffolk——His banishment——and death——Popular insurrection——The parties of York and Lancaster——First armament of the duke of York——First battle of St. Albans——Battle of Blore-heath——of Northampton——A parliament——Battle of Wakefield——Death of the duke of York——Battle of Mortimer's Cross——Second battle of St. Albans——Edward IV. assumes the crown——Miscellaneous transactions of this reign. Page 179

CHAP. XXII.

EDWARD IV.

Battle of Touton——Henry escapes into Scotland——A parliament——Battle of Hexham——Henry taken prisoner, and confined to the Tower——King's marriage with the Lady Elizabeth Grey——Warwic disgusted——Alliance with Burgundy——Insurrection in Yorkshire——Battle of Banbury——Warwic and Clarence banished——Warwic and Clarence return——Edward IV. expelled——Henry VI. restored——Edward IV. returns——Battle of Barnet, and death of Warwic——Battle of Tewkesbury, and murder of prince Edward——Death of Henry VI.——Invasion of France——Peace of Pecquigni——Trial and execution of the duke of Clarence——Death and character of Edward IV. 216

CONTENTS.

CHAP. XXIII.
EDWARD V. and RICHARD III.

Edward V.—*State of the court*—*The earl of Rivers arrested*—*Duke of Glocester protector*—*Execution of Lord Hastings*—*The protector aims at the crown*—*Assumes the crown*—*Murder of Edward V. and of the duke of York*—*Richard III.*—*Duke of Buckingham discontented*—*The earl of Richmond*—*Buckingham executed*—*Invasion by the earl of Richmond*—*Battle of Bosworth*—*Death and character of Richard III.* Page 266

CHAP. XXIV.
HENRY VII.

Accession of Henry VII.—*His title to the crown*—*King's prejudice against the house of York*—*His joyful reception in London*—*His coronation*—*Sweating sickness*—*A parliament*—*Entail of the crown*—*King's marriage*—*An insurrection*—*Discontents of the people*—*Lambert Simnel*—*Revolt of Ireland*—*Intrigues of the duchess of Burgundy*—*Lambert Simnel invades England*—*Battle of Stoke.* 307

CHAP.

CONTENTS.

CHAP. XXV.

State of foreign affairs——State of Scotland——of Spain——of the Low Countries——of France—of Britanny——French invasion of Britanny——French embassy to England——Dissimulation of the French court——An insurrection in the north—suppressed——King sends forces into Britanny——Annexation of Britanny to France—A parliament——War with France——Invasion of France——Peace with France——Perkin Warbec——His imposture——He is avowed by the duchess of Burgundy——and by many of the English nobility——Trial and execution of Stanley——A parliament. Page 332

CHAP. XXVI.

Perkin retires to Scotland——Insurrection in the west——Battle of Blackheath——Truce with Scotland——Perkin taken prisoner——Perkin executed——The earl of Warwic executed——Marriage of prince Arthur with Catherine of Arragon——His death——Marriage of the princess Margaret with the king of Scotland——Oppressions of the people——A parliament——Arrival of the king of Castile——Intrigues of the earl of Suffolk——Sickness of the king——His death——and character——His laws. 370

CHAP.

CONTENTS.

CHAP. XXVII.

HENRY VIII.

Popularity of the new king——His ministers——Punishment of Empson and Dudley—King's marriage——Foreign affairs——Julius II.——League of Cambray——War with France——Expedition to Fontarabia——Deceit of Ferdinand——Return of the English——Leo X.——A parliament——War with Scotland—Wolsey minister——His character——Invasion of France——Battle of Guinegate——Battle of Flouden——Peace with France.   Page 408

THE HISTORY OF ENGLAND.

CHAP. XVII.

RICHARD II.

Government during the minority——Insurrection of the common people——Discontents of the barons——Civil commotions——Expulsion or execution of the king's ministers——Cabals of the duke of Glocester——Murder of the duke of Glocester——Banishment of Henry duke of Hereford——Return of Henry——General insurrection——Deposition of the king——His murder——His character——Miscellaneous transactions during this reign.

THE parliament, which was summoned soon after the king's accession, was both elected and assembled in tranquillity; and the great change, from a sovereign of consummate wisdom and experience to a boy of eleven years of age, was not immediately felt by

CHAP.
XVII.

1377.

by the people. The habits of order and obedience which the barons had been taught during the long reign of Edward, still influenced them; and the authority of the king's three uncles, the dukes of Lancaster, York, and Glocester, sufficed to repress, for a time, the turbulent spirit to which that order, in a weak reign, was so often subject. The dangerous ambition too of these princes themselves was checked by the plain and undeniable title of Richard, by the declaration of it made in parliament, and by the affectionate regard which the people bore to the memory of his father, and which was naturally transferred to the young sovereign upon the throne. The different characters also of these three princes rendered them a counterpoize to each other; and it was natural to expect, that any dangerous designs which might be formed by one brother would meet with opposition from the others. Lancaster, whose age and experience, and authority under the late king, gave him the ascendant among them, though his integrity seemed not proof against great temptations, was neither of an enterprizing spirit, nor of a popular and engaging temper. York was indolent, unactive, and of slender capacity. Glocester was turbulent, bold, and popular; but being the youngest of the family, was restained by the power and authority of his elder brothers. There appeared, therefore, no circumstance in the domestic situation of England which might endanger the public peace, or give any immediate apprehensions to the lovers of their country.

But as Edward, though he had fixed the succession to the crown, had taken no care to establish a plan of government during the minority of his grandson, it behoved the parliament to supply this defect: And the house of commons distinguished themselves by taking the lead on the occasion. This house, which had been rising to consideration during the whole course of the late reign,

naturally

naturally received an accession of power during the minority; and as it was now becoming a scene of business, the members chose, for the first time, a speaker, who might preserve order in their debates, and maintain those forms which are requisite in all numerous assemblies. Peter de la Mare was the man pitched on; the same person that had been imprisoned, and detained in custody by the late king, for his freedom of speech in attacking the mistress and the ministers of that prince. But though this election discovered a spirit of liberty in the commons, and was followed by farther attacks both on these ministers and on Alice Pierce [a], they were still too sensible of their great inferiority, to assume at first any immediate share in the administration of government, or the care of the king's person. They were content to apply by petition to the lords for that purpose, and desire them, both to appoint a council of nine, who might direct the public business, and to chuse men of virtuous life and conversation, who might inspect the conduct and education of the young prince. The lords complied with the first part of this request, and elected the bishops of London, Carlisle, and Salisbury, the earls of Marche and Stafford, Sir Richard de Stafford, Sir Henry le Scrope, Sir John Devereux, and Sir Hugh Segrave, to whom they gave authority, for a year, to conduct the ordinary course of business [b]. But as to the regulation of the king's household, they declined interposing in an office which, they said, both was invidious in itself, and might prove disagreeable to his majesty.

The commons, as they acquired more courage, ventured to proceed a step farther in their applications. They presented a petition, in which they prayed the king to check the prevailing custom among the barons, of forming

[a] Walsing. p. 150.   [b] Rymer, vol. vii. p. 161.

illegal confederacies, and supporting each other, as well as men of inferior rank, in the violations of law and justice. They received from the throne a general and an obliging answer to this petition: But another part of their application, that all the great officers should, during the king's minority, be appointed by parliament, which seemed to require the concurrence of the commons, as well as that of the upper house, in the nomination, was not complied with: The lords alone assumed the power of appointing these officers: The commons tacitly acquiesced in the choice; and thought that, for the present, they themselves had proceeded a sufficient length, if they but advanced their pretensions, though rejected, of interposing in these more important matters of state.

On this foot then the government stood. The administration was conducted entirely in the king's name: No regency was expressly appointed: The nine counsellors and the great officers, named by the peers, did their duty, each in his respective department: And the whole system was for some years kept together by the secret authority of the king's uncles, especially of the duke of Lancaster, who was in reality the regent.

The parliament was dissolved, after the commons had represented the necessity of their being re-assembled once every year, as appointed by law; and after having elected two citizens as their treasurers, to receive and disburse the produce of two fifteenths and tenths, which they had voted to the crown. In the other parliaments called during the minority, the commons still discover a strong spirit of freedom, and a sense of their own authority, which, without breeding any disturbance, tended to secure their independence, and that of the people[c].

[c] See note [A] at the end of the volume.

EDWARD

RICHARD II.

EDWARD had left his grandson involved in many dangerous wars. The pretensions of the duke of Lancaster to the crown of Castile made that kingdom still persevere in hostilities against England. Scotland, whose throne was now filled by Robert Stuart, nephew to David Bruce, and the first prince of that family, maintained such close connections with France, that war with one crown almost inevitably produced hostilities with the other. The French monarch, whose prudent conduct had acquired him the sirname of *wise*, as he had already baffled all the experience and valour of the two Edwards, was likely to prove a dangerous enemy to a minor king: But his genius, which was not naturally enterprising, led him not, at present, to give any disturbance to his neighbours; and he laboured, besides, under many difficulties at home, which it was necessary for him to surmount before he could think of making conquests in a foreign country. England was master of Calais, Bourdeaux, and Bayonne; had lately acquired possession of Cherbourg from the cession of the king of Navarre, and of Brest from that of the duke of Britanny [d]; and having thus an easy entrance into France from every quarter, was able, even in its present situation, to give disturbance to his government. Before Charles could remove the English from these important posts, he died in the flower of his age, and left his kingdom to a minor son, who bore the name of Charles VI.

CHAP. XVII.
1377.

MEANWHILE the war with France was carried on in a manner somewhat languid, and produced no enterpize of great lustre or renown. Sir Hugh Calverly, governor of Calais, making an inroad into Picardy with a detachment of the garrison, set fire to Boulogne [e]. The duke of Lancaster conducted an army into Britanny, but returned

1378.

[d] Rymer, vol. vii. p. 190.   [e] Walsing. p. 209.

without

CHAP.
XVII.

1380.

without being able to perform any thing memorable. In a subsequent year, the duke of Glocester marched out of Calais with a body of 2000 cavalry, and 8000 infantry; and scrupled not with his small army, to enter into the heart of France, and to continue his ravages through Picardy, Champaigne, the Brie, the Beausse, the Gatinois, the Orleanois, till he reached his allies in the province of Britanny[f]. The duke of Burgundy, at the head of a more considerable army, came within sight of him; but the French were so overawed by the former successes of the English, that no superiority of numbers could tempt them to venture a pitched battle with the troops of that nation. As the duke of Britanny, soon after the arrival of these succours, formed an accommodation with the court of France, this enterprize also proved in the issue unsuccessful, and made no durable impression upon the enemy.

THE expences of these armaments, and the usual want of œconomy attending a minority, much exhausted the English treasury, and obliged the parliament, besides making some alterations in the council, to impose a new and unusual tax of three groats on every person, male and female, above fifteen years of age; and they ordained that, in levying that tax, the opulent should relieve the poor by an equitable compensation. This imposition produced a mutiny, which was singular in its circumstances. All history abounds with examples where the great tyrannize over the meaner sort: But here the lowest populace rose against their rulers, committed the most cruel ravages upon them, and took vengeance for all former oppressions.

1381.

THE faint dawn of the arts and of good government in that age had excited the minds of the populace,

[f] Froissard, liv. II, chap. 50, 51. Walsing. p. 239.

In different states of Europe, to wish for a better condition, and to murmur against those chains which the laws, enacted by the haughty nobility and gentry, had so long imposed upon them. The commotions of the people in Flanders, the mutiny of the peasants in France, were the natural effects of this growing spirit of independence; and the report of these events being brought into England, where personal slavery, as we learn from Froissard[g], was more general than in any other country in Europe, had prepared the minds of the multitude for an insurrection. One John Ball also, a seditious preacher, who affected low popularity, went about the country, and inculcated on his audience the principles of the first origin of mankind from one common stock, their equal right to liberty and to all the goods of nature, the tyranny of artificial distinctions, and the abuses which had arisen from the degradation of the more considerable part of the species, and the aggrandizement of a few insolent rulers[h]. These doctrines, so agreeable to the populace, and so conformable to the ideas of primitive equality which are engraven in the hearts of all men, were greedily received by the multitude; and scattered the sparks of that sedition, which the present tax raised into a conflagration[i].

The imposition of three groats a head had been farmed out to tax-gatherers in each county, who levied the money on the people with rigour; and the clause, of making the rich ease their poorer neighbours of some share of the burden, being so vague and undeterminate, had, doubtless, occasioned many partialities, and made the people more

Insurrection of the common people.

[g] Liv. II. chap. 74.   [h] Froissard, liv. ii. chap. 74. Walsingham, p. 275.
[i] There were two verses at that time in the mouths of all the common people, which, in spite of prejudice, one cannot but regard with some degree of approbation:

When Adam delv'd and Eve span,
Where was then the gentleman?

CHAP. XVII.
1381.

sensible of the unequal lot which fortune had assigned them in the distribution of her favours. The first disorder was raised by a blacksmith in a village of Essex. The tax-gatherers came to this man's shop while he was at work; and they demanded payment for his daughter, whom he asserted to be below the age assigned by the statute. One of these fellows offered to produce a very indecent proof to the contrary, and at the same time laid hold of the maid: Which the father resenting, immediately knocked out the ruffian's brains with his hammer. The bystanders applauded the action, and exclaimed, that it was full time for the people to take vengeance on their tyrants, and to vindicate their native liberty. They immediately flew to arms: The whole neighbourhood joined in the sedition: The flame spread in an instant over the county: It soon propagated itself into that of Kent, of Hertford, Surry, Sussex, Suffolk, Norfolk, Cambridge, and Lincoln. Before the government had the least warning of the danger, the disorder had grown beyond controul or opposition: The populace had shaken off all regard to their former masters: And being headed by the most audacious and criminal of their associates, who assumed the feigned names of Wat Tyler, Jack Straw, Hob Carter, and Tom Miller, by which they were fond of denoting their mean origin, they committed every where the most outrageous violence on such of the gentry or nobility as had the misfortune to fall into their hands.

22th June.

THE mutinous populace, amounting to a hundred thousand men, assembled on Blackheath under their leaders, Tyler and Straw; and as the princess of Wales, the king's mother, returning from a pilgrimage to Canterbury, passed through the midst of them, they insulted her attendants; and some of the most insolent among them, to shew their purpose of levelling all mankind, forced kisses from her; but they allowed her to continue her journey,

RICHARD II.

journey, without attempting any farther injury[l]. They sent a message to the king, who had taken shelter in the Tower; and they desired a conference with him. Richard sailed down the river in a barge for that purpose; but on his approaching the shore, he saw such symptoms of tumult and insolence, that he put back and returned to that fortress[m]. The seditious peasants, meanwhile, favoured by the populace of London, had broken into the city; had burned the duke of Lancaster's palace of the Savoy; cut off the heads of all the gentlemen whom they laid hold off; expressed a particular animosity against the lawyers and attornies; and pillaged the warehouses of the rich merchants[n]. A great body of them quartered themselves at Mile-end; and the king, finding no defence in the Tower, which was weakly garrisoned, and ill supplied with provisions, was obliged to go out to them, and ask their demands. They required a general pardon, the abolition of slavery, freedom of commerce in market-towns without toll or impost, and a fixed rent on lands, instead of the services due by villenage. These requests, which, though extremely reasonable in themselves, the nation was not sufficiently prepared to receive, and which it was dangerous to have extorted by violence, were, however, complied with; charters to that purpose were granted them; and this body immediately dispersed, and returned to their several homes[o].

During this transaction, another body of the rebels had broken into the Tower; had murdered Simon Sudbury, the primate, and chancellor, with Sir Robert Hales, the treasurer, and some other persons of distinction; and continued their ravages in the city[p]. The king, passing along Smithfield, very slenderly guarded, met with Wat

[l] Froissard, liv. ii. chap. 74. chap. 76. Walsingham, p. 248, 249.
[m] Ibid. chap. 75.
[n] Ibid.
[o] Froissard, liv. ii. chap. 77.
[p] Walsingham, p. 250, 251.

Tyler,

CHAP. XVII.
1381.

Tyler, at the head of these rioters, and entered into a conference with him. Tyler, having ordered his companions to retire till he should give them a signal, after which they were to murder all the company except the king himself, whom they were to detain prisoner, feared not to come into the midst of the royal retinue. He there behaved himself in such a manner, that Walworth, the mayor of London, not able to bear his insolence, drew his sword, and struck him so violent a blow as brought him to the ground, where he was instantly dispatched by others of the king's attendants. The mutineers, seeing their leader fall, prepared themselves for revenge; and this whole company, with the king himself, had undoubtedly perished on the spot had it not been for an extraordinary presence of mind which Richard discovered on the occasion. He ordered his company to stop; he advanced alone towards the enraged multitude; and accosting them with an affable and intrepid countenance, he asked them, "What is the meaning of this disorder, my good people? Are ye angry that ye have lost your leader? I am your king: I will be your leader." The populace, overawed by his presence, implicitly followed him: He led them into the fields, to prevent any disorder which might have arisen by their continuing in the city: Being there joined by Sir Robert Knolles, and a body of well-armed veteran soldiers, who had been secretly drawn together, he strictly prohibited that officer from falling on the rioters, and committing an undistinguished slaughter upon them; and he peaceably dismissed them with the same charters which had been granted to their fellows [dagger]. Soon after, the nobility and gentry, hearing of the king's danger, in which they were all involved, flocked to London with their adherents and retainers; and Richard took the field at the head of an army 40,000

[dagger] Froissard, vol. ii. chap. 77. Walsingham, p. 250. Knyghton, p. 2637.

strong

strong'. It then behoved all the rebels to submit: The charters of enfranchisement and pardon were revoked by parliament; the low people were reduced to the same slavish condition as before; and several of the ringleaders were severely punished for the late disorders. Some were even executed without process or form of law'. It was pretended, that the intentions of the mutineers had been to seize the king's person, to carry him through England at their head, to murder all the nobility, gentry, and lawyers, and even all the bishops and priests, except the mendicant friars; to dispatch afterwards the king himself; and having thus reduced all to a level, to order the kingdom at their pleasure'. It is not impossible, but many of them, in the delirium of their first success, might have formed such projects: But of all the evils incident to human society, the insurrections of the populace, when not raised and supported by persons of higher quality, are the least to be dreaded: The mischiefs, consequent to an abolition of all rank and distinction, become so great, that they are immediately felt, and soon bring affairs back to their former order and arrangement.

A YOUTH of sixteen (which was at this time the king's age), who had discovered so much courage, presence of mind, and address, and had so dextrously eluded the violence of this tumult, raised great expectations in the nation; and it was natural to hope, that he would, in the course of his life, equal the glories which had so uniformly attended his father and his grandfather in all their undertakings. But in proportion as Richard advanced in years, these hopes vanished; and his want of capacity, at least of solid judgment, appeared in every enterprize which he attempted. The Scots, sensible of their own deficiency in cavalry, had applied to the regency of

r Walsingham, p. 267.   s 5 Rich. II. cap. ult. as quoted in the Observations on ancient Statutes, p. 262.   t Walsingham, p. 265.

Charles

CHAP.
XVII.

1385.

Charles VI.; and John de Vienne, admiral of France, had been sent over with a body of 1500 men at arms, to support them in their incursions against the English. The danger was now deemed by the king's uncles somewhat serious; and a numerous army of 60,000 men was levied; and they marched into Scotland, with Richard himself at their head. The Scots did not pretend to make resistance against so great a force: They abandoned without scruple their country to be pillaged and destroyed by the enemy: And when de Vienne expressed his surprize at this plan of operations, they told him, that all their cattle was driven into the forests and fastnesses; that their houses and other goods were of small value; and that they well knew how to compensate any losses which they might sustain in that respect, by making an incursion into England. Accordingly, when Richard entered Scotland by Berwic and the east coast, the Scots, to the number of 30,000 men, attended by the French, entered the borders of England by the west, and carrying their ravages through Cumberland, Westmoreland, and Lancashire, collected a rich booty, and then returned in tranquillity to their own country. Richard meanwhile advanced towards Edinburgh, and destroyed in his way all the towns and villages on each side of him: He reduced that city to ashes: He treated in the same manner, Perth, Dundee, and other places in the low countries; but when he was advised to march towards the west coast, to await there the return of the enemy, and to take revenge on them for their devastations, his impatience to return to England, and enjoy his usual pleasures and amusements, outweighed every consideration; and he led back his army, without effecting any thing by all these mighty preparations. The Scots, soon after, finding the heavy bodies of French cavalry very useless in that desultory kind of war to which they confined themselves, treated

treated their allies so ill, that the French returned home, much disgusted with the country, and with the manners of its inhabitants [n]. And the English, though they regretted the indolence and levity of their king, saw themselves for the future secured against any dangerous invasion from that quarter.

But it was so material an interest of the French court to wrest the sea-port towns from the hands of their enemy, that they resolved to attempt it by some other expedient, and found no means so likely as an invasion of England itself. They collected a great fleet and army at Sluise; for the Flemings were now in alliance with them: All the nobility of France were engaged in this enterprize: The English were kept in alarm: Great preparations were made for the reception of the invaders: And though the dispersion of the French ships by a storm, and the taking of many of them by the English, before the embarkation of the troops, freed the kingdom from the present danger, the king and council were fully sensible, that this perilous situation might every moment return upon them [o].

There were two circumstances, chiefly, which engaged the French at this time to think of such attempts. The one was the absence of the duke of Lancaster, who had carried into Spain the flower of the English military force, in prosecution of his vain claim to the crown of Castile; an enterprize in which, after some promising success, he was finally disappointed: The other was, the violent dissentions and disorders which had taken place in the English government.

The subjection in which Richard was held by his uncles, particularly by the duke of Glocester, a prince of

[n] Froissard, liv. ii, chap. 149, 150, &c. liv. iii. chap. 52. Walsingham, p. 326, 327. [o] Froissard, liv. iii. chap. 41. 53. Walsingham, p. 322, 323.

CHAP. XVII.

1386.

ambition and genius, though it was not unsuitable to his years and slender capacity, was extremely disagreeable to his violent temper; and he soon attempted to shake off the yoke imposed upon him. Robert de Vere, earl of Oxford, a young man of a noble family, of an agreeable figure, but of dissolute manners, had acquired an entire ascendant over him; and governed him with an absolute authority. The king set so little bounds to his affection, that he first created his favourite marquis of Dublin, a title before unknown in England, then duke of Ireland; and transferred to him by patent, which was confirmed in parliament, the entire sovereignty for life of that island [x]. He gave him in marriage his cousin-german, the daughter of Ingelram de Couci, earl of Bedford; but soon after he permitted him to repudiate that lady, though of an unexceptionable character, and to marry a foreigner, a Bohemian, with whom he had become enamoured [y]. These public declarations of attachment turned the attention of the whole court towards the minion: All favours passed through his hands: Access to the king could only be obtained by his mediation: And Richard seemed to take no pleasure in royal authority, but so far as it enabled him to load with favours and titles and dignities this object of his affections.

Discontent of the barons.

THE jealousy of power immediately produced an animosity between the minion and his creatures on the one hand, and the princes of the blood and chief nobility on the other; and the usual complaints against the insolence of favourites were loudly echoed, and greedily received, in every part of the kingdom. Moubray earl of Nottingham, the mareschal, Fitz-Alan earl of Arundel, Piercy earl of Northumberland, Montacute earl of Salisbury, Beauchamp earl of Warwic, were all connected with each

[x] Cotton, p. 310, 311. Cox's Hist. of Ireland, p. 129. Walsingham, p. 324. [y] Walsingham, p. 328.

other,

other, and with the princes, by friendship or alliance, and still more by their common antipathy to those who had eclipsed them in the king's favour and confidence. No longer kept in awe by the personal character of the prince, they scorned to submit to his ministers; and the method, which they took to redress the grievances complained of, well suited the violence of the age, and proves the desperate extremities to which every opposition was sure to be instantly carried.

CHAP.
XVII.
1386.

MICHAEL DE LA POLE, the present chancellor, and lately created earl of Suffolk, was the son of an eminent merchant; but had risen by his abilities and valour during the wars of Edward III., had acquired the friendship of that monarch, and was esteemed the person of greatest experience and capacity among those who were attached to the duke of Ireland and the king's secret council. The duke of Glocester, who had the house of commons at his devotion, impelled them to exercise that power, which they seem first to have assumed against Lord Latimer during the declining years of the late king; and an impeachment against the chancellor was carried up by them to the house of peers, which was no less at his devotion. The king foresaw the tempest preparing against him and his ministers. After attempting in vain to rouse the Londoners to his defence, he withdrew from parliament, and retired with his court to Eltham. The parliament sent a deputation, inviting him to return, and threatening, that, if he persisted in absenting himself, they would immediately dissolve, and leave the nation, though at that time in imminent danger of a French invasion, without any support or supply for its defence. At the same time, a member was encouraged to call for the record, containing the parliamentary deposition of Edward II.; a plain intimation of the fate which Richard, if he continued refractory, had reason to expect from them.

CHAP. XVII.

1384.

them. The king, finding himself unable to resist, was content to stipulate, that, except finishing the present impeachment against Suffolk, no attack should be made upon any other of his ministers; and, on that condition, he returned to the parliament ª.

NOTHING can prove more fully the innocence of Suffolk, than the frivolousness of the crimes which his enemies, in the present plenitude of their power, thought proper to object against him ᵇ. It was alleged that, being chancellor, and obliged by his oath to consult the king's profit, he had purchased lands of the crown below their true value; that he had exchanged with the king a perpetual annuity of 400 marks a year, which he inherited from his father, and which was assigned upon the customs of the port of Hull for lands of an equal income; that having obtained for his son the priory of St. Anthony, which was formerly possessed by a Frenchman, an enemy, and a schismatic, and a new prior being at the same time named by the pope, he had refused to admit this person, whose title was not legal, till he made a composition with his son, and agreed to pay him a hundred pounds a year from the income of the benefice; that he had purchased, from one Tydeman of Limborch, an old and forfeited annuity of fifty pounds a-year upon the crown, and had engaged the king to admit that bad debt; and that, when created earl of Suffolk, he had obtained a grant of 500 pounds a-year, to support the dignity of that title ᵇ. Even the proof of these articles,

ª See note [B] at the end of the volume.   ᵃ Cotton, p. 315. Knyghton, p. 2683.

ᵇ It is probable that the earl of Suffolk was not rich, nor able to support the dignity without the bounty of the crown: For his father, Michael de la Pole, though a great merchant, had been ruined by lending money to the late king. See Cotton, p. 194. We may remark that the dukes of Glocester and York, though vastly rich, received at the same time each of them a thousand pounds a year, to support their dignity. Rymer, vol. vii. p. 482. Cotton, p. 310.

frivolous

frivolous as they are, was found very deficient upon the trial: It appeared that Suffolk had made no purchase from the crown while he was chancellor, and that all his bargains of that kind were made before he was advanced to that dignity[c]. It is almost needless to add, that he was condemned notwithstanding his defence; and that he was deprived of his office.

GLOCESTER and his associates observed their stipulation with the king, and attacked no more of his ministers: But they immediately attacked himself and his royal dignity, and framed a commission after the model of those which had been attempted almost in every reign since that of Richard I. and which had always been attended with extreme confusion[d]. By this commission, which was ratified by parliament, a council of fourteen persons was appointed, all of Glocester's faction, except Nevil archbishop of York: The sovereign power was transferred to these men for a twelvemonth: The king, who had now reached the twenty-first year of his age, was in reality dethroned: The aristocracy was rendered supreme: And though the term of the commission was limited, it was easy to foresee that the intentions of the party were to render it perpetual, and that power would with great difficulty be wrested from those grasping hands to which it was once committed. Richard, however, was obliged to submit: He signed the commission, which violence had extorted from him; he took an oath never to infringe it; and though at the end of the session he *publicly* entered a protest, that the prerogatives of the crown, notwithstanding his late concession, should still be deemed entire and unimpaired[e], the new commissioners, without regarding this declaration, proceeded to the exercise of their authority.

[c] Cotton, p. 315. 10 Rich. II. chap. 1.
[d] Knyghton, p. 2686. Statutes at Large.
[e] Cotton, p. 318.

CHAP.
XVII.

1387.
Civil commotions.

THE king, thus dispossessed of royal power, was soon sensible of the contempt into which he was fallen. His favourites and ministers, who were as yet allowed to remain about his person, failed not to aggravate the injury, which, without any demerit on his part, had been offered to him. And his eager temper was of itself sufficiently inclined to seek the means, both of recovering his authority, and of revenging himself on those who had invaded it. As the house of commons appeared now of weight in the constitution, he secretly tried some expedients for procuring a favourable election: He founded some of the sheriffs, who, being at that time, both the returning officers and magistrates of great power in the counties, had naturally considerable influence in elections [f]. But, as most of them had been appointed by his uncles, either during his minority, or during the course of the present commission, he found them, in general, averse to his enterprize. The sentiments and inclinations of the judges were more favourable to him. He met, at Nottingham, Sir Robert Tresilian, chief justice of the King's Bench, Sir Robert Belknappe, chief justice of the Common Pleas, Sir John Cary, chief baron of the Exchequer, Holt, Fulthorpe, and Bourg, inferior justices, and Lockton, serjeant at law; and he proposed to them some queries; which these lawyers, either from the influence of his authority, or of reason, made no scruple of answering in the way he desired. They declared that the late commission was derogatory to the royalty and prerogative of the king; that those who procured it, or advised the king to consent to it, were punishable with death; that those who necessitated and compelled him were guilty of treason; that those were equally criminal who should persevere in maintaining it; that the king has the right of dissolving parliaments at pleasure; that the

[f] In the preamble to 5 Henry IV. cap. vii. it is implied, that the sheriffs in a manner appointed the members of the house of commons not only in this parliament, but in many others.

parliament,

RICHARD II.

CHAP. XVII.
1387.

parliament, while it fits, must first proceed upon the king's business; and that this assembly cannot, without his consent, impeach any of his ministers and judges [f]. Even according to our present strict maxims with regard to law and the royal prerogative, all these determinations, except the two last, appear justifiable: And as the great privileges of the commons, particularly that of impeachment, were hitherto new, and supported by few precedents, there want not plausible reasons to justify these opinions of the judges [h]. They signed therefore their answer to the king's queries before the archbishops of York and Dublin, the bishops of Durham, Chichester, and Bangor, the duke of Ireland, the earl of Suffolk, and two other counsellors of inferior quality.

The duke of Glocester and his adherents soon got intelligence of this secret consultation, and were naturally very much alarmed at it. They saw the king's intentions; and they determined to prevent the execution of them. As soon as he came to London, which they knew was well disposed to their party, they secretly assembled their forces, and appeared in arms at Haringay-park, near Highgate, with a power which Richard and his ministers were not able to resist. They sent him a message by the archbishop of Canterbury, and the lords

[f] Knyghton, p. 2694. Ypod. Neust. p. 541.

[h] The parliament, in 1348, enacted of Edward III. that, on the third day of every session, the king should resume all the great offices; and that the ministers should then answer to any accusation that should be brought against them: Which plainly implies that, while ministers, they could not be accused or impeached in parliament. Henry IV. told the commons, that the usage of parliament required them first to go through the king's business in granting supplies; which order the king intended not to alter. Parl. Hist. vol. II. p. 65. Upon the whole, it must be allowed, that, according to ancient practice and principles, there are, at least, plausible grounds for all these opinions of the judges. It must be remarked, that this affirmation of Henry IV. was given deliberately, after consulting the house of peers, who were much better acquainted with the usage of parliament than the ignorant commons. And it has the greater authority, because Henry IV. had made this very principle a considerable article of charge against his predecessor; and that a very few years before. So ill grounded were most of the imputations thrown on the unhappy Richard!

Lovel,

CHAP. XVII.

1387.

Level, Cobham, and Devereux, and demanded that the persons who had seduced him by their pernicious counsel, and were traitors both to him and to the kingdom, should be delivered up to them. A few days after they appeared in his presence, armed and attended with armed followers; and they accused, by name, the archbishop of York, the duke of Ireland, the earl of Suffolk, Sir Robert Tresilian, and Sir Nicholas Brembre, as public and dangerous enemies to the state. They threw down their gauntlets before the king, and fiercely offered to maintain the truth of their charge by duel. The persons accused, and all the other obnoxious ministers, had withdrawn or had concealed themselves.

The duke of Ireland fled to Cheshire, and levied some forces, with which he advanced to relieve the king from the violence of the nobles. Gloceſter encountered him in Oxfordshire with much superior forces; routed him, dispersed his followers, and obliged him to fly into the Low-Countries, where he died in exile a few years after.

1388.
3d Feb.

Expulsion or execution of the king's ministers.

The lords then appeared at London with an army of 40,000 men; and having obliged the king to summon a parliament, which was entirely at their devotion, they had full power, by observing a few legal forms, to take vengeance on all their enemies. Five great peers, men whose combined power was able at any time to shake the throne, the duke of Gloceſter, the king's uncle; the earl of Derby, son of the duke of Lancaſter; the earl of Arundel; the earl of Warwic, and the earl of Nottingham, mareschal of England, entered before the parliament an accusation or appeal, as it was called, against the five counsellors, whom they had already accused before the king. The parliament, who ought to have been judges, were not ashamed to impose an oath on all their members, by which they bound themselves to live and die with the lords appellants, and to defend them against all opposition with their lives and fortunes [b].

[b] Cotton, p. 322.

RICHARD II.

CHAP. XVII.

1388.

THE other proceedings were well suited to the violence and iniquity of the times. A charge, consisting of thirty-nine articles, was delivered in by the appellants; and, as none of the accused counsellors except Sir Nicholas Brembre was in custody, the rest were cited to appear; and, upon their absenting themselves, the house of peers, after a very short interval, without hearing a witness, without examining a fact, or deliberating on one point of law, declared them guilty of high treason. Sir Nicholas Brembre, who was produced in court, had the appearance, and but the appearance, of a trial: The peers, though they were not by law his proper judges, pronounced, in a very summary manner, sentence of death upon him; and he was executed, together with Sir Robert Tresilian, who had been discovered and taken in the interval.

IT would be tedious to recite the whole charge delivered in against the five counsellors; which is to be met with in several collections [1]. It is sufficient to observe, in general, that if we reason upon the supposition, which is the true one, that the royal prerogative was invaded by the commission extorted by the duke of Glocester and his associates, and that the king's person was afterwards detained in custody by rebels, many of the articles will appear, not only to imply no crime in the duke of Ireland and the ministers, but to ascribe to them actions which were laudable, and which they were bound by their allegiance to perform. The few articles, impeaching the conduct of these ministers before that commission, which subverted the constitution, and annihilated all justice and legal authority, are vague and general; such as their engrossing the king's favour, keeping his barons at a distance from him, obtaining unreasonable grants for themselves or their creatures, and dissipating the public treasure by useless expences. No violence is objected to them; no particular illegal act [*]; no breach of any statute; and

[1] Knyghton, p. 2715. Tyrrel, vol. iii. part 2. p. 919, from the records. Parliamentary History, vol. i. p. 414.

[*] See note [C] at the end of the volume.

CHAP. XVII.
1388.

their administration may therefore be concluded to have been so far innocent and inoffensive. All the disorders indeed seem to have proceeded, not from any violation of the laws, or any ministerial tyranny, but merely from a rivalship of power, which the duke of Glocester and the great nobility, agreeably to the genius of the times, carried to the utmost extremity against their opponents, without any regard to reason, justice, or humanity.

But these were not the only deeds of violence committed during the triumph of the party. All the other judges, who had signed the extrajudicial opinions at Nottingham, were condemned to death, and were, as a grace or favour, banished to Ireland; though they pleaded the fear of their lives, and the menaces of the king's ministers as their excuse. Lord Beauchamp of Holt, Sir James Berners, and John Salisbury, were also tried and condemned for high treason; merely because they had attempted to defeat the late commission: But the life of the latter was spared. The fate of Sir Simon Burley was more severe: This gentleman was much beloved for his personal merit, had distinguished himself by many honourable actions [k], was created knight of the garter, and had been appointed governor to Richard, by the choice of the late king and of the Black Prince: He had attended his master from the earliest infancy of that prince, and had ever remained extremely attached to him: Yet all these considerations could not save him from falling a victim to Glocester's vengeance. This execution, more than all the others, made a deep impression on the mind of Richard: His queen too (for he was already married to the sister of the emperor Wincestaus, king of Bohemia), interested herself in behalf of Burley: She remained three

[k] At least this is the character given of him by Froissard, liv. ii who knew him personally; Walsingham, p. 334, gives a very different character of him; but he is a writer somewhat passionate and partial; and the choice made of this gentleman by Edward III. and the Black Prince for the education of Richard, makes the character given him by Froissard much more probable.

hours

hours on her knees before the duke of Glocester, pleading for that gentleman's life; but though she was become extremely popular by her amiable qualities, which had acquired her the appellation of *the good queen Ann*; her petition was sternly rejected by the inexorable tyrant.

THE parliament concluded this violent scene, by a declaration that none of the articles, decided on these trials to be treason, should ever afterwards be drawn into precedent by the judges, who were still to consider the statute of the twenty-fifth of Edward as the rule of their decisions. The house of lords seem not, at that time, to have known or acknowledged the principle, that they themselves were bound, in their judicial capacity, to follow the rules which they, in conjunction with the king and commons, had established in their legislative[*]. It was also enacted, that every one should swear to the perpetual maintenance and support of the forfeitures and attainders, and of all the other acts passed during this parliament. The archbishop of Canterbury added the penalty of excommunication, as a farther security to these violent transactions.

IT might naturally be expected, that the king, being reduced to such slavery by the combination of the princes and chief nobility, and having appeared so unable to defend his servants from the cruel effects of their resentment, would long remain in subjection to them; and never would recover the royal power, without the most violent struggles and convulsions: But the event proved contrary. In less than a twelvemonth, Richard, who was in his twenty-third year, declared in council, that, as he had now attained the full age which entitled him to govern by his own authority his kingdom and household, he resolved to exercise his right of sovereignty;

[*] See note [D] at the end of the volume.

CHAP.
XVII.
1389.

and when no one ventured to contradict so reasonable an intention, he deprived Fitz-Alan, archbishop of Canterbury, of the dignity of chancellor, and bestowed that high office on William of Wickham, bishop of Winchester; the bishop of Hereford was displaced from the office of treasurer, the earl of Arundel from that of admiral; even the duke of Glocester and the earl of Warwic were removed for a time from the council: And no opposition was made to these great changes. The history of this reign is imperfect, and little to be depended on; except where it is supported by public records: And it is not easy for us to assign the reason of this unexpected event. Perhaps some secret animosities, naturally to be expected in that situation, had creeped in among the great men, and had enabled the king to recover his authority. Perhaps the violence of their former proceedings had lost them the affections of the people, who soon repent of any cruel extremities to which they are carried by their leaders. However this may be, Richard exercised with moderation the authority which he had resumed. He seemed to be entirely reconciled to his uncles [1] and the other great men, of whom he had so much reason to complain: He never attempted to recal from banishment the duke of Ireland, whom he found so obnoxious to them: He confirmed, by proclamation, the general pardon which the parliament had passed for all offences: And he courted the affections of the people, by voluntarily remitting some subsidies which had been granted him; a remarkable and almost singular instance of such generosity.

AFTER this composure of domestic differences, and this restoration of the government to its natural state, there passes an interval of eight years, which affords not many remarkable events. The duke of Lancaster re-

[1] Dugdale, vol. II. p. 170.

turned

turned from Spain; having resigned to his rival all pretensions to the crown of Castile upon payment of a large sum of money [m], and having married his daughter, Philippa, to the king of Portugal. The authority of this prince served to counterbalance that of the duke of Gloucester, and secured the power of Richard, who paid great court to his eldest uncle, by whom he had never been offended; and whom he found more moderate in his temper than the younger. He made a cession to him for life of the dutchy of Guienne [n], which the inclinations and changeable humour of the Gascons had restored to the English government; but as they remonstrated loudly against this deed, it was finally, with the duke's consent, revoked by Richard [o]. There happened an incident, which produced a dissention between Lancaster and his two brothers. After the death of the Spanish princess, he espoused Catharine Swineford, daughter of a private knight of Hainault, by whose alliance York and Gloucester thought the dignity of their family much injured: But the king gratified his uncle, by passing in parliament a charter of legitimation to the children whom that lady had born him before marriage, and by creating the eldest earl of Somerset [p].

THE wars, meanwhile, which Richard had inherited with his crown, still continued; though interrupted by frequent truces, according to the practice of that age, and conducted with little vigour, by reason of the weakness of all parties. The French war was scarcely heard of; the tranquillity of the northern borders was only interrupted by one inroad of the Scots, which proceeded more from a rivalship between the two martial families of Piercy and Douglas, than from any national quarrel: A fierce battle or skirmish was fought at Otterborne [q], in

[m] Knyghton, p. 2677. vol. vii. p. 659. Walsingham, p. 352.
Walsingham, p. 342. [o] Ibid. p. 687. 5 15th August, 1388.
[n] Rymer, [p] Cotton, p. 365.

which

CHAP. XVII.

1399.

which young Piercy, firnamed *Hotspur*, from his impetuous valour, was taken prisoner, and Douglas slain; and the victory remained undecided[1]. Some insurrections of the Irish obliged the king to make an expedition into that country, which he reduced to obedience; and he recovered, in some degree, by this enterprize, his character of courage, which had suffered a little by the inactivity of his reign. At last, the English and French

1396.

courts began to think in earnest of a lasting peace; but found it so difficult to adjust their opposite pretensions, that they were content to establish a truce of twenty-five years[2]: Brest and Cherbourg were restored, the former to the duke of Britanny, the latter to the king of Navarre: Both parties were left in possession of all the other places which they held at the time of concluding the truce: And to render the amity between the two crowns more durable, Richard, who was now a widower, was affianced to Isabella, the daughter of Charles[3]. This princess was only seven years of age; but the king agreed to so unequal a match, chiefly that he might fortify himself by this alliance, against the enterprizes of his uncles, and the incurable turbulence as well as inconstancy of his barons.

THE administration of the king, though it was not, in this interval, sullied by any unpopular act, except the seizing of the charter of London[4], which was soon after restored, tended not much to corroborate his authority; and his personal character brought him into contempt, even while his public government appeared, in a good measure, unexceptionable. Indolent, profuse, addicted to low pleasures; he spent his whole time in feasting and jollity, and dissipated, in idle show, or in bounties to favourites of no reputation, that revenue which the people

[1] Froissard, liv. iii. chap. 124, 125, 126. Walsingham. p. 355.
[2] Rymer, vol. vii. p. 820. [4] Ibid. p. 813.
[3] Ibid. p. 727. Walsingham, p. 347.

expected

expected to see him employ in enterprizes directed to
public honour and advantage. He forgot his rank by admitting all men to his familiarity; and he was not sensible, that their acquaintance with the qualities of his
mind was not able to imprefs them with the refpect,
which he neglected to preferve from his birth and station.
The earls of Kent and Huntingdon, his half brothers,
were his chief confidents and favourites; and though he
never devoted himself to them with fo profufe an affection as that with which he had formerly been attached to
the duke of Ireland, it was eafy for men to fee, that every
grace paffed through their hands, and that the king had
rendered himfelf a mere cypher in the government. The
fmall regard, which the public bore to his perfon, difpofed
them to murmur againft his adminiftration, and to receive,
with greedy ears, every complaint which the difcontented
or ambitious grandees fuggefted to them.

CHAP.
XVII.

1396.

GLOCESTER foon perceived the advantages which this
diffolute conduct gave him; and finding, that both refentment and jealoufy on the part of his nephew ftill prevented him from acquiring any afcendant over that prince,
he determined to cultivate his popularity with the nation,
and to revenge himfelf on thofe who eclipfed him in favour and authority. He feldom appeared at court or in
council: He never declared his opinion but in order to
difapprove of the meafures embraced by the king and
his favourites; and he courted the friendfhip of every
man, whom difappointment or private refentment had
rendered an enemy to the adminiftration. The long
truce with France was unpopular with the Englifh, who
breathed nothing but war againft that hoftile nation; and
Glocefter took care to encourage all the vulgar prejudices which prevailed on this fubject. Forgetting the
misfortunes which attended the Englifh arms during the

1397.
Cabals of
the duke of
Glocefter.

later

later years of Edward, he made an invidious comparison between the glories of that reign and the inactivity of the present, and he lamented that Richard should have degenerated so much from the heroic virtues by which his father and his grandfather were distinguished. The military men were inflamed with a desire of war, when they heard him talk of the signal victories formerly obtained, and of the easy prey which might be made of French riches by the superior valour of the English: The populace readily embraced the same sentiments: And all men exclaimed that this prince, whose counsels were so much neglected, was the true support of English honour, and alone able to raise the nation to its former power and splendor. His great abilities, his popular manners, his princely extraction, his immense riches, his high office of constable *; all these advantages, not a little assisted by his want of court-favour, gave him a mighty authority in the kingdom, and rendered him formidable to Richard and his ministers.

FROISSARD[x], a contemporary writer and very impartial, but whose credit is somewhat impaired by his want of exactness in material facts, ascribes to the duke of Glocester more desperate views, and such as were totally incompatible with the government and domestic tranquillity of the nation. According to that historian, he proposed to his nephew, Roger Mortimer, earl of Marche, whom Richard had declared his successor, to give him immediate possession of the throne, by the deposition of a prince so unworthy of power and authority: And when Mortimer declined the project, he resolved to make a partition of the kingdom between himself, his two brothers, and the earl of Arundel; and entirely to dispossess Richard of the crown. The king, it is said, being informed of these designs, saw that either his own ruin

* Rymer, vol. vii. p. 150.   x Liv. iv. chap. 86.

or that of Glocester was inevitable; and he resolved, by a hasty blow, to prevent the execution of such destructive projects. This is certain, that Glocester, by his own confession, had often affected to speak contemptuously of the king's person and government; had deliberated concerning the lawfulness of throwing off allegiance to him; and had even born part in a secret conference, where his deposition was proposed, and talked of, and determined [r]: But it is reasonable to think, that his schemes were not so far advanced as to make him resolve on putting them immediately in execution. The danger, probably, was still too distant to render a desperate remedy entirely necessary for the security of government.

But whatever opinion we may form of the danger arising from Glocester's conspiracies, his aversion to the French truce and alliance was public and avowed; and that court, which had now a great influence over the king, pushed him to provide for his own safety, by punishing the traiterous designs of his uncle. The resentment against his former acts of violence revived; the sense of his refractory and uncompliant behaviour was still recent; and a man, whose ambition had once usurped royal authority, and who had murdered all the faithful servants of the king, was thought capable, on a favourable opportunity, of renewing the same criminal enterprizes. The king's precipitate temper admitted of no deliberation: He ordered Glocester to be unexpectedly arrested; to be hurried on board a ship which was lying in the river; and to be carried over to Calais, where alone, by reason of his nume-

---

[r] Cotton, p. 378. Tyrrel, vol. iii. part 2. p. 971, from the records. Parliamentary History, vol. I. p. 473. That this confession was genuine, and obtained without violence, may be entirely depended on. Judge Rickhill, who brought it over from Calais, was tried on that account, and acquitted in the first parliament of Henry IV. when Glocester's party was prevalent. His acquittal, notwithstanding his innocence, may even appear marvellous, considering the times. See Cotton, p. 393.

rous partizans, he could safely be detained in custody[a]. The earls of Arundel and Warwic were seized at the same time: The malcontents, so suddenly deprived of their leaders, were astonished and overawed: And the concurrence of the dukes of Lancaster and York in those measures, together with the earls of Derby and Rutland, the eldest sons of these princes[b], bereaved them of all possibility of resistance.

A PARLIAMENT was immediately summoned at Westminster; and the king doubted not to find the peers, and still more the commons, very compliant with his will. This house had in a former parliament given him very sensible proofs of their attachment[c]; and the present suppression of Glocester's party made him still more assured of a favourable election. As a farther expedient for that purpose, he is also said to have employed the influence of the sheriffs; a practice which, though not unusual, gave umbrage, but which the established authority of that assembly rendered afterwards still more familiar to the nation. Accordingly the parliament passed whatever acts the king was pleased to dictate to them[d]: They annulled for ever the commission which usurped upon the royal authority, and they declared it treasonable to attempt, in any future period, the revival of any similar commission[e]: They abrogated all the acts which attainted the king's ministers, and which that parliament who passed them, and the whole nation, had sworn inviolably to maintain: And they declared the general pardon then granted to be invalid, as extorted by force, and never ratified by the free consent of the king. Though Richard, after he resumed the government, and lay no longer under constraint,

[a] Froissard, liv. iv. chap. 90. Walsing. p. 354. [c] Rymer, vol. viii. p. 7. [d] See note [E] at the end of the volume.
[b] The nobles brought numerous retainers with them to give them security, as we are told by Walsingham, p. 354. The king had only a few Cheshire men for his guard. [e] Statutes at Large, 21 Richard II.

had

had voluntarily, by proclamation, confirmed that general indemnity; this circumstance seemed not, in their eyes, to merit any consideration. Even a particular pardon granted six years after to the earl of Arundel, was annulled by parliament; on pretence, that it had been procured by surprize, and that the king was not then fully apprized of the degree of guilt incurred by that nobleman.

CHAP.
XVII.
1397.

The commons then preferred an impeachment against Fitz-Alan, archbishop of Canterbury, and brother to Arundel, and accused him for his concurrence in procuring the illegal commission, and in attainting the king's ministers. The primate pleaded guilty; but as he was protected by the ecclesiastical privileges, the king was satisfied with a sentence, which banished him the kingdom, and sequestered his temporalities [d]. An appeal or accusation was presented against the duke of Glocester, and the earls of Arundel and Warwic, by the earls of Rutland, Kent, Huntingdon, Somerset, Salisbury, and Nottingham, together with the lords Spencer and Scrope, and they were accused of the same crimes which had been imputed to the archbishop, as well as of their appearance against the king in a hostile manner at Haringay-park. The earl of Arundel, who was brought to the bar, wisely confined all his defence to the pleading of both the general and particular pardon of the king; but his plea being over-ruled, he was condemned, and executed [e]. The earl of Warwic, who was also convicted of high treason, was, on account of his submissive behaviour, pardoned as to his life, but doomed to perpetual banishment in the Isle of Man. No new acts of treason were imputed to either of these noblemen. The only crimes, for which they were condemned, were the old attempts against the crown, which seemed to be obliterated, both by the distance of

[d] Cotton, p. 368. Walsing. p. 354. [e] Ibid. p. 377. Froissard, liv. iv. chap. 90.

time,

CHAP. XVII.

1397.

time, and by repeated pardons [f]. The reasons of this method of proceeding, it is difficult to conjecture. The recent conspiracies of Glocester seem certain from his own confession: But, perhaps, the king and ministry had not, at that time, in their hands, any satisfactory proof of their reality; perhaps, it was difficult to convict Arundel and Warwic of any participation in them; perhaps, an enquiry into these conspiracies would have involved in the guilt some of those great noblemen who now concurred with the crown, and whom it was necessary to cover from all imputation; or perhaps the king, according to the genius of the age, was indifferent about maintaining even the appearance of law and equity, and was only solicitous by any means to ensure success in these prosecutions. This point, like many others in ancient history, we are obliged to leave altogether undetermined.

Murder of the duke of Glocester.

A WARRANT was issued to the earl mareschal, governor of Calais, to bring over the duke of Glocester, in order to his trial; but the governor returned for answer, that the duke had died suddenly of an apoplexy in that fortress. Nothing could be more suspicious, from the time, than the circumstances of that prince's death: It became immediately the general opinion, that he was murdered by orders from his nephew: In the subsequent reign undoubted proofs were produced in parliament, that he had been suffocated with pillows by his keepers [g]. And it appeared that the king, apprehensive lest the public trial and execution of so popular a prince, and so near a relation, might prove both dangerous and invidious, had taken this base method of gratifying, and, as he fancied, concealing, his revenge upon him. Both parties, in their successive triumphs, seem to have had no farther concern than that of retaliating upon their adversaries;

[f] Tyrrel, vol. iii. part II. p. 968, from the records. [g] Cotton, p. 399, 4to. Dugdale, vol. ii. p. 172.

and neither of them were aware, that, by imitating, they indirectly justified, as far as it lay in their power, all the illegal violence of the opposite party.

THIS session concluded with the creation or advancement of several peers: The earl of Derby was made duke of Hereford; the earl of Rutland, duke of Albemarle; the earl of Kent, duke of Surrey; the earl of Huntingdon, duke of Exeter; the earl of Nottingham, duke of Norfolk; the earl of Somerset, marquis of Dorset; lord Spenser, earl of Glocester; Ralph Nevil, earl of Westmoreland; Thomas Piercy, earl of Worcester; William Scrope, earl of Wiltshire [h]. The parliament, after a session of twelve days, was adjourned to Shrewsbury. The king, before the departure of the members, exacted from them an oath for the perpetual maintenance and establishment of all their acts; an oath, similar to that which had formerly been required by the duke of Glocester and his party, and which had already proved so vain and fruitless.

BOTH king and parliament met in the same dispositions at Shrewsbury. So anxious was Richard for the security of these acts, that he obliged the lords and commons to swear anew to them on the cross of Canterbury [i]; and he soon after procured a bull from the pope, by which they were, as he imagined, perpetually secured and established [k]. The parliament, on the other hand, conferred on him *for life* the duties on wool, wool-fells, and leather, and granted him, besides, a subsidy of one tenth and a half, and one fifteenth and a half. They also reversed the attainder of Tresilian and the other judges; and, with the approbation of the present judges, declared the answers, for which these magistrates had been impeached,

[h] Cotton, p. 370, 371. [i] Ibid. p. 371. [k] Walsing. p. 355.

to be just and legal[l]: And they carried so far their retrospect, as to reverse, on the petition of lord Spenser, earl of Glocester, the attainder pronounced against the two Spensers in the reign of Edward II.[m] The ancient history of England is nothing but a catalogue of reversals: Every thing is in fluctuation and movement: One faction is continually undoing what was established by another: And the multiplied oaths, which each party exacted for the security of the present acts, betray a perpetual consciousness of their instability.

The parliament, before they were dissolved, elected a committee of twelve lords and six commoners[n], whom they invested with the whole power both of lords and commons, and endowed with full authority to finish all business which had been laid before the houses, and which they had not had leisure to bring to a conclusion[o]. This was an unusual concession; and though it was limited in the object, might, either immediately or as a precedent, have proved dangerous to the constitution: But the cause of that extraordinary measure was an event singular and unexpected, which engaged the attention of the parliament.

After the destruction of the duke of Glocester and the heads of that party, a misunderstanding broke out among those noblemen, who had joined in the prosecution; and the king wanted either authority sufficient to appease it, or foresight to prevent it. The duke of Hereford appeared in parliament, and accused the duke of Nor-

---

[l] Statutes at Large, 21 Rich. II. [m] Cotton, p. 372.

[n] The names of the commissioners were, the dukes of Lancaster, York, Aibemarle, Surrey, and Exeter; the marquis of Dorset; the earls of March, Salisbury, Northumberland, Glocester, Winchester, and Wiltshire; John Bussey, Henry Green, John Russel, Robert Teyne, Henry Chelmeswicke, and John Golofre. It is to be remarked, that the duke of Lancaster always concurred with the rest in all their proceedings, even in the banishment of his son, which was afterwards so much complained of.

[o] Cotton, p. 372. Walsing. p. 355.

folk of having spoken to him, in private, many slanderous words of the king, and of having imputed to that prince an intention of subverting and destroying many of his principal nobility[p]. Norfolk denied the charge, gave Hereford the lie, and offered to prove his own innocence by duel. The challenge was accepted: The time and place of combat were appointed: And as the event of this important trial by arms might require the interposition of legislative authority, the parliament thought it more suitable to delegate their power to a committee, than to prolong the session beyond the usual time which custom and general convenience had prescribed to it[q].

THE duke of Hereford was certainly very little delicate in the point of honour, when he revealed a private conversation to the ruin of the person who had entrusted him; and we may thence be more inclined to believe the duke of Norfolk's denial, than the other's asseveration. But Norfolk had in these transactions betrayed an equal neglect of honour, which brings him entirely on a level with his antagonist. Though he had publicly joined with the duke of Glocester and his party in all the former acts of violence against the king; and his name stands among the appellants who accused the duke of Ireland and the other ministers; yet was he not ashamed publicly to impeach his former associates for the very crimes which he had concurred with them in committing; and his name encreases the list of those appellants who brought them to a trial. Such were the principles and practices of those ancient knights and barons during the prevalence of the aristocratical government, and the reign of chivalry.

[p] Cotton, p. 372. Parliamentary History, vol. i. p. 490.
[q] In the first year of Henry VI. when the authority of parliament was great, and when that assembly could least be suspected of lying under violence, a like confession was made to the privy council, from the motives of convenience. See Cotton, p. 564.

CHAP.
XVII.

1398.

The lists for this decision of truth and right were appointed at Coventry before the king: All the nobility of England banded into parties, and adhered either to the one duke or the other: The whole nation was held in suspence with regard to the event: But when the two champions appeared in the field, accoutred for the combat, the king interposed, to prevent both the present effusion of such noble blood, and the future consequences of the quarrel. By the advice and authority of the parliamentary commissioners he stopped the duel; and to show his impartiality, he ordered, by the same authority, both the combatants to leave the kingdom [1]; assigning one country for the place of Norfolk's exile, which he declared perpetual; another for that of Hereford, which he limited to ten years.

Hereford was a man of great prudence and command of temper; and he behaved himself with so much submission in these delicate circumstances, that the king, before his departure, promised to shorten the term of his exile four years; and he also granted him letters patent, by which he was empowered, in case any inheritance should in the interval accrue to him, to enter immediately in possession, and to postpone the doing of homage till his return.

Banishment of Henry duke of Hereford.

The weakness and fluctuation of Richard's counsels appear no where more evident than in the conduct of this affair. No sooner had Hereford left the kingdom, than the king's jealousy of the power and riches of that prince's family revived; and he was sensible, that, by Glocester's death, he had only removed a counterpoise to the Lancastrian interest, which was now become formidable to his crown and kingdom. Being informed that Hereford had entered into a treaty of marriage with the daughter of the duke of Berry, uncle to the French king, he determined

[1] Cotton, p. 380. Walsingham, p. 356.

to prevent the finishing of an alliance, which would so much extend the interest of his cousin in foreign countries; and he sent over the earl of Salisbury to Paris with a commission for that purpose. The death of the duke of Lancaster, which happened soon after, called upon him to take new resolutions with regard to that opulent succession. The present duke, in consequence of the king's patent, desired to be put in possession of the estate and jurisdictions of his father: But Richard, afraid of strengthening the hands of a man, whom he had already so much offended, applied to the parliamentary commissioners, and persuaded them, that this affair was but an appendage to that business which the parliament had delegated to them. By their authority he revoked his letters patent, and retained possession of the estate of Lancaster: And by the same authority, he seized and tried the duke's attorney, who had procured and insisted on the letters, and he had him condemned as a traitor, for faithfully executing that trust to his master [a]. An extravagant act of power! even though the king changed, in favour of the attorney, the penalty of death into that of banishment.

CHAP. XVII.

1399. 3d Feb.

HENRY, the new duke of Lancaster, had acquired, by his conduct and abilities, the esteem of the public; and having served with distinction against the infidels in Lithuania, he had joined to his other praises those of piety and valour, virtues which have at all times a great influence over mankind, and were, during those ages, the qualities chiefly held in estimation [b]. He was connected with most of the principal nobility by blood, alliance, or friendship; and as the injury, done him by the king, might in its consequences affect all of them, he easily brought them, by a sense of common interest, to take part in his resentment. The people, who must have an object of affection, who found nothing in the king's person

[a] Tyrrel, vol. III. part 2, p. 991, from the records. [b] Walsingham, p. 143.

CHAP. XVII.

1399.

which they could love or revere, and who were even disgusted with many parts of his conduct[a], easily transferred to Henry that attachment, which the death of the duke of Glocester had left without any fixed direction. His misfortunes were lamented; the injustice, which he had suffered, was complained of; and all men turned their eyes towards him, as the only person that could retrieve the lost honour of the nation, or redress the supposed abuses in the government.

Return of Henry.

WHILE such were the dispositions of the people, Richard had the imprudence to embark for Ireland, in order to revenge the death of his cousin, Roger earl of Marche, the presumptive heir of the crown, who had lately been slain in a skirmish by the natives; and he thereby left the kingdom of England open to the attempts of his provoked and ambitious enemy. Henry, embarking at Nantz with a retinue of sixty persons, among whom were the archbishop of Canterbury and the young earl of Arundel, nephew to that prelate, landed at Ravenspur in Yorkshire; and was immediately joined by the earls of Northumberland and Westmoreland, two of the most potent barons in England. He here took a solemn oath, that he had no other purpose in this invasion, than to recover the dutchy of Lancaster, unjustly detained from him; and he invited all his friends in England, and all lovers of their country, to second him in this reasonable and moderate pretension. Every place was in commotion: The malcontents in all quarters flew to arms:

4th July.

[a] He levied fines upon those who had ten years before joined the duke of Glocester and his party: They were obliged to pay him money, before he would allow them to enjoy the benefit of the indemnity; and in the articles of charge against him, it is asserted, that the payment of one fine did not suffice. It is indeed likely, that his ministers would abuse the power put into their hands; and this grievance extended to very many people. Historians agree in representing this practice as a great oppression. See Otterbourne, p. 199.

London discovered the strongest symptoms of its disposition to mutiny and rebellion: And Henry's army, encreasing on every day's march, soon amounted to the number of 60,000 combatants.

CHAP. XVII.
1399.

THE duke of York was left guardian of the realm; a place to which his birth intitled him, but which both his slender abilities, and his natural connexions with the duke of Lancaster, rendered him utterly incapable of filling in such a dangerous emergency. Such of the chief nobility as were attached to the crown, and could either have seconded the guardian's good intentions, or have overawed his infidelity, had attended the king into Ireland; and the efforts of Richard's friends were every where more feeble than those of his enemies. The duke of York, however, appointed the rendezvous of his forces at St. Albans, and soon assembled an army of 40,000 men; but found them entirely destitute of zeal and attachment to the royal cause, and more inclined to join the party of the rebels. He hearkened therefore very readily to a message from Henry, who entreated him not to oppose a loyal and humble supplicant in the recovery of his legal patrimony; and the guardian even declared publicly that he would second his nephew in so reasonable a request. His army embraced with acclamations the same measures; and the duke of Lancaster, reinforced by them, was now entirely master of the kingdom. He hastened to Bristol, into which some of the king's ministers had thrown themselves; and soon obliging that place to surrender, he yielded to the popular wishes, and without giving them a trial, ordered the earl of Wiltshire, Sir John Bussy, and Sir Henry Green, whom he there took prisoners, to be led to immediate execution.

General insurrection.

THE king, receiving intelligence of this invasion and insurrection, hastened over from Ireland, and landed in Milford Haven with a body of 20,000 men; But even this

CHAP. XVII.

1399.

this army, so much inferior to the enemy, was either overawed by the general combination of the kingdom, or seized with the same spirit of disaffection; and they gradually deserted him, till he found that he had not above 6000 men who followed his standard. It appeared, therefore, necessary to retire secretly from this small body, which served only to expose him to danger; and he fled to the isle of Anglesea, where he purposed to embark either for Ireland or France, and there await the favourable opportunities, which the return of his subjects to a sense of duty, or their future discontents against the duke of Lancaster, would probably afford him. Henry, sensible of the danger, sent to him the earl of Northumberland with the strongest professions of loyalty and submission; and that nobleman, by treachery and false oaths, made himself master of the king's person, and carried him to his enemy at Flint Castle. Richard was conducted to London, by the duke of Lancaster, who was there received with the acclamations of the mutinous populace. It is pretended that the recorder met him on the road; and in the name of the city, entreated him, for the public safety, to put Richard to death, with all his adherents who were prisoners *; but the duke prudently determined to make many others participate in his guilt, before he would proceed to those extremities. For this purpose, he issued writs of election in the king's name, and appointed the immediate meeting of a parliament at Westminster.

1st Sept.

Such of the peers as were most devoted to the king, were either fled or imprisoned; and no opponents, even among the barons, dared to appear against Henry, amidst that scene of outrage and violence, which commonly attends revolutions, especially in England during those turbulent ages. It is also easy to imagine, that a house of

* Walsingham.

commons,

RICHARD II.

commons, elected during this universal ferment, and this triumph of the Lancastrian party, would be extremely attached to that cause, and ready to second every suggestion of their leaders. That order, being as yet of too little weight to stem the torrent, was always carried along with it, and served only to encrease the violence, which the public interest required it should endeavour to controul. The duke of Lancaster, therefore, sensible that he should be entirely master, began to carry his views to the crown itself; and he deliberated with his partizans concerning the most proper means of effecting his daring purpose. He first extorted a resignation from Richard [s]; but as he knew that this deed would plainly appear the result of force and fear, he also purposed, notwithstanding the danger of the precedent to himself and his posterity, to have him solemnly deposed in parliament, for his pretended tyranny and misconduct. A charge, consisting of thirty-three articles, was accordingly drawn up against him, and presented to that assembly [t].

If we examine these articles, which are expressed with extreme acrimony against Richard, we shall find that, except some rash speeches which are imputed to him [u], and of whose reality, as they are said to have passed in private conversation, we may reasonably entertain some doubt; the chief amount of the charge is contained in his violent conduct during the two last years of his reign, and naturally divides itself into two principal heads. The first and most considerable is the revenge which he took on the princes and great barons, who had formerly usurped, and still persevered in controuling and threatening, his authority; the second is the violation of the laws and general privileges of his people. But the former, however irregular in many of its circumstances, was fully

CHAP.
XVII.

1399.

Deposition of the king.

28th Sept.

[s] Knyghton, p. 2744. Otterbourne, p. 212.   [t] Tyrrel, vol. iii. part 2. p. 1008, from the records. Knyghton, p. 2746. Otterbourne, p. 214.   [u] Art. 16. 26.

supported

supported by authority of parliament, and was but a copy of the violence which the princes and barons themselves, during their former triumph, had exercised against him and his party. The detention of Lancaster's estate was, properly speaking, a revocation, by parliamentary authority, of a grace, which the king himself had formerly granted him. The murder of Glocester (for the secret execution, however merited, of that prince, certainly deserves this appellation) was a private deed, formed not any precedent, and implied not any usurped or arbitrary power of the crown, which could justly give umbrage to the people. It really proceeded from a defect of power in the king, rather than from his ambition; and proves that instead of being dangerous to the constitution, he possessed not even the authority necessary for the execution of the laws.

Concerning the second head of accusation, as it mostly consists of general facts, was framed by Richard's inveterate enemies, and was never allowed to be answered by him or his friends, it is more difficult to form a judgment. The greater part of these grievances, imputed to Richard, seems to be the exertion of arbitrary prerogatives; such as the dispensing power [a], levying purveyance [b], employing the marshal's court [c], extorting loans [d], granting protections from law-suits [e]; prerogatives which, though often complained of, had often been exercised by his predecessors, and still continued to be so by his successors. But whether his irregular acts of this kind were more frequent, and injudicious, and violent than usual, or were only laid hold of and exaggerated by the factions to which the weakness of his reign had given birth, we are not able, at this distance, to determine with certainty. There is, however, one circumstance in which

[a] Art. 13, 17, 18.   [b] Art. 12.   [c] Art. 27.
[d] Art. 14.   [e] Art. 16.

his conduct is visibly different from that of his grandfather: He is not accused of having imposed one arbitrary tax, without consent of parliament, during his whole reign [f]: Scarcely a year passed during the reign of Edward, which was free from complaints with regard to this dangerous exertion of authority. But, perhaps, the ascendant which Edward had acquired over the people, together with his great prudence, enabled him to make a use very advantageous to his subjects of this and other arbitrary prerogatives, and rendered them a smaller grievance in his hands, than a less absolute authority in those of his grandson. This is a point which it would be rash for us to decide positively on either side; but it is certain, that a charge drawn up by the duke of Lancaster, and assented to by a parliament, situated in those circumstances, forms no manner of presumption with regard to the unusual irregularity or violence of the king's conduct in this particular [g].

WHEN the charge against Richard was presented to the parliament, though it was liable, almost in every article, to objections, it was not canvassed, nor examined, nor disputed in either house, and seemed to be received with universal approbation. One man alone, the bishop of Carlisle, had the courage, amidst this general disloyalty and violence, to appear in defence of his unhappy master, and to plead his cause against all the power of the prevailing party. Though some topics, employed by that virtuous prelate, may seem to favour too much the doctrine

---

[f] We learn from Cotton, p. 362, that the king, by his chancellor, told the commons, *that they were severly bound to him, and namely in forbearing to charge them with dismes and fifteens, the which he meant no more to charge them in his own person.* These words we were alledge to the practice of his predecessors. He had not himself imposed any arbitrary taxes: Even the parliament, in the articles of his deposition, though they complain of heavy taxes, affirm not that they were imposed illegally or by arbitrary will.

[g] See note [F] at the end of the volume.

of passive obedience, and to make too large a sacrifice of the rights of mankind; he was naturally pushed into that extreme by his abhorrence of the present licentious factions; and such intrepidity, as well as disinterestedness of behaviour, proves, that whatever his speculative principles were, his heart was elevated far above the meanness and abject submission of a slave. He represented to the parliament, that all the abuses of government which could justly be imputed to Richard, instead of amounting to tyranny, were merely the result of error, youth, or misguided counsel, and admitted of a remedy, more easy and salutary, than a total subversion of the constitution. That even had they been much more violent and dangerous than they really were, they had chiefly proceeded from former examples of resistance, which, making the prince sensible of his precarious situation, had obliged him to establish his throne by irregular and arbitrary expedients. That a rebellious disposition in subjects was the principal cause of tyranny in kings: Laws could never secure the subject, which did not give security to the sovereign: And if the maxim of inviolable loyalty, which formed the basis of the English government, were once rejected, the privileges belonging to the several orders of the state, instead of being fortified by that licentiousness, would thereby lose the surest foundation of their force and stability. That the parliamentary deposition of Edward II. far from making a precedent which could controul this maxim, was only an example of successful violence; and it was sufficiently to be lamented, that crimes were so often committed in the world, without establishing principles which might justify and authorize them. That even that precedent, false and dangerous as it was, could never warrant the present excesses, which were so much greater, and which would entail distraction and misery on the nation, to the latest posterity. That the succession,

cession, at least, of the crown, was then preserved inviolate: The lineal heir was placed on the throne: And the people had an opportunity, by their legal obedience to him, of making atonement for the violence which they had committed against his predecessor. That a descendant of Lionel duke of Clarence, the elder brother of the late duke of Lancaster, had been declared in parliament successor to the crown: He had left posterity: And their title, however it might be overpowered by present force and faction, could never be obliterated from the minds of the people. That if the turbulent disposition alone of the nation had overturned the well-established throne of so good a prince as Richard; what bloody commotions must ensue, when the same cause was united to the motive of restoring the legal and undoubted heir to his authority? That the new government, intended to be established, would stand on no principle; and would scarcely retain any pretence, by which it could challenge the obedience of men of sense and virtue. That the claim of lineal descent was so gross as scarcely to deceive the most ignorant of the populace: Conquest could never be pleaded by a rebel against his sovereign: The consent of the people had no authority in a monarchy not derived from consent, but established by hereditary right; and however the nation might be justified in deposing the misguided Richard, it could never have any reason for setting aside his lawful heir and successor, who was plainly innocent. And that the duke of Lancaster would give them but a bad specimen of the legal moderation, which might be expected from his future government, if he added to the crime of his past rebellion, the guilt of excluding the family, which, both by right of blood, and by declaration of parliament, would, in case of Richard's demise, or voluntary resignation, have been received as the undoubted heirs of the monarchy [b].

[b] Sir John Hayward, p. 101.

ALL

ALL the circumstances of this event, compared to those which attended the late revolution in 1688, show the difference between a great and civilized nation, deliberately vindicating its established privileges, and a turbulent and barbarous aristocracy, plunging headlong from the extremes of one faction into those of another. This noble freedom of the bishop of Carlisle, instead of being applauded, was not so much as tolerated: He was immediately arrested, by order of the duke of Lancaster, and sent a prisoner to the abbey of St. Albans. No farther debate was attempted: Thirty-three long articles of charge were, in one meeting, voted against Richard; and voted unanimously by the same peers and prelates, who, a little before had, voluntarily and unanimously, authorized those very acts of violence, of which they now complained. That prince was deposed by the suffrages of both houses; and the throne being now vacant, the duke of Lancaster stepped forth, and having crossed himself on the forehead, and on the breast, and called upon the name of Christ [i], he pronounced these words, which we shall give in the original language, because of their singularity:

In the name of Fadher, Son, and Holy Ghost, I Henry of Lancaster, challenge this rewme of Ynglonde, and the croun, with all the membres, and the appurtenances; als I that am descendit by right line of the blode, coming fro the gude king Henry therde, and throge that right that God of his grace hath sent me, with helpe of kyn, and of my frendes to recover it; the which rewme was in poynt to be ondone by defaut of governance, and ondoying of the gude lawes [k].

IN order to understand this speech, it must be observed, that there was a silly story, received among some of the lowest vulgar, that Edmond, earl of Lancaster, son of Henry III. was really the elder brother of Edward I.; but

[i] Cotton, p. 389. [k] Knyghton, p. 2757.

that, by reason of some deformity in his person, he had been postponed in the succession, and his younger brother imposed on the nation in his stead. As the present duke of Lancaster inherited from Edmond by his mother, this genealogy made him the true heir of the monarchy; and it is therefore insinuated in Henry's speech: But the absurdity was too gross to be openly avowed either by him, or by the parliament. The case is the same with regard to his right of conquest: He was a subject who rebelled against his sovereign: He entered the kingdom with a retinue of no more than sixty persons: He could not therefore be the conqueror of England; and this right is accordingly insinuated, not avowed. Still there is a third claim derived from his merits in saving the nation from tyranny and oppression; and this claim is also insinuated: But as it seemed, by its nature, better calculated as a reason for his being *elected* king by a free choice, than for giving him an immediate right of possession, he durst not speak openly even on this head; and to obviate any notion of election, he challenges the crown as his due, either by acquisition or inheritance. The whole forms such a piece of jargon and nonsense, as is almost without example: No objection, however, was made to it in parliament: The unanimous voice of lords and commons placed Henry on the throne: He became king, nobody could tell how or wherefore: The title of the house of Marche, formerly recognized by parliament, was neither invalidated nor repealed; but passed over in total silence: And as a concern for the liberties of the people seems to have had no hand in this revolution, their right to dispose of the government, as well as all their other privileges, was left precisely on the same footing as before. But Henry having, when he claimed the crown, dropped some obscure hint concerning conquest, which, it was thought, might endanger these privileges, he soon after made a public declaration, that he did not thereby intend

to

to deprive any one of his franchises or liberties[1]: Which was the only circumstance, where we shall find meaning or common sense, in all these transactions.

THE subsequent events discover the same headlong violence of conduct, and the same rude notions of civil government. The deposition of Richard dissolved the parliament: It was necessary to summon a new one: And Henry, in six days after, called together, without any new election, the same members; and this assembly he denominated a new parliament. They were employed in the usual task of reversing every deed of the opposite party. All the acts of the last parliament of Richard, which had been confirmed by their oaths, and by a papal bull, were abrogated: All the acts which had passed in the parliament where Glocester prevailed, which had also been confirmed by their oaths, but which had been abrogated by Richard, were anew established[m]: The answers of Tresilian, and the other judges, which a parliament had annulled, but which a new parliament, and new judges, had approved, here received a second condemnation. The peers, who had accused Glocester, Arundel, and Warwic, and who had received higher titles for that piece of service, were all of them degraded from their new dignities: Even the practice of prosecuting appeals in parliament, which bore the air of a violent confederacy against an individual, rather than of a legal indictment, was wholly abolished; and trials were restored to the course of common law[n]. The natural effect of this conduct was to render the people giddy with such rapid and perpetual changes, and to make them lose all notions of right and wrong in the measures of government.

THE earl of Northumberland made a motion, in the house of peers, with regard to the unhappy prince whom they had deposed. He asked them what advice they

[l] Knyghton, p. 2759. Otterbourne, p. 220. [m] Cotton, p. 390. [n] Henry IV. cap. 14.

would give the king for the future treatment of him; since Henry was resolved to spare his life. They unanimously replied, that he should be imprisoned under a secure guard, in some secret place, and should be deprived of all commerce with any of his friends or partizans. It was easy to foresee, that he would not long remain alive in the hands of such barbarous and sanguinary enemies. Historians differ with regard to the manner in which he was murdered. It was long the prevailing opinion, that Sir Piers Exton, and others of his guards, fell upon him in the castle of Pomfret, where he was confined, and dispatched him with their halberts. But it is more probable, that he was starved to death in prison; and after all sustenance was denied him, he prolonged his unhappy life, it is said, for a fortnight, before he reached the end of his miseries. This account is more consistent with the story, that his body was exposed in public, and that no marks of violence were observed upon it. He died in the thirty-fourth year of his age, and the twenty-third of his reign. He left no posterity, either legitimate or illegitimate.

CHAP. XVII.
1399.

Murder of the king.

ALL the writers, who have transmitted to us the history of Richard, lived during the reigns of the Lancastrian princes; and candor requires, that we should not give entire credit to the reproaches which they have thrown upon his memory. But after making all proper allowances, he still appears to have been a weak prince, and unfit for government, less for want of natural parts and capacity, than of solid judgment and a good education. He was violent in his temper; profuse in his expence; fond of idle show and magnificence; devoted to favourites; and addicted to pleasure: Passions, all of them, the most inconsistent with a prudent œconomy, and consequently dangerous in a limited and mixed government. Had he possessed the talents of gaining, and still

His character.

CHAP. still more those of overawing, his great barons, he might
XVII.
~~~~~ have escaped all the misfortunes of his reign, and been
1399. allowed to carry much farther his oppressions over the
people, if he really was guilty of any, without their
daring to rebel, or even to murmur against him. But
when the grandees were tempted, by his want of prudence and of vigour, to resist his authority, and execute
the most violent enterprizes upon him, he was naturally
led to seek an opportunity of retaliation; justice was
neglected; the lives of the chief nobility were sacrificed;
and all these enormities seem to have proceeded less from
a settled design of establishing arbitrary power, than from
the insolence of victory, and the necessities of the king's
situation. The manners indeed of the age were the chief
source of such violence: Laws, which were feebly executed in peaceable times, lost all their authority during
public convulsions: Both parties were alike guilty: Or
if any difference may be remarked between them, we shall
find, that the authority of the crown, being more legal,
was commonly carried, when it prevailed, to less desperate extremities than was that of the aristocracy.

On comparing the conduct and events of this reign,
with those of the preceding, we shall find equal reason
to admire Edward, and to blame Richard; but the circumstance of opposition, surely, will not lie in the strict
regard paid by the former to national privileges, and the
neglect of them by the latter. On the contrary, the
prince of small abilities, as he felt his want of power,
seems to have been more moderate in this respect than the
other. Every parliament, assembled during the reign of
Edward, remonstrates against the exertion of some arbitrary prerogative or other: We hear not any complaints
of that kind during the reign of Richard, till the assembling of his last parliament, which was summoned by his
inveterate enemies, which dethroned him, which framed

their

their complaints during the time of the most furious convulsions, and whose testimony must therefore have, on that account, much less authority with every equitable judge*. Both these princes experienced the encroachments of the Great upon their authority. Edward, reduced to necessities, was obliged to make an express bargain with his parliament, and to sell some of his prerogatives for present supply; but as they were acquainted with his genius and capacity, they ventured not to demand any exorbitant concessions, or such as were incompatible with regal and sovereign power: The weakness of Richard tempted the parliament to extort a commission, which, in a manner, dethroned the prince, and transferred the sceptre into the hands of the nobility. The events of these encroachments were also suitable to the character of each. Edward had no sooner gotten the supply, than he departed from the engagements which had induced the parliament to grant it; he openly told his people, that he had but *dissembled* with them when he seemed to make them these concessions; and he resumed and retained all his prerogatives. But Richard, because he was detected in consulting and deliberating with the judges on the lawfulness of restoring the constitution, found his barons immediately in arms against him; was deprived of his liberty; saw his favourites, his ministers, his tutor, butchered before his face, or banished and attainted; and was obliged to give way to all this violence. There cannot be a more remarkable contrast between the fortunes of two princes: It were happy for society, did this contrast always depend on the justice or injustice of the measures which men embrace; and not rather on the different degrees of prudence and vigour with which those measures are supported.

* Peruse, in this view, the abridgment of the records, by Sir Robert Cotton, during these two reigns.

CHAP. XVII.

1199.
Miscellaneous transactions during this reign.

THERE was a sensible decay of ecclesiastical authority during this period. The disgust, which the laity had received from the numerous usurpations both of the court of Rome, and of their own clergy, had very much weaned the kingdom from superstition; and strong symptoms appeared, from time to time, of a general desire to shake off the bondage of the Romish church. In the committee of eighteen, to whom Richard's last parliament delegated their whole power, there is not the name of one ecclesiastic to be found; a neglect which is almost without example, while the catholic religion subsisted in England [p].

THE aversion entertained against the established church soon found principles and tenets and reasonings, by which it could justify and support itself. John Wickliffe, a secular priest, educated at Oxford, began in the latter end of Edward III. to spread the doctrine of reformation by his discourses, sermons, and writings; and he made many disciples among men of all ranks and stations. He seems to have been a man of parts and learning; and has the honour of being the first person in Europe, that publicly called in question those principles, which had universally passed for certain and undisputed during so many ages. Wickliffe himself, as well as his disciples, who received the name of Wickliffites, or Lollards, was distinguished by a great austerity of life and manners; a circumstance common to almost all those who dogmatize in any new way; both because men, who draw to them the attention of the public, and expose themselves to the odium of great multitudes, are obliged to be very guarded in their conduct, and because few, who have a strong propensity to pleasure or business, will enter upon so difficult and laborious an undertaking. The doctrines of Wickliffe, being derived from his search into the scrip-

[p] See note [G] at the end of the volume.

tures

tures and into ecclesiastical antiquity, were nearly the same with those which were propagated by the reformers in the sixteenth century: He only carried some of them farther than was done by the more sober part of these reformers. He denied the doctrine of the real presence, the supremacy of the church of Rome, the merit of monastic vows: He maintained, that the scriptures were the sole rule of faith; that the church was dependant on the state, and should be reformed by it; that the clergy ought to possess no estates; that the begging friars were a nuisance, and ought not to be supported [q]; that the numerous ceremonies of the church were hurtful to true piety: He asserted, that oaths were unlawful, that dominion was founded in grace, that every thing was subject to fate and destiny, and that all men were preordained either to eternal salvation or reprobation [r]. From the whole of his doctrines, Wickliffe appears to have been strongly tinctured with enthusiasm, and to have been thereby the better qualified to oppose a church, whose chief characteristic is superstition.

THE propagation of these principles gave great alarm to the clergy; and a bull was issued by pope Gregory XI. for taking Wickliffe into custody, and examining into the scope of his opinions [s]. Courteney, bishop of London, cited him before his tribunal; but the reformer had now acquired powerful protectors, who screened him from the ecclesiastical jurisdiction. The duke of Lancaster, who then governed the kingdom, encouraged the principles of Wickliffe; and he made no scruple, as well as lord Piercy, the mareschal, to appear openly in court with him, in order to give him countenance upon his trial: He even insisted, that Wickliffe should sit in the bishop's

[q] Walsingham, p. 191. 208. 283, 284. Spelman. Concil. vol. ii. p. 630. Knyght n, p. 2657. [r] Harpsfield, p. 669. 673, 674. Waldens. tom. i. lib. 3. art. 1. cap. 8. [s] Spelm. Conc. vol. ii. p. 621. Walsingham, p. 201, 202, 203.

presence, while his principles were examined: Courtenay exclaimed against the insult: The Londoners, thinking their prelate affronted, attacked the duke and mareschal, who escaped from their hands with some difficulty[1]. And the populace, soon after, broke into the houses of both these noblemen, threatened their persons, and plundered their goods. The bishop of London had the merit of appeasing their fury and resentment.

The duke of Lancaster, however, still continued his protection to Wickliffe, during the minority of Richard; and the principles of that reformer had so far propagated themselves, that, when the pope sent to Oxford a new bull against these doctrines, the university deliberated for some time, whether they should receive the bull; and they never took any vigorous measures in consequence of the papal orders[2]. Even the populace of London were at length brought to entertain favourable sentiments of this reformer: When he was cited before a synod at Lambeth, they broke into the assembly, and so overawed the prelates, who found both the people and the court against them, that they dismissed him without any farther censure.

The clergy, we may well believe, were more wanting in power, than in inclination to punish this new heresy, which struck at all their credit, possessions, and authority. But there was hitherto no law in England, by which the secular arm was authorised to support orthodoxy; and the ecclesiastics endeavoured to supply the defect by an extraordinary and unwarrantable artifice. In the year 1381, there was an act passed, requiring sheriffs to apprehend the preachers of heresy and their abettors; but this statute had been surreptitiously obtained by the clergy, and had the formality of an enrolment without the consent of

---

[1] Harpsfield in Hist. Wickl. p. 685. Lib. i. p. 191, &c. Walsingham, p. 201.
[2] Wood's Ant. Oxon.

RICHARD II.

the commons. In the subsequent session the lower house complained of the fraud; affirmed, that they had no intention to bind themselves to the prelates farther than their ancestors had done before them; and required that the pretended statute should be repealed; which was done accordingly [w]. But it is remarkable that, notwithstanding this vigilance of the commons, the clergy had so much art and influence that the repeal was suppressed; and the act, which never had any legal authority, remains to this day upon the statute-book [x]: Though the clergy still thought proper to keep it in reserve, and not proceed to the immediate execution of it.

But, besides this defect of power in the church, which saved Wickliffe, that reformer himself, notwithstanding his enthusiasm, seems not to have been actuated by the spirit of martyrdom; and, in all subsequent trials before the prelates, he so explained away his doctrine by tortured meanings, as to render it quite innocent and inoffensive [y]. Most of his followers imitated his cautious disposition, and saved themselves either by recantations or explanations. He died of a palsy, in the year 1385, at his rectory of Lutterworth, in the county of Leicester; and the clergy, mortified that he should have escaped their vengeance, took care, besides assuring the people of his eternal damnation, to represent his last distemper as a visible judgment of heaven upon him for his multiplied heresies and impieties [z].

The proselytes, however, of Wickliffe's opinions still encreased in England [a]: Some monkish writers represent one half of the kingdom as infected by those principles: They were carried over to Bohemia by some youth of that nation, who studied at Oxford: But though the age

[w] Cotton's Abridgment, p. 285. [x] 5 Rich. II. chap. 5.
[y] Walsingham, p. 206. Knyghton, p. 2655, 2656.   [z] Walsingham, p. 312. Ypod. Neust. p. 337.   [a] Knyghton, p. 2663.

CHAP. XVII.

1399.

seemed strongly disposed to receive them, affairs were not yet fully ripe for this great revolution; and the finishing blow to ecclesiastical power was reserved to a period of more curiosity, literature, and inclination for novelties.

MEANWHILE the English parliament continued to check the clergy and the court of Rome, by more sober and more legal expedients. They enacted anew the statute of *provisors*, and affixed higher penalties to the transgression of it, which, in some instances, was even made capital[b]. The court of Rome had fallen upon a new device, which encreased their authority over the prelates: The pope, who found that the expedient of arbitrarily depriving them was violent and liable to opposition, attained the same end, by transferring such of them as were obnoxious to poorer sees, and even to nominal sees, *in partibus infidelium*. It was thus that the archbishop of York, and the bishops of Durham and Chichester, the king's ministers, had been treated after the prevalence of Glocester's faction: The bishop of Carlisle met with the same fate after the accession of Henry IV. For the pope always joined with the prevailing powers when they did not thwart his pretensions. The parliament, in the reign of Richard, enacted a law against this abuse: And the king made a general remonstrance to the court of Rome against all those usurpations which he calls *horrible excesses* of that court[c].

IT was usual for the church, that they might elude the mortmain act, to make their votaries leave lands in trust to certain persons, under whose name the clergy enjoyed the benefit of the bequest; The parliament also stopped the progress of this abuse[d]. In the 17th of the king, the commons prayed, *that remedy might be had against such religious persons as cause their villains to*

[b] 13 Rich. II. cap. 3. 16 Rich. II. cap. 4. [c] Rymer, vol. vii. p. 670. [d] Knyghton, p. 27. 38. Cotton, p. 355.

marry

marry free women inheritable, whereby the estate comes to those religious bands by collusion[e]. This was a new device of the clergy.

The papacy was, at this time, somewhat weakened by a schism, which lasted during forty years, and gave great scandal to the devoted partizans of the holy see. After the pope had resided many years at Avignon, Gregory XI. was persuaded to return to Rome; and upon his death, which happened in 1380, the Romans, resolute to fix, for the future, the seat of the papacy in Italy, besieged the cardinals in the conclave, and compelled them, though they were mostly Frenchmen, to elect Urban VI. an Italian, into that high dignity. The French cardinals, as soon as they recovered their liberty, fled from Rome, and protesting against the forced election, chose Robert, son of the count of Geneva, who took the name of Clement VII. and resided at Avignon. All the kingdoms of Christendom, according to the several interests and inclinations, were divided between these two pontiffs. The court of France adhered to Clement, and was followed by its allies, the king of Castile, and the king of Scotland: England, of course, was thrown into the other party, and declared for Urban. Thus the appellation of *Clementines* and *Urbanists* distracted Europe for several years; and each party damned the other as schismatics, and as rebels to the true vicar of Christ. But this circumstance, though it weakened the papal authority, had not so great an effect as might naturally be imagined. Though any king could easily at first make his kingdom embrace the party of one pope or the other, or even keep it some time in suspence between them, he could not so easily transfer his obedience at pleasure: The people attached themselves to their own party, as to a religious opinion; and conceived an extreme abhorrence to the opposite party.

[e] Cotton, p. 355.

party, whom they regarded as little better than Saracens or infidels. Crusades were even undertaken in this quarrel; and the zealous bishop of Norwich in particular led over, in 1382, near 60,000 bigots into Flanders against the Clementines; but, after losing a great part of his followers, he returned with disgrace into England[f]. Each pope, sensible, from this prevailing spirit among the people, that the kingdom which once embraced his cause would always adhere to him, boldly maintained all the pretensions of his see, and stood not much more in awe of the temporal sovereigns, than if his authority had not been endangered by a rival.

We meet with this preamble to a law enacted at the very beginning of this reign: " Whereas divers persons of " small garrison of land or other possessions, do make great " retinue of people, as well of esquires as of others, in " many parts of the realm, giving to them hats and " other livery of one suit by year, taking again towards " them the value of the same livery, or percase the double " value, by such covenant and assurance, that every of " them shall maintain other in all quarrels, be they " reasonable or unreasonable, to the great mischief and " oppression of the people, &c.[g]" This preamble contains a true picture of the state of the kingdom. The laws had been so feebly executed, even during the long, active, and vigilant reign of Edward III. that no subject could trust to their protection. Men openly associated themselves, under the patronage of some great baron, for their mutual defence. They wore public badges, by which their confederacy was distinguished. They supported each other in all quarrels, iniquities, extortions, murders, robberies, and other crimes. Their chief was more their sovereign than the king himself; and their

[f] Froissard, lib. II. chap. 133, 134. Walsingham, p. 298, 299, 300, &c. Knyghton, p. 2673.   [g] 1 Rich. II. chap. 7.

own

own band was more connected with them than their country. Hence the perpetual turbulence, disorders, factions, and civil wars of those times: Hence the small regard paid to a character or the opinion of the public: Hence the large discretionary prerogatives of the crown, and the danger which might have ensued from the too great limitation of them. If the king had possessed no arbitrary powers, while all the nobles assumed and exercised them, there must have ensued an absolute anarchy in the state.

ONE great mischief attending these confederacies, was the extorting from the king pardons for the most enormous crimes. The parliament often endeavoured, in the last reign, to deprive the prince of this prerogative; but, in the present, they were content with an abridgment of it. They enacted, that no pardon for rapes or for murder from malice prepense should be valid, unless the crime were particularly specified in it[b]. There were also some other circumstances required for passing any pardon of this kind: An excellent law; but ill observed, like most laws that thwart the manners of the people, and the prevailing customs of the times.

IT is easy to observe, from these voluntary associations among the people, that the whole force of the feudal system was in a manner dissolved, and that the English had nearly returned, in that particular, to the same situation in which they stood before the Norman conquest. It was, indeed, impossible that that system could long subsist under the perpetual revolutions to which landed property is every where subject. When the great feudal baronies were first erected, the lord lived in opulence in the midst of his vassals: He was in a situation to protect and cherish and defend them: The quality of patron naturally united itself to that of superior: And these two principles

[b] 13 Rich. II. chap. 1.

of authority mutually supported each other. But when, by the various divisions and mixtures of property, a man's superior came to live at a distance from him, and could no longer give him shelter or countenance; the tie gradually became more fictitious than real: New connexions from vicinity or other causes were formed: Protection was sought by voluntary services and attachment: The appearance of valour, spirit, abilities in any great man, extended his interest very far: And if the sovereign were deficient in these qualities, he was no less, if not more exposed to the usurpations of the aristocracy, than even during the vigour of the feudal system.

The greatest novelty introduced into the civil government during this reign was the creation of peers by patent. Lord Beauchamp of Holt was the first peer that was advanced to the house of lords in this manner. The practice of levying benevolences is also first mentioned in the present reign.

This prince lived in a more magnificent manner than perhaps any of his predecessors or successors. His household consisted of 10,000 persons: He had 300 in his kitchen; and all the other offices were furnished in proportion[i]. It must be remarked, that this enormous train had tables supplied them at the king's expence, according to the mode of that age. Such prodigality was probably the source of many exactions, by purveyors, and was one chief reason of the public discontents.

[i] Harding: This poet says, that he speaks from the authority of a clerk of the green cloth.

CHAP. XVIII.

HENRY IV.

Title of the king——An insurrection——An insurrection in Wales——The earl of Northumberland rebels ——Battle of Shrewsbury——State of Scotland —— Parliamentary transactions——Death ——and character of the king.

THE English had so long been familiarized to the hereditary succession of their monarchs, the instances of departure from it had always borne such strong symptoms of injustice and violence, and so little of a national choice or election, and the returns to the true line had ever been deemed such fortunate incidents in their history, that Henry was afraid lest, in resting his title on the consent of the people, he should build on a foundation to which the people themselves were not accustomed, and whose solidity they would with difficulty be brought to recognize. The idea too of choice seemed always to imply that of conditions, and a right of recalling the consent upon any supposed violation of them; an idea which was not naturally agreeable to a sovereign, and might, in England, be dangerous to the subjects, who, lying so much under the influence of turbulent nobles, had ever paid but an imperfect obedience even to their hereditary princes. For these reasons, Henry was determined never to have recourse to this claim; the only one on which his authority could confidently stand: He rather chose to patch up his title in the best manner he could from other pretensions: And, in the end, he left himself,

CHAP. XVIII.

1399.
Title of the king.

CHAP.
XVIII.

1399.

himself, in the eyes of men of sense, no ground of right but his present possession; a very precarious foundation, which, by its very nature, was liable to be overthrown by every faction of the great, or prejudice of the people. He had indeed a present advantage over his competitor: The heir of the house of Mortimer, who had been declared, in parliament, heir to the crown, was a boy of seven years of age[k]: His friends consulted his safety, by keeping silence with regard to his title: Henry detained him and his younger brother in an honourable custody at Windsor castle: But he had reason to dread, that, in proportion as that nobleman grew to man's estate, he would draw to him the attachment of the people, and make them reflect on the fraud, violence, and injustice, by which he had been excluded from the throne. Many favourable topics would occur in his behalf: He was a native of England; possessed an extensive interest from the greatness and alliances of his family; however criminal the deposed monarch, this youth was entirely innocent; he was of the same religion, and educated in the same manners with the people, and could not be governed by any separate interest: These views would all concur to favour his claim; and though the abilities of the present prince might ward off any dangerous revolution, it was justly to be apprehended, that his authority could with difficulty be brought to equal that of his predecessors.

HENRY, in his very first parliament, had reason to see the danger attending that station which he had assumed, and the obstacles which he would meet with in governing an unruly aristocracy, always divided by faction, and at present inflamed with the resentments consequent on such recent convulsions. The peers, on their assembling, broke out into violent animosities against each other; forty gauntlets, the pledges of furious battle, were thrown on

[k] Dugdale, vol. i. p. 151.

the

the floor of the house by noblemen who gave mutual challenges; and *liar* and *traitor* resounded from all quarters. The king had so much authority with these doughty champions, as to prevent all the combats which they threatened; but he was not able to bring them to a proper composure, or to an amicable disposition towards each other.

It was not long before these passions broke into action. The earls of Rutland, Kent, and Huntingdon, and lord Spencer, who were now degraded from the respective titles of Albemarle, Surrey, Exeter, and Glocester, conferred on them by Richard, entered into a conspiracy, together with the earl of Salisbury and lord Lumley, for raising an insurrection, and for seizing the king's person at Windsor[l]; but the treachery of Rutland gave him warning of the danger. He suddenly withdrew to London; and the conspirators, who came to Windsor with a body of 500 horse, found that they had missed this blow, on which all the success of their enterprize depended. Henry appeared next day at Kingston upon Thames, at the head of 20,000 men, mostly drawn from the city; and his enemies, unable to resist his power, dispersed themselves, with a view of raising their followers in the several counties which were the seat of their interest. But the adherents of the king were hot in the pursuit, and every where opposed themselves to their progress. The earls of Kent and Salisbury were seized at Cirencester by the citizens; and were next day beheaded without farther ceremony, according to the custom of the times[m]. The citizens of Bristol treated Spencer and Lumley in the same manner. The earl of Huntingdon, Sir Thomas Blount, and Sir Benedict Sely, who were also taken prisoners, suffered

[l] Walsingham p. 362. Outhbourne, p. 214. Ypod. Neust. p. 556.
[m] Walsingham, p. 363.

death,

CHAP. XVIII.

1400.

death, with many others of the conspirators, by orders from Henry. And when the quarters of these unhappy men were brought to London, no less than eighteen bishops and thirty-two mitred abbots joined the populace, and met them with the most indecent marks of joy and exultation.

But the spectacle, the most shocking to every one who retained any sentiment either of honour or humanity, still remained. The earl of Rutland appeared, carrying on a pole the head of lord Spencer, his brother-in-law, which he presented in triumph to Henry as a testimony of his loyalty. This infamous man, who was soon after duke of York by the death of his father, and first prince of the blood, had been instrumental in the murder of his uncle the duke of Glocester[a], had then deserted Richard, by whom he was trusted; had conspired against the life of Henry, to whom he had sworn allegiance; had betrayed his associates, whom he had seduced into this enterprize; and now displayed, in the face of the world, these badges of his multiplied dishonour.

1401.

Henry was sensible, that though the execution of these conspirators might seem to give security to his throne, the animosities, which remain after such bloody scenes, are always dangerous to royal authority; and he therefore determined not to encrease, by any hazardous enterprize, those numerous enemies with whom he was every where environed. While a subject, he was believed to have strongly imbibed all the principles of his father, the duke of Lancaster, and to have adopted the prejudices which the Lollards inspired against the abuses of the established church: But, finding himself possessed of the throne by so precarious a title, he thought superstition a necessary implement of public authority; and he resolved, by every

[a] Dugdale, vol. ii. p. 171.

expedient,

expedient, to pay court to the clergy. There were hitherto no penal laws enacted against heresy; an indulgence which had proceeded, not from a spirit of toleration in the Romish church, but from the ignorance and simplicity of the people, which had rendered them unfit either for starting or receiving any new or curious doctrines, and which needed not to be restrained by rigorous penalties. But when the learning and genius of Wickliffe had once broken, in some measure, the fetters of prejudice, the ecclesiastics called aloud for the punishment of his disciples; and the king, who was very little scrupulous in his conduct, was easily induced to sacrifice his principles to his interest, and to acquire the favour of the church by that most effectual method, the gratifying of their vengeance against opponents. He engaged the parliament to pass a law for that purpose: It was enacted, that when any heretic, who relapsed or refused to abjure his opinions, was delivered over to the secular arm by the bishop or his commissaries, he should be committed to the flames by the civil magistrate before the whole people[o]. This weapon did not long remain unemployed in the hands of the clergy: William Sautré, rector of St. Osithes in London, had been condemned by the convocation of Canterbury; his sentence was ratified by the house of peers; the king issued his writ for the execution[p]; and the unhappy man atoned for his erroneous opinions by the penalty of fire. This is the first instance of that kind in England; and thus one horror more was added to those dismal scenes which at that time were already but too familiar to the people.

But the utmost precaution and prudence of Henry could not shield him from those numerous inquietudes which assailed him from every quarter. The connexions of Richard with the royal family of France made that

[o] 2 Henry IV. chap. vii.   [p] Rymer, vol. viii. p. 178.

CHAP.
XVIII.

1401.

court exert its activity to recover his authority, or revenge his death [q]; but though the confusions in England tempted the French to engage in some enterprize by which they might distress their ancient enemy, the greater confusions which they experienced at home obliged them quickly to accommodate matters; and Charles, content with recovering his daughter from Henry's hands, laid aside his preparations, and renewed the truce between the kingdoms [r]. The attack of Guienne was also an inviting attempt, which the present factions that prevailed among the French obliged them to neglect. The Gascons, affectionate to the memory of Richard, who was born among them, refused to swear allegiance to a prince that had dethroned and murdered him; and the appearance of a French army on their frontiers would probably have tempted them to change masters [s]. But the earl of Worcester, arriving with some English troops, gave countenance to the partizans of Henry, and overawed their opponents. Religion too was here found a cement to their union with England. The Gascons had been engaged, by Richard's authority, to acknowledge the pope of Rome; and they were sensible that, if they submitted to France, it would be necessary for them to pay obedience to the pope of Avignon, whom they had been taught to detest as a schismatic. Their principles on this head were too fast rooted to admit of any sudden or violent alteration.

Insurrection in Wales.

THE revolution in England proved likewise the occasion of an insurrection in Wales. Owen Glendour, or Glendourduy, descended from the ancient princes of that country, had become obnoxious on account of his attachment to Richard; and Reginald, lord Gray of Ruthyn, who was closely connected with the new king, and who

[q] Rymer, vol. viii. p. 193.   [r] Ibid. vol. viii. p. 142. 152. 229.
[s] Ibid. vol. viii. p. 120, 111.

enjoyed

enjoyed a great fortune in the marches of Wales, thought the opportunity favourable for oppressing his neighbour, and taking possession of his estate[t]. Glendour, provoked at the injustice, and still more at the indignity, recovered possession by the sword[u]: Henry sent assistance to Gray[w]; the Welsh took part with Glendour: A troublesome and tedious war was kindled, which Glendour long sustained by his valour and activity, aided by the natural strength of the country, and the untamed spirit of its inhabitants.

As Glendour committed devastations promiscuously on all the English, he infested the estate of the earl of Marche; and Sir Edmund Mortimer, uncle to that nobleman, led out the retainers of the family, and gave battle to the Welsh chieftain: His troops were routed, and he was taken prisoner[x]: At the same time, the earl himself, who had been allowed to retire to his castle of Wigmore, and who, though a mere boy, took the field with his followers, fell also into Glendour's hands, and was carried by him into Wales[y]. As Henry dreaded and hated all the family of Marche, he allowed the earl to remain in captivity; and though that young nobleman was nearly allied to the Piercies, to whose assistance he himself had owed his crown, he refused to the earl of Northumberland permission to treat of his ransom with Glendour.

The uncertainty in which Henry's affairs stood during a long time with France, as well as the confusions incident to all great changes in government, tempted the Scots to make incursions into England; and Henry, desirous of taking revenge upon them, but afraid of rendering his new government unpopular by requiring great supplies from his subjects, summoned at Westminster a council of the peers, without the commons, and laid before them

[t] Vita Ric. sec. p. 171, 172.
[u] Vita Ric. sec. p. 172, 173.
[y] Ibid. vol. I. p. 151.
[w] Walsingham, p. 364.
[x] Dugdale, vol. I. p. 150.

the state of his affairs[e]. The military part of the feudal constitution was now much decayed: There remained only so much of that fabric as affected the civil rights and properties of men: And the peers here undertook, but voluntarily, to attend the king in an expedition against Scotland, each of them at the head of a certain number of his retainers[a]. Henry conducted this army to Edinburgh, of which he easily made himself master; and he there summoned Robert III. to do homage to him for his crown[b]. But finding that the Scots would neither submit nor give him battle, he returned in three weeks, after making this useless bravado; and he disbanded his army.

In the subsequent season, Archibald earl of Douglas, at the head of 12,000 men, and attended by many of the principal nobility of Scotland, made an irruption into England, and committed devastations on the northern counties. On his return home, he was overtaken by the Piercies at Homeldon, on the borders of England, and a fierce battle ensued, where the Scots were totally routed. Douglas himself was taken prisoner; as was Mordac earl of Fife, son of the duke of Albany, and nephew of the Scottish king, with the earls of Angus, Murray, and Orkney, and many others of the gentry and nobility[c]. When Henry received intelligence of this victory, he sent the earl of Northumberland orders not to ransom his prisoners, which that nobleman regarded as his right by the laws of war received in that age. The king intended to detain them, that he might be able, by their means, to make an advantageous peace with Scotland; but by this policy he gave a fresh disgust to the family of Piercy.

[a] Rymer, vol. viii. p. 125, 126.   [d] Ibid. p. 125.
[b] Ibid. p. 155, 156, &c.   [c] Walsingham, p. 366. Vita Ric. &c. p. 180. Chron. Otterbourne, p. 237.

HENRY IV.

CHAP. XVIII.

1403. The earl of Northumberland revolts.

THE obligations which Henry had owed to Northumberland were of a kind the most likely to produce ingratitude on the one side, and discontent on the other. The sovereign naturally became jealous of that power which had advanced him to the throne; and the subject was not easily satisfied in the returns which he thought so great a favour had merited. Though Henry, on his accession, had bestowed the office of constable on Northumberland for life[a], and conferred other gifts on that family, these favours were regarded as their due; the refusal of any other request was deemed an injury. The impatient spirit of Harry Piercy, and the factious disposition of the earl of Worcester, younger brother of Northumberland, inflamed the discontents of that nobleman; and the precarious title of Henry tempted him to seek revenge, by overturning that throne which he had at first established. He entered into a correspondence with Glendour: He gave liberty to the earl of Douglas, and made an alliance with that martial chief: He rouzed up all his partizans to arms; and such unlimited authority at that time belonged to the great families, that the same men whom, a few years before, he had conducted against Richard, now followed his standard in opposition to Henry. When war was ready to break out, Northumberland was seized with a sudden illness at Berwic; and young Piercy, taking the command of the troops, marched towards Shrewsbury, in order to join his forces with those of Glendour. The king had happily a small army on foot, with which he had intended to act against the Scots; and knowing the importance of celerity in all civil wars, he instantly hurried down, that he might give battle to the rebels. He approached Piercy near Shrewsbury, before that nobleman was joined by Glendour;

[a] Rymer, vol. viii. p. 89.

CHAP. XVIII.

1403.

and the policy of one leader, and impatience of the other, made them hasten to a general engagement.

THE evening before the battle, Piercy sent a manifesto to Henry, in which he renounced his allegiance, set that prince at defiance, and, in the name of his father and uncle, as well as his own, enumerated all the grievances of which, he pretended, the nation had reason to complain. He upbraided him with the perjury of which he had been guilty, when, on landing at Ravenspur, he had sworn upon the gospels, before the earl of Northumberland, that he had no other intention than to recover the dutchy of Lancaster, and that he would ever remain a faithful subject to king Richard. He aggravated his guilt in first dethroning, then murdering that prince, and in usurping on the title of the house of Mortimer, to whom, both by lineal succession, and by declarations of parliament, the throne, when vacant by Richard's demise, did of right belong. He complained of his cruel policy in allowing the young earl of Marche, whom he ought to regard as his sovereign, to remain a captive in the hands of his enemies, and in even refusing to all his friends permission to treat of his ransom. He charged him again with perjury in loading the nation with heavy taxes, after having sworn, that, without the utmost necessity, he would never levy any impositions upon them. And he reproached him with the arts employed in procuring favourable elections into parliament; arts which he himself had before imputed as a crime to Richard, and which he had made one chief reason of that prince's arraignment and deposition[a]. This manifesto was well calculated to inflame the quarrel between the parties: The bravery of the two leaders promised an obstinate engagement: And the equality of the armies, being each about 12,000. men, a number which was not unmanageable by the

[a] Hall, fol. 23, 21, &c.

commanders,

HENRY IV.

commanders, gave reason to expect a great effusion of blood on both sides, and a very doubtful issue to the combat.

CHAP. XVIII.
1403.

We shall scarcely find any battle in those ages where the shock was more terrible, and more constant. Henry exposed his person in the thickest of the fight: His gallant son, whose military atchievements were afterwards so renowned, and who here performed his noviciate in arms, signalized himself on his father's footsteps, and even a wound, which he received in the face with an arrow, could not oblige him to quit the field [f]. Piercy supported that fame which he had acquired in many a bloody combat: And Douglas, his ancient enemy, and now his friend, still appeared his rival, amidst the horror and confusion of the day. This nobleman performed feats of valour which are almost incredible: He seemed determined that the king of England should that day fall by his arm: He fought him all over the field of battle: And as Henry, either to elude the attacks of the enemy upon his person, or to encourage his own men by the belief of his presence every where, had accoutered several captains in the royal garb, the sword of Douglas rendered this honour fatal to many [g]. But while the armies were contending in this furious manner, the death of Piercy, by an unknown hand, decided the victory, and the royalists prevailed. There are said to have fallen that day on both sides near two thousand three hundred gentlemen; but the persons of greatest distinction were on the king's; the earl of Stafford, Sir Hugh Shirley, Sir Nicholas Gausel, Sir Hugh Mortimer, Sir John Massey, Sir John Calverly. About six thousand private men perished, of whom two thirds were of Piercy's army [h]. The earls of Worcester and Douglas were taken prisoners: The former was be-

21st July. Battle of Shrewsbury.

[f] T. Livii, p. 3. [g] Walsingham, p. 366, 367. Hall, fol. 22.
[h] Chron. Otterbourne, p. 224. Ypod Neust. p. 560.

F 4   headed

headed at Shrewsbury; the latter was treated with the courtesy due to his rank and merit.

The earl of Northumberland, having recovered from his sickness, had levied a fresh army, and was on his march to join his son; but being opposed by the earl of Westmoreland, and bearing of the defeat at Shrewsbury, he dismissed his forces, and came with a small retinue to the king at York¹. He pretended that his sole intention in arming was to mediate between the parties: Henry thought proper to accept of the apology, and even granted him a pardon for his offence: All the other rebels were treated with equal lenity; and, except the earl of Worcester and Sir Richard Vernon, who were regarded as the chief authors of the insurrection, no person engaged in this dangerous enterprize seems to have perished by the hands of the executioner².

But Northumberland, though he had been pardoned, knew that he never should be trusted, and that he was too powerful to be cordially forgiven by a prince whose situation gave him such reasonable grounds of jealousy. It was the effect either of Henry's vigilance or good fortune, or of the narrow genius of his enemies, that no proper concert was ever formed among them: They rose in rebellion one after another; and thereby afforded him an opportunity of suppressing singly those insurrections, which, had they been united, might have proved fatal to his authority. The earl of Nottingham, son of the duke of Norfolk, and the archbishop of York, brother to the earl of Wiltshire, whom Henry, then duke of Lancaster, had beheaded at Bristol, though they had remained quiet while Piercy was in the field, still harboured in their breast a violent hatred against the enemy of their families; and they determined, in conjunction with the earl

¹ Chron. Otterbourne, p. 225.   ² Rymer, vol. viii. p. 353.

of Northumberland, to seek revenge against him. They betook themselves to arms before that powerful nobleman was prepared to join them; and publishing a manifesto, In which they reproached Henry with his usurpation of the crown, and the murder of the late king, they required that the right line should be restored, and all public grievances be redressed. The earl of Westmoreland, whose power lay in the neighbourhood, approached them with an inferior force at Shipton, near York; and being afraid to hazard an action, he attempted to subdue them by a stratagem, which nothing but the greatest folly and simplicity on their part could have rendered successful. He desired a conference with the archbishop and earl between the armies: He heard their grievances with great patience: He begged them to propose the remedies: He approved of every expedient which they suggested: He granted them all their demands: He also engaged that Henry should give them entire satisfaction; and when he saw them pleased with the facility of his concessions, he observed to them, that since amity was now, in effect, restored between them, it were better on both sides to dismiss their forces, which otherwise would prove an insupportable burden to the country. The archbishop and the earl of Nottingham immediately gave directions to that purpose; Their troops disbanded upon the field: But Westmoreland, who had secretly issued contrary orders to *his* army, seized the two rebels without resistance, and carried them to the king, who was advancing with hasty marches to suppress the insurrection[1]. The trial and punishment of an archbishop might have proved a troublesome and dangerous undertaking, had Henry proceeded regularly, and allowed time for an opposition to form itself against that unusual measure: The celerity of the execution alone could here render it safe and prudent.

CHAP. XVIII.

1405.

[1] Walsingham, p. 373. Otterbourne, p. 255.

CHAP. XVIII.
1405.

Finding that Sir William Gascoigne, the chief justice, made some scruple of acting on this occasion, he appointed Sir William Fulthorpe for judge; who, without any indictment, trial, or defence, pronounced sentence of death upon the prelate, which was presently executed. This was the first instance in England of a capital punishment inflicted on a bishop; whence the clergy of that rank might learn that their crimes, more than those of laics, were not to pass with impunity. The earl of Nottingham was condemned and executed in the same summary manner: But though many other persons of condition, such as lord Falconberg, Sir Ralph Hastings, Sir John Colville, were engaged in this rebellion, no others seem to have fallen victims to Henry's severity.

THE earl of Northumberland, on receiving this intelligence, fled into Scotland, together with lord Bardolf[l]; and the king, without opposition, reduced all the castles and fortresses belonging to these noblemen. He thence turned his arms against Glendour, over whom his son, the prince of Wales, had obtained some advantages: But that enemy, more troublesome than dangerous, still found means of defending himself in his fastnesses, and of eluding, though not resisting, all the force of England. In a subsequent season, the earl of Northumberland and lord Bardolf, impatient of their exile, entered the north, in hopes of raising the people to arms; but found the country in such a posture as rendered all their attempts unsuccessful. Sir Thomas Rokesby, sheriff of Yorkshire, levied some forces, attacked the invaders at Bramham, and gained a victory, in which both Northumberland and Bardolf were slain[m]. This prosperous event, joined to the death of Glendour, which happened soon after, freed Henry from all his domestic enemies; and this prince, who had mounted the throne by such unjustifiable means,

1407.

[l] Walsingham, p. 374.   [m] Ibid. p. 377. Chron. Otterb. p. 261.

and

and held it by such an exceptionable title, had yet, by his valour, prudence, and address, accustomed the people to the yoke, and had obtained a greater ascendant over his haughty barons than the law alone, not supported by these active qualities, was ever able to confer.

ABOUT the same time, fortune gave Henry an advantage over that neighbour who, by his situation, was most enabled to disturb his government. Robert III. king of Scots, was a prince, though of slender capacity, extremely innocent and inoffensive in his conduct: But Scotland, at that time, was still less fitted than England for cherishing, or even enduring, sovereigns of that character. The duke of Albany, Robert's brother, a prince of more abilities, at least of a more boisterous and violent disposition, had assumed the government of the state; and, not satisfied with present authority, he entertained the criminal purpose of extirpating his brother's children, and of acquiring the crown to his own family. He threw in prison David, his eldest nephew, who there perished by hunger: James alone, the younger brother of David, stood between that tyrant and the throne; and king Robert, sensible of his son's danger, embarked him on board a ship, with a view of sending him to France, and entrusting him to the protection of that friendly power. Unfortunately, the vessel was taken by the English; prince James, a boy about nine years of age, was carried to London; and though there subsisted at that time a truce between the kingdoms, Henry refused to restore the young prince to his liberty. Robert, worn out with cares and infirmities, was unable to bear the shock of this last misfortune; and he soon after died, leaving the government in the hands of the duke of Albany[e]. Henry was now more sensible than ever of the importance of the acquisition which he had made: While he re-

[e] Buchanan, lib. 19.

tained such a pledge, he was sure of keeping the duke of Albany in dependance; or, if offended, he could easily, by restoring the true heir, take ample revenge upon the usurper. But though the king, by detaining James in the English court, had shown himself somewhat deficient in generosity, he made ample amends by giving that prince an excellent education, which afterwards qualified him, when he mounted the throne, to reform, in some measure, the rude and barbarous manners of his native country.

The hostile dispositions which of late had prevailed between France and England were restrained, during the greater part of this reign, from appearing in action. The jealousies and civil commotions with which both nations were disturbed kept each of them from taking advantage of the unhappy situation of its neighbour. But as the abilities and good fortune of Henry had sooner been able to compose the English factions, this prince began, in the later part of his reign, to look abroad, and to foment the animosities between the families of Burgundy and Orleans, by which the government of France was, during that period, so much distracted. He knew that one great source of the national discontent against his predecessor was the inactivity of his reign; and he hoped, by giving a new direction to the restless and unquiet spirits of his people, to prevent their breaking out in domestic wars and disorders. That he might unite policy with force, he first entered into treaty with the duke of Burgundy, and sent that prince a small body of troops, which supported him against his enemies [p]. Soon after, he hearkened to more advantageous proposals made him by the duke of Orleans, and dispatched a greater body to support that party [q]. But the leaders of the opposite factions having made temporary accommodation,

[p] Walsingham, p. 380. [q] Rymer, vol. viii. p. 715. 738.

the interests of the English were sacrificed; and this effort of Henry proved, in the issue, entirely vain and fruitless. The declining state of his health, and the shortness of his reign, prevented him from renewing the attempt, which his more fortunate son carried to so great a length against the French monarchy.

Such were the military and foreign transactions of this reign: The civil and parliamentary are somewhat more memorable, and more worthy of our attention. During the two last reigns, the elections of the commons had appeared a circumstance of government not to be neglected; and Richard was even accused of using unwarrantable methods for procuring to his partizans a seat in that house. This practice formed one considerable article of charge against him in his deposition; yet Henry scrupled not to tread in his footsteps, and to encourage the same abuses in elections. Laws were enacted against such undue influence, and even a sheriff was punished for an iniquitous return which he had made[f]: But laws were commonly, at that time, very ill executed; and the liberties of the people, such as they were, stood on a surer basis than on laws and parliamentary elections. Though the house of commons was little able to withstand the violent currents which perpetually ran between the monarchy and the aristocracy, and though that house might easily be brought, at a particular time, to make the most unwarrantable concessions to either; the general institutions of the state still remained invariable; the interests of the several members continued on the same footing; the sword was in the hands of the subject; and the government, though thrown into temporary disorder, soon settled itself on its ancient foundations.

During the greater part of this reign, the king was obliged to court popularity; and the house of commons,

[f] Cotton, p. 429.

sensible

CHAP. XVIII.

1411.

sensible of their own importance, began to assume powers, which had not usually been exercised by their predecessors. In the first year of Henry, they procured a law, that no judge, in concurring with any iniquitous measure, should be excused by pleading the orders of the king, or even the danger of his own life from the menaces of the sovereign[s]. In the second year, they insisted on maintaining the practice of not granting any supply before they received an answer to their petitions; which was a tacit manner of bargaining with the prince[t]. In the fifth year, they desired the king to remove from his household four persons who had displeased them, among whom was his own confessor; and Henry, though he told them, that he knew of no offence which these men had committed, yet, in order to gratify them, complied with their request[u]. In the sixth year, they voted the king supplies, but appointed treasurers of their own, to see the money disbursed for the purposes intended, and required them to deliver in their accounts to the house[w]. In the eighth year, they proposed, for the regulation of the government and household, thirty important articles, which were all agreed to; and they even obliged all the members of council, all the judges, and all the officers of the household, to swear to the observance of them[x]. The abridger of the records remarks the unusual liberties taken by the speaker and the house during this period[y]. But the great authority of the commons was but a temporary advantage, arising from the present situation. In a subsequent parliament, when the speaker made his customary application to the throne for liberty of speech, the king, having now overcome all his domestic difficulties, plainly told him, that he would have no novelties introduced, and would enjoy his prerogatives. But on

[s] Cotton, p. 364.   [t] Ibid. p. 406.   [u] Ibid. p. 426.
[w] Ibid. p. 438.   [x] Ibid. p. 456, 457.   [y] Ibid. p. 462.

the

the whole, the limitations of the government seem to have been more sensibly felt, and more carefully maintained by Henry, than by any of his predecessors.

During this reign, when the house of commons were, at any time, brought to make unwary concessions to the crown, they also shewed their freedom by a speedy retractation of them. Henry, though he entertained a perpetual and well-grounded jealousy of the family of Mortimer, allowed not their name to be once mentioned in parliament; and as none of the rebels had ventured to declare the earl of Marche king, he never attempted to procure, what would not have been refused him, an express declaration against the claim of that nobleman; because he knew that such a declaration, in the present circumstances, would have no authority, and would only serve to revive the memory of Mortimer's title in the minds of the people. He proceeded in his purpose after a more artful and covert manner. He procured a settlement of the crown on himself and his heirs-male [r], thereby tacitly excluding the females, and transferring the Salic law into the English government. He thought, that though the house of Plantagenet had at first derived their title from a female, this was a remote event, unknown to the generality of the people; and if he could once accustom them to the practice of excluding women, the title of the earl of Marche would gradually be forgotten and neglected by them. But he was very unfortunate in this attempt. During the long contests with France, the injustice of the Salic law had been so much exclaimed against by the nation, that a contrary principle had taken deep root in the minds of men; and it was now become impossible to eradicate it. The same house of commons, therefore, in a subsequent session, apprehensive that they had overturned the foundations of the English govern-

[r] Cotton. p. 454.

ment,

CHAP. XVIII.

1411.

ment, and that they had opened the door to more civil wars than might enfue even from the irregular elevation of the houfe of Lancafter, applied with fuch earneftnefs for a new fettlement of the crown, that Henry yielded to their requeft, and agreed to the fucceffion of the princeffes of his family[a]. A certain proof, that nobody was, in his heart, fatisfied with the king's title to the crown, or knew on what principle to reft it.

But though the commons, during this reign, fhowed a laudable zeal for liberty in their tranfactions with the crown; their efforts againft the church were ftill more extraordinary, and feemed to anticipate very much the fpirit which became fo general in little more than a century afterwards. I know, that the credit of thefe paffages refts entirely on one ancient hiftorian[b]; but that hiftorian was contemporary, was a clergyman, and it was contrary to the interefts of his order to preferve the memory of fuch tranfactions, much more to forge precedents, which pofterity might, fome time, be tempted to imitate. This is a truth fo evident, that the moft likely way of accounting for the filence of the records on this head, is by fuppofing, that the authority of fome churchmen was fo great as to procure a razure, with regard to thefe circumftances, which the indifcretion of one of that order has happily preferved to us.

In the fixth of Henry, the commons, who had been required to grant fupplies, propofed in plain terms to the king, that he fhould feize all the temporalities of the church, and employ them as a perpetual fund to ferve the exigencies of the ftate. They infifted, that the clergy poffeffed a third of the lands of the kingdom; that they contributed nothing to the public burdens; and that their riches tended only to difqualify them from performing their minifterial functions with proper zeal and atten-

[a] Rymer, vol. viii. p. 462. [b] Walfingham.

tion.

HENRY IV.

tion. When this address was presented, the archbishop of Canterbury, who then attended the king, objected that the clergy, though they went not in person to the wars, sent their vassals and tenants in all cases of necessity; while, at the same time, they themselves who staid at home, were employed night and day in offering up their prayers for the happiness and prosperity of the state. The speaker smiled, and answered, without reserve, that he thought the prayers of the church but a very slender supply. The archbishop, however, prevailed in the dispute: The king discouraged the application of the commons: And the lords rejected the bill which the lower house had framed for stripping the church of her revenues [c].

THE commons were not discouraged by this repulse: In the eleventh of the king they returned to the charge with more zeal than before: They made a calculation of all the ecclesiastical revenues, which, by their account, amounted to 485,000 marks a-year, and contained 18,400 ploughs of land. They proposed to divide this property among fifteen new earls, 1500 knights, 6000 esquires, and a hundred hospitals; besides 20,000 pounds a-year, which the king might take for his own use: And they insisted, that the clerical functions would be better performed than at present, by 15,000 parish priests, paid at the rate of seven marks a-piece of yearly stipend [d]. This application was accompanied with an address for mitigating the statutes enacted against the Lollards, which shows from what source the address came. The king gave the commons a severe reply; and farther to satisfy the church, and to prove that he was quite in earnest, he ordered a Lollard to be burned before the dissolution of the parliament [e].

[c] Walsingham, p. 371. Ypod. Neust. p. 563. [d] Walsingham, p. 379. Tit. Livius. [e] Rymer, vol. viii. p. 627. Otterbourne, p. 267.

CHAP.
XVIII.

1413.

We have now related almoſt all the memorable tranſactions of this reign, which was buſy and active; but produced few events that deſerve to be tranſmitted to poſterity. The king was ſo much employed in defending his crown, which he had obtained by unwarrantable means, and poſſeſſed by a bad title, that he had little leiſure to look abroad, or perform any action, which might redound to the honour or advantage of the nation. His health declined ſome months before his death; He was ſubject to fits, which bereaved him, for the time, of his ſenſes: And, though he was yet in the flower of his age, his end was viſibly approaching. He expired at Weſtminſter in the forty-ſixth year of his age, and the thirteenth of his reign.

ſeth Mſrch.
Death,

and character of the king.

The great popularity which Henry enjoyed before he attained the crown, and which had ſo much aided him in the acquiſition of it, was entirely loſt many years before the end of his reign; and he governed his people more by terror than by affection, more by his own policy than by their ſenſe of duty or allegiance. When men came to reflect, in cool blood, on the crimes which had led him to the throne; the rebellion againſt his prince; the depoſition of a lawful king, guilty ſometimes, perhaps, of oppreſſion, but more frequently of indiſcretion; the excluſion of the true heir; the murder of his ſovereign and near relation; theſe were ſuch enormities as drew on him the hatred of his ſubjects, ſanctified all the rebellions againſt him, and made the executions, though not remarkably ſevere, which he found neceſſary for the maintenance of his authority, appear cruel as well as iniquitous to the people. Yet, without pretending to apologize for theſe crimes, which muſt ever be held in deteſtation, it may be remarked, that he was inſenſibly led into this blameable conduct by a train of incidents, which few men poſſeſs virtue enough to withſtand. The injuſtice with

with which his predecessor had treated him, in first condemning him to banishment, then despoiling him of his patrimony, made him naturally think of revenge, and of recovering his lost rights; the headlong zeal of the people hurried him into the throne; the care of his own security, as well as his ambition, made him an usurper; and the steps have always been so few between the prisons of princes and their graves, that we need not wonder that Richard's fate was no exception to the general rule. All these considerations make Henry's situation, if he retained any sense of virtue, much to be lamented; and the inquietude with which he possessed his envied greatness, and the remorses by which, it is said, he was continually haunted, render him an object of our pity, even when seated upon the throne. But it must be owned, that his prudence and vigilance and foresight, in maintaining his power, were admirable: His command of temper remarkable: His courage, both military and political, without blemish: And he possessed many qualities which fitted him for his high station, and which rendered his usurpation of it, though pernicious in after-times, rather salutary, during his own reign, to the English nation.

HENRY was twice married: By his first wife, Mary de Bohun, daughter and co-heir of the earl of Hereford, he had four sons, Henry, his successor in the throne, Thomas, duke of Clarence, John, duke of Bedford, and Humphrey, duke of Glocester; and two daughters, Blanche and Philippa, the former married to the duke of Bavaria, the latter to the king of Denmark. His second wife, Jane, whom he married after he was king, and who was daughter of the king of Navarre, and widow of the duke of Britanny, brought him no issue.

BY an act of the fifth of this reign, it is made felony to cut out any person's tongue, or put out his eyes; crimes which, the act says, were very frequent. This savage spirit of revenge denotes a barbarous people; though,

perhaps,

CHAP. XVIII.

1413.

perhaps, it was encreased by the prevailing factions and civil commotions.

COMMERCE was very little understood in this reign, as in all the preceding. In particular, a great jealousy prevailed against *merchant strangers*; and many restraints were, by law, imposed upon them; namely, that they should lay out in English manufactures or commodities all the money acquired by the sale of their goods; that they should not buy or sell with one another, and that all their goods should be disposed of three months after importation[f]. This last clause was found so inconvenient, that it was soon after repealed by parliament.

IT appears that the expence of this king's household amounted to the yearly sum of 19,500l. money of that age[g].

GUICCIARDIN tells us, that the Flemings, in this century, learned from Italy all the refinements in arts which they taught the rest of Europe. The progress, however, of the arts was still very slow and backward in England.

[f] 4 Hen. IV. cap. 15. and 5 Hen. IV. cap. 9. [g] Rymer, tom. viii. p. 510.

CHAP. XIX.

HENRY V.

The king's former disorders——His reformation——The Lollards——Punishment of lord Cobham——State of France——Invasion of that kingdom——Battle of Azincour——State of France——New invasion of France——Assassination of the duke of Burgundy——Treaty of Troye——Marriage of the king——His death——and character——Miscellaneous transactions during this reign.

THE many jealousies, to which Henry IV.'s situation naturally exposed him, had so infected his temper, that he had entertained unreasonable suspicions with regard to the fidelity of his eldest son; and, during the latter years of his life, he had excluded that prince from all share in public business, and was even displeased to see him at the head of armies, where his martial talents, though useful to the support of government, acquired him a renown, which, he thought, might prove dangerous to his own authority. The active spirit of young Henry, restrained from its proper exercise, broke out in extravagancies of every kind; and the riot of pleasure, the frolic of debauchery, the outrage of wine, filled the vacancies of a mind, better adapted to the pursuits of ambition, and the cares of government. This course of life threw him among companions, whose disorders, if accompanied with spirit and humour, he indulged and seconded; and he was detected in many sallies, which, to severer eyes, appeared totally unworthy his rank and station. There even remains a tradition, that,

CHAP. XIX.

1413. The king's former disorders.

CHAP. XIX.
1413.

that, when heated with liquor and jollity, he scrupled not to accompany his riotous associates in attacking the passengers on the streets and highways, and despoiling them of their goods; and he found an amusement in the incidents which the terror and regret of these defenceless people produced on such occasions. This extreme of dissoluteness proved equally disagreeable to his father, as that eager application to business which had at first given him occasion of jealousy; and he saw, in his son's behaviour, the same neglect of decency, the same attachment to low company, which had degraded the personal character of Richard, and which, more than all his errors in government, had tended to overturn his throne. But the nation, in general, considered the young prince with more indulgence; and observed so many gleams of generosity, spirit, and magnanimity, breaking continually through the cloud, which a wild conduct threw over his character, that they never ceased hoping for his amendment; and they ascribed all the weeds, which shot up in that rich soil, to the want of proper culture and attention in the king and his ministers. There happened an incident which encouraged these agreeable views, and gave much occasion for favourable reflections to all men of sense and candour. A riotous companion of the prince's had been indicted before Gascoigne, the chief justice, for some disorders; and Henry was not ashamed to appear at the bar with the criminal, in order to give him countenance and protection. Finding that his presence had not over-awed the chief justice, he proceeded to insult that magistrate on his tribunal; but Gascoigne, mindful of the character which he then bore, and the majesty of the sovereign and of the laws, which he sustained, ordered the prince to be carried to prison for his rude behaviour[b]. The spectators were agreeably disappointed when

[b] Hall, fol. 33.

they saw the heir of the crown submit peaceably to this sentence, make reparation for his error by acknowledging it, and check his impetuous nature in the midst of its extravagant career.

The memory of this incident, and of many others of a like nature, rendered the prospect of the future reign nowise disagreeable to the nation, and encreased the joy which the death of so unpopular a prince as the late king naturally occasioned. The first steps taken by the young prince confirmed all those prepossessions entertained in his favour [i]. He called together his former companions, acquainted them with his intended reformation, exhorted them to imitate his example, but strictly inhibited them, till they had given proofs of their sincerity in this particular, from appearing any more in his presence; and he thus dismissed them with liberal presents [k]. The wise ministers of his father, who had checked his riots, found that they had unknowingly been paying the highest court to him; and were received with all the marks of favour and confidence. The chief justice himself, who trembled to approach the royal presence, met with praises instead of reproaches for his past conduct, and was exhorted to persevere in the same rigorous and impartial execution of the laws. The surprize of those who expected an opposite behaviour, augmented their satisfaction; and the character of the young king appeared brighter than if it had never been shaded by any errors.

But Henry was anxious not only to repair his own misconduct, but also to make amends for those iniquities into which policy or the necessity of affairs had betrayed his father. He expressed the deepest sorrow for the fate of the unhappy Richard, did justice to the memory of that unfortunate prince, even performed his funeral obse-

[i] Walsing. p. 382.   [k] Hall, fol. 33. Holingshed, p. 543. Godwin's Life of Henry V. p. 1.

quiet with pomp and solemnity, and cherished all those who had distinguished themselves by their loyalty and attachment towards him[1]. Instead of continuing the restraints which the jealousy of his father had imposed on the earl of Marche, he received that young nobleman with singular courtesy and favour; and by this magnanimity so gained on the gentle and unambitious nature of his competitor, that he remained ever after sincerely attached to him, and gave him no disturbance in his future government. The family of Piercy was restored to its fortune and honours[m]. The king seemed ambitious to bury all party-distinctions in oblivion: The instruments of the preceding reign, who had been advanced from their blind zeal for the Lancastrian interests, more than from their merits, gave place every where to men of more honourable characters: Virtue seemed now to have an open career, in which it might exert itself: The exhortations, as well as example, of the prince gave it encouragement: All men were unanimous in their attachment to Henry; and the defects of his title were forgotten amidst the personal regard which was universally paid to him.

The Lollards. THERE remained among the people only one party distinction, which was derived from religious differences, and which, as it is of a peculiar, and commonly a very obstinate nature, the popularity of Henry was not able to overcome. The Lollards were every day encreasing in the kingdom, and were become a formed party, which appeared extremely dangerous to the church, and even formidable to the civil authority[n]. The enthusiasm by which these sectaries were generally actuated, the great alterations which they pretended to introduce, the hatred which they expressed against the established hierarchy,

[1] Hist. Croyland. contin. Hall, fol. 34. Holingshed, p. 544. [m] Ho. lingshed, p. 545. [n] Walsingham, p. 382.

gave an alarm to Henry; who, either from a sincere attachment to the ancient religion, or from a dread of the unknown consequences which attend all important changes, was determined to execute the laws against such bold innovators. The head of this sect was Sir John Oldcastle, lord Cobham, a nobleman who had distinguished himself by his valour and his military talents, and had, on many occasions, acquired the esteem both of the late and of the present king [o]. His high character and his zeal for the new sect pointed him out to Arundel, archbishop of Canterbury, as the proper victim of ecclesiastical severity; whose punishment would strike a terror into the whole party, and teach them that they must expect no mercy under the present administration. He applied to Henry for a permission to indict lord Cobham [p]; but the generous nature of the prince was averse to such sanguinary methods of conversion. He represented to the primate, that reason and conviction were the best expedients for supporting truth; that all gentle means ought first to be tried in order to reclaim men from error; and that he himself would endeavour, by a conversation with Cobham, to reconcile him to the catholic faith. But he found that nobleman obstinate in his opinions, and determined not to sacrifice truths of such infinite moment to his complaisance for sovereigns [q]. Henry's principles of toleration, or rather his love of the practice, could carry him no farther; and he then gave full reins to ecclesiastical severity against the inflexible heresiarch. The primate indicted Cobham; and, with the assistance of his three suffragans, the bishops of London, Winchester, and St. David's, condemned him to the flames for his erroneous opinions. Cobham, who was confined in the Tower, made his escape before the day appointed for his

[o] Walsingham, p. 382.　　[p] Fox's Acts and Monuments, p. 513.
[q] Rymer, vol. ix. p. 61. Walsingham, p. 383.

execution.

CHAP. XIX.

1413.

1414.
6th Jan.

Punishment of lord Cobham.

execution. The bold spirit of the man, provoked by persecution, and stimulated by zeal, was urged to attempt the most criminal enterprizes; and his unlimited authority over the new sect proved, that he well merited the attention of the civil magistrate. He formed in his retreat very violent designs against his enemies; and dispatching his emissaries to all quarters, appointed a general rendezvous of the party, in order to seize the person of the king at Eltham, and put their persecutors to the sword [f]. Henry, apprized of their intention, removed to Westminster: Cobham was not discouraged by this disappointment; but changed the place of rendezvous to the field near St. Giles's: The king, having shut the gates of the city, to prevent any reinforcement to the Lollards from that quarter, came into the field in the night-time, seized such of the conspirators as appeared, and afterwards laid hold of the several parties, who were hastening to the place appointed. It appeared, that a few only were in the secret of the conspiracy: The rest implicitly followed their leaders: But upon the trial of the prisoners, the treasonable designs of the sect were rendered certain, both from evidence, and from the confession of the criminals themselves [g]. Some were executed; the greater number pardoned [h]. Cobham, himself, who made his escape by flight, was not brought to justice till four years after, when he was hanged as a traitor; and his body was burnt on the gibbet, in execution of the sentence pronounced against him as a heretic [i]. This criminal design, which was perhaps somewhat aggravated by the clergy, brought discredit upon the party, and checked the progress of that sect, which had embraced the speculative doctrines of Wickliffe, and at the same time aspired to a reformation of ecclesiastical abuses.

[f] Walsingham, p. 385. [g] Cotton, p. 554. Hall, fol. 35. Holingshed, p. 544. [h] Rymer, vol. ix. p. 119. 129. 193. [i] Walsingham, p. 410. Otterbourne, p. 280. Holingshed, p. 561.

THESE

THESE two points were the great objects of the Lollards; but the bulk of the nation was not affected in the same degree by both of them. Common sense, and obvious reflection, had discovered to the people the advantages of a reformation in discipline; but the age was not yet so far advanced as to be seized with the spirit of controversy, or to enter into those abstruse doctrines, which the Lollards endeavoured to propagate throughout the kingdom. The very notion of heresy alarmed the generality of the people: Innovation in fundamental principles was suspicious: Curiosity was not, as yet, a sufficient counterpoize to authority: And even many, who were the greatest friends to the reformation of abuses, were anxious to express their detestation of the speculative tenets of the Wickliffites, which, they feared, threw disgrace on so good a cause. This turn of thought appears evidently in the proceedings of the parliament, which was summoned immediately after the detection of Cobham's conspiracy. That assembly passed severe laws against the new heretics: They enacted, that whoever was convicted of Lollardy before the Ordinary, besides suffering capital punishment according to the laws formerly established, should also forfeit his lands and goods to the king; and that the chancellor, treasurer, justices of the two benches, sheriffs, justices of the peace, and all the chief magistrates in every city and borough, should take an oath to use their utmost endeavours for the extirpation of heresy [v]. Yet this very parliament, when the king demanded supply, renewed the offer formerly pressed upon his father, and entreated him to seize all the ecclesiastical revenues, and convert them to the use of the crown [x]. The clergy were alarmed: They could offer the king no bribe which was equivalent: They only agreed to confer on him all the priories alien, which

[v] 2 Hen. V. chap. 7. [x] Hall, fol. 35.

depended

CHAP.
XIX.

1414.

depended on capital abbies in Normandy, and had been bequeathed to these abbies, when that province remained united to England: And Chicheley, now archbishop of Canterbury, endeavoured to divert the blow, by giving occupation to the king, and by persuading him to undertake a war against France, in order to recover his lost rights to that kingdom [y].

It was the dying injunction of the late king to his son, not to allow the English to remain long in peace, which was apt to breed intestine commotions; but to employ them in foreign expeditions, by which the prince might acquire honour; the nobility, in sharing his dangers, might attach themselves to his person; and all the restless spirits find occupation for their inquietude. The natural disposition of Henry sufficiently inclined him to follow this advice, and the civil disorders of France, which had been prolonged beyond those of England, opened a full career to his ambition.

1415.
State of
France.

The death of Charles V. which followed soon after that of Edward III. and the youth of his son, Charles VI. put the two kingdoms for some time in a similar situation; and it was not to be apprehended, that either of them, during a minority, would be able to make much advantage of the weakness of the other. The jealousies also between Charles's three uncles, the dukes of Anjou, Berri, and Burgundy, had distracted the affairs of France rather more than those between the dukes of Lancaster, York, and Gloucester, Richard's three uncles, disordered those of England; and had carried off the attention of the French nation from any vigorous enterprize against foreign states. But in proportion as Charles advanced in years, the factions were composed; his two uncles, the dukes of Anjou and Burgundy, died; and the king him-

[y] Hall, fol. 35, 36.

self,

self, assuming the reins of government, discovered symptoms of genius and spirit, which revived the drooping hopes of his country. This promising state of affairs was not of long duration: The unhappy prince fell suddenly into a fit of frenzy, which rendered him incapable of exercising his authority; and though he recovered from this disorder, he was so subject to relapses, that his judgment was gradually, but sensibly impaired, and no steady plan of government could be pursued by him. The administration of affairs was disputed between his brother, Lewis duke of Orleans, and his cousin-german, John duke of Burgundy: The propinquity to the crown pleaded in favour of the former: The latter, who, in right of his mother, had inherited the county of Flanders, which he annexed to his father's extensive dominions, derived a lustre from his superior power: The people were divided between these contending princes: And the king, now resuming, now dropping his authority, kept the victory undecided, and prevented any regular settlement of the state by the final prevalence of either party.

At length, the dukes of Orleans and Burgundy, seeming to be moved by the cries of the nation and by the interposition of common friends, agreed to bury all past quarrels in oblivion, and to enter into strict amity: They swore before the altar the sincerity of their friendship; the priest administered the sacrament to both of them; they gave to each other every pledge which could be deemed sacred among men: But all this solemn preparation was only a cover for the basest treachery, which was deliberately premeditated by the duke of Burgundy. He procured his rival to be assassinated in the streets of Paris: He endeavoured for some time to conceal the part which he took in the crime: But being detected, he embraced a resolution still more criminal and more dangerous to society, by openly avowing and justifying it it [a]. The parliament itself of Paris, the tribunal of justice, heard the harangues of the duke's advocate in defence of assassination, which he termed tyrannicide; and that assembly, partly influenced by faction, partly overawed by power, pronounced no sentence of condemnation against this detestable doctrine [b]. The same question was afterwards agitated before the council of Constance; and it was with difficulty that a feeble decision, in favour of the contrary opinion, was procured from these fathers of the church, the ministers of peace and of religion. But the mischievous effects of that tenet, had they been before anywise doubtful, appeared sufficiently from the present incidents. The commission of this crime, which destroyed all trust and security, rendered the war implacable between the French parties, and cut off every means of peace and accommodation. The princes of the blood, combining with the young duke of Orleans and his brothers, made violent war on the duke of Burgundy; and the unhappy king, seized sometimes by one party, sometimes by the other, transferred alternately to each of them the appearance of legal authority. The provinces were laid waste by mutual depredations: Assassinations were every where committed from the animosity of the several leaders; or, what was equally terrible, executions were ordered, without any legal or free trial, by pretended courts of judicature. The whole kingdom was distinguished into two parties, the Burgundians, and the Armagnacs; so the adherents of the young duke of Orleans were called, from the count of Armagnac, father-in-law to that prince. The city of Paris, distracted between them, but inclining more to the Burgundians, was a perpetual scene of blood and violence; the king and royal family were often detained captives in the hands of the populace; their

[a] La Laboureur, liv. xvii. chap. 23, 24.
[b] Ibid. liv. 27. chap. 27. Monstrelet, chap. 39.

faithful

faithful ministers were butchered or imprisoned before their face; and it was dangerous for any man, amidst these enraged factions, to be distinguished by a strict adherence to the principles of probity and honour.

DURING this scene of general violence, there rose into some consideration a body of men, which usually makes no figure in public transactions even during the most peaceful times; and that was the university of Paris, whose opinion was sometimes demanded, and more frequently offered, in the multiplied disputes between the parties. The schism, by which the church was at that time divided, and which occasioned frequent controversies in the university, had raised the professors to an unusual degree of importance; and this connection between literature and superstition had bestowed on the former a weight, to which reason and knowledge are not, of themselves, any wise entitled among men. But there was another society whose sentiments were much more decisive at Paris, the fraternity of butchers, who, under the direction of their ringleaders, had declared for the duke of Burgundy, and committed the most violent outrages against the opposite party. To counterbalance their power, the Armagnacs made interest with the fraternity of carpenters; the populace ranged themselves on one side or the other; and the fate of the capital depended on the prevalence of either party.

THE advantage, which might be made of these confusions, was easily perceived in England; and, according to the maxims which usually prevail among nations, it was determined to lay hold of the favourable opportunity. The late king, who was courted by both the French parties, fomented the quarrel, by alternately sending assistance to each; but the present sovereign, impelled by the vigour of youth and the ardour of ambition, determined to push his advantages to a greater length, and to

carry

carry violent war into that distracted kingdom. But while he was making preparations for this end, he tried to effect his purpose by negociation; and he sent over ambassadors to Paris, offering a perpetual peace and alliance; but demanding Catharine, the French king's daughter, in marriage, two millions of crowns as her portion, one million six hundred thousand as the arrears of king John's ransom, and the immediate possession and full sovereignty of Normandy and of all the other provinces, which had been ravished from England by the arms of Philip Augustus; together with the superiority of Britanny and Flanders [b]. Such exorbitant demands show, that he was sensible of the present miserable condition of France; and the terms, offered by the French court, though much inferior, discover their consciousness of the same melancholy truth. They were willing to give him the princess in marriage, to pay him eight hundred thousand crowns, to resign the entire sovereignty of Guienne, and to annex to that province the country of Perigord, Rovergue, Xaintonge, the Angoumois, and other territories [c]. As Henry rejected these conditions, and scarcely hoped that his own demands would be complied with, he never intermitted a moment his preparations for war, and having assembled a great fleet and army at Southampton, having invited all the nobility and military men of the kingdom to attend him by the hopes of glory and of conquest, he came to the sea-side, with a purpose of embarking on his expedition.

[b] Rymer, vol. ix. p. 208.
[c] Ibid. p. 211. It is reported by some historians (See H R. Croyl. Cont. p. 500.) that the Dauphin, in derision of Henry's claims and dissolute character, sent him a box of tennis balls, intimating that these implements of play were better adapted to him than the instruments of war. But this story is by no means credible; the great offers made by the court of France, show that they had already entertained a just idea of Henry's character, as well as of their own situation.

But while Henry was meditating conquests upon his neighbours, he unexpectedly found himself in danger from a conspiracy at home, which was happily detected in its infancy. The earl of Cambridge, second son of the late duke of York, having espoused the sister of the earl of Marche, had zealously embraced the interests of that family; and had held some conferences with lord Scrope of Masham, and Sir Thomas Grey of Heton, about the means of recovering to that nobleman his right to the crown of England. The conspirators, as soon as detected, acknowledged their guilt to the king[d]; and Henry proceeded without delay to their trial and condemnation. The utmost that could be expected of the best king in those ages, was, that he would so far observe the essentials of justice, as not to make an innocent person a victim to his severity: But as to the formalities of law, which are often as material as the essentials themselves, they were sacrificed without scruple to the least interest or convenience. A jury of commoners was summoned: The three conspirators were indicted before them: The constable of Southampton castle swore, that they had separately confessed their guilt to him: Without other evidence, Sir Thomas Grey was condemned and executed: But as the earl of Cambridge and lord Scrope pleaded the privilege of their peerage, Henry thought proper to summon a court of eighteen barons, in which the duke of Clarence presided: The evidence, given before the jury, was read to them: The prisoners, though one of them was a prince of the blood, were not examined, nor produced in court, nor heard in their own defence; but received sentence of death upon this proof, which was every way irregular and unsatisfactory; and the sentence was soon after executed. The earl of Marche was accused of having given his approbation to the conspi-

[d] Rymer, vol. ix. p. 300. T. Livii, p. 8.

CHAP. XIX.

1415.

Invasion of France.

14th Aug.

racy, and received a general pardon from the king[e]. He was probably either innocent of the crime imputed to him, or had made reparation by his early repentance and discovery[f].

THE successes which the arms of England have, in different ages, obtained over those of France, have been much owing to the favourable situation of the former kingdom. The English, happily seated in an island, could make advantage of every misfortune which attended their neighbours, and were little exposed to the danger of reprizals. They never left their own country but when they were conducted by a king of extraordinary genius, or found their enemy divided by intestine factions, or were supported by a powerful alliance on the continent; and as all these circumstances concurred at present to favour their enterprize, they had reason to expect from it proportionable success. The duke of Burgundy, expelled France by a combination of the princes, had been secretly soliciting the alliance of England[g]; and Henry knew, that this prince, though he scrupled at first to join the inveterate enemy of his country, would willingly, if he saw any probability of success, both assist him with his Flemish subjects, and draw over to the same side all his numerous partizans in France. Trusting therefore to this circumstance, but without establishing any concert with the duke, he put to sea, and landed near Harfleur, at the head of an army of 6000 men at arms, and 24,000 foot, mostly archers. He immediately began the siege of that place, which was valiantly defended by d'Estoüteville, and under him by de Guitri, de Gaucourt, and others of the French nobility: But as the garrison was weak, and the fortifications in bad repair, the governor was at last obliged to capitulate; and he promised to surrender the

[e] Rymer, vol. ix. p. 303. [f] St. Remi, chap. lv. Goodwin, p. 65.
[g] Rymer, vol. ix. p. 137, 153.

HENRY V.

CHAP. XIX.

1415.

place if he received no succour before the eighteenth of September. The day came, and there was no appearance of a French army to relieve him. Henry, taking possession of the town, placed a garrison in it, and expelled all the French inhabitants, with an intention of peopling it anew with English.

THE fatigues of this siege, and the unusual heat of the season, had so wasted the English army, that Henry could enter on no farther enterprise; and was obliged to think of returning into England. He had dismissed his transports, which could not anchor in an open road upon the enemy's coasts: And he lay under a necessity of marching by land to Calais, before he could reach a place of safety. A numerous French army of 14,000 men at arms, and 40,000 foot, was by this time assembled in Normandy under the constable d'Albret; a force which, if prudently conducted, was sufficient either to trample down the English in the open field, or to harass and reduce to nothing their small army, before they could finish so long and difficult a march. Henry, therefore, cautiously offered to sacrifice his conquest of Harfleur for a safe passage to Calais; but his proposal being rejected, he determined to make his way by valour and conduct through all the opposition of the enemy[i]. That he might not discourage his army by the appearance of flight, or expose them to those hazards which naturally attend precipitate marches, he made slow and deliberate journies[k], till he reached the Somme, which he purposed to pass at the ford of Blanquetague, the same place where Edward, in a like situation, had before escaped from Philip de Valois. But he found the ford rendered impassable by the precaution of the French general, and guarded by a strong body on the opposite

[i] De Laboureur, liv. 35. chap. 6.   [k] T. Livii, p. 12.

CHAP. XIX.

1415.

Battle of Azincour.

25 h Oo.

bank¹; and he was obliged to march higher up the river, in order to seek for a safe passage. He was continually harassed on his march by flying parties of the enemy; saw bodies of troops on the other side ready to oppose every attempt; his provisions were cut off; his soldiers languished with sickness and fatigue; and his affairs seemed to be reduced to a desperate situation: When he was so dexterous or so fortunate as to seize by surprise a passage near St. Quintin, which had not been sufficiently guarded; and he safely carried over his army ⁿ.

HENRY then bent his march northwards to Calais; but he was still exposed to great and imminent danger from the enemy, who had also passed the Somme, and threw themselves full in his way, with a purpose of intercepting his retreat. After he had passed the small river of Ternois at Blangi, he was surprised to observe from the heights the whole French army drawn up in the plains of Azincour, and so posted, that it was impossible for him to proceed on his march without coming to an engagement. Nothing in appearance could be more unequal than the battle, upon which his safety and all his fortunes now depended. The English army was little more than half the number, which had disembarked at Harfleur; and they laboured under every discouragement and necessity. The enemy was four times more numerous, was headed by the dauphin and all the princes of the blood; and was plentifully supplied with provisions of every kind. Henry's situation was exactly similar to that of Edward at Cressy, and that of the Black Prince at Poictiers; and the memory of these great events, inspiring the English with courage, made them hope for a like deliverance from their present difficulties. The king

¹ St. Reml, chap. 58.   ⁿ T. Livii, p. 13.

likewise

likewise observed the same prudent conduct which had been followed by these great commanders: He drew up his army on a narrow ground between two woods, which guarded each flank; and he patiently expected in that posture the attack of the enemy[a].

HAD the French constable been able, either to reason justly upon the present circumstances of the two armies, or to profit by past experience, he had declined a combat, and had waited, till necessity, obliging the English to advance, had made them relinquish the advantages of their situation. But the impetuous valour of the nobility, and a vain confidence in superior numbers, brought on this fatal action, which proved the source of infinite calamities to their country. The French archers on horseback and their men at arms, crowded in their ranks, advanced upon the English archers, who had fixed pallisadoes in their front to break the impression of the enemy, and who safely plyed them, from behind that defence, with a shower of arrows, which nothing could resist[o]. The clay soil, moistened by some rain which had lately fallen, proved another obstacle to the force of the French cavalry: The wounded men and horses discomposed their ranks: The narrow compass, in which they were pent, hindered them from recovering any order: The whole army was a scene of confusion, terror, and dismay: And Henry, perceiving his advantage, ordered the English archers, who were light and unincumbered, to advance upon the enemy, and seize the moment of victory. They fell with their battle-axes upon the French, who, in their present posture, were incapable either of flying or of making defence: They hewed them in pieces without resistance[p]. And being seconded by the men at arms, who also

C H A P.
XIX.

1415.

[a] St. Remi, chap. 62. [o] Walsingham, p. 392. T. Livii, p. 19. Le Laboureur, liv. 35. chap. 7. Monstrelet, chap. 147. [p] Walsingham, p. 393. Yped. Neust. p. 584.

pushed

pushed on against the enemy, they covered the field with the killed, wounded, dismounted, and overthrown. After all appearance of opposition was over, the English had leisure to make prisoners; and having advanced with uninterrupted success to the open plain, they there saw the remains of the French rear guard, which still maintained the appearance of a line of battle. At the same time, they heard an alarm from behind: Some gentlemen of Picardy, having collected about 600 peasants, had fallen upon the English baggage, and were doing execution on the unarmed followers of the camp, who fled before them. Henry, seeing the enemy on all sides of him, began to entertain apprehensions from his prisoners; and he thought it necessary to issue general orders for putting them to death: But on discovering the truth, he stopped the slaughter, and was still able to save a great number.

No battle was ever more fatal to France, by the number of princes and nobility, slain or taken prisoners. Among the former were the constable himself, the count of Nevers and the duke of Brabant, brothers to the duke of Burgundy, the count of Vaudemont, brother to the duke of Lorraine, the duke of Alençon, the duke of Barre, the count of Marle. The most eminent prisoners were the dukes of Orleans and Bourbon, the counts d'Eu, Vendôme, and Richemont, and the mareschal of Boucicaut. An archbishop of Sens also was slain in this battle. The killed are computed on the whole to have amounted to ten thousand men; and as the slaughter fell chiefly upon the cavalry, it is pretended, that of these eight thousand were gentlemen. Henry was master of 14,000 prisoners. The person of chief note, who fell among the English, was the duke of York, who perished fighting by the king's side, and had an end more honourable than his life. He was succeeded in his honours and fortune by his

nephew,

nephew, son of the earl of Cambridge, executed in the beginning of the year. All the English, who were slain, exceeded not forty; though some writers, with greater probability, make the number more considerable.

CHAP. XIX.
1415.

THE three great battles of Cressy, Poictiers, and Azincour bear a singular resemblance to each other in their most considerable circumstances. In all of them, there appears the same temerity in the English princes, who without any object of moment, merely for the sake of plunder, had ventured so far into the enemies' country as to leave themselves no retreat; and unless saved by the utmost imprudence in the French commanders, were, from their very situation, exposed to inevitable destruction. Due allowance being made for this temerity, which, according to the irregular plans of war followed in those ages, seems to have been, in some measure, unavoidable; there appears, in the day of action, the same presence of mind, dexterity, courage, firmness, and precaution on the part of the English: The same precipitation, confusion, and vain confidence on the part of the French: And the events were such as might have been expected from such opposite conduct. The immediate consequences too of these three great victories were similar: Instead of pushing the French with vigour, and taking advantage of their consternation, the English princes, after their victory, seem rather to have relaxed their efforts, and to have allowed the enemy leisure to recover from his losses. Henry interrupted not his march a moment after the battle of Azincour; he carried his prisoners to Calais, thence to England; he even concluded a truce with the enemy; and it was not till after an interval of two years that any body of English troops appeared in France.

THE poverty of all the European princes, and the small resources of their kingdoms, were the cause of these continual interruptions in their hostilities; and though the

CHAP. XIX.

1415.

maxims of war were in general destructive, their military operations were mere incursions, which, without any settled plan, they carried on against each other. The lustre, however, attending the victory of Azincour, procured some supplies from the English parliament, though still unequal to the expences of a campaign. They granted Henry an entire fifteenth of moveables; and they conferred on him, *for life,* the duties of tonnage and poundage, and the subsidies on the exportation of wool and leather. This concession is more considerable than that which had been granted to Richard II. by his last parliament, and which was afterwards, on his deposition, made so great an article of charge against him.

State of France.

But during this interruption of hostilities from England, France was exposed to all the furies of civil war; and the several parties became every day more enraged against each other. The duke of Burgundy, confident that the French ministers and generals were entirely discredited by the misfortune at Azincour, advanced with a great army to Paris, and attempted to re-instate himself in possession of the government, as well as of the person of the king. But his partizans in that city were overawed by the court, and kept in subjection: The duke despaired of success; and he retired with his forces, which he immediately disbanded in the Low-Countries [9].

1417.

He was soon after invited to make a new attempt, by some violent quarrels which broke out in the royal family. The queen, Isabella, daughter of the duke of Bavaria, who had been hitherto an inveterate enemy to the Burgundian faction, had received a great injury from the other party, which the implacable spirit of that princess was never able to forgive. The public necessities obliged the count of Armagnac, created constable of France in the place of d'Albret, to seize the great treasures which Isa-

[9] Le Laboureur, liv. 35. chap. 10.

bella

bells had amassed: And when she expressed her displeasure at this injury, he inspired into the weak mind of the king some jealousies concerning her conduct, and pushed him to seize, and put to the torture, and afterwards throw into the Seine, Bois-bourdon, her favourite, whom he accused of a commerce of gallantry with that princess. The queen herself was sent to Tours, and confined under a guard[r]; and, after suffering these multiplied insults, she no longer scrupled to enter into a correspondence with the duke of Burgundy. As her son, the dauphin Charles, a youth of sixteen, was entirely governed by the faction of Armagnac, she extended her animosity to him, and sought his destruction with the most unrelenting hatred. She had soon an opportunity of rendering her unnatural purpose effectual. The duke of Burgundy, in concert with her, entered France at the head of a great army: He made himself master of Amiens, Abbeville, Dourlens, Montreüil, and other towns in Picardy; Senlis, Rheims, Chalons, Troye, and Auxerre, declared themselves of his party[s]. He got possession of Beaumont, Pontoise, Vernon, Meulant, Montlheri, towns in the neighbourhood of Paris; and carrying farther his progress towards the west, he seized Etampes, Chartres, and other fortresses; and was at last able to deliver the queen, who fled to Troye, and openly declared against those ministers who, she said, detained her husband in captivity[t].

Meanwhile, the partizans of Burgundy raised a commotion in Paris, which always inclined to that faction. Lile-Adam, one of the duke's captains, was received into the city in the night-time, and headed the insurrection of the people, which in a moment became so impetuous that nothing could oppose it. The person of the king was seized: The dauphin made his escape with difficulty:

[r] St. Remi, chap. 74. Monstrelet, chap. 167. [s] St. Remi, chap. 79. [t] Ibid, chap. 81. Monstrelet, chap. 178, 179.

Great

CHAP. XIX.

1417.

Great numbers of the faction of Armagnac were immediately butchered: The count himself, and many persons of note, were thrown into prison: Murders were daily committed from private animosity, under pretence of faction: And the populace, not satiated with their fury, and deeming the course of public justice too dilatory, broke into the prisons, and put to death the count of Armagnac, and all the other nobility who were there confined [u].

New invasion of France.
18 August.

WHILE France was in such furious combustion, and was so ill prepared to resist a foreign enemy, Henry, having collected some treasure, and levied an army, landed in Normandy at the head of 25,000 men; and met with no considerable opposition from any quarter. He made himself master of Falaise; Evreux and Caen submitted to him; Pont de l'Arche opened its gates; and Henry, having subdued all the lower Normandy, and having received a reinforcement of 15,000 men from England [w], formed the siege of Roüen, which was defended by a garrison of 4000 men, seconded by the inhabitants, to the number of 15,000 [x]. The cardinal des Ursins here attempted to incline him towards peace, and to moderate his pretensions: But the king replied to him in such terms, as shewed that he was fully sensible of all his present advantages: "Do you not see," said he, "that God has led me hither as by the hand? France has no sovereign: I have just pretensions to that kingdom: Every thing is here in the utmost confusion: No one thinks of resisting me. Can I have a more sensible proof, that the Being who disposes of empires, has determined to put the crown of France upon my head [y]?"

1418.

BUT though Henry had opened his mind to this scheme of ambition, he still continued to negociate with his ene-

[u] St. Remi, chap. 35, 86. Monstrelet, chap. 118.   [w] Wolsingham, p. 400.   [x] St. Remi, chap. 91.   [y] Juvenal des Ursins.

mies

mies, and endeavoured to obtain more secure, though less considerable advantages. He made, at the same time, offers of peace to both parties; to the queen and duke of Burgundy on the one hand, who, having possession of the king's person, carried the appearance of legal authority [a]; and to the dauphin on the other, who, being the undoubted heir of the monarchy, was adhered to by every one that payed any regard to the true interests of their country [b]. These two parties also carried on a continual negociation with each other. The terms proposed on all sides were perpetually varying; The events of the war, and the intrigues of the cabinet, intermingled with each other: And the fate of France remained long in this uncertainty. After many negociations, Henry offered the queen and the duke of Burgundy to make peace with them, to espouse the princess Catharine, and to accept of all the provinces ceded to Edward III. by the treaty of Bretigni, with the addition of Normandy, which he was to receive in full and entire sovereignty [c]. These terms were submitted to; There remained only some circumstances to adjust, in order to the entire completion of the treaty: But in this interval the duke of Burgundy secretly finished his treaty with the dauphin; and these two princes agreed to share the royal authority during king Charles's lifetime, and to unite their arms in order to expel foreign enemies [d].

THIS alliance, which seemed to cut off from Henry all hopes of farther success, proved, in the issue, the most favourable event that could have happened for his pretensions. Whether the dauphin and the duke of Burgundy were ever sincere in their mutual engagements, is uncertain; but very fatal effects resulted from their momentary and seeming union. The two princes agreed to an interview, in order to concert the means of rendering effec-

[a] Rymer, vol. ix. p. 717. 749. [c] Ibid. p. 626, &c.
[b] Ibid. p. 761. [d] Ibid. p. 776. St. Remi, chap. 95.

CHAP.
XIX.

1419.

tual their common attack on the English; but how both or either of them could with safety venture upon this conference, it seemed somewhat difficult to contrive. The assassination perpetrated by the duke of Burgundy, and still more, his open avowal of the deed, and defence of the doctrine, tended to dissolve all the bands of civil society; and even men of honour, who detested the example, might deem it just, on a favourable opportunity, to retaliate upon the author. The duke, therefore, who neither dared to give, nor could pretend to expect, any trust, agreed to all the contrivances for mutual security which were proposed by the ministers of the dauphin. The two princes came to Montereau: The duke lodged in the castle: The dauphin in the town, which was divided from the castle by the river Yonne: The bridge between them was chosen for the place of interview: Two high rails were drawn across the bridge: The gates on each side were guarded, one by the officers of the dauphin, the other by those of the duke: The princes were to enter into the intermediate space by the opposite gates, accompanied each by ten persons; and, with all these marks of diffidence, to conciliate their mutual friendship. But it appeared that no precautions are sufficient where laws have no place, and where all principles of honour are utterly abandoned. Tannegui de Chatel, and others of the dauphin's retainers, had been zealous partizans of the late duke of Orleans; and they determined to seize the opportunity of revenging on the assassin the murder of that prince: They no sooner entered the rails, than they drew their swords and attacked the duke of Burgundy: His friends were astonished, and thought not of making any defence; and all of them either shared his fate, or were taken prisoners by the retinue of the dauphin [a].

Assassination of the duke of Burgundy.

[a] St. Remi, chap. 97. Monstrelet, chap. 212.

THE

HENRY V.

THE extreme youth of this prince made it doubtful whether he had been admitted into the secret of the conspiracy: But as the deed was committed under his eye, by his most intimate friends, who still retained their connexions with him, the blame of the action, which was certainly more imprudent than criminal, fell entirely upon him. The whole state of affairs was every where changed by this unexpected incident. The city of Paris, passionately devoted to the family of Burgundy, broke out into the highest fury against the dauphin. The court of king Charles entered from interest into the same views; and as all the ministers of that monarch had owed their preferment to the late duke, and foresaw their downfal if the dauphin should recover possession of his father's person, they were concerned to prevent, by any means, the success of his enterprize. The queen, persevering in her unnatural animosity against her son, encreased the general flame, and inspired into the king, as far as he was susceptible of any sentiment, the same prejudices by which she herself had long been actuated. But above all, Philip count of Charolois, now duke of Burgundy, thought himself bound, by every tie of honour and of duty, to revenge the murder of his father, and to prosecute the assassin to the utmost extremity. And in this general transport of rage, every consideration of national and family interest was buried in oblivion by all parties: The subjection to a foreign enemy, the expulsion of the lawful heir, the slavery of the kingdom, appeared but small evils if they led to the gratification of the present passion.

THE king of England had, before the death of the duke of Burgundy, profited extremely by the distractions of France, and was daily making a considerable progress in Normandy. He had taken Rouen after an obstinate siege[a]: He had made himself master of Pontoise and Gi-

[a] T. Livii, p. 69. Monstrelet, chap. 201.

CHAP. XIX.
1419.

fors: He even threatened Paris, and by the terror of his arms, had obliged the court to remove to Troye: And in the midst of his successes, he was agreeably surprised to find his enemies, instead of combining against him for their mutual defence, disposed to rush into his arms, and to make him the instrument of their vengeance upon each other. A league was immediately concluded at Arras between him and the duke of Burgundy. This prince, without stipulating any thing for himself, except the prosecution of his father's murder, and the marriage of the duke of Bedford with his sister, was willing to sacrifice the kingdom to Henry's ambition; and he agreed to every

1420.

demand made by that monarch. In order to finish this astonishing treaty, which was to transfer the crown of France to a stranger, Henry went to Troye, accompanied by his brothers, the dukes of Clarence and Glocester; and was there met by the duke of Burgundy. The imbecility into which Charles had fallen made him incapable of seeing any thing but through the eyes of those who attended him; as they, on their part, saw every thing through the medium of their passions. The treaty, being already concerted among the parties, was immediately drawn, and signed, and ratified: Henry's will seemed to be a law throughout the whole negociation: Nothing was attended to but his advantages.

Treaty of Troye.

THE principal articles of the treaty were, that Henry should espouse the princess Catharine: That king Charles, during his life-time, should enjoy the title and dignity of king of France: That Henry should be declared and acknowledged heir of the monarchy, and be entrusted with the present administration of the government: That that kingdom should pass to his heirs general: That France and England should for ever be united under one king; but should still retain their several usages, customs, and privileges: That all the princes, peers, vassals, and communities

munities of France should swear, that they would both adhere to the future succession of Henry, and pay him present obedience as regent: That this prince should unite his arms to those of king Charles and the duke of Burgundy, in order to subdue the adherents of Charles, the pretended dauphin: And that these three princes should make no peace or truce with him but by common consent and agreement [f].

SUCH was the tenor of this famous treaty; a treaty which, as nothing but the most violent animosity could dictate it, so nothing but the power of the sword could carry into execution. It is hard to say whether its consequences, had it taken effect, would have proved more pernicious to England or to France. It must have reduced the former kingdom to the rank of a province: It would have entirely disjointed the succession of the latter, and have brought on the destruction of every descendant of the royal family; as the houses of Orleans, Anjou, Alençon, Britanny, Bourbon, and of Burgundy itself, whose titles were preferable to that of the English princes, would, on that account, have been exposed to perpetual jealousy and persecution from the sovereign. There was even a palpable deficiency in Henry's claim, which no art could palliate. For, besides the insuperable objections to which Edward IIId's pretensions were exposed, he was not heir to that monarch: If female succession were admitted, the right had devolved on the house of Mortimer: Allowing that Richard II. was a tyrant, and that Henry IVth's merits in deposing him were so great towards the English, as to justify that nation in placing him on the throne; Richard had nowise offended France, and his rival had merited nothing of that kingdom: It could not possibly be pretended that the crown of France was become an appendage to that of England; and that a

[f] Rymer, vol. ix. p. 895. St. Remi, chap. 101. Monstrelet, chap. 213.

prince

CHAP. XIX.

1420.

prince who, by any means, got possession of the latter, was, without farther question, entitled to the former. So that, on the whole, it must be allowed that Henry's claim to France was, if possible, still more unintelligible than the title by which his father had mounted the throne of England.

BUT though all these considerations were overlooked, amidst the hurry of passion by which the courts of France and Burgundy were actuated, they would necessarily revive during times of more tranquillity; and it behoved Henry to push his present advantages, and allow men no leisure for reason or reflection. In a few days

Marriage of the king.

days after he espoused the princess Catharine: He carried his father-in-law to Paris, and put himself in possession of that capital: He obtained, from the parliament and the three estates, a ratification of the treaty of Troye: He supported the duke of Burgundy in procuring a sentence against the murderers of his father: And he immediately turned his arms, with success, against the adherents of the dauphin, who, as soon as he heard of the treaty of Troye, took on him the style and authority of regent, and appealed to God and his sword for the maintenance of his title.

THE first place that Henry subdued was Sens, which opened its gates after a slight resistance. With the same facility he made himself master of Montereau. The defence of Melun was more obstinate: Barbasan, the governor, held out for the space of four months against the besiegers; and it was famine alone which obliged him to capitulate. Henry stipulated to spare the lives of all the garrison, except such as were accomplices in the murder of the duke of Burgundy; and as Barbasan himself was suspected to be of the number, his punishment was demanded by Philip: But the king had the generosity to intercede for him, and to prevent his execution [a].

[a] Holingshed, p. 577.

THE

THE neceffity of providing fupplies, both of men and money, obliged Henry to go over to England; and he left the duke of Exeter, his uncle, governor of Paris during his abfence. The authority which naturally attends fuccefs, procured from the Englifh parliament a fubfidy of a fifteenth; but, if we may judge by the fcantinefs of the fupply, the nation was nowife fanguine on their king's victories; and in proportion as the profpect of their union with France became nearer, they began to open their eyes, and to fee the dangerous confequences with which that event muft neceffarily be attended. It was fortunate for Henry, that he had other refources, befides pecuniary fupplies from his native fubjects. The provinces which he had already conquered maintained his troops; and the hopes of farther advantages allured to his ftandard all men of ambitious fpirits in England, who defired to fignalize themfelves by arms. He levied a new army of 24,000 archers, and 4000 horfemen [b], and marched them to Dover, the place of rendezvous. Every thing had remained in tranquillity at Paris, under the duke of Exeter; but there had happened, in another quarter of the kingdom, a misfortune which haftened the king's embarkation.

THE detention of the young king of Scots in England had hitherto proved advantageous to Henry; and, by keeping the regent in awe, had preferved, during the whole courfe of the French war, the northern frontier in tranquillity. But when intelligence arrived in Scotland of the progrefs made by Henry, and the near profpect of his fucceffion to the crown of France, the nation was alarmed, and forefaw their own inevitable ruin, if the fubjection of their ally left them to combat alone a victorious enemy, who was already fo much fuperior in power and riches. The regent entered into the fame views;

[b] Monftrelet, chap. 241.

and though he declined an open rupture with England, he permitted a body of seven thousand Scots, under the command of the earl of Buchan, his second son, to be transported into France for the service of the dauphin. To render this aid ineffectual, Henry had, in his former expedition, carried over the king of Scots, whom he obliged to send orders to his countrymen to leave the French service; but the Scottish general replied, that he would obey no commands which came from a king in captivity, and that a prince, while in the hands of his enemy, was nowise entitled to authority. These troops, therefore, continued still to act under the earl of Buchan; and were employed by the dauphin to oppose the progress of the duke of Clarence in Anjou. The two armies encountered at Baugé: The English were defeated: The duke himself was slain by Sir Allan Swinton, a Scotch knight, who commanded a company of men at arms: And the earls of Somerset[i], Dorset, and Huntingdon, were taken prisoners[k]. This was the first action that turned the tide of success against the English; and the dauphin, that he might both attach the Scotch to his service, and reward the valour and conduct of the earl of Buchan, honoured that nobleman with the office of constable.

But the arrival of the king of England, with so considerable an army, was more than sufficient to repair this loss. Henry was received at Paris with great expressions of joy; so obstinate were the prejudices of the people: And he immediately conducted his army to Chartres, which had long been besieged by the dauphin. That prince raised the siege on the approach of the English; and being resolved to decline a battle, he retired

---

[i] His name was John, and he was afterwards created duke of Somerset. He was grandson of John of Gaunt duke of Lancaster. The earl of Dorset was brother to Somerset, and succeeded him in that title.

[k] St. Remi, chap. 110. Monstrelet, chap. 239. Hall, fol. 76.

with his army [1]. Henry made himself master of Dreux without a blow: He laid siege to Meaux at the solicitation of the Parisians, who were much incommoded by the garrison of that place. This enterprize employed the English arms during the space of eight months: The bastard of Vaurus, governor of Meaux, distinguished himself by an obstinate defence; but was at last obliged to surrender at discretion. The cruelty of this officer was equal to his bravery: He was accustomed to hang, without distinction, all the English and Burgundians who fell into his hands: And Henry, in revenge of his barbarity, ordered him immediately to be hanged on the same tree which he had made the instrument of his inhuman executions [m].

THIS success was followed by the surrender of many other places in the neighbourhood of Paris, which held for the dauphin: That prince was chased beyond the Loire, and he almost totally abandoned all the northern provinces: He was even pursued into the south by the united arms of the English and Burgundians, and threatened with total destruction. Notwithstanding the bravery and fidelity of his captains, he saw himself unequal to his enemies in the field; and found it necessary to temporize, and to avoid all hazardous actions with a rival, who had gained so much the ascendant over him. And to crown all the other prosperities of Henry, his queen was delivered of a son, who was called by his father's name, and whose birth was celebrated by rejoicings no less pompous, and no less sincere, at Paris than at London. The infant prince seemed to be universally regarded as the future heir of both monarchies.

BUT the glory of Henry, when it had nearly reached the summit, was stopped short by the hand of nature;

[1] St. Remi, chap. 3. p. 91, 53. St. Remi, chap. 116. [m] Rymer, vol. x. p. 212. T. Livii, Monstrelet, chap. 260.

CHAP. XIX.
1422.

and all his mighty projects vanished into smoke. He was seized with a fistula, a malady which the surgeons at that time had not skill enough to cure; and he was at last sensible that his distemper was mortal, and that his end was approaching. He sent for his brother the duke of Bedford, the earl of Warwic, and a few noblemen more, whom he had honoured with his friendship; and he delivered to them, in great tranquillity, his last will with regard to the government of his kingdom and family. He entreated them to continue, towards his infant son, the same fidelity and attachment which they had always professed to himself during his lifetime, and which had been cemented by so many mutual good offices. He expressed his indifference on the approach of death; and, though he regretted that he must leave unfinished a work so happily begun, he declared himself confident, that the final acquisition of France would be the effect of their prudence and valour. He left the regency of that kingdom to his elder brother, the duke of Bedford; that of England to his younger, the duke of Glocester; and the care of his son's person to the earl of Warwic. He recommended to all of them a great attention to maintain the friendship of the duke of Burgundy; and advised them never to give liberty to the French princes taken at Azincour, till his son were of age, and could himself hold the reins of government. And he conjured them, if the success of their arms should not enable them to place young Henry on the throne of France, never, at least, to make peace with that kingdom, unless the enemy, by the cession of Normandy, and its annexation to the crown of England, made compensation for all the hazard and expence of his enterprize [a].

He next applied himself to his devotions, and ordered his chaplain to recite the seven penitential psalms. When

[a] Monstrelet, chap. 265. Hall, fol. 80.

that

that paſſage of the fifty-firſt pſalm was read, *build thou the walls of Jeruſalem*; he interrupted the chaplain, and declared his ſerious intention, after he ſhould have fully ſubdued France, to conduct a cruſade againſt the infidels, and recover poſſeſſion of the Holy Land[*]. So ingenious are men in deceiving themſelves, that Henry forgot, in thoſe moments, all the blood ſpilt by his ambition; and received comfort from this late and feeble reſolve, which, as the mode of theſe enterprizes was now paſt, he certainly would never have carried into execution. He expired in the thirty-fourth year of his age and the tenth of his reign.

CHAP. XIX.
1422.

31ſt Aug.

THIS prince poſſeſſed many eminent virtues; and if we give indulgence to ambition in a monarch, or rank it, as the vulgar are inclined to do, among his virtues, they were unſtained by any conſiderable blemiſh. His abilities appeared equally in the cabinet and in the field: The boldneſs of his enterprizes was no leſs remarkable than his perſonal valour in conducting them. He had the talent of attaching his friends by affability, and of gaining his enemies by addreſs and clemency. The Engliſh, dazzled by the luſtre of his character, ſtill more than by that of his victories, were reconciled to the defects in his title: The French almoſt forgot that he was an enemy: And his care in maintaining juſtice in his civil adminiſtration, and preſerving diſcipline in his armies, made ſome amends to both nations for the calamities inſeparable from thoſe wars, in which his ſhort reign was almoſt entirely occupied. That he could forgive the earl of Marche, who had a better title to the crown than himſelf, is a ſure indication of his magnanimity; and that the earl relied ſo entirely on his friendſhip, is no leſs a proof of his eſtabliſhed character for candour and ſincerity. There remain in hiſtory few inſtances of

and character of the king.

[*] St. Remi, chap. 118. Monſtrelet, chap. 265.

CHAP. XIX.

1422.

such mutual trust; and still fewer where neither party found reason to repent it.

THE exterior figure of this great prince, as well as his deportment, was engaging. His stature was somewhat above the middle size; his countenance beautiful; his limbs genteel and slender, but full of vigour; and he excelled in all warlike and manly exercises[p]. He left, by his queen, Catherine of France, only one son, not full nine months old; whose misfortunes, in the course of his life, surpassed all the glories and successes of his father.

IN less than two months after Henry's death, Charles VI. of France, his father-in-law, terminated his unhappy life. He had, for several years, possessed only the appearance of royal authority: Yet was this mere appearance of considerable advantage to the English; and divided the duty and affections of the French between them and the dauphin. This prince was proclaimed and crowned king of France at Poictiers, by the name of Charles VII. Rheims, the place where this ceremony is usually performed, was at that time in the hands of his enemies.

CATHERINE of France, Henry's widow, married, soon after his death, a Welsh gentleman, Sir Owen Tudor, said to be descended from the ancient princes of that country: She bore him two sons, Edmund and Jasper, of whom the eldest was created earl of Richmond; the second earl of Pembroke. The family of Tudor, first raised to distinction by this alliance, mounted afterwards the throne of England.

Miscellaneous transactions.

THE long schism, which had divided the Latin church for near forty years, was finally terminated in this reign by the council of Constance; which deposed the pope, John XXIII. for his crimes, and elected Martin V. in

[p] T. Livii, p. 4.

his

his place, who was acknowledged by almost all the kingdoms of Europe. This great and unusual act of authority in the council gave the Roman pontiffs ever after a mortal antipathy to those assemblies. The same jealousy which had long prevailed in most European countries, between the civil aristocracy and monarchy, now also took place between these powers in the ecclesiastical body. But the great separation of the bishops in the several states, and the difficulty of assembling them, gave the pope a mighty advantage, and made it more easy for him to centre all the powers of the hierarchy in his own person. The cruelty and treachery which attended the punishment of John Huss and Jerome of Prague, the unhappy disciples of Wickliffe, who, in violation of a safe-conduct, were burned alive for their errors by the council of Constance, prove this melancholy truth, that toleration is none of the virtues of priests in any form of ecclesiastical government. But as the English nation had little or no concern in these great transactions, we are here the more concise in relating them.

The first commission of array, which we meet with, was issued in this reign [t]. The military part of the feudal system, which was the most essential circumstance of it, was entirely dissolved; and could no longer serve for the defence of the kingdom. Henry, therefore, when he went to France, in 1415, impowered certain commissioners to take, in each county, a review of all the freemen able to bear arms, to divide them into companies, and to keep them in readiness for resisting an enemy. This was the æra, when the feudal militia in England gave place to one which was perhaps still less orderly and regular.

We have an authentic and exact account of the ordinary revenue of the crown during this reign; and it

[t] Rymer, vol. ix. p. 254, 255.

amounts

amounts only to 55,714 pounds 10 shillings and 10 pence a year[r]. This is nearly the same with the revenue of Henry III. and the kings of England had neither become much richer nor poorer in the course of so many years. The ordinary expence of the government amounted to 42,507 pounds 16 shillings and 10 pence: So that the king had a surplus only of 13,206 pounds 14 shillings for the support of his household; for his wardrobe; for the expence of embassies; and other articles. This sum was no-wise sufficient: He was therefore obliged to have frequent recourse to parliamentary supplies, and was thus, even in time of peace, not altogether independent of his people. But wars were attended with a great expence, which neither the prince's ordinary revenue, nor the extraordinary supplies were able to bear; and the sovereign was always reduced to many miserable shifts, in order to make any tolerable figure in them. He commonly borrowed money from all quarters; he pawned his jewels, and sometimes the crown itself[s]; he ran in arrears to his army; and he was often obliged, notwithstanding all these expedients, to stop in the midst of his career of victory, and to grant truces to the enemy. The high pay which was given to soldiers agreed very ill with this low income. All the extraordinary supplies, granted by parliament to Henry during the course of his reign, were only seven tenths and fifteenths, about 203,000 pounds[t]. It is easy to compute how soon this money must be exhausted by armies of 24,000 archers, and 6000 horse; when each archer had six pence a day[u], and each horseman two shillings. The most splendid successes proved commonly fruitless, when supported by so poor a revenue; and

[r] Rymer, vol. x. p. 113. [s] Ibid. p. 190. [t] Parliamentary History, vol. ii. p. 168.

[u] It appears from many passages of Rymer, particularly vol. iv. p. 258. that the king paid 10 marks a year for an archer, which is a good deal above six pence a day. The price had risen, as is natural, by raising the denomination of money.

the debts and difficulties, which the king thereby incurred, made him pay dear for his victories. The civil administration, likewise, even in time of peace, could never be very regular, where the government was so ill enabled to support itself. Henry, till within a year of his death, owed debts, which he had contracted when prince of Wales [w]. It was in vain that the parliament pretended to restrain him from arbitrary practices, when he was reduced to such necessities. Though the right of levying purveyance, for instance, had been expressly guarded against by the Great Charter itself, and was frequently complained of by the commons, it was found absolutely impracticable to abolish it; and the parliament at length, submitting to it as a legal prerogative, contented themselves with enacting laws to limit and confine it. The duke of Gloucester, in the reign of Richard II. possessed a revenue of 60,000 crowns (about 30,000 pounds a year of our present money), as we learn from Froissard [x], and was, consequently, richer than the king himself, if all circumstances be duly considered.

It is remarkable, that the city of Calais alone was an annual expence to the crown of 19,119 pounds [y]; that is, above a third of the common charge of the government in time of peace. This fortress was of no use to the defence of England, and only gave that kingdom an inlet to annoy France. Ireland cost two thousand pounds a-year, over and above its own revenue; which was certainly very low. Every thing conspires to give us a very mean idea of the state of Europe in those ages.

From the most early times, till the reign of Edward III. the denomination of money had never been altered: A pound sterling was still a pound troy; that is, about three pounds of our present money. That conqueror was the first that innovated in this important article.

[w] Rymer, vol. x. p. 114. vol. xi. p. 113.   [x] Liv. iv. chap. 86.   [y] Rymer,

CHAP. XIX.

1422.

In the twentieth of his reign, he coined twenty-two shillings from a pound troy; in his twenty-seventh year he coined twenty-five shillings. But Henry V. who was also a conqueror, raised still farther the denomination, and coined thirty shillings from a pound troy[a]: His revenue, therefore, must have been about 110,000 pounds of our present money; and, by the cheapness of provisions, was equivalent to above 330,000 pounds.

NONE of the princes of the house of Lancaster ventured to impose taxes without consent of parliament: Their doubtful or bad title became so far of advantage to the constitution. The rule was then fixed, and could not safely be broken afterwards, even by more absolute princes.

[a] Fleetwood's Chronicon Preciosum, p. 52.

CHAP. XX.

HENRY VI.

Government during the minority——State of France ——Military operations——Battle of Verneüil ——Siege of Orleans——The maid of Orleans—— The siege of Orleans raised—— The king of France crowned at Rheims——Prudence of the duke of Bedford — Execution of the maid of Orleans—— Defection of the duke of Burgundy——Death of the duke of Bedford——Decline of the English in France——Truce with France——Marriage of the king with Margaret of Anjou——Murder of the duke of Glocester——State of France ——Renewal of the war with France——The English expelled France.

DURING the reigns of the Lancastrian princes, the authority of parliament seems to have been more confirmed, and the privileges of the people more regarded, than during any former period; and the two preceding kings, though men of great spirit and abilities, abstained from such exertions of prerogative, as even weak princes, whose title was undisputed, were tempted to think they might venture upon with impunity. The long minority, of which there was now the prospect, encouraged still farther the lords and commons to extend their influence; and, without paying much regard to the verbal destination of Henry V. they assumed the power of giving a new arrangement to the whole administration. They declined altogether

altogether the name of *Regent* with regard to England: They appointed the duke of Bedford *protector* or *guardian* of that kingdom, a title which they supposed to imply less authority: They invested the duke of Glocester with the same dignity during the absence of his elder brother[a]: And, in order to limit the power of both these princes, they appointed a council, without whose advice and approbation no measure of importance could be determined[b]. The person and education of the infant prince was committed to Henry Beaufort, bishop of Winchester, his great uncle, and the legitimated son of John of Gaunt, duke of Lancaster; a prelate, who, as his family could never have any pretensions to the crown, might safely, they thought, be intrusted with that important charge[c]. The two princes, the dukes of Bedford and Glocester, who seemed injured by this plan of government, yet, being persons of great integrity and honour, acquiesced in any appointment which tended to give security to the public; and as the wars in France appeared to be the object of greatest moment, they avoided every dispute which might throw an obstacle in the way of foreign conquests.

State of France.

WHEN the state of affairs between the English and French kings was considered with a superficial eye, every advantage seemed to be on the side of the former; and the total expulsion of Charles appeared to be an event which might naturally be expected from the superior power of his competitor. Though Henry was yet in his infancy, the administration was devolved on the duke of Bedford, the most accomplished prince of his age; whose experience, prudence, valour, and generosity qualified him for his high office, and enabled him both to maintain union among his friends, and to gain the confidence of his

[a] Rymer, vol. 8. p. 261. Cotton, p. 564.   [b] Cotton, p. 564.
[c] Hall, fol. 53. Monstrelet, vol. ii. p. 27.

enemies,

enemies. The whole power of England was at his command: He was at the head of armies enured to victory: He was seconded by the most renowned generals of the age, the earls of Somerset, Warwic, Salisbury, Suffolk, and Arundel, Sir John Talbot, and Sir John Fastolfe: And besides Guienne, the ancient inheritance of England, he was master of the capital, and of almost all the northern provinces, which were well enabled to furnish him with supplies, both of men and money, and to assist and support his English forces.

But Charles, notwithstanding the present inferiority of his power, possessed some advantages, derived partly from his situation, partly from his personal character, which promised him success, and served, first to controul, then to overbalance the superior force and opulence of his enemies. He was the true and undoubted heir of the monarchy: All Frenchmen, who knew the interests, or desired the independence of their country, turned their eyes towards him as its sole resource: The exclusion given him, by the imbecility of his father, and the forced or precipitate consent of the states, had plainly no validity: That spirit of faction, which had blinded the people, could not long hold them in so gross a delusion: Their national and inveterate hatred against the English, the authors of all their calamities, must soon revive, and inspire them with indignation at bending their necks under the yoke of that hostile people: Great nobles and princes, accustomed to maintain an independence against their native sovereigns, would never endure a subjection to strangers: And though most of the princes of the blood were, since the fatal battle of Azincour, detained prisoners in England, the inhabitants of their demesnes, their friends, their vassals, all declared a zealous attachment to the king, and exerted themselves in resisting the violence of foreign invaders.

Charles

CHAP.
XX.

1422.

CHARLES himself, though only in his twentieth year, was of a character well calculated to become the object of these benevolent sentiments; and, perhaps, from the favour which naturally attends youth, was the more likely, on account of his tender age, to acquire the good-will of his native subjects. He was a prince of the most friendly and benign disposition, of easy and familiar manners, and of a just and sound, though not a very vigorous understanding. Sincere, generous, affable, he engaged, from affection, the services of his followers, even while his low fortunes might make it their interest to desert him; and the lenity of his temper could pardon in them those sallies of discontent, to which princes in his situation are so frequently exposed. The love of pleasure often seduced him into indolence; but, amidst all his irregularities, the goodness of his heart still shone forth; and, by exerting at intervals his courage and activity, he proved, that his general remissness proceeded not from the want, either of a just spirit of ambition, or of personal valour.

Though the virtues of this amiable prince lay some time in obscurity, the duke of Bedford knew that his title alone made him formidable, and that every foreign assistance would be requisite, ere an English regent could hope to complete the conquest of France; an enterprize which, however it might seem to be much advanced, was still exposed to many and great difficulties. The chief circumstance, which had procured to the English all their present advantages, was the resentment of the duke of Burgundy against Charles; and as that prince seemed intent rather on gratifying his passion than consulting his interests, it was the more easy for the regent, by demonstrations of respect and confidence, to retain him in the alliance of England. He bent therefore all his endeavours to that purpose: He gave the duke every proof of friendship and regard: He even offered him the regency

of

of France, which Philip declined: And that he might corroborate national connexions by private ties, he concluded his own marriage with the princess of Burgundy, which had been stipulated by the treaty of Arras.

BEING sensible, that next to the alliance of Burgundy, the friendship of the duke of Britanny was of the greatest importance towards forwarding the English conquests; and that, as the provinces of France, already subdued, lay between the dominions of these two princes, he could never hope for any security, without preserving his connexions with them; he was very intent on strengthening himself also from that quarter. The duke of Britanny, having received many just reasons of displeasure from the ministers of Charles, had already acceded to the treaty of Troye, and had, with other vassals of the crown, done homage to Henry V. in quality of heir to the kingdom: But as the regent knew, that the duke was much governed by his brother, the count of Richemont, he endeavoured to fix his friendship, by paying court and doing services to this haughty and ambitious prince.

ARTHUR, count of Richemont, had been taken prisoner at the battle of Azincour, had been treated with great indulgence by the late king, and had even been permitted on his parole to take a journey into Britanny, where the state of affairs required his presence. The death of that victorious monarch happened before Richemont's return; and this prince pretended, that, as his word was given personally to Henry V. he was not bound to fulfil it towards his son and successor: A chicane which the regent, as he could not force him to compliance, deemed it prudent to overlook. An interview was settled at Amiens between the dukes of Bedford, Burgundy, and Britanny, at which the count of Richemont was also present[d]: The alliance was renewed between these princes:

[d] Hall, fol. 84. Monstrelet, vol. l. p. 4. Stowe, p. 364.

CHAP. XX.
1423.

And the regent perfuaded Philip to give in marriage to Richemont his eldeft fifter, widow of the deceafed dauphin, Lewis, the elder brother of Charles. Thus Arthur was connected both with the regent and the duke of Burgundy, and feemed engaged by intereft to profecute the fame object, in forwarding the fuccefs of the Englifh arms.

WHILE the vigilance of the duke of Bedford was employed in gaining or confirming thefe allies, whofe vicinity rendered them fo important, he did not overlook the ftate of more remote countries. The duke of Albany, regent of Scotland, had died; and his power had devolved on Murdac, his fon, a prince of a weak underftanding and indolent difpofition; who, far from poffeffing the talents requifite for the government of that fierce people, was not even able to maintain authority in his own family, or reftrain the petulance and infolence of his fons. The ardour of the Scots to ferve in France, where Charles treated them with great honour and diftinction, and where the regent's brother enjoyed the dignity of conftable, broke out afrefh under this feeble adminiftration: New fuccours daily came over, and filled the armies of the French king: The earl of Douglas conducted a reinforcement of 5000 men to his affiftance: And it was juftly to be dreaded that the Scots, by commencing open hoftilities in the north, would occafion a diverfion ftill more confiderable of the Englifh power, and would eafe Charles, in part, of that load, by which he was at prefent fo grievoufly oppreffed. The duke of Bedford, therefore, perfuaded the Englifh council to form an alliance with James their prifoner; to free that prince from his long captivity; and to connect him with England, by marrying him to a daughter of the earl of Somerfet and coufin of the young king^e. As the Scottifh regent,

^e Hall, fol. 86. Stowe, p. 364. Grafton, p. 501.

tired

tired of his present dignity, which he was not able to support, was now become entirely sincere in his applications for James's liberty, the treaty was soon concluded; a ransom of forty thousand pounds was stipulated [f]; and the king of Scots was restored to the throne of his ancestors, and proved, in his short reign, one of the most illustrious princes that had ever governed that kingdom. He was murdered, in 1437, by his traiterous kinsman the earl of Athole. His affections inclined to the side of France; but the English had never reason, during his life-time, to complain of any breach of the neutrality by Scotland.

BUT the regent was not so much employed in these political negociations as to neglect the operations of war, from which alone he could hope to succeed in expelling the French monarch. Though the chief seat of Charles's power lay in the southern provinces beyond the Loire; his partizans were possessed of some fortresses in the northern, and even in the neighbourhood of Paris; and it behoved the duke of Bedford first to clear these countries from the enemy, before he could think of attempting more distant conquests. The castle of Dorsoy was taken, after a siege of six weeks: That of Noyelle and the town of Rüe in Picardy underwent the same fate: Pont sur Seine, Vertus, Montaigu, were subjected by the English arms: And a more considerable advantage was soon after gained by the united forces of England and Burgundy. John Stuart, constable of Scotland, and the lord of Estissac, had formed the siege of Crevant in Burgundy: The earls of Salisbury and Suffolk, with the count of Toulongeon, were sent to its relief: A fierce and well-disputed action ensued: The Scots and French were defeated: The constable of Scotland, and the count of Ventadour were taken prisoners: And above a thousand men, among whom was Sir Wil-

[f] Rymer, vol. x. p. 299, 300. 326.

CHAP. liam Hamilton, were left on the field of battleʳ. The
XX. taking of Gaillon upon the Seine, and of la Charité upon
1423. the Loire, was the fruit of this victory: And as this latter
place opened an entrance into the southern provinces, the
acquisition of it appeared on that account of the greater
importance to the duke of Bedford, and seemed to promise
a successful issue to the war.

1424. THE more Charles was threatened with an invasion in those provinces which adhered to him, the more
necessary it became that he should retain possession of
every fortress, which he still held within the quarters of
the enemy. The duke of Bedford had besieged in person,
during the space of three months, the town of Yvri in
Normandy; and the brave governor, unable to make any
longer defence, was obliged to capitulate; and he agreed
to surrender the town, if, before a certain term, no relief arrived. Charles, informed of these conditions, determined to make an attempt for saving the place. He
collected, with some difficulty, an army of 14,000 men,
of whom one half were Scots; and he sent them thither
under the command of the earl of Buchan, constable of
France; who was attended by the earl of Douglas, his
countryman, the duke of Alençon, the mareschal de la
Fayette, the count of Aumale, and the viscount of Narbonne. When the constable arrived within a few leagues
of Yvri, he found that he was come too late, and that
the place was already surrendered. He immediately
turned to the left, and sat down before Verneüil, which
the inhabitants, in spite of the garrison, delivered up to
himˢ. Buchan might now have returned in safety, and
with the glory of making an acquisition no less important than the place which he was sent to relieve: But
hearing of Bedford's approach, he called a council of war,

ʳ Hall, fol. 85. Monstrelet, vol. II. p. 8. Hollingshed, p. 586. Grafton,
p. 500.   ˢ Monstrelet, vol. II. p. 14. Grafton, p. 504.

in

in order to deliberate concerning the conduct which he should hold in this emergence. The wiser part of the council declared for a retreat; and represented, that all the past misfortunes of the French had proceeded from their rashness in giving battle when no necessity obliged them; that this army was the last resource of the king, and the only defence of the few provinces which remained to him; and that every reason invited him to embrace cautious measures, which might leave time for his subjects to return to a sense of their duty, and give leisure for discord to arise among his enemies, who, being united by no common band of interest or motive of alliance, could not long persevere in their animosity against him. All these prudential considerations were overborne by a vain point of honour, not to turn their backs to the enemy; and they resolved to await the arrival of the duke of Bedford.

The numbers were nearly equal in this action; and as the long continuance of war had introduced discipline, which, however imperfect, sufficed to maintain some appearance of order in such small armies, the battle was fierce, and well disputed, and attended with bloodshed on both sides. The constable drew up his forces under the walls of Verneüil, and resolved to abide the attack of the enemy: But the impatience of the viscount of Narbonne, who advanced precipitately, and obliged the whole line to follow him in some hurry and confusion, was the cause of the misfortune which ensued. The English archers, fixing their palisadoes before them, according to their usual custom, sent a volley of arrows amidst the thickest of the French army; and though beaten from their ground, and obliged to take shelter among the baggage, they soon rallied, and continued to do great execution upon the enemy. The duke of Bedford, meanwhile, at the head of the men at arms, made impression on the French, broke their ranks, chafed them off the field, and rendered the victory entirely complete and decisive[i]. The constable himself perished in battle, as well as the earl of Douglas and his son, the counts of Aumale, Tonnerre, and Ventadour, with many other considerable nobility. The duke of Alençon, the mareschal de la Fayette, the lords of Gaucour and Mortemar were taken prisoners. There fell about four thousand of the French, and sixteen hundred of the English; a loss esteemed, at that time, so unusual on the side of the victors, that the duke of Bedford forbad all rejoicings for his success. Verneüil was surrendered next day by capitulation[k].

THE condition of the king of France now appeared very terrible, and almost desperate. He had lost the flower of his army, and the bravest of his nobles in this fatal action: He had no resource either for recruiting or subsisting his troops: He wanted money even for his personal subsistence; and though all parade of a court was banished, it was with difficulty he could keep a table, supplied with the plainest necessaries, for himself and his few followers: Every day brought him intelligence of some loss or misfortune: Towns, which were bravely defended, were obliged at last to surrender for want of relief or supply: He saw his partizans entirely chaced from all the provinces which lay north of the Loire: And he expected soon to lose, by the united efforts of his enemies, all the territories of which he had hitherto continued master; when an incident happened which saved him on the brink of ruin, and lost the English such an opportunity for completing their conquests as they never afterwards were able to recal.

JAQUELINE, countess of Hainault and Holland, and heir of these provinces, had espoused John duke of Bra-

[i] Hall, fol. 88, 89, 90. Monstrelet, vol. ii. p. 15. Stowe, p. 365. Hollingshed, p. 583. [k] Monstrelet, vol. ii. p. 15.

bant,

bant, cousin-german to the duke of Burgundy; but, having made this choice from the usual motives of princes, she soon found reason to repent of the unequal alliance. She was a princess of a masculine spirit and uncommon understanding; the duke of Brabant was of a sickly complexion and weak mind: She was in the vigour of her age; he had only reached his fifteenth year: These causes had inspired her with such contempt for her husband, which soon proceeded to antipathy, that she determined to dissolve a marriage, where, it is probable, nothing but the ceremony had as yet intervened. The court of Rome was commonly very open to applications of this nature, when seconded by power and money; but, as the princess foresaw great opposition from her husband's relations, and was impatient to effect her purpose, she made her escape into England, and threw herself under the protection of the duke of Glocester. That prince, with many noble qualities, had the defect of being governed by an impetuous temper and vehement passions; and he was rashly induced, as well by the charms of the countess herself, as by the prospect of possessing her rich inheritance, to offer himself to her as a husband. Without waiting for a papal dispensation; without endeavouring to reconcile the duke of Burgundy to the measure, he entered into a contract of marriage with Jaqueline, and immediately attempted to put himself in possession of her dominions. Philip was disgusted with so precipitate a conduct: He resented the injury done to the duke of Brabant, his near relation: He dreaded to have the English established on all sides of him: And he foresaw the consequences which must attend the extensive and uncontrouled dominion of that nation, if, before the full settlement of their power, they insulted and injured an ally, to whom they had already been so much indebted, and who was still so necessary for supporting them in their farther progress. He encouraged,

couraged, therefore, the duke of Brabant to make refiſtance: He engaged many of Jaqueline's ſubjects to adhere to that prince: He himſelf marched troops to his ſupport: And as the duke of Gloceſter ſtill perſevered in his purpoſe, a ſharp war was ſuddenly kindled in the Low Countries. The quarrel ſoon became perſonal as well as political. The Engliſh prince wrote to the duke of Burgundy, complaining of the oppoſition made to his pretenſions; and though, in the main, he employed amicable terms in his letter, he took notice of ſome falſehoods into which, he ſaid, Philip had been betrayed during the courſe of theſe tranſactions. This unguarded expreſſion was highly reſented: The duke of Burgundy inſiſted that he ſhould retract it: And mutual challenges and defiances paſſed between them on this occaſion[1].

THE duke of Bedford could eaſy foreſee the bad effects of ſo ill-timed and imprudent a quarrel. All the ſuccours which he expected from England, and which were ſo neceſſary in this critical emergence, were intercepted by his brother, and employed in Holland and Hainault: The forces of the duke of Burgundy, which he alſo depended on, were diverted by the ſame wars: And, beſides this double loſs, he was in imminent danger of alienating, for ever, that confederate, whoſe friendſhip was of the utmoſt importance, and whom the late king had enjoined him, with his dying breath, to gratify by every mark of regard and attachment. He repreſented all theſe topics to the duke of Gloceſter: He endeavoured to mitigate the reſentment of the duke of Burgundy: He interpoſed with his good offices between theſe princes: But was not ſucceſsful in any of his endeavours; and he found that the impetuoſity of his brother's temper was ſtill the chief obſtacle to all accommodation[m]. For this reaſon, inſtead of puſhing the victory gained at

[1] Monſtrelet, vol. ii. p. 19, 20, 21. [m] Monſtrelet, p. 18.

Verneüil,

Verneüil, he found himself obliged to take a journey into England, and to try, by his counsels and authority, to moderate the measures of the duke of Glocester.

There had likewise broken out some differences among the English ministry, which had proceeded to great extremities, and which required the regent's presence to compose them[n]. The bishop of Winchester, to whom the care of the king's person and education had been entrusted, was a prelate of great capacity and experience, but of an intriguing and dangerous character; and, as he aspired to the government of affairs, he had continual disputes with his nephew the protector; and he gained frequent advantages over the vehement and impolitic temper of that prince. The duke of Bedford employed the authority of parliament to reconcile them; and these rivals were obliged to promise, before that assembly, that they would bury all quarrels in oblivion[o]. Time also seemed to open expedients for composing the difference with the duke of Burgundy. The credit of that prince had procured a bull from the pope; by which not only Jaqueline's contract with the duke of Glocester was annulled; but it was also declared, that even in case of the duke of Brabant's death, it should never be lawful for her to espouse the English prince. Humphrey, despairing of success, married another lady of inferior rank, who had lived some time with him as his mistress[p]. The duke of Brabant died; and his widow, before she could recover possession of her dominions, was obliged to declare the duke of Burgundy her heir, in case she should die without issue, and to promise never to marry without his consent. But though the affair was thus terminated to the satisfaction of Philip, it left a disagreeable impression on

CHAP. XX.
1424.

1425.

[n] Stowe, p. 368. Hollingshed, p. 590. [o] Hall, fol. 98, 99. Hollingshed, p. 593, 594. Polydore Virgil, p. 466. Grafton, p. 512, 519. [p] Stowe, p. 367.

K 4   his

CHAP. XX.

1425.

his mind: It excited an extreme jealousy of the English, and opened his eyes to his true interests: And as nothing but his animosity against Charles had engaged him in alliance with them, it counterbalanced that passion by another of the same kind, which, in the end, became prevalent, and brought him back, by degrees, to his natural connexions with his family and his native country.

ABOUT the same time the duke of Britanny began to withdraw himself from the English alliance. His brother, the count of Richemont, though connected by marriage with the dukes of Burgundy and Bedford, was extremely attached by inclination to the French interest; and he willingly hearkened to all the advances which Charles made him for obtaining his friendship. The staff of constable, vacant by the earl of Buchan's death, was offered him; and, as his martial and ambitious temper aspired to the command of armies, which he had in vain attempted to obtain from the duke of Bedford, he not only accepted that office, but brought over his brother to an alliance with the French monarch. The new constable, having made this one change in his measures, firmly adhered, ever after, to his engagements with France. Though his pride and violence, which would admit of no rival in his master's confidence, and even prompted him to assassinate the other favourites, had so much disgusted Charles, that he once banished him the court, and refused to admit him to his presence, he still acted with vigour for the service of that monarch, and obtained, at last, by his perseverance, the pardon of all past offences.

1426.

IN this situation the duke of Bedford, on his return, found the affairs of France, after passing eight months in England. The duke of Burgundy was much disgusted. The duke of Britanny had entered into engagements with Charles,

Charles, and had done homage to that prince for his dutchy. The French had been allowed to recover from the aftonishment into which their frequent difasters had thrown them. An incident too had happened, which ferved extremely to raife their courage. The earl of Warwic had befieged Montargis with a fmall army of 3000 men, and the place was reduced to extremity, when the baftard of Orleans undertook to throw relief into it. This general, who was natural fon to the prince affaffinated by the duke of Burgundy, and who was afterwards created count of Dunois, conducted a body of 1600 men to Montargis; and made an attack on the enemy's trenches with fo much valour, prudence, and good fortune, that he not only penetrated into the place, but gave a fevere blow to the Englifh, and obliged Warwic to raife the fiege [q]. This was the firft fignal action that raifed the fame of Dunois, and opened him the road to thofe great honours, which he afterwards attained.

But the regent, foon after his arrival, revived the reputation of the Englifh arms, by an important enterprize which he happily atchieved. He fecretly brought together, in feparate detachments, a confiderable army to the frontiers of Britanny; and fell fo unexpectedly upon that province, that the duke, unable to make refiftance, yielded to all the terms required of him: He renounced the French alliance; he engaged to maintain the treaty of Troye; he acknowledged the duke of Bedford for regent of France; and promifed to do homage for his dutchy to king Henry [r]. And the Englifh prince, having thus freed himfelf from a dangerous enemy who lay behind him, refolved on an undertaking which, if fuccefsful, would, he hoped, caft the balance between the two nations, and prepare the way for the final conqueft of France.

[p] Monftrelet, vc'. ii. p. 32, 33. Hollingfhed, p. 597.
[r] Monftrelet, vol. ii. p. 35, 36.

CHAP. XX.

1428.
Siege of Orleans.

The city of Orleans was so situated between the provinces commanded by Henry, and those possessed by Charles, that it opened an easy entrance to either; and as the duke of Bedford intended to make a great effort for penetrating into the south of France, it behoved him to begin with this place, which, in the present circumstances, was become the most important in the kingdom. He committed the conduct of the enterprize to the earl of Salisbury, who had newly brought him a reinforcement of 6000 men from England, and who had much distinguished himself, by his abilities, during the course of the present war. Salisbury, passing the Loire, made himself master of several small places, which surrounded Orleans on that side[*]; and as his intentions were thereby known, the French king used every expedient to supply the city with a garrison and provisions, and enable it to maintain a long and obstinate siege. The lord of Gaucour, a brave and experienced captain, was appointed governor: Many officers of distinction threw themselves into the place: The troops which they conducted were enured to war, and were determined to make the most obstinate resistance: And even the inhabitants, disciplined by the long continuance of hostilities, were well qualified, in their own defence, to second the efforts of the most veteran forces. The eyes of all Europe were turned towards this scene; where, it was reasonably supposed, the French were to make their last stand for maintaining the independence of their monarchy, and the rights of their sovereign.

The earl of Salisbury at last approached the place with an army, which consisted only of 10,000 men; and not being able, with so small a force, to invest so great a city, that commanded a bridge over the Loire, he stationed himself on the southern side towards Sologne, leav-

[*] Monstrelet, vol. II. p. 38, 39. Polyd. Virg. p. 488.

HENRY VI.

ing the other, towards the Beauffe, still open to the enemy. He there attacked the fortifications which guarded the entrance to the bridge; and after an obstinate resistance he carried several of them: But was himself killed by a cannon ball as he was taking a view of the enemy[f]. The earl of Suffolk succeeded to the command; and being reinforced with great numbers of English and Burgundians, he passed the river with the main body of his army, and invested Orleans on the other side. As it was now the depth of winter, Suffolk, who found it difficult, in that season, to throw up intrenchments all around, contented himself, for the present, with erecting redoubts at different distances, where his men were lodged in safety, and were ready to intercept the supplies, which the enemy might attempt to throw into the place. Though he had several pieces of artillery in his camp (and this is among the first sieges in Europe, where cannon were found to be of importance), the art of engineering was hitherto so imperfect, that Suffolk trusted more to famine than to force for subduing the city; and he purposed in the spring to render the circumvallation more complete, by drawing intrenchments from one redoubt to another. Numberless feats of valour were performed both by the besiegers and besieged during the winter: Bold sallies were made, and repulsed with equal boldness: Convoys were sometimes introduced and often intercepted: The supplies were still unequal to the consumption of the place: And the English seemed daily, though slowly, to be advancing towards the completion of their enterprize.

BUT while Suffolk lay in this situation, the French parties ravaged all the country around; and the besiegers, who were obliged to draw their provisions from a distance, were themselves exposed to the danger of want and famine.

---

[f] Hall, fol. 105. Monstrelet, vol. ii. p. 39. Stowe, p. 369. Hollingshed, p. 599. Grafton, p. 531.

CHAP.
XX.

1429.

Sir John Faſtolffe was bringing up a large convoy, of every kind of ſtores, which he eſcorted with a detachment of 2500 men; when he was attacked by a body of 4000 French, under the command of the counts of Clermont and Dunois. Faſtolffe drew up his troops behind the waggons; but the French generals, afraid of attacking him in that poſture, planted a battery of cannon againſt him, which threw every thing into confuſion, and would have inſured them the victory, had not the impatience of ſome Scottiſh troops, who broke the line of battle, brought on an engagement, in which Faſtolffe was victorious. The count of Dunois was wounded; and about 500 French were left on the field of battle. This action, which was of great importance in the preſent conjuncture, was commonly called the battle of *Herrings*; becauſe the convoy brought a great quantity of that kind of proviſions, for the uſe of the Engliſh army during the Lent ſeaſon ".

CHARLES ſeemed now to have but one expedient for ſaving this city, which had been ſo long inveſted. The duke of Orleans, who was ſtill priſoner in England, prevailed on the protector and the council to conſent, that all his demeſnes ſhould be allowed to preſerve a neutrality during the war, and ſhould be ſequeſtered, for greater ſecurity, into the hands of the duke of Burgundy. This prince, who was much leſs cordial in the Engliſh intereſts than formerly, went to Paris, and made the propoſal to the duke of Bedford; but the regent coldly replied, That he was not of a humour to beat the buſhes, while others ran away with the game: An anſwer which ſo diſguſted the duke, that he recalled all the troops of Burgundy that acted in the ſiege *. The place however was

" Hall, fol. 106. Monſtrelet, vol. ii. p. 41, 42. Stowe, p. 369. Holingſhed, p. 610. Polyd Virg. p. 469. Grafton, p. 532.

" Hall, fol. 106. Monſtrelet, vol. ii. p. 42. Stowe, p. 369. Grafton, p. 533.

every

every day more and more closely invested by the English: Great scarcity began already to be felt by the garrison and inhabitants: Charles, in despair of collecting an army, which should dare to approach the enemy's entrenchments, not only gave the city for lost, but began to entertain a very dismal prospect with regard to the general state of his affairs. He saw that the country, in which he had hitherto, with great difficulty, subsisted, would be laid entirely open to the invasion of a powerful and victorious enemy; and he already entertained thoughts of retiring with the remains of his forces into Languedoc and Dauphiny, and defending himself as long as possible in those remote provinces. But it was fortunate for this good prince, that, as he lay under the dominion of the fair, the women, whom he consulted, had the spirit to support his sinking resolution in this desperate extremity. Mary of Anjou, his queen, a princess of great merit and prudence, vehemently opposed this measure, which, she foresaw, would discourage all his partizans, and serve as a general signal for deserting a prince, who seemed himself to despair of success. His mistress too, the fair Agnes Sorel, who lived in entire amity with the queen, seconded all her remonstrances, and threatened that, if he thus pusillanimously threw away the sceptre of France, she would seek in the court of England a fortune more correspondent to her wishes. Love was not able to rouze in the breast of Charles that courage, which ambition had failed to excite: He resolved to dispute every inch of ground with an imperious enemy; and rather to perish with honour in the midst of his friends, than yield ingloriously to his bad fortune: When relief was unexpectedly brought him by another female of a very different character, who gave rise to one of the most singular revolutions that is to be met with in history.

CHAP. XX.
1429.

IN the village of Domremi near Vaucouleurs, on the borders of Lorraine, there lived a country girl of twenty-seven

The maid of Orleans.

seven years of age, called Joan d'Arc, who was servant in a small inn, and who in that station had been accustomed to tend the horses of the guests, to ride them without a saddle to the watering-place, and to perform other offices, which, in well-frequented inns, commonly fall to the share of the men-servants [n]. This girl was of an irreproachable life, and had not hitherto been remarked for any singularity; whether that she had met with no occasion to excite her genius, or that the unskilful eyes of those who conversed with her, had not been able to discern her uncommon merit. It is easy to imagine, that the present situation of France was an interesting object even to persons of the lowest rank, and would become the frequent subject of conversation: A young prince expelled his throne by the sedition of native subjects, and by the arms of strangers, could not fail to move the compassion of all his people, whose hearts were uncorrupted by faction; and the peculiar character of Charles, so strongly inclined to friendship and the tender passions, naturally rendered him the hero of that sex, whose generous minds know no bounds in their affections. The siege of Orleans, the progress of the English before that place, the great distress of the garrison and inhabitants, the importance of saving this city and its brave defenders, had turned thither the public eye; and Joan, inflamed by the general sentiment, was seized with a wild desire of bringing relief to her sovereign in his present distresses. Her unexperienced mind, working day and night on this favourite object, mistook the impulses of passion for heavenly inspirations; and she fancied, that she saw visions, and heard voices, exhorting her to re-establish the throne of France, and to expel the foreign invaders. An uncommon intrepidity of temper made her overlook all

[n] Hall, fol. 107. Monstrelet, vol. II. p. 42. Grafton, p. 534.

the

the dangers which might attend her in such a path; and thinking herself destined by Heaven to this office, she threw aside all that bashfulness and timidity, so natural to her sex, her years, and her low station. She went to Vaucouleurs; procured admission to Baudricourt, the governor; informed him of her inspirations and intentions; and conjured him not to neglect the voice of God, who spoke through her, but to second those heavenly revelations, which impelled her to this glorious enterprize. Baudricourt treated her at first with some neglect; but on her frequent returns to him, and importunate solicitations, he began to remark something extraordinary in the maid, and was inclined, at all hazards, to make so easy an experiment. It is uncertain, whether this gentleman had discernment enough to perceive, that great use might be made with the vulgar of so uncommon an engine; or, what is more likely, in that credulous age, was himself a convert to this visionary: But he adopted at last the schemes of Joan; and he gave her some attendants, who conducted her to the French court, which at that time resided at Chinon.

It is the business of history to distinguish between the *miraculous* and the *marvellous*: to reject the first in all narrations merely profane and human; to doubt the second; and when obliged by unquestionable testimony, as in the present case, to admit of something extraordinary, to receive as little of it as is consistent with the known facts and circumstances. It is pretended, that Joan, immediately on her admission, knew the king, though she had never seen his face before, and though he purposely kept himself in the crowd of courtiers, and had laid aside every thing in his dress and apparel which might distinguish him: That she offered him, in the name of the supreme Creator, to raise the siege of Orleans, and conduct him to Rheims to be there crowned and anointed; and on his

expressing

expressing doubts of her mission, revealed to him, before some sworn confidents, a secret, which was unknown to all the world beside himself, and which nothing but a heavenly inspiration could have discovered to her: And that she demanded, as the instrument of her future victories, a particular sword, which was kept in the church of St. Catharine of Fierbois, and which, though she had never seen it, she described by all its marks, and by the place in which it had long lain neglected [r]. This is certain, that all these miraculous stories were spread abroad, in order to captivate the vulgar. The more the king and his ministers were determined to give into the illusion, the more scruples they pretended. An assembly of grave doctors and theologians cautiously examined Joan's mission, and pronounced it undoubted and supernatural. She was sent to the parliament, then residing at Poictiers; and was interrogated before that assembly: The presidents, the counsellors, who came persuaded of her imposture, went away convinced of her inspiration. A ray of hope began to break through that despair, in which the minds of all men were before enveloped. Heaven had now declared itself in favour of France, and had laid bare its outstretched arm to take vengeance on her invaders. Few could distinguish between the impulse of inclination and the force of conviction; and none would submit to the trouble of so disagreeable a scrutiny.

AFTER these artificial precautions and preparations had been for some time employed, Joan's requests were at last complied with: She was armed cap-a-pee, mounted on horseback, and shown in that martial habiliment before the whole people. Her dexterity in managing her steed, though acquired in her former occupation, was regarded as a fresh proof of her mission; and she was received with the loudest acclamations by the spectators.

[r] Hall, fol. 107. Hollingshed, p. 600.

Her

Her former occupation was even denied: She was no longer the servant of an inn: She was converted into a shepherdess, an employment much more agreeable to the imagination. To render her still more interesting, near ten years were substracted from her age; and all the sentiments of love and of chivalry were thus united to those of enthusiasm, in order to inflame the fond fancy of the people with prepossessions in her favour.

WHEN the engine was thus dressed up in full splendor, it was determined to essay its force against the enemy. Joan was sent to Blois, where a large convoy was prepared for the supply of Orleans, and an army of ten thousand men, under the command of St. Severe, assembled to escort it. She ordered all the soldiers to confess themselves before they set out on the enterprize: She banished from the camp all women of bad fame: She displayed in her hands a consecrated banner; where the Supreme Being was represented grasping the globe of earth, and surrounded with flower de luces: And she insisted, in right of her prophetic mission, that the convoy should enter Orleans by the direct road from the side of Beausse: But the count of Dunois, unwilling to submit the rules of the military art to her inspirations, ordered it to approach by the other side of the river, where, he knew, the weakest part of the English army was stationed.

PREVIOUS to this attempt, the maid had written to the regent, and to the English generals before Orleans, commanding them, in the name of the omnipotent Creator, by whom she was commissioned, immediately to raise the siege, and to evacuate France; and menacing them with divine vengeance in case of their disobedience. All the English affected to speak with derision of the maid, and of her heavenly commission; and said, that the French king was now indeed reduced to a sorry pass, when he had re-

course

course to such ridiculous expedients: But they felt their imagination secretly struck with the vehement persuasion which prevailed in all around them; and they waited with an anxious expectation, not unmixed with horror, for the issue of these extraordinary preparations.

As the convoy approached the river, a sally was made by the garrison on the side of Beausse, to prevent the English general from sending any detachment to the other side: The provisions were peaceably embarked in boats, which the inhabitants of Orleans had sent to receive them: The maid covered with her troops the embarkation: Suffolk did not venture to attack her: And the French general carried back the army in safety to Blois; an alteration of affairs which was already visible to all the world, and which had a proportional effect on the minds of both parties.

THE maid entered the city of Orleans arrayed in her military garb, and displaying her consecrated standard; and was received as a celestial deliverer by all the inhabitants. They now believed themselves invincible under her influence; and Dunois himself, perceiving such a mighty alteration both in friends and foes, consented that the next convoy, which was expected in a few days, should enter by the side of Beausse. The convoy approached: No sign of resistance appeared in the besiegers: The waggons and troops passed without interruption between the redoubts of the English: A dead silence and astonishment reigned among those troops, formerly so elated with victory, and so fierce for the combat.

THE earl of Suffolk was in a situation very unusual and extraordinary, and which might well confound the man of the greatest capacity and firmest temper. He saw his troops overawed, and strongly impressed with the idea of a divine influence accompanying the maid. Instead

stead of banishing these vain terrors by hurry, and action, and war, he waited till the soldiers should recover from the panic; and he thereby gave leisure for those prepossessions to sink still deeper into their minds. The military maxims, which are prudent in common cases, deceived him in these unaccountable events. The English felt their courage daunted and overwhelmed; and thence inferred a divine vengeance hanging over them. The French drew the same inference from an inactivity so new and unexpected. Every circumstance was now reversed in the opinions of men, on which all depends: The spirit resulting from a long course of uninterrupted success was on a sudden transferred from the victors to the vanquished.

The maid called aloud, that the garrison should remain no longer on the defensive; and she promised her followers the assistance of heaven in attacking those redoubts of the enemy which had so long kept them in awe, and which they had never hitherto dared to insult. The generals seconded her ardour: An attack was made on one redoubt, and it proved successful[a]: All the English who defended the entrenchments were put to the sword, or taken prisoners: And Sir John Talbot himself, who had drawn together, from the other redoubts, some troops to bring them relief, durst not appear in the open field against so formidable an enemy.

Nothing, after this success, seemed impossible to the maid and her enthusiastic votaries. She urged the generals to attack the main body of the English in their entrenchments: But Dunois, still unwilling to hazard the fate of France by too great temerity, and sensible that the least reverse of fortune would make all the present visions evaporate, and restore every thing to its former condition, checked her vehemence, and proposed to her

[a] Monstrelet, vol. ii. p. 45.

first to expel the enemy from their forts on the other side of the river, and thus lay the communication with the country entirely open, before she attempted any more hazardous enterprize. Joan was perfuaded, and thefe forts were vigoroufly affailed. In one attack the French were repulfed; the maid was left almoft alone; fhe was obliged to retreat, and join the runaways; but difplaying her facred ftandard, and animating them with her countenance, her geftures, her exhortations, fhe led them back to the charge, and overpowered the Englifh in their entrenchments. In the attack of another fort, fhe was wounded in the neck with an arrow; fhe retreated a moment behind the affailants; fhe pulled out the arrow with her own hands; fhe had the wound quickly dreffed; and fhe haftened back to head the troops, and to plant her victorious banner on the ramparts of the enemy.

By all thefe fucceffes, the Englifh were entirely chaced from their fortifications on that fide: They had loft above fix thoufand men in thefe different actions; and, what was ftill more important, their wonted courage and confidence was wholly gone, and had given place to amazement and defpair. The maid returned triumphant over the bridge, and was again received as the guardian angel of the city. After performing fuch miracles, fhe convinced the moft obdurate incredulity of her divine miffion: Men felt themfelves animated as by a fuperior energy, and thought nothing impoffible to that divine band which fo vifibly conducted them. It was in vain even for the Englifh generals to oppofe with their foldiers the prevailing opinion of fupernatural influence: They themfelves were probably moved by the fame belief: The utmoft they dared to advance was, that Joan was not an inftrument of God; fhe was only the implement of the Devil: But as the Englifh had felt, to their fad experience, that the Devil might be allowed fometimes to prevail, they derived not much confolation from the enforcing of this opinion.

It might prove extremely dangerous for Suffolk, with fuch intimidated troops, to remain any longer in the prefence of fo courageous and victorious an enemy; he therefore raifed the fiege, and retreated with all the precaution imaginable. The French refolved to pufh their conquefts, and to allow the Englifh no leifure to recover from their confternation. Charles formed a body of fix thoufand men, and fent them to attack Jergeau, whither Suffolk had retired with a detachment of his army. The fiege lafted ten days; and the place was obftinately defended. Joan difplayed her wonted intrepidity on the occafion. She defcended into the foffee in leading the attack; and fhe there received a blow on the head with a ftone, by which fhe was confounded and beaten to the ground: But fhe foon recovered herfelf, and in the end rendered the affault fuccefsful: Suffolk was obliged to yield himfelf prifoner to a Frenchman called Renaud; but, before he fubmitted, he afked his adverfary, whether he were a gentleman? On receiving a fatisfactory anfwer, he demanded, whether he were a knight? Renaud replied, that he had not yet attained that honour. *Then I make you one,* replied Suffolk: Upon which he gave him the blow with his fword, which dubbed him into that fraternity; and he immediately furrendered himfelf his prifoner.

The remainder of the Englifh army was commanded by Faftolffe, Scales, and Talbot, who thought of nothing but of making their retreat, as foon as poffible, into a place of fafety; while the French efteemed the overtaking them equivalent to a victory. So much had the events which paffed before Orleans altered every thing between the two nations! The vanguard of the French, under Richemont and Xaintrailles, attacked the rear of

CHAP. XX.

1429.
The fiege of Orleans raifed.
8th May.

the enemy at the village of Patay. The battle lasted not a moment: The English were discomfited, and fled: The brave Fastolffe himself showed the example of flight to his troops; and the order of the garter was taken from him, as a punishment for this instance of cowardice[b]. Two thousand men were killed in this action, and both Talbot and Scales taken prisoners.

In the account of all these successes, the French writers, to magnify the wonder, represent the maid (who was now known by the appellation of *the Maid of Orleans*) as not only active in combat, but as performing the office of general; directing the troops, conducting the military operations, and swaying the deliberations in all councils of war. It is certain, that the policy of the French court endeavoured to maintain this appearance with the public: But it is much more probable, that Dunois and the wiser commanders prompted her in all her measures, than that a country girl, without experience or education, could, on a sudden, become expert in a profession which requires more genius and capacity than any other active scene of life. It is sufficient praise that she could distinguish the persons on whose judgment she might rely; that she could seize their hints and suggestions, and, on a sudden, deliver their opinions as her own; and that she could curb, on occasion, that visionary and enthusiastic spirit with which she was actuated, and could temper it with prudence and discretion.

The raising of the siege of Orleans was one part of the maid's promise to Charles: The crowning of him at Rheims was the other: And she now vehemently insisted that he should forthwith set out on that enterprize. A few weeks before, such a proposal would have appeared the most extravagant in the world. Rheims lay in a

---

[b] Monstrelet, vol. ii. p. 46.

distant

distant quarter of the kingdom; was then in the hands of a victorious enemy; the whole road which led to it was occupied by their garrisons; and no man could be so sanguine as to imagine that such an attempt could so soon come within the bounds of possibility. But as it was extremely the interest of Charles to maintain the belief of something extraordinary and divine in these events, and to avail himself of the present consternation of the English, he resolved to follow the exhortations of his warlike prophetess, and to lead his army upon this promising adventure. Hitherto he had kept remote from the scene of war: As the safety of the state depended upon his person, he had been persuaded to restrain his military ardour: But observing this prosperous turn of affairs, he now determined to appear at the head of his armies, and to set the example of valour to all his soldiers. And the French nobility saw at once their young sovereign assuming a new and more brilliant character, seconded by fortune, and conducted by the hand of heaven; and they caught fresh zeal to exert themselves in replacing him on the throne of his ancestors.

CHARLES set out for Rheims at the head of twelve thousand men: He passed by Troye, which opened its gates to him: Chalons imitated the example: Rheims sent him a deputation with its keys, before his approach to it: And he scarcely perceived, as he passed along, that he was marching through an enemy's country. The ceremony of his coronation was here performed [c] with the holy oil, which a pigeon had brought to king Clovis from heaven on the first establishment of the French monarchy: The maid of Orleans stood by his side in complete armour, and displayed her sacred ban-

[c] Monstrelet, vol. II. p. 48.

CHAP. XX.
1429.

ner, which had so often dissipated and confounded his fiercest enemies: And the people shouted with the most unfeigned joy on viewing such a complication of wonders. After the completion of the ceremony, the maid threw herself at the king's feet, embraced his knees, and with a flood of tears, which pleasure and tenderness extorted from her, she congratulated him on this singular and marvellous event.

CHARLES, thus crowned and anointed, became more respectable in the eyes of all his subjects, and seemed, in a manner, to receive anew, from a heavenly commission, his title to their allegiance. The inclinations of men swaying their belief, no one doubted of the inspirations and prophetic spirit of the maid: So many incidents, which passed all human comprehension, left little room to question a superior influence: And the real and undoubted facts brought credit to every exaggeration, which could scarcely be rendered more wonderful. Laon, Soissons, Chateau-Thierri, Provins, and many other towns and fortresses in that neighbourhood, immediately after Charles's coronation, submitted to him on the first summons; and the whole nation was disposed to give him the most zealous testimonies of their duty and affection.

Prudence of the duke of Bedford.

NOTHING can impress us with a higher idea of the wisdom, address, and resolution of the duke of Bedford, than his being able to maintain himself in so perilous a situation, and to preserve some footing in France, after the defection of so many places, and amidst the universal inclination of the rest to imitate that contagious example. This prince seemed present every where by his vigilance and foresight: He employed every resource which fortune had yet left him: He put all the English garrisons in a posture of defence: He kept a watchful eye over every attempt

tempt among the French towards an infurrection: He retained the Parifians in obedience, by alternately employing careffes and feverity: And knowing that the duke of Burgundy was already wavering in his fidelity, he acted with fo much fkill and prudence, as to renew, in this dangerous crifis, his alliance with that prince; an alliance of the utmoft importance to the credit and fupport of the Englifh government.

CHAP.
XX.

1429.

THE fmall fupplies which he received from England fet the talents of this great man in ftill a ftronger light. The ardour of the Englifh for foreign conquefts was now extremely abated by time and reflection: The parliament feems even to have become fenfible of the danger which might attend their farther progrefs: No fupply of money could be obtained by the regent during his greateft diftreffes: And men enlifted flowly under his ftandard, or foon deferted, by reafon of the wonderful accounts which had reached England, of the magic, and forcery, and diabolical power of the maid of Orleans [d]. It happened fortunately, in this emergency, that the bifhop of Winchefter, now created a cardinal, landed at Calais with a body of 5000 men, which he was conducting into Bohemia, on a crufade againft the Huffites. He was perfuaded to lend thefe troops to his nephew during the prefent difficulties [e]; and the regent was thereby enabled to take the field, and to oppofe the French king, who was advancing with his army to the gates of Paris.

THE extraordinary capacity of the duke of Bedford appeared alfo in his military operations. He attempted to reftore the courage of his troops by boldly advancing to the face of the enemy; but he chofe his pofts with fo much caution, as always to decline a combat, and to render it impoffible for Charles to attack him. He ftill at-

[d] Rymer, vol. x. p. 459. 472.   [e] Ibid. vol. x. p. 421.

tended

tended that prince in all his movements; covered his own towns and garrisons; and kept himself in a posture to reap advantage from every imprudence or false step of the enemy. The French army, which consisted mostly of volunteers, who served at their own expence, soon after retired, and was disbanded: Charles went to Bourges, the ordinary place of his residence; but not till he made himself master of Compiegne, Beauvais, Senlis, Sens, Laval, Lagni, St. Denis, and of many places in the neighbourhood of Paris, which the affections of the people had put into his hands.

The regent endeavoured to revive the declining state of his affairs by bringing over the young king of England, and having him crowned and anointed at Paris[f]. All the vassals of the crown who lived within the provinces possessed by the English, swore a new allegiance, and did homage to him. But this ceremony was cold and insipid, compared with the lustre which had attended the coronation of Charles at Rheims; and the duke of Bedford expected more effect from an accident, which put into his hands the person that had been the author of all his calamities.

The maid of Orleans, after the coronation of Charles, declared to the count of Dunois, that her wishes were now fully gratified, and that she had no farther desire than to return to her former condition, and to the occupations and course of life which became her sex: But that nobleman, sensible of the great advantages which might still be reaped from her presence in the army, exhorted her to persevere, till, by the final expulsion of the English, she had brought all her prophecies to their full completion. In pursuance of this advice, she threw herself into the town of Compiegne, which was at that time besieged by the duke

[f] Rymer, vol. x. p. 432.

of Burgundy, assisted by the earls of Arundel and Suffolk; and the garrison, on her appearance, believed themselves thenceforth invincible. But their joy was of short duration. The maid, next day after her arrival, headed a sally upon the quarters of John of Luxembourg; she twice drove the enemy from their entrenchments; finding their numbers to encrease every moment, she ordered a retreat; when hard pressed by the pursuers, she turned upon them, and made them again recoil; but being here deserted by her friends, and surrounded by the enemy, she was at last, after exerting the utmost valour, taken prisoner by the Burgundians[s]. The common opinion was, that the French officers, finding the merit of every victory ascribed to her, had, in envy to her renown, by which they themselves were so much eclipsed, willingly exposed her to this fatal accident.

THE envy of her friends, on this occasion, was not a greater proof of her merit than the triumph of her enemies. A complete victory would not have given more joy to the English and their partizans. The service of *Te Deum*, which has so often been profaned by princes, was publicly celebrated, on this fortunate event, at Paris. The duke of Bedford fancied, that, by the captivity of that extraordinary woman, who had blasted all his successes, he should again recover his former ascendant over France; and, to push farther the present advantage, he purchased the captive from John of Luxembourg, and formed a prosecution against her, which, whether it proceeded from vengeance or policy, was equally barbarous and dishonourable.

THERE was no possible reason, why Joan should not be regarded as a prisoner of war, and be entitled to all the

[s] Stowe, p. 371.

courtesy and good usage, which civilized nations practise towards enemies on these occasions. She had never, in her military capacity, forfeited, by any act of treachery or cruelty, her claim to that treatment: She was unstained by any civil crime: Even the virtues and the very decorums of her sex had ever been rigidly observed by her: And though her appearing in war, and leading armies to battle, may seem an exception, she had thereby performed such signal service to her prince, that she had abundantly compensated for this irregularity; and was, on that very account, the more an object of praise and admiration. It was necessary, therefore, for the duke of Bedford to interest religion some way in the prosecution; and to cover, under that cloak, his violation of justice and humanity.

THE bishop of Beauvais, a man wholly devoted to the English interests, presented a petition against Joan, on pretence that she was taken within the bounds of his diocese; and he desired to have her tried by an ecclesiastical court for sorcery, impiety, idolatry, and magic: The university of Paris was so mean as to join in the same request: Several prelates, among whom the cardinal of Winchester was the only Englishman, were appointed her judges: They held their court in Roüen, where the young king of England then resided: And the Maid, clothed in her former military apparel, but loaded with irons, was produced before this tribunal.

SHE first desired to be eased of her chains: Her judges answered, that she had once already attempted an escape, by throwing herself from a tower: She confessed the fact, maintained the justice of her intention, and owned that, if she could, she would still execute that purpose. All her other speeches shewed the same firmness and intrepidity; Though harassed with interrogatories during the course

course of near four months, she never betrayed any weakness or womanish submission; and no advantage was gained over her. The point, which her judges pushed most vehemently, was her visions and revelations and intercourse with departed saints; and they asked her, whether she would submit to the church the truth of these inspirations: She replied, that she would submit them to God, the fountain of truth. They then exclaimed, that she was a heretic, and denied the authority of the church. She appealed to the pope: They rejected her appeal.

They asked her, why she put trust in her standard, which had been consecrated by magical incantations: She replied, that she put trust in the Supreme Being alone, whose image was impressed upon it. They demanded, why she carried in her hand that standard at the anointment and coronation of Charles at Rheims: She answered, that the person who had shared the danger, was entitled to share the glory. When accused of going to war, contrary to the decorums of her sex, and of assuming government and command over men; she scrupled not to reply, that her sole purpose was to defeat the English, and to expel them the kingdom. In the issue, she was condemned for all the crimes of which she had been accused, aggravated by heresy; her revelations were declared to be inventions of the devil to delude the people; and she was sentenced to be delivered over to the secular arm.

Joan, so long surrounded by inveterate enemies, who treated her with every mark of contumely; brow-beaten and overawed by men of superior rank, and men invested with the ensigns of a sacred character, which she had been accustomed to revere, felt her spirit at last subdued; and those visionary dreams of inspiration, in which she had been buoyed up by the triumphs of success, and the

applauses

applauses of her own party, gave way to the terrors of that punishment to which she was sentenced. She publicly declared herself willing to recant; she acknowledged the illusion of those revelations which the church had rejected; and she promised never more to maintain them. Her sentence was then mitigated: She was condemned to perpetual imprisonment, and to be fed during life on bread and water.

ENOUGH was now done to fulfil all political views, and to convince both the French and the English, that the opinion of divine influence, which had so much encouraged the one, and daunted the other, was entirely without foundation. But the barbarous vengeance of Joan's enemies was not satisfied with this victory. Suspecting, that the female dress, which she had now consented to wear, was disagreeable to her, they purposely placed in her apartment a suit of men's apparel; and watched for the effects of that temptation upon her. On the sight of a dress in which she had acquired so much renown, and which, she once believed, she wore by the particular appointment of heaven, all her former ideas and passions revived; and she ventured in her solitude to clothe herself again in the forbidden garment. Her insidious enemies caught her in that situation: Her fault was interpreted to be no less than a relapse into heresy: No recantation would now suffice, and no pardon could be granted her. She was condemned to be burned in the market-place of Roüen; and the infamous sentence was accordingly executed. This admirable heroine, to whom the more generous superstition of the ancients would have erected altars, was, on pretence of heresy and magic, delivered over alive to the flames, and expiated, by that dreadful punishment, the signal services which she had rendered to her prince and to her native country.

The affairs of the English, far from being advanced by this execution, went every day more and more to decay: The great abilities of the regent were unable to resist the strong inclination, which had seized the French, to return under the obedience of their rightful sovereign, and which that act of cruelty was ill fitted to remove. Chartres was surprized by a stratagem of the count of Dunois: A body of the English, under lord Willoughby, was defeated at St. Celerin upon the Sarte [i]: The fair in the suburbs of Caën, seated in the midst of the English territories, was pillaged by de Lore, a French officer: The duke of Bedford himself was obliged by Dunois to raise the siege of Lagni, with some loss of reputation: And all these misfortunes, though light, yet being continued and uninterrupted, brought discredit on the English, and menaced them with an approaching revolution. But the chief detriment, which the regent sustained, was by the death of his duchess, who had hitherto preserved some appearance of friendship between him and her brother, the duke of Burgundy [i]: And his marriage soon afterwards, with Jaqueline of Luxembourg, was the beginning of a breach between them [k]. Philip complained, that the regent had never had the civility to inform him of his intentions, and that so sudden a marriage was a slight on his sister's memory. The cardinal of Winchester mediated a reconciliation between these princes, and brought both of them to St. Omers for that purpose. The duke of Bedford here expected the first visit, both as he was son, brother, and uncle to a king, and because he had already made such advances as to come into the duke of Burgundy's territories, in order to have an interview with him: But Philip, proud of his great power and independent dominions, refused to pay this compli-

[i] Monstrelet, vol. ii. p. 100. p. 373. Grafton, p. 551. [i] Ibid. p. 87. [k] Stowe,

ment to the regent: And the two princes, unable to adjust the ceremonial, parted without seeing each other [m]. A bad prognostic of their cordial intentions to renew past amity!

Defection of the duke of Burgundy.

NOTHING could be more repugnant to the interests of the house of Burgundy, than to unite the crowns of France and England on the same head; an event which, had it taken place, would have reduced the duke to the rank of a petty prince, and have rendered his situation entirely dependant and precarious. The title also to the crown of France, which, after the failure of the elder branches, might accrue to the duke or his posterity, had been sacrificed by the treaty of Troye; and strangers and enemies were thereby irrevocably fixed upon the throne. Revenge alone had carried Philip into these impolitic measures; and a point of honour had hitherto induced him to maintain them. But as it is the nature of passion gradually to decay, while the sense of interest maintains a permanent influence and authority; the duke had, for some years, appeared sensibly to relent in his animosity against Charles, and to hearken willingly to the apologies made by that prince for the murder of the late duke of Burgundy. His extreme youth was pleaded in his favour; his incapacity to judge for himself; the ascendant gained over him by his ministers; and his inability to resent a deed, which, without his knowledge, had been perpetrated by those under whose guidance he was then placed. The more to flatter the pride of Philip, the king of France had banished from his court and presence Tanegui de Chatel, and all those who were concerned in that assassination; and had offered to make every other atonement which could be required of him. The distress which Charles had already suffered, had tended to gratify the duke's revenge; the miseries, to which France had

[m] Monstrelet, vol. ii. p. 90. Grafton, p. 561.

been

been so long exposed, had begun to move his compassion; and the cries of all Europe admonished him, that his resentment, which might hitherto be deemed pious, would, if carried farther, be universally condemned as barbarous and unrelenting. While the duke was in this disposition, every disgust, which he received from England, made a double impression upon him; the entreaties of the count of Richemont and the duke of Bourbon, who had married his two sisters, had weight; and he finally determined to unite himself to the royal family of France, from which his own was descended. For this purpose, a congress was appointed at Arras under the mediation of deputies from the pope and the council of Basle: The duke of Burgundy came thither in person: The duke of Bourbon, the count of Richemont, and other persons of high rank, appeared as ambassadors from France: And the English having also been invited to attend, the cardinal of Winchester, the bishops of Norwich and St. David's, the earls of Huntingdon and Suffolk, with others, received from the protector and council a commission for that purpose [m].

CHAP.
XX.

1431.

1135.

The conferences were held in the abbey of St. Vaast; and began with discussing the proposals of the two crowns, which were so wide of each other as to admit of no hopes of accommodation. France offered to cede Normandy with Guienne, but both of them loaded with the usual homage and vassalage to the crown. As the claims of England upon France were universally unpopular in Europe, the mediators declared the offers of Charles very reasonable; and the cardinal of Winchester, with the other English ambassadors, without giving a particular detail of their demands, immediately left the congress. There remained nothing but to discuss the mutual pretensions of Charles and Philip. These were easily adjusted:

August.

[m] Rymer, vol. x. p. 611, 612.

The vassal was in a situation to give law to his superior; and he exacted conditions, which, had it not been for the present necessity, would have been deemed, to the last degree, dishonourable and disadvantageous to the crown of France. Besides making repeated atonements and acknowledgments for the murder of the duke of Burgundy, Charles was obliged to cede all the towns of Picardy which lay between the Somme and the Low Countries; he yielded several other territories; he agreed, that these and all the other dominions of Philip should be held by him, during his life, without doing any homage, or swearing fealty to the present king; and he freed his subjects from all obligations to allegiance, if ever he infringed this treaty [a]. Such were the conditions upon which France purchased the friendship of the duke of Burgundy.

The duke sent a herald to England with a letter, in which he notified the conclusion of the treaty of Arras, and apologized for his departure from that of Troye. The council received the herald with great coldness: they even assigned him his lodgings in a shoemaker's house, by way of insult; and the populace were so incensed, that, if the duke of Glocester had not given him guards, his life had been exposed to danger, when he appeared in the streets. The Flemings, and other subjects of Philip, were insulted, and some of them murdered by the Londoners; and every thing seemed to tend towards a rupture between the two nations [b]. These violences were not disagreeable to the duke of Burgundy; as they afforded him a pretence for the farther measures which he intended to take against the English, whom he now regarded as implacable and dangerous enemies.

[a] Monstrelet, vol. II. p. 131. Grafton, p. 565. [b] Monstrelet, vol. II. p. 124. Hollingshed, p. 612.

A FEW

HENRY VI.

CHAP. XX.

A FEW days after the duke of Bedford received intelligence of this treaty, so fatal to the interests of England, he died at Roüen; a prince of great abilities, and of many virtues; and whose memory, except from the barbarous execution of the maid of Orleans, was unsullied by any considerable blemish. Isabella, queen of France, died a little before him, despised by the English, detested by the French, and reduced in her later years to regard, with an unnatural horror, the progress and successes of her own son, in recovering possession of his kingdom. This period was also signalized by the death of the earl of Arundel[p], a great English general, who, though he commanded three thousand men, was foiled by Xaintrailles at the head of six hundred, and soon after expired of the wounds which he received in the action.

1435. 14th Sept. Death of the duke of Bedford.

THE violent factions, which prevailed between the duke of Glocester and the cardinal of Winchester, prevented the English from taking the proper measures for repairing these multiplied losses, and threw all their affairs into confusion. The popularity of the duke, and his near relation to the crown, gave him advantages in the contest, which he often lost by his open and unguarded temper, unfit to struggle with the politic and interested spirit of his rival. The balance, meanwhile, of these parties, kept every thing in suspence: Foreign affairs were much neglected: And though the duke of York, son to that earl of Cambridge who was executed in the beginning of the last reign, was appointed successor to the duke of Bedford, it was seven months before his commission passed the seals; and the English remained so long in an enemy's country, without a proper head or governor.

1436.

[p] Monstrelet, vol. II. p. 105. Hollingshed, p. 610.

CHAP.
XX.

1436.
Decline of the English in France.

THE new governor, on his arrival, found the capital already lost. The Parisians had always been more attached to the Burgundian than to the English interest; and after the conclusion of the treaty of Arras, their affections, without any farther controul, universally led them to return to their allegiance under their native sovereign. The constable, together with Lile-Adam, the same person who had before put Paris into the hands of the duke of Burgundy, was introduced in the night-time by intelligence with the citizens: Lord Willoughby, who commanded only a small garrison of 1500 men, was expelled: This nobleman discovered valour and presence of mind on the occasion; but unable to guard so large a place against such multitudes, he retired into the Bastile, and being there invested, he delivered up that fortress, and was contended to stipulate for the safe retreat of his troops into Normandy[q].

IN the same season, the duke of Burgundy openly took part against England, and commenced hostilities by the siege of Calais, the only place which now gave the English any sure hold of France, and still rendered them dangerous. As he was beloved among his own subjects, and had acquired the epithet of *Good*, from his popular qualities, he was able to interest all the inhabitants of the Low Countries in the success of this enterprize; and he invested that place with an army, formidable from its numbers, but without experience, discipline, or military spirit[r]. On the first alarm of this siege, the duke of Glocester assembled some forces, sent a defiance to Philip, and challenged him to wait the event of a battle, which he promised to give, as soon as the wind would permit him to reach Calais. The warlike genius of the English had at that time rendered them terrible to all the northern

[q] Monstrelet, vol. ii. p. 117. Grafton, p. 568.   [r] Monstrelet, vol. ii. p. 126. 130. 132. Hollingshed, p. 613. Grafton, p. 571.

parts

parts of Europe; especially to the Flemings, who were more expert in manufactures than in arms; and the duke of Burgundy, being already foiled in some attempts before Calais, and observing the discontent and terror of his own army, thought proper to raise the siege, and to retreat before the arrival of the enemy [a].

CHAP.
XX.

1436.

THE English were still masters of many fine provinces in France; but retained possession, more by the extreme weakness of Charles, than by the strength of their own garrisons, or the force of their armies. Nothing indeed can be more surprising than the feeble efforts made, during the course of several years, by these two potent nations against each other; while the one struggled for independence, and the other aspired to a total conquest of its rival. The general want of industry, commerce, and police, in that age, had rendered all the European nations, and France and England no less than the others, unfit for bearing the burthens of war, when it was prolonged beyond one season; and the continuance of hostilities had, long ere this time, exhausted the force and patience of both kingdoms. Scarcely could the appearance of an army be brought into the field on either side; and all the operations consisted in the surprisal of places, in the rencounter of detached parties, and in incursions upon the open country; which were performed by small bodies, assembled on a sudden from the neighbouring garrisons. In this method of conducting the war, the French king had much the advantage: The affections of the people were entirely on his side: Intelligence was early brought him of the state and motions of the enemy: The inhabitants were ready to join in any attempts against the garrisons: And thus ground was continually, though flowly, gained upon the English. The duke of York, who was a prince of abilities, struggled against these difficulties dur-

26th June.

[a] Monstrelet, vol. ii. p. 136. Hollingshed, p. 614.

ing the course of five years; and being assisted by the valour of lord Talbot, soon after created earl of Shrewsbury, he performed actions which acquired him honour, but merit not the attention of posterity. It would have been well, had this feeble war, in sparing the blood of the people, prevented likewise all other oppressions; and had the fury of men, which reason and justice cannot restrain, thus happily received a check from their impotence and inability. But the French and English, though they exerted such small force, were, however, stretching beyond their resources, which were still smaller; and the troops, destitute of pay, were obliged to subsist by plundering and oppressing the country, both of friends and enemies. The fields in all the north of France, which was the seat of war, were laid waste and left uncultivated [1]. The cities were gradually depopulated, not by the blood spilt in battle, but by the more destructive pillage of the garrisons [2]: And both parties, weary of hostilities, which decided nothing, seemed at last desirous of peace, and they set on foot negociations for that purpose. But the proposals of France, and the demands of England, were still so wide of each other, that all hope of accommodation immediately vanished. The English ambassadors demanded restitution of all the provinces which had once been annexed to England, together with the final cession of Calais and its district; and required the possession of these extensive territories without the burthen of any fealty or homage on the part of their prince: The French offered only part of Guienne, part of Normandy, and Calais, loaded with the usual burthens. It appeared in vain to

[1] Grafton, p. 361.

[2] Fortescue, who soon after this period, visited France, in the train of prince Henry, speaks of that kingdom as a desart in comparison of England. See his Treatise *de laudibus Angliæ*. Though we make allowance for the partialities of Fortescue, there must have been some foundation for his account; and these destructive wars are the most likely reason to be assigned for the difference remarked by this author.

continue

continue the negociation, while there was so little prospect of agreement. The English were still too haughty to stoop from the vast hopes which they had formerly entertained, and to accept of terms more suitable to the present condition of the two kingdoms.

THE duke of York soon after resigned his government to the earl of Warwic, a nobleman of reputation, whom death prevented from long enjoying this dignity. The duke, upon the demise of that nobleman, returned to his charge, and, during his administration, a truce was concluded between the king of England and the duke of Burgundy, which had become necessary for the commercial interests of their subjects[u]. The war with France continued in the same languid and feeble state as before.

THE captivity of five princes of the blood, taken prisoners in the battle of Azincour, was a considerable advantage which England long enjoyed over its enemy; but this superiority was now entirely lost. Some of these princes had died; some had been ransomed; and the duke of Orleans, the most powerful among them, was the last that remained in the hands of the English. He offered the sum of 54,000 nobles[r] for his liberty; and when this proposal was laid before the council of England, as every question was there an object of faction, the party of the duke of Glocester, and that of the cardinal of Winchester, were divided in their sentiments with regard to it. The duke reminded the council of the dying advice of the late king, that none of these prisoners should on any account be released,

[u] Grafton, p. 573. [r] Rymer, vol. x. p. 764. 776. 782. 795. 796. This sum was equal to 36,000 pounds sterling of our present money. A subsidy of a tenth and fifteenth was fixed by Edward III. at 29,000 pounds, which, in the reign of Henry VI. made only 38,000 pounds of our present money. The parliament granted only one subsidy during the course of seven years, from 1437 to 1444.

till his son should be of sufficient age to hold, himself, the reins of government. The cardinal insisted on the greatness of the sum offered, which, in reality, was near equal to two-thirds of all the extraordinary supplies that the parliament, during the course of seven years, granted for the support of the war. And he added, that the release of this prince was more likely to be advantageous than prejudicial to the English interests; by filling the court of France with faction, and giving a head to those numerous malcontents whom Charles was at present able, with great difficulty, to restrain. The cardinal's party, as usual, prevailed: The duke of Orleans was released, after a melancholy captivity of twenty-five years[a]: And the duke of Burgundy, as a pledge of his entire reconciliation with the family of Orleans, facilitated to that prince the payment of his ransom. It must be confessed, that the princes and nobility, in those ages, went to war on very disadvantageous terms. If they were taken prisoners, they either remained in captivity during life, or purchased their liberty at the price which the victors were pleased to impose, and which often reduced their families to want and beggary.

1443.

The sentiments of the cardinal, some time after, prevailed in another point of still greater moment. That prelate had always encouraged every proposal of accommodation with France; and had represented the utter impossibility, in the present circumstances, of pushing farther the conquests in that kingdom, and the great difficulty of even maintaining those which were already made. He insisted on the extreme reluctance of the parliament to grant supplies; the disorders in which the English affairs in Normandy were involved; the daily progress made by the French king; and the advantage

[a] Grafton, p. 578.

of stopping his hand by a temporary accommodation, which might leave room for time and accidents to operate in favour of the English. The duke of Glocester, high-spirited and haughty, and educated in the lofty pretensions which the first successes of his two brothers had rendered familiar to him, could not yet be induced to relinquish all hopes of prevailing over France; much less could he see, with patience, his own opinion thwarted and rejected by the influence of his rival in the English council. But, notwithstanding his opposition, the earl of Suffolk, a nobleman who adhered to the cardinal's party, was dispatched to Tours, in order to negociate with the French ministers. It was found impossible to adjust the terms of a lasting peace; but a truce for twenty-two months was concluded, which left every thing on the present footing between the parties. The numerous disorders under which the French government laboured, and which time alone could remedy, induced Charles to assent to this truce; and the same motives engaged him afterwards to prolong it[a]. But Suffolk, not content with executing this object of his commission, proceeded also to finish another business; which seems rather to have been implied than expressed in the powers that had been granted him[b].

In proportion as Henry advanced in years, his character became fully known in the court, and was no longer ambiguous to either faction. Of the most harmless, inoffensive, simple manners; but of the most slender capacity; he was fitted, both by the softness of his temper, and the weakness of his understanding, to be perpetually governed by those who surrounded him; and it was easy to foresee that his reign would prove a perpetual minority. As he had now reached the twenty-third year of his age, it was natural to think of choosing him a queen;

[a] Rymer, vol. xi. p. 101. 108. 206. 214.   [b] Ibid. p. 53.

and

170   HISTORY OF ENGLAND.

CHAP. XX.
1443.

and each party was ambitious of having him receive one from their hand; as it was probable that this circumstance would decide, for ever, the victory between them. The duke of Glocester proposed a daughter of the count of Armagnac; but had not credit to effect his purpose. The cardinal and his friends had cast their eye on Margaret of Anjou, daughter of Regnier, titular king of Sicily, Naples, and Jerusalem, descended from the count of Anjou, brother of Charles V. who had left these magnificent titles, but without any real power or possessions, to his posterity. This princess herself was the most accomplished of her age both in body and mind; and seemed to possess those qualities which would equally qualify her to acquire the ascendant over Henry, and to supply all his defects and weaknesses. Of a masculine, courageous spirit, of an enterprizing temper, endowed with solidity as well as vivacity of understanding, she had not been able to conceal these great talents even in the privacy of her father's family; and it was reasonable to expect, that when she should mount the throne, they would break out with still superior lustre. The earl of Suffolk, therefore, in concert with his associates of the English council, made proposals of marriage to Margaret, which were accepted. But this nobleman, besides preoccupying the princess's favour, by being the chief means of her advancement, endeavoured to ingratiate himself with her and her family, by very extraordinary concessions: Though Margaret brought no dowry with her, he ventured, of himself, without any direct authority from the council, but probably with the approbation of the cardinal and the ruling members, to engage, by a secret article, that the province of Maine, which was at that time in the hands of the English, should be ceded to Charles of Anjou, her uncle[t], who was prime mini-

Marriage of the king with Margaret of Anjou.

[t] *Grafton*, p. 597.

ster

HENRY VI.

fter and favourite of the French king, and who had already received from his master the grant of that province as his appanage.

This treaty of marriage was ratified in England: Suffolk obtained first the title of marquis, then that of duke; and even received the thanks of parliament for his services in concluding it[d]. The princess fell immediately into close connections with the cardinal and his party, the dukes of Somerset, Suffolk, and Buckingham[e]; who, fortified by her powerful patronage, resolved on the final ruin of the duke of Glocester.

This generous prince, worsted in all court intrigues, for which his temper was not suited; but possessing, in a high degree, the favour of the public, had already received from his rivals a cruel mortification, which he had hitherto borne without violating public peace, but which it was impossible that a person of his spirit and humanity could ever forgive. His duchess, the daughter of Reginald, lord Cobham, had been accused of the crime of witchcraft, and it was pretended that there was found in her possession a waxen figure of the king, which she and her associates, Sir Roger Bolingbroke a priest, and one Margery Jordan of Eye, melted in a magical manner before a slow fire, with an intention of making Henry's force and vigour waste away by like insensible degrees. The accusation was well calculated to affect the weak and credulous mind of the king, and to gain belief in an ignorant age; and the duchess was brought to trial with her confederates. The nature of this crime, so opposite to all common sense, seems always to exempt the accusers from observing the rules of common sense in their evidence: The prisoners were pronounced guilty; the duchess was condemned to do public penance, and to suffer perpetual

CHAP. XI.

1443.

1447.

[d] Cotton, p. 630. [e] Hollingshed, p. 626.

imprison-

imprisonment; the others were executed [f]. But, as these violent proceedings were ascribed solely to the malice of the duke's enemies, the people, contrary to their usual practice in such marvellous trials, acquitted the unhappy sufferers; and encreased their esteem and affection towards a prince, who was thus exposed, without protection, to those mortal injuries.

THESE sentiments of the public made the cardinal of Winchester and his party sensible that it was necessary to destroy a man whose popularity might become dangerous, and whose resentment they had so much cause to apprehend. In order to effect their purpose, a parliament was summoned to meet, not at London, which was supposed to be too well affected to the duke, but at St. Edmondsbury, where they expected that he would lie entirely at their mercy. As soon as he appeared, he was accused of treason, and thrown into prison. He was soon after found dead in his bed [g]; and though it was pretended that his death was natural, and though his body, which was exposed to public view, bore no marks of outward violence, no one doubted but he had fallen a victim to the vengeance of his enemies. An artifice, formerly practised in the case of Edward II. Richard II. and Thomas of Woodstock, duke of Glocester, could deceive no body. The reason of this assassination of the duke seems not, that the ruling party apprehended his acquittal in parliament on account of his innocence, which, in such times, was seldom much regarded; but that they imagined his public trial and execution would have been more invidious than his private murder, which they pretended to deny. Some gentlemen of his retinue were afterwards tried as accomplices in his treasons, and were condemned to be hanged, drawn, and quartered. They

[f] Stowe, p. 381. Hollingshed, p. 622. Grafton, p. 587.
[g] Grafton, p. 597.

were

were hanged and cut down; but just as the executioner was proceeding to quarter them, their pardon was produced, and they were recovered to life [h]. The most barbarous kind of mercy that can possibly be imagined!

THIS prince is said to have received a better education than was usual in his age, to have founded one of the first public libraries in England, and to have been a great patron of learned men. Among other advantages which he reaped from this turn of mind, it tended much to cure him of credulity; of which the following instance is given by Sir Thomas More. There was a man who pretended, that, though he was born blind, he had recovered his sight by touching the shrine of St. Albans. The duke, happening soon after to pass that way, questioned the man, and, seeming to doubt of his sight, asked him the colours of several cloaks, worn by persons of his retinue. The man told them very readily. *You are a knave*, cried the prince; *had you been born blind, you could not so soon have learned to distinguish colours*: And immediately ordered him to be set in the stocks as an impostor [i].

THE cardinal of Winchester died six weeks after his nephew, whose murder was universally ascribed to him as well as to the duke of Suffolk, and which, it is said, gave him more remorse in his last moments, than could naturally be expected from a man hardened, during the course of a long life, in falsehood and in politics. What share the queen had in this guilt is uncertain; her usual activity and spirit made the public conclude, with some reason, that the duke's enemies durst not have ventured on such a deed without her privity. But there happened, soon after, an event, of which she and her favourite, the duke of Suffolk, bore incontestibly the whole odium.

THAT article of the marriage treaty, by which the province of Maine was to be ceded to Charles of Anjou,

[h] ... n Chron. anno 1447. [i] Grafton, p. 597.

the

the queen's uncle, had probably been hitherto kept secret; and, during the lifetime of the duke of Glocester, it might have been dangerous to venture on the execution of it. But, as the court of France strenuously insisted on performance, orders were now dispatched, under Henry's hand, to Sir Francis Surienne, governor of Mans, commanding him to surrender that place to Charles of Anjou. Surienne, either questioning the authenticity of the order, or regarding his government as his sole fortune, refused compliance; and it became necessary for a French army, under the count of Dunois, to lay siege to the city. The governor made as good a defence as his situation could permit; but, receiving no relief from Edmund duke of Somerset, who was at that time governor of Normandy, he was at last obliged to capitulate, and to surrender not only Mans, but all the other fortresses of that province, which was thus entirely alienated from the crown of England.

THE bad effects of this measure stopped not here. Surienne, at the head of all his garrisons, amounting to 2500 men, retired into Normandy, in expectation of being taken into pay, and of being quartered in some towns of that province. But Somerset, who had no means of subsisting such a multitude, and who was probably incensed at Surienne's disobedience, refused to admit him; and this adventurer, not daring to commit depredations on the territories either of the king of France or of England, marched into Britanny, seized the town of Fougeres, repaired the fortifications of Pontorson and St. James de Beuvron, and subsisted his troops by the ravages which he exercised on that whole province [k]. The duke of Britanny complained of this violence to the king of France, his liege lord: Charles remonstrated with the

[k] Monstrelet, vol. iii. p. 6.

duke of Somerset: That nobleman replied, that the injury was done without his privity, and that he had no authority ever Surienne and his companions[1]. Though this anfwer ought to have appeared fatisfactory to Charles, who had often felt feverely the licentious, independent spirit of such mercenary foldiers, he never would admit of the apology. He still infifted that thefe plunderers fhould be recalled, and that reparation fhould be made to the duke of Britanny for all the damages which he had fuftained: And, in order to render an accommodation abfolutely impracticable, he made the eftimation of damages amount to no lefs a fum than 1,600,000 crowns. He was fenfible of the fuperiority which the prefent ftate of his affairs gave him over England; and he determined to take advantage of it.

No fooner was the truce concluded between the two kingdoms, than Charles employed himfelf, with great induftry and judgment, in repairing thofe numberlefs ills to which France, from the continuance of wars both foreign and domeftic, had fo long been expofed. He reftored the courfe of public juftice; he introduced order into the finances; he eftablifhed difcipline in his troops; he repreffed faction in his court; he revived the languid ftate of agriculture and the arts; and, in the courfe of a few years, he rendered his kingdom flourifhing within itfelf, and formidable to its neighbours. Meanwhile, affairs in England had taken a very different turn. The court was divided into parties, which were enraged againft each other: The people were difcontented with the government: Conquefts in France, which were an object more of glory than of intereft, were overlooked amidft domeftic incidents, which engroffed the attention of all men: The governor of Normandy, ill fupplied with money, was obliged to difmifs the greater part of his troops, and to allow

State of France.

[1] Monftrelet, vol. iii. p. 7. Hollingfhed, p. 629.

CHAP. XX.

1449.

Renewal of the war with France.

4th Nov.

the fortifications of the towns and castles to become ruinous: And the nobility and people of that province had, during the late open communication with France, enjoyed frequent opportunities of renewing connexions with their ancient master, and of concerting the means for expelling the English. The occasion, therefore, seemed favourable to Charles for breaking the truce. Normandy was at once invaded by four powerful armies; one commanded by the king himself; a second by the duke of Britanny; a third by the duke of Alençon; and a fourth by the count of Dunois. The places opened their gates almost as soon as the French appeared before them: Verneüil, Nogent, Chateau Gaillard, Ponteau de Mer, Gisors, Mante, Vernon, Argentan, Lisieux, Fecamp, Coutances, Belesme, Pont de l'Arche, fell in an instant into the hands of the enemy. The duke of Somerset, so far from having an army which could take the field, and relieve these places, was not able to supply them with the necessary garrisons and provisions. He retired with the few troops, of which he was master, into Rouen; and thought it sufficient, if, till the arrival of succours from England, he could save that capital from the general fate of the province. The king of France, at the head of a formidable army, fifty thousand strong, presented himself before the gates: The dangerous example of revolt had infected the inhabitants; and they called aloud for a capitulation. Somerset, unable to resist, at once, both the enemies within and from without, retired with his garrison into the palace and castle; which, being places not tenable, he was obliged to surrender: He purchased a retreat to Harfleur by the payment of 56,000 crowns, by engaging to surrender Arques, Tancarville, Caudebec, Honfleur, and other places in the higher Normandy, and by delivering hostages for the performance of articles[n]. The governor of Honfleur refused to obey his orders;

[n] Monstrelet, vol. III. p. 11. Grafton, p. 643.

orders; upon which the earl of Shrewsbury, who was one of the hostages, was detained prisoner; and the English were thus deprived of the only general capable of recovering them from their present distressed situation. Harfleur made a better defence under Sir Thomas Curson the governor; but was finally obliged to open its gates to Dunois. Succours at last appeared from England under Sir Thomas Kyriel, and landed at Cherbourg: But these came very late, amounted only to 4000 men, and were soon after put to rout at Fourmigni by the count of Clermont [a]. This battle, or rather skirmish, was the only action fought by the English for the defence of their dominions in France, which they had purchased at such an expence of blood and treasure. Somerset, shut up in Caën without any prospect of relief, found it necessary to capitulate: Falaise opened its gates, on condition that the earl of Shrewsbury should be restored to liberty: And Cherbourg, the last place of Normandy which remained in the hands of the English, being delivered up, the conquest of that important province was finished in a twelvemonth by Charles, to the great joy of the inhabitants and of his whole kingdom [b].

A LIKE rapid success attended the French arms in Guienne; though the inhabitants of that province were, from long custom, better inclined to the English government. Dunois was dispatched thither, and met with no resistance in the field, and very little from the towns. Great improvements had been made, during this age, in the structure and management of artillery, and none in fortification; and the art of defence was by that means more unequal, than either before or since, to the art of attack. After all the small places about Bourdeaux were reduced, that city agreed to submit, if not relieved by a certain time; and as no one in England thought seriously

[a] Hollingshed, p. 631. [b] Grafton, p. 646.

of these distant concerns, no relief appeared; the place surrendered; and Bayonne being taken soon after, this whole province, which had remained united to England, since the accession of Henry II. was, after a period of three centuries, finally swallowed up in the French monarchy.

Though no peace or truce was concluded between France and England, the war was, in a manner, at an end. The English, torn in pieces by the civil dissensions which ensued, made but one feeble effort more for the recovery of Guienne: And Charles, occupied at home in regulating the government, and fencing against the intrigues of his factious son, Lewis the Dauphin, scarcely ever attempted to invade them in their island, or to retaliate upon them, by availing himself of their intestine confusions.

CHAP. XXI.

HENRY VI.

Claim of the duke of York to the crown—— The earl of Warwic —— Impeachment of the duke of Suffolk —— His banishment —— and death —— Popular insurrection —— The parties of York and Lancaster —— First armament of the duke of York —— First battle of St. Albans —— Battle of Blore-heath —— of Northampton —— A parliament —— Battle of Wakefield —— Death of the duke of York —— Battle of Mortimer's Cross —— Second Battle of St. Albans —— Edward IV. assumes the crown —— Miscellaneous transactions of this reign.

A WEAK prince, seated on the throne of England, had never failed, how gentle soever and innocent, to be infested with faction, discontent, rebellion, and civil commotions; and as the incapacity of Henry appeared every day in a fuller light, these dangerous consequences began, from past experience, to be universally and justly apprehended. Men also of unquiet spirits, no longer employed in foreign wars, whence they were now excluded by the situation of the neighbouring states, were the more likely to excite intestine disorders, and, by their emulation, rivalship, and animosities, to tear the bowels of their native country. But though these causes alone were sufficient to breed confusion, there concurred another circumstance of the most dangerous nature: A pretender to the crown appeared: The title itself of the weak prince, who enjoyed the name of sovereignty, was disputed:

CHAP. XXI.

1450.

CHAP. XXI.

1450.

Claim of the duke of York to the crown.

puted: And the English were now to pay the severe, though late, penalty of their turbulence under Richard II. and of their levity in violating, without any necessity or just reason, the lineal succession of their monarchs.

ALL the males of the house of Mortimer were extinct; but Anne, the sister of the last earl of Marche, having espoused the earl of Cambridge, beheaded in the reign of Henry V. had transmitted her latent, but not yet forgotten, claim to her son, Richard, duke of York. This prince, thus descended by his mother from Philippa, only daughter of the duke of Clarence, second son of Edward III. stood plainly in the order of succession before the king, who derived his descent from the duke of Lancaster, third son of that monarch; and that claim could not, in many respects, have fallen into more dangerous hands than those of the duke of York. Richard was a man of valour and abilities, of a prudent conduct and mild dispositions: He had enjoyed an opportunity of displaying these virtues in his government of France: And though recalled from that command by the intrigues and superior interest of the duke of Somerset, he had been sent to suppress a rebellion in Ireland; had succeeded much better in that enterprize than his rival in the defence of Normandy; and had even been able to attach to his person and family the whole Irish nation, whom he was sent to subdue*. In the right of his father, he bore the rank of first prince of the blood; and by this station he gave a lustre to his title derived from the family of Mortimer, which, though of great nobility, was equalled by other families in the kingdom, and had been eclipsed by the royal descent of the house of Lancaster. He possessed an immense fortune from the union of so many successions, those of Cambridge and York on the one hand, with those of Mor-

*Stowe, p. 387.

timer

timer on the other: Which last inheritance had before been augmented by an union of the estates of Clarence and Ulster, with the patrimonial possessions of the family of Marche. The alliances too of Richard, by his marrying the daughter of Ralph Nevil, earl of Westmoreland, had widely extended his interest among the nobility, and had procured him many connexions in that formidable order.

THE family of Nevil was, perhaps, at this time the most potent, both from their opulent possessions, and from the characters of the men, that has ever appeared in England. For, besides the earl of Westmoreland, and the lords Latimer, Fauconberg, and Abergavenny; the earls of Salisbury and Warwic were of that family, and were of themselves, on many accounts, the greatest noblemen in the kingdom. The earl of Salisbury, brother-in-law to the duke of York, was the eldest son by a second marriage of the earl of Westmoreland; and inherited by his wife, daughter and heir of Montacute, earl of Salisbury, killed before Orleans, the possessions and title of that great family. His eldest son, Richard, had married Anne, the daughter and heir of Beauchamp, earl of Warwic, who died governor of France; and by this alliance he enjoyed the possessions, and had acquired the title, of that other family, one of the most opulent, most ancient, and most illustrious in England. The personal qualities also of these two earls, especially of Warwic, enhanced the splendour of their nobility, and encreased their influence over the people. This latter nobleman, commonly known, from the subsequent events, by the appellation of the *King-maker*, had distinguished himself by his gallantry in the field, by the hospitality of his table, by the magnificence, and still more by the generosity of his expence, and by the spirited and bold manner which attended him in all his actions. The undesigning frankness and openness of his character rendered his conquest over men's affections

affections the more certain and infallible: His presents were regarded as sure testimonies of esteem and friendship; and his professions as the overflowings of his genuine sentiments. No less than 30,000 persons are said to have daily lived at his board in the different manors and castles which he possessed in England: The military men, allured by his munificence and hospitality, as well as by his bravery, were zealously attached to his interests: The people in general bore him an unlimited affection: His numerous retainers were more devoted to his will, than to the prince or to the laws: And he was the greatest, as well as the last, of those mighty barons, who formerly overawed the crown, and rendered the people incapable of any regular system of civil government.

But the duke of York, besides the family of Nevil, had many other partizans among the great nobility. Courtney, earl of Devonshire, descended from a very noble family of that name in France, was attached to his interests: Moubray, duke of Norfolk, had, from his hereditary hatred to the family of Lancaster, embraced the same party: And the discontents, which universally prevailed among the people, rendered every combination of the great the more dangerous to the established government.

Though the people were never willing to grant the supplies necessary for keeping possession of the conquered provinces in France, they repined extremely at the loss of these boasted acquisitions; and fancied, because a sudden irruption could make conquests, that, without steady counsels, and a uniform expence, it was possible to maintain them. The voluntary cession of Maine to the queen's uncle, had made them suspect treachery in the loss of Normandy and Guienne. They still considered Margaret as a French woman and a latent enemy of the kingdom. And when they saw her father and all her relations active

in

In promoting the succefs of the French, they could not be perfuaded that fhe, who was all powerful in the Englifh council, would very zealoufly oppofe them in their enterprizes.

But the moft fatal blow given to the popularity of the crown, and to the interefts of the houfe of Lancafter, was by the affaffination of the virtuous duke of Glocefter, whofe character, had he been alive, would have intimidated the partizans of York; but whofe memory, being extremely cherifhed by the people, ferved to throw an odium on all his murderers. By this crime the reigning family fuffered a double prejudice: It was deprived of its firmeft fupport; and it was loaded with all the infamy of that imprudent and barbarous affaffination.

As the duke of Suffolk was known to have had an active hand in the crime, he partook deeply of the hatred attending it; and the clamours, which neceffarily rofe againft him, as prime minifter, and declared favourite of the queen, were thereby augmented to a tenfold pitch, and became abfolutely uncontrolable. The great nobility could ill brook to fee a fubject exalted above them; much more one who was only great grandfon to a merchant, and who was of a birth fo much inferior to theirs. The people complained of his arbitrary meafures; which were, in fome degree, a neceffary confequence of the irregular power then poffeffed by the prince, but which the leaft difaffection eafily magnified into tyranny. The great acquifitions which he daily made were the object of envy; and as they were gained at the expence of the crown, which was itfelf reduced to poverty, they appeared, on that account, to all indifferent perfons, the more exceptionable and invidious.

The revenues of the crown, which had long been difproportioned to its power and dignity, had been extremely dilapidated during the minority of Henry [a]; both by the

[a] Cotton, p. 604.

CHAP. XXI.
1450.

rapacity of the courtiers, which the king's uncles could not controul, and by the necessary expences of the French war, which had always been very ill supplied by the grants of parliament. The royal demesnes were dissipated; and at the same time the king was loaded with a debt of 372,000 pounds, a sum so great, that the parliament could never think of discharging it. This unhappy situation forced the ministers upon many arbitrary measures: The household itself could not be supported without stretching to the utmost the right of purveyance, and rendering it a kind of universal robbery upon the people: The public clamour rose high upon this occasion, and no one had the equity to make allowance for the necessity of the king's situation. Suffolk, once become odious, bore the blame of the whole; and every grievance, in every part of the administration, was universally imputed to his tyranny and injustice.

Impeachment of the duke of Suffolk.

THIS nobleman, sensible of the public hatred under which he laboured, and foreseeing an attack from the commons, endeavoured to overawe his enemies by boldly presenting himself to the charge, and by insisting upon his own innocence, and even upon his merits, and those of his family, in the public service. He rose in the house of peers; took notice of the clamours propagated against him; and complained, that, after serving the crown in thirty-four campaigns; after living abroad seventeen years without once returning to his native country; after losing a father and three brothers in the wars with France; after being himself a prisoner, and purchasing his liberty by a great ransom; it should yet be suspected, that he had been debauched from his allegiance by that enemy whom he had ever opposed with such zeal and fortitude, and that he had betrayed his prince, who had rewarded his services by the highest honours and greatest offices, that it was in his power to confer [r]. This speech did not an-

[r] Cotton, p. 641.

swer

HENRY VI.

swer the purpose intended. The commons, rather provoked at his challenge, opened their charge against him, and sent up to the peers an accusation of high treason, divided into several articles. They insisted, that he had persuaded the French king to invade England with an armed force, in order to depose the king, and to place on the throne his own son, John de la Pole, whom he intended to marry to Margaret, the only daughter of the late John duke of Somerset, and to whom, he imagined, he would by that means acquire a title to the crown: That he had contributed to the release of the duke of Orleans, in hopes that that prince would assist king Charles in expelling the English from France, and recovering full possession of his kingdom: That he had afterwards encouraged that monarch to make open war on Normandy and Guienne, and had promoted his conquests by betraying the secrets of England, and obstructing the succours intended to be sent to those provinces: And that he had, without any powers or commission, promised by treaty to cede the province of Maine to Charles of Anjou, and had accordingly ceded it; which proved in the issue the chief cause of the loss of Normandy [a].

It is evident, from a review of these articles, that the commons adopted, without enquiry, all the popular clamours against the duke of Suffolk, and charged him with crimes, of which none but the vulgar could seriously believe him guilty. Nothing can be more incredible, than that a nobleman, so little eminent by his birth and character, could think of acquiring the crown to his family, and of deposing Henry by foreign force, and, together with him, Margaret, his patron, a princess of so much spirit and penetration. Suffolk appealed to many noblemen in the house, who knew, that he had intended to

[a] Cotton, p. 642. Hall, fol. 157. Hollingshed, p. 631. Grafton, p. 607.

CHAP. XXI.

1452.

marry his son to one of the co-heirs of the earl of Warwic, and was disappointed in his views, only by the death of that lady: And he observed, that Margaret of Somerset could bring to her husband no title to the crown; because she herself was not so much as comprehended in the entail, settled by act of parliament. It is easy to account for the loss of Normandy and Guienne, from the situation of affairs in the two kingdoms, without supposing any treachery in the English ministers; and it may safely be affirmed, that greater vigour was requisite to defend these provinces from the arms of Charles VII. than to conquer them at first from his predecessor. It could never be the interest of any English minister to betray and abandon such acquisitions; much less of one, who was so well established in his master's favour, who enjoyed such high honours and ample possessions in his own country, who had nothing to dread but the effects of popular hatred, and who could never think, without the most extreme reluctance, of becoming a fugitive and exile in a foreign land. The only article which carries any face of probability, is his engagement for the delivery of Maine to the queen's uncle: But Suffolk maintained, with great appearance of truth, that this measure was approved of by several at the council table[1]; and it seems hard to ascribe to it, as is done by the commons, the subsequent loss of Normandy, and expulsion of the English. Normandy lay open on every side to the invasion of the French: Maine, an inland province, must soon after have fallen without any attack: And as the English possessed in other parts more fortresses than they could garrison or provide for, it seemed no bad policy to contract their force, and to render the defence practicable, by reducing it within a narrower compass.

[1] Cotton, p. 642.

THE

THE commons were probably sensible, that this charge CHAP. XXI.
of treason against Suffolk would not bear a strict scrutiny;
and they, therefore, soon after, sent up against him a 1450.
new charge of misdemeanors, which they also divided into
several articles. They affirmed, among other imputations,
that he had procured exorbitant grants from the crown,
had embezzled the public money, had conferred offices
on improper persons, had perverted justice by maintaining
iniquitous causes, and had procured pardons for notorious
offenders [a]. The articles are mostly general; but are not
improbable: And as Suffolk seems to have been a bad
man and a bad minister, it will not be rash in us to think
that he was guilty, and that many of these articles could
have been proved against him. The court was alarmed
at the prosecution of a favourite minister, who lay under
such a load of popular prejudices; and an expedient was
fallen upon to save him from present ruin. The king summoned all the lords, spiritual and temporal, to his apartment: The prisoner was produced before them, and
asked what he could say in his own defence? He denied
the charge; but submitted to the king's mercy: Henry
expressed himself not satisfied with regard to the first impeachment for treason; but in consideration of the second,
for misdemeanors, he declared, that, by virtue of Suffolk's own submission, not by any judicial authority, he
banished him the kingdom during five years. The lords His banishment.
remained silent; but as soon as they returned to their own
house, they entered a protest, that this sentence should
nowise infringe their privileges; and that, if Suffolk had
insisted upon his right, and had not voluntarily submitted
to the king's commands, he was intitled to a trial by his
peers in parliament.

IT was easy to see, that these irregular proceedings
were meant to favour Suffolk, and that, as he still pos-

[a] Cotton, p. 643.

sessed

CHAP.
XXI.
1450.

and death.

Popular insurrections.

sessed the queen's confidence, he would, on the first favourable opportunity, be restored to his country, and be re-instated in his former power and credit. A captain of a vessel was therefore employed by his enemies to intercept him in his passage to France: He was seized near Dover; his head struck off on the side of a long-boat; and his body thrown into the sea [w]. No enquiry was made after the actors and accomplices in this atrocious deed of violence.

The duke of Somerset succeeded to Suffolk's power in the ministry, and credit with the queen; and as he was the person under whose government the French provinces had been lost, the public, who always judge by the event, soon made him equally the object of their animosity and hatred. The duke of York was absent in Ireland during all these transactions; and however it might be suspected, that his partizans had excited and supported the prosecution against Suffolk, no immediate ground of complaint could, on that account, lie against him. But there happened, soon after, an incident which roused the jealousy of the court, and discovered to them the extreme danger to which they were exposed from the pretensions of that popular prince.

The humours of the people, set afloat by the parliamentary impeachment, and by the fall of so great a favourite as Suffolk, broke out in various commotions, which were soon suppressed; but there arose one in Kent, which was attended with more dangerous consequences. A man of low condition, one John Cade, a native of Ireland, who had been obliged to fly into France for crimes, observed, on his return to England, the discontents of the people; and he laid on them the foundation of projects, which were at first crowned with surprising success.

[w] Hall, fol. 158. Hist. Croyland, contin. p. 525. Stowe, p. 388. Grafton, p. 610.

3

ſucceſs. He took the name of John Mortimer; intending, as is ſuppoſed, to paſs himſelf for a ſon of that Sir John Mortimer who had been ſentenced to death by parliament, and executed, in the beginning of this reign, without any trial or evidence, merely upon an indictment of high treaſon given in againſt him [x]. On the firſt mention of that popular name, the common people of Kent, to the number of 20,000, flocked to Cade's ſtandard; and he excited their zeal by publiſhing complaints againſt the numerous abuſes in government, and demanding a redreſs of grievances. The court, not yet fully ſenſible of the danger, ſent a ſmall force againſt the rioters, under the command of Sir Humphry Stafford, who was defeated and ſlain in an action near Sevenoke [y]; and Cade, advancing with his followers towards London, encamped on Blackheath. Though elated by his victory, he ſtill maintained the appearance of moderation; and ſending to the court a plauſible liſt of grievances [z], he promiſed that, when theſe ſhould be redreſſed, and when lord Say, the treaſurer, and Cromer, ſheriff of Kent, ſhould be puniſhed for their malverſations, he would immediately lay down his arms. The council, who obſerved that nobody was willing to fight againſt men ſo reaſonable in their pretenſions, carried the king, for preſent ſafety, to Kenilworth; and the city immediately opened its gates to Cade, who maintained, during ſome time, great order and diſcipline among his followers. He al-

[x] Stowe, p. 363. Cotton, p. 564. This author admires that ſuch a piece of injuſtice ſhould have been committed in peaceable times. He might have added, and by ſuch virtuous princes as Bedford and Gloceſter. But it is to be preſumed that Mortimer was guilty; though his condemnation was highly irregular and illegal. The people had at this time a very feeble ſenſe of law and a conſtitution; and power was very imperfectly reſtrained by theſe limits. When the proceedings of a parliament were ſo irregular, it is eaſy to imagine that thoſe of a king would be come ſo.

[y] Hall, fol. 159. Holingſhed, p. 634.   [z] Stowe, p. 388, 389. Holingſhed, p. 633.

CHAP.
XXI.

1450.

ways led them into the fields during the night-time; and published severe edicts against plunder and violence of every kind: But being obliged, in order to gratify their malevolence against Say and Cromer, to put these men to death without a legal trial [a], he found, that, after the commission of this crime, he was no longer master of their riotous disposition, and that all his orders were neglected [b]. They broke into a rich house, which they plundered; and the citizens, alarmed at this act of violence, shut their gates against them; and being seconded by a detachment of soldiers sent them by lord Scales, governor of the Tower, they repulsed the rebels with great slaughter [c]. The Kentishmen were so discouraged by the blow, that, upon receiving a general pardon from the primate, then chancellor, they retreated towards Rochester, and there dispersed. The pardon was soon after annulled, as extorted by violence: A price was set on Cade's head [d], who was killed by one Iden, a gentleman of Sussex; and many of his followers were capitally punished for their rebellion.

It was imagined by the court, that the duke of York had secretly instigated Cade to this attempt, in order to try, by that experiment, the dispositions of the people towards his title and family [e]: And as the event had so far succeeded to his wish, the ruling party had greater reason than ever to apprehend the future consequences of his pretensions. At the same time, they heard that he intended to return from Ireland; and fearing that he meant to bring an armed force along with him, they issued orders, in the king's name, for opposing him, and for debarring him entrance into England [f]. But the duke refuted his enemies by coming attended with no more than

[a] Grafton, p. 622. Holinshed. p. 126. Stowe, p. 391.
[b] Hall, fol. 160.
[d] Rymer, vol. xi. p. 275.
[f] Stowe, p. 394.
[c] Hist. Croyland.
[e] Cotton, p. 661.

HENRY VI.

his ordinary retinue: The precautions of the ministers served only to shew him their jealousy and malignity against him: He was sensible that his title, by being dangerous to the king, was also become dangerous to himself: He now saw the impossibility of remaining in his present situation, and the necessity of proceeding forward in support of his claim. His partizans, therefore, were instructed to maintain, in all companies, his right by succession, and by the established laws and constitution of the kingdom: These questions became every day more and more the subject of conversation: The minds of men were insensibly sharpened against each other by disputes, before they came to more dangerous extremities: And various topics were pleaded in support of the pretensions of each party.

THE partizans of the house of Lancaster maintained, that though the elevation of Henry IV. might at first be deemed somewhat irregular, and could not be justified by any of those principles on which that prince chose to rest his title, it was yet founded on general consent, was a national act, and was derived from the voluntary approbation of a free people, who, being loosened from their allegiance by the tyranny of the preceding government, were moved by gratitude, as well as by a sense of public interest, to entrust the sceptre into the hands of their deliverer: That, even if that establishment were allowed to be at first invalid, it had acquired solidity by time; the only principle which ultimately gives authority to government, and removes those scruples which the irregular steps attending almost all revolutions naturally excite in the minds of the people: That the right of succession was a rule admitted only for general good, and for the maintenance of public order; and could never be pleaded to the overthrow of national tranquillity, and the subversion of regular establishments:

CHAP. XXI.

1450.

The parties of Lancaster and York.

That

CHAP. XXI.

1450.

That the principles of liberty, no less than the maxims of internal peace, were injured by these pretensions of the house of York; and if so many reiterated acts of the legislature, by which the crown was entailed on the present family, were now invalidated, the English must be considered, not as a free people, who could dispose of their own government, but as a troop of slaves, who were implicitly transmitted by succession from one master to another: That the nation was bound to allegiance under the house of Lancaster by moral, no less than by political duty; and were they to infringe those numerous oaths of fealty which they had sworn to Henry and his predecessors, they would thenceforth be thrown loose from all principles, and it would be found difficult ever after to fix and restrain them: That the duke of York himself had frequently done homage to the king as his lawful sovereign, and had thereby, in the most solemn manner, made an indirect renunciation of those claims with which he now dares to disturb the tranquillity of the public: That, even though the violation of the rights of blood, made on the deposition of Richard, was perhaps rash and imprudent, it was too late to remedy the mischief; the danger of a disputed succession could no longer be obviated; the people, accustomed to a government which, in the hands of the late king, had been so glorious, and in that of his predecessor so prudent and salutary, would still ascribe a right to it; by causing multiplied disorders, and by shedding an inundation of blood, the advantage would only be obtained of exchanging one pretender for another; and the house of York itself, if established on the throne, would, on the first opportunity, be exposed to those revolutions which the giddy spirit, excited in the people, gave so much reason to apprehend: And that though the present king enjoyed not the shining talents which had appeared

in

in his father and grandfather, he might still have a son CHAP.
who should be endowed with them; he is himself XXI.
eminent for the most harmless and inoffensive manners; 1450.
and if active princes were dethroned on pretence of tyranny, and indolent ones on the plea of incapacity, there would thenceforth remain, in the constitution, no established rule of obedience to any sovereign.

THESE strong topics, in favour of the house of Lancaster, were opposed by arguments no less convincing on the side of the house of York. The partizans of this latter family asserted, that the maintenance of order in the succession of princes, far from doing injury to the people, or invalidating their fundamental title to good government, was established only for the purposes of government, and served to prevent those numberless confusions which must ensue, if no rule were followed but the uncertain and disputed views of present convenience and advantage: That the same maxims which ensured public peace, were also salutary to national liberty; the privileges of the people could only be maintained by the observance of laws; and if no account were made of the rights of the sovereign, it could less be expected that any regard would be paid to the property and freedom of the subject: That it was never too late to correct any pernicious precedent; an unjust establishment, the longer it stood, acquired the greater sanction and validity; it could, with more appearance of reason, be pleaded as an authority for a like injustice, and the maintenance of it, instead of favouring public tranquillity, tended to disjoint every principle by which human society was supported: That usurpers would be happy, if their present possession of power, or their continuance for a few years, could convert them into legal princes; but nothing would be more miserable than the people, if all restraints on violence and ambition were thus removed,

CHAP. XXI.
1450.

removed, and a full scope given to the attempts of every turbulent innovator: That time, indeed, might bestow solidity on a government whose first foundations were the most infirm; but it required both a long course of time to produce this effect, and the total extinction of those claimants, whose title was built on the original principles of the constitution: That the deposition of Richard II. and the advancement of Henry IV. were not deliberate national acts, but the result of the levity and violence of the people, and proceeded from those very defects in human nature, which the establishment of political society, and of an order in succession, was calculated to prevent: That the subsequent entails of the crown were a continuance of the same violence and usurpation; they were not ratified by the legislature, since the consent of the rightful king was still wanting; and the acquiescence, first of the family of Mortimer, then of the family of York, proceeded from present necessity, and implied no renunciation of their pretensions: That the restoration of the true order of succession could not be considered as a change which familiarized the people to revolutions; but as the correction of a former abuse, which had, itself, encouraged the giddy spirit of innovation, rebellion, and disobedience: And that, as the original title of Lancaster stood only in the person of Henry IV. on present conveniency, even this principle, unjustifiable as it was, when not supported by laws, and warranted by the constitution, had now entirely gone over to the other side; nor was there any comparison between a prince utterly unable to sway the sceptre, and blindly governed by corrupt ministers, or by an imperious queen, engaged in foreign and hostile interests; and a prince of mature years, of approved wisdom and experience, a native of England, the lineal heir of the crown, who, by his restoration, would replace every thing on ancient foundations.

So

So many plausible arguments could be urged on both sides of this interesting question, that the people were extremely divided in their sentiments; and though the noblemen of greatest power and influence seem to have espoused the party of York, the opposite cause had the advantage of being supported by the present laws, and by the immediate possession of royal authority. There were also many great noblemen in the Lancastrian party, who balanced the power of their antagonists, and kept the nation in suspense between them. The earl of Northumberland adhered to the present government: The earl of Westmoreland, in spite of his connexions with the duke of York, and with the family of Nevil, of which he was the head, was brought over to the same party; and the whole north of England, the most warlike part of the kingdom, was by means of these two potent noblemen, warmly engaged in the interests of Lancaster. Edmund Beaufort, duke of Somerset, and his brother Henry, were great supports of that cause; as were also Henry Holland duke of Exeter, Stafford duke of Buckingham, the earl of Shrewsbury, the lords Clifford, Dudley, Scales, Audley, and other noblemen.

WHILE the kingdom was in this situation, it might naturally be expected that so many turbulent barons, possessed of so much independent authority, would immediately have flown to arms, and have decided the quarrel, after their usual manner, by war and battle, under the standards of the contending princes. But there still were many causes which retarded these desperate extremities, and made a long train of faction, intrigue, and cabal, precede the military operations. By the gradual progress of arts in England, as well as in other parts of Europe, the people were now become of some importance; laws were beginning to be respected by them; and it was requisite, by various pretences, previously to reconcile

CHAP.
XXI.

1450.

reconcile their minds to the overthrow of such an ancient establishment as that of the house of Lancaster, ere their concurrence could reasonably be expected. The duke of York himself, the new claimant, was of a moderate and cautious character, an enemy to violence, and disposed to trust rather to time and policy, than to sanguinary measures, for the success of his pretensions. The very imbecility itself of Henry, tended to keep the factions in suspense, and make them stand long in awe of each other: It rendered the Lancastrian party unable to strike any violent blow against their enemies; it encouraged the Yorkists to hope, that, after banishing the king's ministers, and getting possession of his person, they might gradually undermine his authority, and be able, without the perilous expedient of a civil war, to change the succession by parliamentary and legal authority.

1451.
6th Nov.

THE dispositions, which appeared in a parliament assembled soon after the arrival of the duke of York from Ireland, favoured these expectations of his partizans, and both discovered an unusual boldness in the commons, and were a proof of the general discontents which prevailed against the administration. The lower house, without any previous enquiry or examination, without alleging any other ground of complaint than common fame, ventured to present a petition against the duke of Somerset, the duchess of Suffolk, the bishop of Chester, Sir John Sutton lord Dudley, and several others of inferior rank; and they prayed the king to remove them for ever from his person and councils, and to prohibit them from approaching within twelve miles of the court [s]. This was a violent attack, somewhat arbitrary, and supported but by few precedents, against the ministry; yet the king durst not openly oppose

[s] Parliamentary History, vol. ii. p. 163.

it: He replied, that, except the lords, he would banish all the others from court during a year, unless he should have occasion for their service in suppressing any rebellion. At the same time, he rejected a bill which had passed both houses, for attainting the late duke of Suffolk, and which, in several of its clauses, discovered a very general prejudice against the measures of the court.

CHAP. XXI.

1451.

THE duke of York, trusting to these symptoms, raised an army of 10,000 men, with which he marched towards London; demanding a reformation of the government, and the removal of the duke of Somerset from all power and authority [b]. He unexpectedly found the gates of the city shut against him; and, on his retreating into Kent, he was followed by the king at the head of a superior army; in which several of Richard's friends, particularly Salisbury and Warwic, appeared; probably with a view of mediating between the parties, and of seconding, on occasion, the duke of York's pretensions. A parley ensued; Richard still insisted upon the removal of Somerset, and his submitting to a trial in parliament: The court pretended to comply with his demand; and that nobleman was put in arrest: The duke of York was then persuaded to pay his respects to the king in his tent; and, on repeating his charge against the duke of Somerset, he was surprised to see that minister step from behind the curtain, and offer to maintain his innocence. Richard now found that he had been betrayed; that he was in the hands of his enemies; and that it was become necessary, for his own safety, to lower his pretensions. No violence, however, was attempted against him: The nation was not in a disposition to bear the destruction of so popular a prince: He had many friends in Henry's camp: And his son, who was not in the power of the court,

1450. The first armament of the duke of York.

[b] Stowe, p. 394.

might

CHAP. XXI.

1452.

might still be able to revenge his death on all his enemies: He was therefore dismissed; and he retired to his seat of Wigmore on the borders of Wales[i].

WHILE the duke of York lived in this retreat, there happened an incident, which, by encreasing the public discontents, proved favourable to his pretensions. Several Gascon lords, affectionate to the English government, and disgusted at the new dominion of the French, came to London, and offered to return to their allegiance under Henry[k]. The earl of Shrewsbury, with a body of 8000

1454. 20th July.

men, was sent over to support them. Bourdeaux opened its gates to him: He made himself master of Fronsac, Castillon, and some other places: Affairs began to wear a favourable aspect: But, as Charles hastened to resist this dangerous invasion, the fortunes of the English were soon reversed: Shrewsbury, a venerable warrior, above fourscore years of age, fell in battle; his conquests were lost; Bourdeaux was again obliged to submit to the French king[l]; and all hopes of recovering the province of Gascony were for ever extinguished.

THOUGH the English might deem themselves happy to to be fairly rid of distant dominions which were of no use to them, and which they never could defend against the growing power of France, they expressed great discontent on the occasion; and they threw all the blame on the ministry, who had not been able to effect impossibilities. While they were in this disposition, the queen's

13th Oct.

delivery of a son, who received the name of Edward, was deemed no joyful incident; and as it removed all hopes of the peaceable succession of the duke of York, who was otherwise, in the right of his father, and, by the laws enacted since the accession of the house of Lancaster, next heir to the crown, it had rather a tendency to inflame the

[i] Grafton, p. 620. [k] Hollingshed, p. 640.
[l] Polyd. Virg. p. 501. Grafton, p. 613.

quarrel

quarrel between the parties. But the duke was incapable CHAP.
of violent counsels; and even when no visible obstacle XXI.
lay between him and the throne, he was prevented by his
own scruples from mounting it. Henry, always unfit to 1454.
exercise the government, fell at this time into a distemper,
which so far encreased his natural imbecility, that it rendered him incapable of maintaining even the appearance of
royalty. The queen and the council, destitute of this support, found themselves unable to resist the York party;
and they were obliged to yield to the torrent. They sent
Somerset to the Tower; and appointed Richard lieutenant of the kingdom, with powers to open and hold a
session of parliament ⁿ. That assembly also, taking into
consideration the state of the kingdom, created him protector during pleasure. Men who thus entrusted sovereign authority to one that had such evident and strong
pretensions to the crown, were not surely averse to his
taking immediate and full possession of it: Yet the duke,
instead of pushing them to make farther concessions, appeared somewhat timid and irresolute, even in receiving
the power which was tendered to him. He desired that
it might be recorded in parliament, that this authority
was conferred on him from their own free motion, without any application on his part: He expressed his hopes
that they would assist him in the exercise of it: He made
it a condition of his acceptance, that the other lords,
who were appointed to be of his council, should also accept of the trust, and should exercise it: And he required that all the powers of his office should be specified
and defined by act of parliament. This moderation of
Richard was certainly very unusual and very amiable;
yet was it attended with bad consequences in the present
juncture, and, by giving time to the animosities of faction

ⁿ Rymer, vol. xi. p. 344.

CHAP. XXI.

to rise and ferment, it proved the source of all those furious wars and commotions which ensued.

1454.

The enemies of the duke of York soon found it in their power to make advantage of his excessive caution. Henry, being so far recovered from his distemper as to carry the appearance of exercising the royal power; they moved him to resume his authority, to annul the protectorship of the duke, to release Somerset from the Tower [a], and to commit the administration into the hands of that nobleman. Richard, sensible of the dangers which might attend his former acceptance of the parliamentary commission, should he submit to the annulling of it, levied an army; but still without advancing any pretensions to the crown. He complained only of the king's ministers, and demanded a reformation of the government. A battle was fought at St. Albans, in which the Yorkists were superior, and, without suffering any material loss, slew about 5000 of their enemies; among whom were the duke of Somerset, the earl of Northumberland, the earl of Stafford, eldest son of the duke of Buckingham, lord Clifford, and many other persons of distinction [b]. The king himself fell into the hands of the duke of York, who treated him with great respect and tenderness: He was only obliged (which he regarded as no hardship) to commit the whole authority of the crown into the hands of his rival.

1455.

First battle of St. Albans, 22d May.

This was the first blood spilt in that fatal quarrel, which was not finished in less than a course of thirty years, which was signalized by twelve pitched battles, which opened a scene of extraordinary fierceness and cruelty, is computed to have cost the lives of eighty princes of the blood, and almost entirely annihilated the ancient nobility of England. The strong attachments

[a] Rymer, vol. xi. p. 361. Hollingshed, p. 642. Grafton, p. 636.
[b] Stowe, p. 309. Hollingshed, p. 643.

which,

which, at that time, men of the same kindred bore to each
other, and the vindictive spirit, which was considered as
a point of honour, rendered the great families implacable
in their resentments, and every moment widened the
breach between the parties. Yet affairs did not immediately proceed to the last extremities: The nation was
kept some time in suspense: The vigour and spirit of
queen Margaret, supporting her small power, still proved
a balance to the great authority of Richard, which was
checked by his irresolute temper. A parliament, which
was soon after assembled, plainly discovered, by the contrariety of their proceedings, the contrariety of the motives by which they were actuated. They granted the
Yorkists a general indemnity; and they restored the protectorship to the duke, who, in accepting it, still persevered in all his former precautions: But at the same time
they renewed their oaths of fealty to Henry, and fixed the
continuance of the protectorship to the majority of his
son Edward, who was vested with the usual dignities of
prince of Wales, duke of Cornwal, and earl of Chester.
The only decisive act, passed in this parliament, was a
full resumption of all the grants which had been made
since the death of Henry V. and which had reduced the
crown to great poverty.

CHAP.
XXI.

1455.

9th July.

It was not found difficult to wrest power from hands
so little tenacious as those of the duke of York. Margaret, availing herself of that prince's absence, produced
her husband before the house of lords; and, as his state of
health permitted him, at that time, to act his part with
some tolerable decency, he declared his intentions of resuming the government, and of putting an end to Richard's authority. This measure, being unexpected, was
not opposed by the contrary party: The house of lords,
who were many of them disgusted with the late act of resumption,

1456.

sumption, assented to Henry's proposal: And the king was declared to be reinstated in sovereign authority. Even the duke of York acquiesced in this irregular act of the peers; and no disturbance ensued. But that prince's claim to the crown was too well known, and the steps which he had taken to promote it, were too evident ever to allow sincere trust and confidence to have place between the parties. The court retired to Coventry, and invited the duke of York and the earls of Salisbury and Warwic to attend the king's person. When they were on the road they received intelligence that designs were formed against their liberties and lives. They immediately separated themselves: Richard withdrew to his castle of Wigmore: Salisbury to Middleham in Yorkshire: And Warwic to his government of Calais, which had been committed to him after the battle of St. Albans, and which, as it gave him the command of the only regular military force maintained by England, was of the utmost importance in the present juncture. Still, men of peaceable dispositions, and among the rest, Bourchier, archbishop of Canterbury, thought it not too late to interpose with their good offices, in order to prevent that effusion of blood with which the kingdom was threatened; and the awe, in which each party stood of the other, rendered the mediation for some time successful. It was agreed that all the great leaders on both sides should meet in London, and be solemnly reconciled. The duke of York and his partizans came thither with numerous retinues, and took up their quarters near each other for mutual security. The leaders of the Lancastrian party used the same precaution. The mayor, at the head of 5000 men, kept a strict watch night and day; and was extremely vigilant in maintaining peace between them *p*. Terms were adjusted, which removed

---

p Fabian Chron. anno 1458. The author says, that some lords brought 900 retainers, some 600, none less than 400. See also Grafton, p. 633.

not the ground of difference. An outward reconciliation only was procured: And in order to notify this accord to the whole people, a solemn procession to St. Paul's was appointed, where the duke of York led queen Margaret, and a leader of one party marched hand in hand with a leader of the opposite. The less real cordiality prevailed, the more were the exterior demonstrations of amity redoubled. But it was evident, that a contest for a crown could not thus be peaceably accommodated; that each party watched only for an opportunity of subverting the other; and that much blood must yet be spilt, ere the nation could be restored to perfect tranquillity, or enjoy a settled and established government.

CHAP.
XXI.

1456.

EVEN the smallest accident, without any formed design, was sufficient, in the present disposition of men's minds, to dissolve the seeming harmony between the parties; and had the intentions of the leaders been ever so amicable, they would have found it difficult to restrain the animosity of their followers. One of the king's retinue insulted one of the earl of Warwic's: Their companions on both sides took part in the quarrel: A fierce combat ensued: The earl apprehended his life to be aimed at: He fled to his government of Calais; and both parties, in every county of England, openly made preparations for deciding the contest by war and arms.

1459.

THE earl of Salisbury, marching to join the duke of York, was overtaken, at Blore-heath, on the borders of Staffordshire, by lord Audley, who commanded much superior forces; and a small rivulet with steep banks ran between the armies. Salisbury here supplied his defect in numbers by stratagem; a refinement, of which there occur few instances in the English civil wars, where a headlong courage, more than military conduct, is commonly

Battle of Blore-heath 23d Sept.

monly to be remarked. He feigned a retreat, and allured Audley to follow him with precipitation: But when the van of the royal army had passed the brook, Salisbury suddenly turned upon them; and partly by the surprize, partly by the division, of the enemies' forces, put this body to rout: The example of flight was followed by the rest of the army: And Salisbury, obtaining a complete victory, reached the general rendezvous of the Yorkists at Ludlow [q].

The earl of Warwic brought over to this rendezvous a choice body of veterans from Calais, on whom, it was thought, the fortune of the war would much depend; but this reinforcement occasioned, in the issue, the immediate ruin of the duke of York's party. When the royal army approached, and a general action was every hour expected, Sir Andrew Trollop, who commanded the veterans, deserted to the king in the night-time; and the Yorkists were so dismayed at this instance of treachery, which made every man suspicious of his fellow, that they separated next day without striking a stroke [r]: The duke fled to Ireland: The earl of Warwic, attended by many of the other leaders, escaped to Calais; where his great popularity among all orders of men, particularly among the military, soon drew to him partizans, and rendered his power very formidable. The friends of the house of York, in England, kept themselves every where in readiness to rise on the first summons from their leaders.

1460. After meeting with some successes at sea, Warwic landed in Kent, with the earl of Salisbury, and the earl of Marche, eldest son of the duke of York; and being met by the primate, by lord Cobham, and other persons

[q] Hollingshed, p. 649. Grafton, p. 936. [r] Hollingshed, p. 650. Grafton, p. 537.

HENRY VI.

of distinction, he marched, amidst the acclamations of the people, to London. The city immediately opened its gates to him; and his troops encreasing on every day's march, he soon found himself in a condition to face the royal army, which hastened from Coventry to attack him. The battle was fought at Northampton; and was soon decided against the royalists by the infidelity of lord Grey of Ruthin, who, commanding Henry's van, deserted to the enemy during the heat of action, and spread a consternation through the troops. The duke of Buckingham, the earl of Shrewsbury, the lords Beaumont and Egremont, and Sir William Lucie, were killed in the action or pursuit: The slaughter fell chiefly on the gentry and nobility; the common people were spared by orders of the earls of Warwic and Marche[t]. Henry himself, that empty shadow of a king, was again taken prisoner; and as the innocence and simplicity of his manners, which bore the appearance of sanctity, had procured him the tender regard of the people[t], the earl of Warwic and the other leaders took care to distinguish themselves by their respectful demeanour towards him.

A PARLIAMENT was summoned in the king's name, and met at Westminster; where the duke soon after appeared from Ireland. This prince had never hitherto advanced openly any claim to the crown: He had only complained of ill ministers, and demanded a redress of grievances: And even, in the present crisis, when the parliament was surrounded by his victorious army, he showed such a regard to law and liberty, as is unusual during the prevalence of a party in any civil dissentions; and was still less to be expected in those violent and licentious times. He advanced towards the throne; and being met by the archbishop of Canterbury, who asked him, whether he had yet paid his respects to the king? he replied,

CHAP. XXI.

1460.

Battle of Northampton. 10th July.

A parliament. 7th Oct.

[t] Stowe, p. 409. [t] Hall, fol. 169. Grafton, p. 195.

that

CHAP.
XXI.

1460.

that he knew of none to whom he owed that title. He then stood near the throne, and addressing himself to the house of peers, he gave them a deduction of his title by descent, mentioned the cruelties by which the house of Lancaster had paved their way to sovereign power, insisted on the calamities which had attended the government of Henry, exhorted them to return into the right path, by doing justice to the lineal successor, and thus pleaded his cause before them as his natural and legal judges. This cool and moderate manner of demanding a crown, intimidated his friends, and encouraged his enemies: The lords remained in suspense; and no one ventured to utter a word on the occasion. Richard, who had probably expected that the peers would have invited him to place himself on the throne, was much disappointed at their silence; but desiring them to reflect on what he had proposed to them, he departed the house. The peers took the matter into consideration, with as much tranquillity as if it had been a common subject of debate: They desired the assistance of some considerable members among the commons in their deliberations: They heard, in several successive days, the reasons alleged for the duke of York: They even ventured to propose objections to his claim, founded on former entails of the crown, and on the oaths of fealty sworn to the house of Lancaster: They also observed, that, as Richard had all along borne the arms of York, not those of Clarence, he could not claim as successor to the latter family: And after receiving answers to these objections, derived from the violence and power by which the house of Lancaster supported their present possession of the crown, they proceeded to give a decision. Their sentence was calculated, as far as possible, to please both parties: They

^t Hollingshed, p. 655.   ^u Cotton, p. 665.   Grafton, p. 643.
^x Hollingshed, p. 657.   Grafton, p. 645.   ^y Cotton, p. 666.

declared

declared the title of the duke of York to be certain and indefeasible; but in consideration that Henry had enjoyed the crown, without dispute or controversy, during the course of thirty-eight years, they determined, that he should continue to possess the title and dignity during the remainder of his life; that the administration of the government, meanwhile, should remain with Richard; that he should be acknowledged the true and lawful heir of the monarchy; that every one should swear to maintain his succession, and it should be treason to attempt his life; and that all former settlements of the crown, in this and the two last reigns, should be abrogated and rescinded[e]. The duke acquiesced in this decision: Henry himself, being a prisoner, could not oppose it: Even if he had enjoyed his liberty, he would not probably have felt any violent reluctance against it: And the act thus passed with the unanimous consent of the whole legislative body. Though the mildness of this compromise is chiefly to be ascribed to the moderation of the duke of York, it is impossible not to observe in those transactions visible marks of a higher regard to law, and of a more fixed authority, enjoyed by parliament, than has appeared in any former period of English history.

It is probable that the duke, without employing either menaces or violence, could have obtained from the commons a settlement more consistent and uniform: But as many, if not all the members of the upper house, had received grants, concessions, or dignities, during the last sixty years, when the house of Lancaster was possessed of the government: They were afraid of invalidating their own titles by too sudden and violent an overthrow of that family; and in thus temporizing between the parties, they fixed the throne on a basis, upon which it could not possibly stand. The duke, apprehending his chief dan-

[e] Cotton, p. 666. Grafton, p. 647.

CHAP.
XXI.

1460.

ger to arise from the genius and spirit of queen Margaret, sought a pretence for banishing her the kingdom: He sent her, in the king's name, a summons to come immediately to London; intending, in case of her disobedience, to proceed to extremities against her. But the queen needed not this menace to excite her activity in defending the rights of her family. After the defeat at Northampton, she had fled with her infant son to Durham, thence to Scotland; but soon returning, she applied to the northern barons, and employed every motive to procure their assistance. Her affability, insinuation, and address, qualities in which she excelled; her caresses, her promises wrought a powerful effect on every one who approached her: The admiration of her great qualities was succeeded by compassion towards her helpless condition: The nobility of that quarter, who regarded themselves as the most warlike in the kingdom, were moved by indignation to find the southern barons pretend to dispose of the crown and settle the government: And that they might allure the people to their standard, they promised them the spoils of all the provinces on the other side of the Trent. By these means, the queen had collected an army twenty thousand strong, with a celerity which was neither expected by her friends, nor apprehended by her enemies.

THE duke of York, informed of her appearance in the north, hastened thither with a body of 5000 men, to suppress, as he imagined, the beginnings of an insurrection; when, on his arrival at Wakefield, he found himself so much outnumbered by the enemy. He threw himself into Sandal castle, which was situated in the neighbourhood; and he was advised by the earl of Salisbury, and other prudent counsellors, to remain in that fortress, till his son, the earl of Marche, who was levying forces in the borders of Wales, could advance to his assistance.

assistance[a]. But the duke, though deficient in political courage, possessed personal bravery in an eminent degree; and notwithstanding his wisdom and experience, he thought, that he should be for ever disgraced, if, by taking shelter behind walls, he should for a moment resign the victory to a woman. He descended into the plain, and offered battle to the enemy, which was instantly accepted. The great inequality of numbers was sufficient alone to decide the victory; but the queen, by sending a detachment, who fell on the back of the duke's army, rendered her advantage still more certain and undisputed. The duke himself was killed in the action; and as his body was found among the slain, the head was cut off by Margaret's orders, and fixed on the gates of York, with a paper crown upon it, in derision of his pretended title. His son, the earl of Rutland, a youth of seventeen, was brought to lord Clifford; and that barbarian, in revenge of his father's death, who had perished in the battle of St. Albans, murdered in cool blood, and with his own hands, this innocent prince, whose exterior figure, as well as other accomplishments, are represented by historians as extremely amiable. The earl of Salisbury was wounded and taken prisoner, and immediately beheaded, with several other persons of distinction, by martial law at Pomfret[b]. There fell near three thousand Yorkists in this battle: The duke himself was greatly and justly lamented by his own party; a prince who merited a better fate, and whose errors in conduct proceeded entirely from such qualities, as render him the more an object of esteem and affection. He perished in the fiftieth year of his age, and left three sons, Edward, George, and Richard, with three daughters, Anne, Elizabeth, and Margaret.

CHAP. XXI.

1460.

Battle of Wakefield, 24th Dec.

Death of the duke of York.

[a] Stowe, p. 412. [b] Polyd. Virg. p. 510.

CHAP. XXI.
1461.

Battle of Mortimer's Cross.

Second battle of St. Albans.

The queen, after this important victory, divided her army. She sent the smaller division under Jasper Tudor, earl of Pembroke, half brother to the king, against Edward, the new duke of York. She herself marched with the larger division towards London, where the earl of Warwic had been left with the command of the Yorkists. Pembroke was defeated by Edward at Mortimer's Cross in Herefordshire, with the loss of near 4000 men: His army was dispersed; he himself escaped by flight; but his father, Sir Owen Tudor, was taken prisoner, and immediately beheaded by Edward's orders. This barbarous practice, being once begun, was continued by both parties, from a spirit of revenge, which covered itself under the pretence of retaliation[e].

Margaret compensated this defeat by a victory which she obtained over the earl of Warwic. That nobleman, on the approach of the Lancastrians, led out his army, re-inforced by a strong body of the Londoners, who were affectionate to his cause; and he gave battle to the queen at St. Albans. While the armies were warmly engaged, Lovelace, who commanded a considerable body of the Yorkists, withdrew from the combat; and this treacherous conduct, of which there are many instances in those civil wars, decided the victory in favour of the queen. About 2300 of the vanquished perished in the battle and pursuit; and the person of the king fell again into the hands of his own party. This weak prince was sure to be almost equally a prisoner whichever faction had the keeping of him; and scarcely any more decorum was observed by one than by the other, in their method of treating him. Lord Bonville, to whose care he had been entrusted by the Yorkists, remained with him after the defeat, on assurances of pardon given him by Henry: But Margaret, regardless of her husband's promise, immediately

[e] Hollingshed, p. 660. Grafton, p. 650.

ordered

ordered the head of that nobleman to be ſtruck off by the executioner[c]. Sir Thomas Kiriel, a brave warrior, who had ſignalized himſelf in the French wars, was treated in the ſame manner.

THE queen made no great advantage of this victory: Young Edward advanced upon her from the other ſide; and collecting the remains of Warwic's army, was ſoon in a condition of giving her battle with ſuperior forces. She was ſenſible of her danger, while ſhe lay between the enemy and the city of London; and ſhe found it neceſſary to retreat with her army to the north[d]. Edward entered the capital amidſt the acclamations of the citizens, and immediately opened a new ſcene to his party. This prince, in the bloom of youth, remarkable for the beauty of his perſon, for his bravery, his activity, his affability, and every popular quality, found himſelf ſo much poſſeſſed of public favour, that, elated with the ſpirit natural to his age, he reſolved no longer to confine himſelf within thoſe narrow limits which his father had preſcribed to himſelf, and which had been found by experience ſo prejudicial to his cauſe. He determined to aſſume the name and dignity of king; to inſiſt openly on his claim; and thenceforth to treat the oppoſite party as traitors and rebels to his lawful authority. But as a national conſent, or the appearance of it, ſtill ſeemed, notwithſtanding his plauſible title, requiſite to precede this bold meaſure, and as the aſſembling of a parliament might occaſion too many delays, and be attended with other inconveniencies, he ventured to proceed in a leſs regular manner, and to put it out of the power of his enemies to throw obſtacles in the way of his elevation. His army was ordered to aſſemble in St. John's Fields; great numbers of people ſurrounded them; an harangue was pronounced to this mixed multitude, ſetting forth the

[c] Halling‍ſh‍ed, p. 660.   [d] Grafton, p. 652.

CHAP. XXI.
1461.

CHAP. XXI.

1461.

Edward IV. assumes the crown.

5th March.

title of Edward, and inveighing against the tyranny and usurpation of the rival family; and the people were then asked, whether they would have Henry of Lancaster for king? They unanimously exclaimed against the proposal. It was then demanded, whether they would accept of Edward, eldest son of the late duke of York? They expressed their assent by loud and joyful acclamations [r]. A great number of bishops, lords, magistrates, and other persons of distinction were next assembled at Baynard's castle, who ratified the popular election; and the new king was on the subsequent day proclaimed in London, by the title of Edward IV [s].

In this manner ended the reign of Henry VI. a monarch, who, while in his cradle, had been proclaimed king both of France and England, and who began his life with the most splendid prospects that any prince in Europe had ever enjoyed. The revolution was unhappy for his people, as it was the source of civil wars; but was almost entirely indifferent to Henry himself, who was utterly incapable of exercising his authority, and who, provided he personally met with good usage, was equally easy, as he was equally enslaved in the hands of his enemies and of his friends. His weakness and his disputed title were the chief causes of the public calamities: But whether his queen, and his ministers, were not also guilty of some great abuses of power, it is not easy for us at this distance of time to determine: There remain no proofs on record of any considerable violation of the laws, except in the assassination of the duke of Glocester, which was a private crime, formed no precedent, and was but too much of a piece with the usual ferocity and cruelty of the times.

Miscellaneous transactions of this reign.

The most remarkable law, which passed in this reign, was that for the due election of members of parliament in

[r] Stowe, p. 415. Hollingshed, p. 661.   [s] Grafton, p. 653.

counties,

counties. After the fall of the feudal system, the distinction of tenures was in some measure lost; and every freeholder, as well those who held of mesne lords, as the immediate tenants of the crown, were by degrees admitted to give their votes at elections. This innovation (for such it may probably be esteemed) was indirectly confirmed by a law of Henry IV.[h]; which gave right to such a multitude of electors, as was the occasion of great disorder. In the eighth and tenth of this king, therefore, laws were enacted, limiting the electors to such as possessed forty shillings a-year in land, free from all burdens within the county[i]. This sum was equivalent to near twenty pounds a-year of our present money; and it were to be wished, that the spirit, as well as letter of this law, had been maintained.

THE preamble of the statute is remarkable: "Whereas the elections of knights have of late, in many "counties of England, been made by outrages and "excessive numbers of people, many of them of small "substance and value, yet pretending to a right equal to "the best knights and esquires; whereby manslaughters, "riots, batteries, and divisions among the gentlemen "and other people of the same counties, shall very likely "rise and be, unless due remedy be provided in this behalf, &c." We may learn from these expressions, what an important matter the election of a member of parliament was now become in England: That assembly was beginning in this period to assume great authority: The commons had it much in their power to enforce the execution of the laws; and if they failed of success in this particular, it proceeded less from any exorbitant power of the crown, than from the licentious spirit of the aristocracy, and perhaps from the rude education of the age,

[h] Statutes at Large, 7 Henry IV. cap. 15. cap. 7. 10 Henry VI. cap. 2. [i] Ibid. 8 Henry VI.

CHAP.
XXI.

1461.

and their own ignorance of the advantages resulting from a regular administration of justice.

WHEN the duke of York, the earls of Salisbury and Warwic, fled the kingdom upon the desertion of their troops, a parliament was summoned at Coventry in 1460, by which they were all attainted. This parliament seems to have been very irregularly constituted, and scarcely deserves the name: Insomuch, that an act passed in it, "that all such knights of any county, as were returned "by virtue of the king's letters, without any other elec- "tion, should be valid, and that no sheriff should, for "returning them, incur the penalty of the statute of "Henry IV.*" All the acts of that parliament were afterwards reversed; "because it was unlawfully sum- "moned, and the knights and barons not duly chosen¹."

THE parliaments in this reign, instead of relaxing their vigilance against the usurpations of the court of Rome, endeavoured to enforce the former statutes enacted for that purpose. The commons petitioned, that no foreigner should be capable of any church preferment, and that the patron might be allowed to present anew upon the non-residence of any incumbent ᵐ: But the king eluded these petitions. Pope Martin wrote him a severe letter against the statute of provisors; which he calls an abominable law, that would infallibly damn every one who observed it ⁿ. The cardinal of Winchester was legate; and as he was also a kind of prime minister, and immensely rich from the profits of his clerical dignities, the parliament became jealous lest he should extend the papal power; and they protested, that the cardinal should absent himself in all affairs and councils of the king, whenever the pope or see of Rome was touched upon °.

ᵏ Cotton, p. 664.
ᵐ Cotton, p. 585.
° Cotton, p. 593.

ˡ Statutes at Large, 39 Henry VI. cap. 1.
ⁿ Burnet's Collection of Records, vol. i. p. 59.

PERMISSION

PERMISSION was given by parliament to export corn when it was at low prices; wheat at six shillings and eight pence a quarter, money of that age; barley at three shillings and four pence [p]. It appears from these prices, that corn still remained at near half its present value; though other commodities were much cheaper. The inland commerce of corn was also opened in the eighteenth of the king, by allowing any collector of the customs to grant a licence for carrying it from one county to another [q]. The same year a kind of navigation act was proposed with regard to all places within the Streights; but the king rejected it [r].

THE first instance of debt contracted upon parliamentary security occurs in this reign [s]. The commencement of this pernicious practice deserves to be noted; a practice, the more likely to become pernicious, the more a nation advances in opulence and credit. The ruinous effects of it are now become but too apparent, and threaten the very existence of the nation.

[p] Statutes at Large, 15 Henry VI. cap. 2. 23 Henry VI. cap. 6.
[q] Cotton, p. 625. [r] Ibid. p. 626. [s] Ibid. p. 593. 614. 639.

CHAP. XXII.

EDWARD IV.

Battle of Touton—Henry escapes into Scotland—A parliament.—Battle of Hexham—Henry taken prisoner, and confined to the Tower—King's marriage with the Lady Elizabeth Gray—Warwic disgusted—Alliance with Burgundy—Insurrection in Yorkshire.—Battle of Banbury—Warwic and Clarence banished—Warwic and Clarence return—Edward IV. expelled—Henry VI. restored—Edward IV. returns—Battle of Barnet, and death of Warwic—Battle of Teukesbury, and murder of prince Edward—Death of Henry VI.—Invasion of France—Peace of Pecquigni—Trial and execution of the duke of Clarence—Death and character of Edward IV.

CHAP. XXII.
1461.

YOUNG Edward, now in his twentieth year, was of a temper well fitted to make his way through such a scene of war, havoc, and devastation, as must conduct him to the full possession of that crown, which he claimed from hereditary right, but which he had assumed from the tumultuary election alone of his own party. He was bold, active, enterprising; and his hardness of heart and severity of character rendered him impregnable to all those movements of compassion, which might relax his vigour in the prosecution of the most bloody revenges upon his enemies. The very commencement

ment of his reign gave symptoms of his sanguinary disposition. A tradesman of London, who kept shop at the sign of the Crown, having said that he would make his son heir to the Crown; this harmless pleasantry was interpreted to be spoken in derision of Edward's assumed title; and he was condemned and executed for the offence[t]. Such an act of tyranny was a proper prelude to the events which ensued. The scaffold, as well as the field, incessantly streamed with the noblest blood of England, spilt in the quarrel between the two contending families, whose animosity was now become implacable. The people, divided in their affections, took different symbols of party: The partizans of the house of Lancaster chose the red rose as their mark of distinction; those of York were denominated from the white; and these civil wars were thus known, over Europe, by the name of the quarrel between the two roses.

THE licence, in which queen Margaret had been obliged to indulge her troops, infused great terror and aversion into the city of London, and all the southern parts of the kingdom; and as she there expected an obstinate resistance, she had prudently retired northwards among her own partizans. The same licence, joined to the zeal of faction, soon brought great multitudes to her standard; and she was able, in a few days, to assemble an army, sixty thousand strong, in Yorkshire. The king and the earl of Warwic hastened with an army of forty thousand men, to check her progress; and when they reached Pomfret they dispatched a body of troops, under the command of lord Fitzwalter, to secure the passage of Ferrybridge over the river Are, which lay between them and the enemy. Fitzwalter took possession of the post assigned him; but was not able to maintain it against lord Clifford, who attacked him with superior numbers. The

[t] Habington in Kennet, p. 435. Grafton, p. 791.

Yorkists

CHAP.
XXII.

1461.

Yorkists were chased back with great slaughter; and lord Fitzwalter himself was slain in the action ⁿ. The earl of Warwic, dreading the consequences of this disaster, at a time when a decisive action was every hour expected, immediately ordered his horse to be brought him, which he stabbed before the whole army; and, kissing the hilt of his sword, swore that he was determined to share the fate of the meanest soldier ʷ. And to shew the greater security, a proclamation was at the same time issued, giving to every one full liberty to retire; but menacing the severest punishment to those who should discover any symptoms of cowardice in the ensuing battle ˣ. Lord Falconberg was sent to recover the post which had been lost: He passed the river some miles above Ferrybridge, and, falling unexpectedly on lord Clifford, revenged the former disaster by the defeat of the party, and the death of their leader ʸ.

Battle of Touton, 29th of March.

THE hostile armies met at Touton; and a fierce and bloody battle ensued. While the Yorkists were advancing to the charge, there happened a great fall of snow, which, driving full in the faces of their enemies, blinded them; and this advantage was improved by a stratagem of lord Falconberg's. That nobleman ordered some infantry to advance before the line, and, after having sent a volley of flight-arrows, as they were called, amidst the enemy, immediately to retire. The Lancastrians, imagining that they were gotten within reach of the opposite army, discharged all their arrows, which thus fell short of the Yorkists ᶻ. After the quivers of the enemy were emptied, Edward advanced his line, and did execution with impunity on the dismayed Lancastrians: The bow, however, was soon laid aside, and the sword decided the

ᵘ W. Wyrcester, p. 489. Hall, fol. 186. Hollingshed, p. 654.
ʷ Habington, p. 418.   ˣ Hollingshed, p. 664.   ʸ Hist. Croyl. contin. p. 532.   ᶻ Hall, fol. 186.

combat,

combat, which ended in a total victory on the side of the Yorkists. Edward issued orders to give no quarter[a]. The routed army was pursued to Tadcaster with great bloodshed and confusion; and above thirty-six thousand men are computed to have fallen in the battle and pursuit[b]: Among these were the earl of Westmoreland, and his brother, Sir John Nevil, the earl of Northumberland, the lords Dacres and Welles, and Sir Andrew Trollop[c]. The earl of Devonshire, who was now engaged in Henry's party, was brought a prisoner to Edward; and was, soon after, beheaded by martial law at York. His head was fixed on a pole erected over a gate of that city; and the head of duke Richard, and that of the earl of Salisbury, were taken down, and buried with their bodies. Henry and Margaret had remained at York during the action; but, learning the defeat of their army, and being sensible that no place in England could now afford them shelter, they fled with great precipitation into Scotland. They were accompanied by the duke of Exeter, who, though he had married Edward's sister, had taken part with the Lancastrians, and by Henry duke of Somerset, who had commanded in the unfortunate battle of Touton, and who was the son of that nobleman killed in the first battle of St. Albans.

NOTWITHSTANDING the great animosity which prevailed between the kingdoms, Scotland had never exerted itself with vigour, to take advantage, either of the wars which England carried on with France, or of the civil commotions, which arose between the contending families. James I. more laudably employed, in civilizing his subjects, and taming them to the salutary yoke of law and justice, avoided all hostilities with foreign nations; and though he seemed interested to maintain a balance between

CHAP.
XXII.

1461.

Henry escapes into Scotland.

[a] Habington, p. 438. Hist. Croyl. cont. p. 533.
[b] Hollingshed, p. 665. Grafton, p. 656.
[c] Hall, fol. 187. Habington, p. 433.

CHAP.
XXII.
1461.

tween France and England, he gave no farther assistance to the former kingdom in its greatest distresses, than permitting, and perhaps encouraging, his subjects to enlist in the French service. After the murder of that excellent prince, the minority of his son and successor, James II. and the distractions incident to it, retained the Scots in the same state of neutrality; and the superiority, visibly acquired by France, rendered it then unnecessary for her ally to interpose in her defence. But, when the quarrel commenced between the houses of York and Lancaster, and became absolutely incurable, but by the total extinction of one party; James, who had now risen to man's estate, was tempted to seize the opportunity, and he endeavoured to recover those places which the English had formerly conquered from his ancestors. He laid siege to the castle of Roxborough in 1460, and had provided himself with a small train of artillery for that enterprize: But his cannon were so ill framed, that one of them burst as he was firing it, and put an end to his life in the flower of his age. His son and successor, James III. was also a minor on his accession: The usual distractions ensued in the government: The queen-dowager, Anne of Gueldres, aspired to the regency: The family of Douglas opposed her pretensions: And queen Margaret, when she fled into Scotland, found there a people little less divided by faction, than those by whom she had been expelled. Though she pleaded the connexions between the royal family of Scotland and the house of Lancaster, by the young king's grandmother, a daughter of the earl of Somerset; she could engage the Scottish council to go no farther than to express their good wishes in her favour: But, on her offer to deliver to them immediately the important fortress of Berwic, and to contract her son in marriage with a sister of king James, she found a better reception; and the Scots

promised

promised the assistance of their arms to re-instate her family upon the throne[d]. But, as the danger from that quarter seemed not very urgent to Edward, he did not pursue the fugitive king and queen into their retreat; but returned to London, where a parliament was summoned for settling the government.

On the meeting of this assembly, Edward found the good effects of his vigorous measure in assuming the crown, as well as of his victory at Touton, by which he had secured it: The parliament no longer hesitated between the two families, or proposed any of those ambiguous decisions, which could only serve to perpetuate and inflame the animosities of party. They recognized the title of Edward, by hereditary descent, through the family of Mortimer; and declared that he was king by right, from the death of his father, who had also the same lawful title; and that he was in possession of the crown from the day that he assumed the government, tendered to him by the acclamations of the people[e]. They expressed their abhorrence of the usurpation and intrusion of the house of Lancaster, particularly that of the earl of Derby, otherwise called Henry IV. which, they said, had been attended with every kind of disorder, the murder of the sovereign and the oppression of the subject. They annulled every grant which had passed in those reigns; they reinstated the king in all the possessions which had belonged to the crown at the pretended deposition of Richard II. and though they confirmed judicial deeds, and the decrees of inferior courts, they reversed all attainders passed in any pretended parliament; particularly the attainder of the earl of Cambridge, the king's grandfather; as well as that of the earls of Salisbury, and Glocester, and of lord Lumley, who had been forfeited for adhering to Richard II.[f]

[d] Hall, fol. 137. Habington, p. 434. [e] Cotton, p. 670.
[f] Cotton, p. 672. Statutes at Large, 1 Edw. IV. cap. 1.

MANY

CHAP. XXII.
1461.

MANY of these votes were the result of the usual violence of party: The common sense of mankind, in more peaceable times, repealed them: And the statutes of the house of Lancaster, being the deeds of an established government, and enacted by princes long possessed of authority, have always been held as valid and obligatory. The parliament, however, in subverting such deep foundations, had still the pretence of replacing the government on its ancient and natural basis: But, in their subsequent measures, they were more guided by revenge, at least by the views of convenience, than by the maxims of equity and justice. They passed an act of forfeiture and attainder against Henry VI. and queen Margaret, and their infant son, prince Edward: The same act was extended to the dukes of Somerset and Exeter; to the earls of Northumberland, Devonshire, Pembroke, Wilts; to the viscount Beaumont; the lords Roos, Nevil, Clifford, Welles, Dacre, Gray of Rugemont, Hungerford; to Alexander Hedie, Nicholas Latimer, Edmond Mountfort, John Heron, and many other persons of distinction [f]. The parliament vested the estates of all these attainted persons in the crown; though their sole crime was the adhering to a prince, whom every individual of the parliament had long recognized, and whom that very king himself, who was now seated on the throne, had acknowledged and obeyed as his lawful sovereign.

THE necessity of supporting the government established will more fully justify some other acts of violence; though the method of conducting them may still appear exceptionable. John earl of Oxford, and his son, Aubrey de Vere, were detected in a correspondence with Margaret, were tried by martial law before the constable, were condemned and executed [h]. Sir William Tyrrel,

[f] Cotton, p. 670. W. Wyrcester, p. 490.   [h] W. de Wyrcester, p. 492. Hall, fol. 189. Grafton, p. 658. Fabian, fol. 215. Fragm. ad finem T. Sproll.

Sir

EDWARD IV.

Sir Thomas Tudenham, and John Montgomery, were convicted in the same arbitrary court; were executed, and their estates forfeited. This introduction of martial law into civil government was a high strain of prerogative; which, were it not for the violence of the times, would probably have appeared exceptionable to a nation so jealous of their liberties as the English were now become[l]. It was impossible but such a great and sudden revolution must leave the roots of discontent and dissatisfaction in the subject, which would require great art, or in lieu of it, great violence to extirpate them. The latter was more suitable to the genius of the nation in that uncultivated age.

But the new establishment still seemed precarious and uncertain; not only from the domestic discontents of the people, but from the efforts of foreign powers. Lewis, the eleventh of the name, had succeeded to his father, Charles, in 1460; and was led, from the obvious motives of national interest, to feed the flames of civil discord among such dangerous neighbours, by giving support to the weaker party. But the intriguing and politic genius of this prince was here checked by itself: having attempted to subdue the independent spirit of his own vassals, he had excited such an opposition at home, as prevented him from making all the advantage which the opportunity afforded, of the dissentions among the English. He sent, however, a small body to Henry's assistance under Varenne, Seneschal of Normandy[k]; who landed in Northumberland, and got possession of the castle of Alnewic: But as the indefatigable Margaret went in person to France, where she solicited larger supplies; and promised Lewis to deliver up Calais, if her family should by his means be restored to the throne of England; he

---
[l] See note [H] at the end of the volume.
[k] Monstrelet, vol. iii. p. 95.

was induced to send along with her a body of 2000 men at arms, which enabled her to take the field, and to make an inroad into England. Though reinforced by a numerous train of adventurers from Scotland, and by many partizans of the family of Lancaster; she received a check at Hedgley-more from lord Montacute or Montague, brother to the earl of Warwic, and warden of the east Marches between Scotland and England. Montague was so encouraged with this success, that, while a numerous reinforcement was on their march to join him by orders from Edward, he yet ventured, with his own troops alone, to attack the Lancastrians at Hexham; and he obtained a complete victory over them. The duke of Somerset, the lords Roos and Hungerford, were taken in the pursuit, and immediately beheaded by martial law at Hexham. Summary justice was in like manner executed at Newcastle on Sir Humphrey Nevil, and several other gentlemen. All those who were spared in the field suffered on the scaffold; and the utter extermination of their adversaries was now become the plain object of the York party; a conduct which received but too plausible an apology from the preceding practice of the Lancastrians.

THE fate of the unfortunate royal family, after this defeat, was singular. Margaret, flying with her son into a forest, where she endeavoured to conceal herself, was beset, during the darkness of the night, by robbers, who, either ignorant or regardless of her quality, despoiled her of her rings and jewels, and treated her with the utmost indignity. The partition of this rich booty raised a quarrel among them; and while their attention was thus engaged, she took the opportunity of making her escape with her son, into the thickest of the forest, where she wandered for some time, over-spent with hunger and fatigue, and sunk with terror and affliction. While in this wretched condition, she saw a robber approach with his naked

naked fword; and finding that fhe had no means of
efcape, fhe fuddenly embraced the refolution of trufting
entirely for protection to his faith and generofity. She
advanced towards him; and prefenting to him the young
prince, called out to him, *Here, my friend, I commit to
your care the fafety of your king's fon.* The man, whofe
humanity and generous fpirit had been obfcured, not entirely loft by his vicious courfe of life, was ftruck with
the fingularity of the event, was charmed with the confidence repofed in him; and vowed, not only to abftain
from all injury againft the princefs, but to devote himfelf entirely to her fervice[l]. By his means fhe dwelt
fome time concealed in the foreft, and was at laft conducted to the fea-coaft, whence fhe made her efcape into
Flanders. She paffed thence into her father's court,
where fhe lived feveral years in privacy and retirement.
Her hufband was not fo fortunate or fo dexterous in finding the means of efcape. Some of his friends took him
under their protection, and conveyed him into Lanca-
fhire; where he remained concealed during a twelvemonth; but he was at laft detected, delivered up to Edward, and thrown into the Tower[m]. The fafety of his
perfon was owing lefs to the generofity of his enemies,
than to the contempt which they had entertained of his
courage and his underftanding.

THE imprifonment of Henry, the expulfion of Margaret, the execution and confifcation of all the moft
eminent Lancaftrians, feemed to give full fecurity to
Edward's government; whofe title by blood being now
recognized by parliament, and univerfally fubmitted to
by the people, was no longer in danger of being impeached by any antagonift. In this profperous fituation,
the king delivered himfelf up, without controul, to thofe
pleafures which his youth, his high fortune, and his na-

[l] Monftrelet, vol. iii. p. 96.   [m] Hall, fol. 191. Fragm. ad
Annum Sprott.

tural temper invited him to enjoy; and the cares of royalty were less attended to, than the dissipation of amusement, or the allurements of passion. The cruel and unrelenting spirit of Edward, though enured to the ferocity of civil wars, was at the same time extremely devoted to the softer passions, which, without mitigating his severe temper, maintained a great influence over him, and shared his attachment with the pursuits of ambition, and the thirst of military glory. During the present interval of peace, he lived in the most familiar and sociable manner with his subjects[n], particularly with the Londoners; and the beauty of his person, as well as the gallantry of his address, which, even unassisted by his royal dignity, would have rendered him acceptable to the fair, facilitated all his applications for their favour. This easy and pleasurable course of life augmented every day his popularity among all ranks of men: He was the peculiar favourite of the young and gay of both sexes. The disposition of the English, little addicted to jealousy, kept them from taking umbrage at these liberties: And his indulgence in amusements, while it gratified his inclination, was thus become, without design, a means of supporting and securing his government. But as it is difficult to confine the ruling passion within strict rules of prudence, the amorous temper of Edward led him into a snare, which proved fatal to his repose, and to the stability of his throne.

King's marriage with the lady Elizabeth Gray.

JAQUELINE OF LUXEMBOURG, dutchess of Bedford, had, after her husband's death, so far sacrificed her ambition to love, that she espoused, in second marriage, Sir Richard Woodeville, a private gentleman, to whom she bore several children; and among the rest, Elizabeth, who was remarkable for the grace and beauty of her person, as well as for other amiable accomplishments. This young

[n] Polyd. Virg. p. 513. Biondi.

lady had married Sir John Gray of Groby, by whom she had children; and her husband being slain in the second battle of St. Albans, fighting on the side of Lancaster, and his estate being for that reason confiscated, his widow retired to live with her father, at his seat of Grafton in Northamptonshire. The king came accidentally to the house after a hunting party, in order to pay a visit to the dutchess of Bedford; and as the occasion seemed favourable for obtaining some grace from this gallant monarch, the young widow flung herself at his feet, and with many tears entreated him to take pity on her impoverished and distressed children. The sight of so much beauty in affliction strongly affected the amorous Edward; love stole insensibly into his heart under the guise of compassion; and her sorrow, so becoming a virtuous matron, made his esteem and regard quickly correspond to his affection. He raised her from the ground with assurances of favour; he found his passion encrease every moment by the conversation of the amiable object; and he was soon reduced, in his turn, to the posture and stile of a supplicant at the feet of Elizabeth. But the lady, either averse to dishonourable love from a sense of duty, or perceiving that the impression, which she had made, was so deep as to give her hopes of obtaining the highest elevation, obstinately refused to gratify his passion; and all the endearments, caresses, and importunities of the young and amiable Edward, proved fruitless against her rigid and inflexible virtue. His passion, irritated by opposition, and encreased by his veneration for such honourable sentiments, carried him at last beyond all bounds of reason; and he offered to share his throne, as well as his heart, with the woman, whose beauty of person, and dignity of character, seemed so well to entitle her to both. The marriage was privately celebrated at Grafton[o]. The secret was carefully

---

[o] Hall, fol. 193. Fabian, fol. 216.

CHAP. XXII.

1464.

kept for some time: No one suspected, that so libertine a prince could sacrifice so much to a romantic passion: And there were in particular strong reasons, which at that time rendered this step to the highest degree dangerous and imprudent.

THE king, desirous to secure his throne, as well by the prospect of issue, as by foreign alliances, had, a little before, determined to make application to some neighbouring princes; and he had cast his eye on Bona of Savoy, sister of the queen of France, who, he hoped, would, by her marriage, ensure him the friendship of that power, which was alone both able and inclined to give support and assistance to his rival. To render the negociation more successful, the earl of Warwic had been dispatched to Paris, where the princess then resided; he had demanded Bona in marriage for the king; his proposals had been accepted; the treaty was fully concluded; and nothing remained but the ratification of the terms agreed on, and the bringing over the princess to England[p]. But when the secret of Edward's marriage broke out, the haughty earl, deeming himself affronted, both by being employed in this fruitless negociation, and by being kept a stranger to the king's intentions, who had owed every thing to his friendship, immediately returned to England, inflamed with rage and indignation. The influence of passion over so young a man as Edward might have served as an excuse for his imprudent conduct, had he deigned to acknowledge his error, or had pleaded his weakness as an apology: But his faulty shame or pride prevented him from so much as mentioning the matter to Warwic; and that nobleman was allowed to depart the court, full of the same ill-humour and discontent which he brought to it.

Warwic disgusted.

[p] Hall, fol. 193. Habington, p. 437. Hollingshed, p. 667. Grafton, p. 665. Polyd. Virg. p. 513.

EVERY

EDWARD IV.

EVERY incident now tended to widen the breach between the king and this powerful subject. The queen, who lost not her influence by marriage, was equally solicitous to draw every grace and favour to her own friends and kindred, and to exclude those of the earl, whom she regarded as her mortal enemy. Her father was created earl of Rivers: He was made treasurer in the room of lord Mountjoy[s]: He was invested in the office of constable for life; and his son received the survivance of that high dignity[t]. The same young nobleman was married to the only daughter of lord Scales, enjoyed the great estate of that family, and had the title of Scales conferred upon him. Catherine, the queen's sister, was married to the young duke of Buckingham, who was a ward of the crown[v]: Mary, another of her sisters, espoused William Herbert, created earl of Huntingdon: Ann, a third sister, was given in marriage to the son and heir of Gray, lord Ruthyn, created earl of Kent[t]. The daughter and heir of the duke of Exeter, who was also the king's niece, was contracted to Sir Thomas Gray, one of the queen's sons by her former husband; and as lord Montague was treating of a marriage between his son and this lady, the preference given to young Gray was deemed an injury and affront to the whole family of Nevil.

THE earl of Warwic could not suffer with patience the least diminution of that credit, which he had long enjoyed, and which, he thought, he had merited by such important services. Though he had received so many grants from the crown, that the revenue arising from them amounted, besides his patrimonial estate, to 80,000 crowns a-year, according to the computation of Philip de Comines[u]; his ambitious spirit was still dissatisfied, so long

---

s W. Wyrcester, p. 506.
t W. Wyrc. p. 505.
v Liv. lii. chap. 4.

r Rymer, vol. xi. p. 581.
t Ibid. p. 506.

CHAP. XXII.
1466.

as he saw others surpass him in authority and influence with the king[w]. Edward also, jealous of that power which had supported him, and which he himself had contributed still higher to exalt, was well pleased to raise up rivals in credit to the earl of Warwic; and he justified, by this political view, his extreme partiality to the queen's kindred. But the nobility of England, envying the sudden growth of the Woodevilles[x], were more inclined to take part with Warwic's discontent, to whose grandeur they were already accustomed, and who had reconciled them to his superiority by his gracious and popular manners. And as Edward obtained from parliament a general resumption of all grants which he had made since his accession, and which had extremely impoverished the crown[y]; this act, though it passed with some exceptions, particularly one in favour of the earl of Warwic, gave a general alarm to the nobility, and disgusted many, even zealous partizans of the family of York.

But the most considerable associate that Warwic acquired to his party, was George, duke of Clarence, the king's second brother. This prince deemed himself no less injured than the other grandees, by the uncontrouled influence of the queen and her relations; and as his fortunes were still left on a precarious footing, while theirs were fully established, this neglect, joined to his unquiet and restless spirit, inclined him to give countenance to all the malcontents[z]. The favourable opportunity of gaining him was espied by the earl of Warwic, who offered him in marriage his elder daughter, and co-heir of his immense fortunes; a settlement which, as it was superior to any that the king himself could confer upon him, immediately attached him to the party of the earl[a]. Thus an extensive and

[w] Polyd. Virg. p. 514.
[y] W. Wyrcester, p. 508.
[x] Hist. Croyl. cont. p. 539.
[z] Grafton, p. 673.
[a] W. Wyrcester, p. 511. Hall, fol. 200. Habington, p. 439. Hollingshed, p. 671. Polyd. Virg. p. 515.

dangerous

dangerous combination was insensibly formed against Edward and his ministry. Though the immediate object of the malcontents was not to overturn the throne, it was difficult to foresee the extremities to which they might be carried: And as opposition to government was usually in those ages prosecuted by force of arms, civil convulsions and disorders were likely to be soon the result of these intrigues and confederacies.

CHAP. XXII.
1466.

WHILE this cloud was gathering at home, Edward carried his views abroad, and endeavoured to secure himself against his factious nobility by entering into foreign alliances. The dark and dangerous ambition of Lewis XI. the more it was known, the greater alarm it excited among his neighbours and vassals; and as it was supported by great abilities, and unrestrained by any principle of faith or humanity, they found no security to themselves but by a jealous combination against him. Philip, duke of Burgundy, was now dead: His rich and extensive dominions were devolved to Charles, his only son, whose martial disposition acquired him the sirname of *Bold*, and whose ambition, more outrageous than that of Lewis, but seconded by less power and policy, was regarded with a more favourable eye by the other potentates of Europe. The opposition of interests, and still more, a natural antipathy of character, produced a declared animosity between these bad princes; and Edward was thus secure of the sincere attachment of either of them, for whom he should choose to declare himself. The duke of Burgundy, being descended by his mother, a daughter of Portugal, from John of Gaunt, was naturally inclined to favour the house of Lancaster [b]: But this consideration was easily overbalanced by political motives; and Charles, perceiving the interests of that house to be extremely decayed in England, sent over his natural brother, com-

Alliance with the duke of Burgundy.

[b] Comines, liv. iii. chap. 4. 6.

monly

monly called the bastard of Burgundy, to carry in his name proposals of marriage to Margaret, the king's sister. The alliance of Burgundy was more popular among the English than that of France; the commercial interests of the two nations invited the princes to a close union; their common jealousy of Lewis was a natural cement between them; and Edward, pleased with strengthening himself by so potent a confederate, soon concluded the alliance, and bestowed his sister upon Charles[c]. A league, which Edward at the same time concluded with the duke of Britanny, seemed both to encrease his security, and to open to him the prospect of rivalling his predecessors in those foreign conquests, which, however short-lived and unprofitable, had rendered their reigns so popular and illustrious[d].

Insurrection in Yorkshire.

But whatever ambitious schemes the king might have built on these alliances, they were soon frustrated by intestine commotions, which engrossed all his attention. These disorders probably arose not immediately from the intrigues of the earl of Warwic, but from accident, aided by the turbulent spirit of the age, by the general humour of discontent which that popular nobleman had instilled into the nation, and perhaps by some remains of attachment to the house of Lancaster. The hospital of St. Leonard's near York had received, from an ancient grant of king Athelstane, a right of levying a thrave of corn upon every plough-land in the county; and as these charitable establishments are liable to abuse, the country people complained, that the revenue of the hospital was no longer expended for the relief of the poor, but was secreted by the managers, and employed to their private purposes. After long repining at the contribution, they

[c] Hall, fol. 169. 197. Hist. vol. ii. p. 338.
[d] W. Wyrcester, p. 5. Parliament. refused

refused payment: Ecclesiastical and civil censures were issued against them: Their goods were distrained, and their persons thrown into jail: Till, as their ill-humour daily encreased, they rose in arms; fell upon the officers of the hospital, whom they put to the sword; and proceeded in a body, fifteen thousand strong, to the gates of York. Lord Montague, who commanded in those parts, opposed himself to their progress; and having been so fortunate in a skirmish as to seize Robert Hulderne their leader, he ordered him immediately to be led to execution; according to the practice of the times. The rebels, however, still continued in arms; and being soon headed by men of greater distinction, Sir Henry Nevil, son of lord Latimer, and Sir John Coniers, they advanced southwards, and began to appear formidable to government. Herbert, earl of Pembroke, who had received that title on the forfeiture of Jasper Tudor, was ordered by Edward to march against them at the head of a body of Welshmen; and he was joined by five thousand archers under the command of Stafford, earl of Devonshire, who had succeeded in that title to the family of Courtney, which had also been attainted. But a trivial difference about quarters having begotten an animosity between these two noblemen, the earl of Devonshire retired with his archers, and left Pembroke alone to encounter the rebels, The two armies approached each other near Banbury; and Pembroke, having prevailed in a skirmish, and having taken Sir Henry Nevil prisoner, ordered him immediately to be put to death, without any form of process. This execution enraged, without terrifying, the rebels: They attacked the Welsh army, routed them, put them to the sword without mercy; and having seized Pembroke, they took immediate revenge upon him for the death of their leader, The king, imputing this misfortune to the earl of Devonshire, who had deserted Pembroke,

broke, ordered him to be executed in a like summary manner. But these speedy executions, or rather open murders, did not stop there: The northern rebels, sending a party to Grafton, seized the earl of Rivers and his son John; men who had become obnoxious by their near relation to the king, and his partiality towards them: And they were immediately executed by orders from Sir John Coniers[e].

THERE is no part of English history since the Conquest so obscure, so uncertain, so little authentic or consistent, as that of the wars between the two Roses: Historians differ about many material circumstances; some events of the utmost consequence, in which they almost all agree, are incredible and contradicted by records[f]; and it is remarkable, that this profound darkness falls upon us just on the eve of the restoration of letters, and when the art of Printing was already known in Europe. All we can distinguish with certainty through the deep cloud, which covers that period, is a scene of horror and bloodshed, savage manners, arbitrary executions, and treacherous, dishonourable conduct in all parties. There is no possibility, for instance, of accounting for the views and intentions of the earl of Warwic at this time. It is agreed, that he resided, together with his son-in-law, the duke of Clarence, in his government of Calais, during the commencement of this rebellion; and that his brother Montague acted with vigour against the northern rebels. We may thence presume, that the insurrection had not proceeded from the secret counsels and instigation of Warwic; though the murder, committed by the rebels on the earl of Rivers, his capital enemy, forms, on the other hand, a violent presumption against him. He and Clarence came over to England, offered their service to Edward, were received without any suspicion, were

[e] Fabian, fol. 217.   [f] See note [I] at the end of the volume.

entrusted

entrusted by him in the highest commands [g], and still perseverd in their fidelity. Soon after, we find the rebels quieted and dispersed by a general pardon granted by Edward from the advice of the earl of Warwic: But why so courageous a prince, if secure of Warwic's fidelity, should have granted a general pardon to men, who had been guilty of such violent and personal outrages against him, is not intelligible; nor why that nobleman, if unfaithful, should have endeavoured to appease a rebellion, of which he was able to make such advantages. But it appears that, after this insurrection, there was an interval of peace, during which the king loaded the family of Nevil with honours and favours of the highest nature: He made lord Montague a Marquess, by the same name: He created his son, George, duke of Bedford [h]: He publicly declared his intention of marrying that young nobleman to his eldest daughter, Elizabeth, who, as he had yet no sons, was presumptive heir of the crown: Yet we find, that soon after being invited to a feast by the archbishop of York, a younger brother of Warwic and Montague, he entertained a sudden suspicion that they intended to seize his person or to murder him: And he abruptly left the entertainment [i].

SOON after, there broke out another rebellion, which is as unaccountable as all the preceding events; chiefly because no sufficient reason is assigned for it, and because, so far as appears, the family of Nevil had no hand in exciting and fomenting it. It arose in Lincolnshire, and was headed by Sir Robert Welles, son to the lord of that name. The army of the rebels amounted to 30,000 men; but lord Welles himself, far from giving countenance to them, fled into a sanctuary, in order to secure

[g] Rymer, vol. xi. p. 647, 649, 652.   [h] Cotton, p. 702.
[i] Fragm. Ed. IV, ad fin. Sprotti.

CHAP.
XXII.

1470.
15th March.

his person against the king's anger or suspicions. He was allured from this retreat by a promise of safety; and was soon after, notwithstanding this assurance, beheaded, along with Sir Thomas Dymoc, by orders from Edward [h]. The king fought a battle with the rebels, defeated them, took Sir Robert Welles and Sir Thomas Launde prisoners, and ordered them immediately to be beheaded.

EDWARD, during these transactions, had entertained so little jealousy of the earl of Warwic or duke of Clarence, that he sent them with commissions of array to levy forces against the rebels [i]: But these malcontents, as soon as they left the court, raised troops in their own name, issued declarations against the government, and complained of grievances, oppressions, and bad ministers. The unexpected defeat of Welles disconcerted all their measures; and they retired northwards into Lancashire, where they expected to be joined by lord Stanley, who had married the earl of Warwic's sister. But as that nobleman refused all concurrence with them, and as lord Montague also remained quiet in Yorkshire; they were obliged to disband their army, and to fly into Devonshire, where they embarked and made sail towards Calais [m].

Warwic and Clarence banished.

THE deputy-governor, whom Warwic had left at Calais, was one Vaucler, a Gascon, who seeing the earl return in this miserable condition, refused him admittance; and would not so much as permit the dutchess of Clarence to land; though, a few days before, she had been delivered on ship-board of a son, and was at that time extremely disordered by sickness. With diffi-

[h] Hall, fol. 204. Fabian, fol. 218. Habington, p. 442. Hollingshed, p. 674.   [i] Rymer, vol. xi. p. 652.

[m] The king offered by proclamation a reward of 1000 pounds, or 100 pounds a year in land, to any that would seize them. Whence we may learn that land was at that time sold for about ten years purchase. See Rymer, vol. xi. p. 654.

culty,

culty, he would allow a few flaggons of wine to be carried to the ship for the use of the ladies: But as he was a man of sagacity, and well acquainted with the revolutions to which England was subject, he secretly apologized to Warwic for this appearance of infidelity, and represented it as proceeding entirely from zeal for his service. He said, that the fortress was ill supplied with provisions; that he could not depend on the attachment of the garrison; that the inhabitants, who lived by the English commerce, would certainly declare for the established government; that the place was at present unable to resist the power of England on the one hand, and that of the duke of Burgundy on the other; and that, by seeming to declare for Edward, he would acquire the confidence of that prince, and still keep it in his power, when it should become safe and prudent, to restore Calais to its ancient master[n]. It is uncertain, whether Warwic was satisfied with this apology, or suspected a double infidelity in Vaucler; but he feigned to be entirely convinced by him; and having seized some Flemish vessels which he found lying off Calais, he immediately made sail towards France.

THE king of France, uneasy at the close conjunction between Edward and the duke of Burgundy, received with the greatest demonstrations of regard the unfortunate Warwic[o], with whom he had formerly maintained a secret correspondence, and whom he hoped still to make his instrument, in overturning the government of England, and re-establishing the house of Lancaster. No animosity was ever greater than that which had long prevailed between that house and the earl of Warwic. His father had been executed by orders from Margaret: He himself had twice reduced Henry to cap-

[n] Cominæs, liv. lii. sap. 4. Hall, fol. 205. p. 519.   [o] Polyd. Virg.

CHAP. XXII.
1470.

tivity, had banished the queen, had put to death all their most zealous partizans either in the field or on the scaffold, and had occasioned innumerable ills to that unhappy family. For this reason, believing that such inveterate rancour could never admit of any cordial reconciliation, he had not mentioned Henry's name, when he took arms against Edward; and he rather endeavoured to prevail by means of his own adherents, than revive a party which he sincerely hated. But his present distresses and the entreaties of Lewis, made him hearken to terms of accommodation; and Margaret being sent for from Angers, where she then resided, an agreement was from common interest soon concluded between them. It was stipulated, that Warwic should espouse the cause of Henry, and endeavour to restore him to liberty, and to re-establish him on the throne; that the administration of the government, during the minority of young Edward, Henry's son, should be entrusted conjointly to the earl of Warwic and the duke of Clarence; that prince Edward should marry the lady Anne, second daughter of that nobleman; and that the crown, in case of the failure of male issue in that prince, should descend to the duke of Clarence, to the entire exclusion of king Edward and his posterity. Never was confederacy, on all sides, less natural or more evidently the work of necessity: But Warwic hoped, that all former passions of the Lancastrians might be lost in present political views; and that at worst, the independent power of his family, and the affections of the people, would suffice to give him security, and enable him to exact the full performance of all the conditions agreed on. The marriage of prince Edward with the lady Anne was immediately celebrated in France.

EDWARD foresaw, that it would be easy to dissolve an alliance, composed of such discordant parts. For this

this purpose, he sent over a lady of great sagacity and address, who belonged to the train of the dutchess of Clarence, and who, under colour of attending her mistress, was empowered to negociate with the duke, and to renew the connexions of that prince with his own family[p]. She represented to Clarence, that he had unwarily, to his own ruin, become the instrument of Warwic's vengeance, and had thrown himself entirely in the power of his most inveterate enemies; that the mortal injuries which the one royal family had suffered from the other, were now past all forgiveness, and no imaginary union of interests could ever suffice to obliterate them; that even if the leaders were willing to forget past offences, the animosity of their adherents would prevent a sincere coalition of parties, and would, in spite of all temporary and verbal agreements, preserve an eternal opposition of measures between them; and that a prince, who deserted his own kindred, and joined the murderers of his father, left himself single, without friends, without protection, and would not, when misfortunes inevitably fell upon him, be so much as entitled to any pity or regard from the rest of mankind. Clarence was only one and twenty years of age, and seems to have possessed but a slender capacity; yet could he easily see the force of these reasons; and upon the promise of forgiveness from his brother, he secretly engaged, on a favourable opportunity, to desert the earl of Warwic, and abandon the Lancastrian party.

DURING this negociation, Warwic was secretly carrying on a correspondence of the same nature with his brother, the marquess of Montague, who was entirely trusted by Edward; and like motives produced a like resolution in that nobleman. The marquess also, that he might render the projected blow the more deadly and

[p] Comines, vol. iii, chap. 5. Hall, fol. 207. Hollingshed, p. 675.

incurable,

incurable, resolved, on his side, to watch a favourable opportunity for committing *his* perfidy, and still to maintain the appearance of being a zealous adherent to the house of York.

AFTER these mutual snares were thus carefully laid, the decision of the quarrel advanced apace. Lewis prepared a fleet to escort the earl of Warwic, and granted him a supply of men and money [q]. The duke of Burgundy, on the other hand, enraged at that nobleman for his seizure of the Flemish vessels before Calais, and anxious to support the reigning family in England, with whom his own interests were now connected, fitted out a larger fleet, with which he guarded the Channel; and he incessantly warned his brother-in-law of the imminent perils, to which he was exposed. But Edward, though always brave and often active, had little foresight or penetration. He was not sensible of his danger: He made no suitable preparations against the earl of Warwic [r]: He even said, that the duke might spare himself the trouble of guarding the seas, and that he wished for nothing more than to see Warwic set foot on English ground [s]. A vain confidence in his own prowess, joined to the immoderate love of pleasure, had made him incapable of all sound reason and reflection.

September. Warwic and Clarence return.

THE event soon happened, of which Edward seemed so desirous. A storm dispersed the Flemish navy, and left the sea open to Warwic [t]. That nobleman seized the opportunity, and setting sail, quickly landed at Dartmouth, with the duke of Clarence, the earls of Oxford and Pembroke, and a small body of troops; while the king was in the north, engaged in suppressing an insurrection which had been raised by lord Fitz-Hugh,

[q] Comines, liv. iii. chap. 4. Hall, fol. 207. [r] Grafton, p. 687.
[s] Comines, liv. iii. chap. 5. Hall, fol. 208. [t] Comines, liv. iii. chap. 5.

brother-

brother-in-law to Warwic. The scene, which ensues, resembles more the fiction of a poem or romance than an event in true history. The prodigious popularity of Warwic[a], the zeal of the Lancastrian party, the spirit of discontent with which many were infected, and the general instability of the English nation, occasioned by the late frequent revolutions, drew such multitudes to his standard, that, in a very few days, his army amounted to sixty thousand men, and was continually encreasing. Edward hastened southwards to encounter him; and the two armies approached each other near Nottingham, where a decisive action was every hour expected. The rapidity of Warwic's progress had incapacitated the duke of Clarence from executing *his* plan of treachery; and the marquis of Montague had here the opportunity of striking the first blow. He communicated the design to his adherents, who promised him their concurrence: They took to arms in the night-time, and hastened with loud acclamations to Edward's quarters: The king was alarmed at the noise, and starting from bed, heard the cry of war usually employed by the Lancastrian party. Lord Hastings, his chamberlain, informed him of the danger, and urged him to make his escape by speedy flight, from an army where he had so many concealed enemies, and where few seemed zealously attached to his service. He had just time to get on horseback, and to hurry with a small retinue, to Lynne in Norfolk, where he luckily found some ships ready, on board of which he instantly embarked[w]. And after this manner the earl of Warwic, in no longer space than eleven days after his first landing, was left entire master of the kingdom.

CHAP. XXII.
1470.

Edward IV. expelled.

But Edward's danger did not end with his embarkation. The Easterlings, or Hanse-Towns were then at

[a] Hall, fol. 205.   [w] Comines, liv. 3. chap. 5. Hall, fol. 208.

CHAP.
XXII.

1470.

war both with France and England; and some ships of these people, hovering on the English coast, espied the king's vessels, and gave chace to them; nor was it without extreme difficulty that he made his escape into the port of Alcmaer in Holland. He had fled from England with such precipitation, that he had carried nothing of value along with him; and the only reward which he could bestow on the captain of the vessel that brought him over, was a robe lined with sables; promising him an ample recompence, if fortune should ever become more propitious to him [x].

It is not likely, that Edward could be very fond of presenting himself in this lamentable plight before the duke of Burgundy; and that having so suddenly, after his mighty vaunts, lost all footing in his own kingdom, he could be insensible to the ridicule which must attend him in the eyes of that prince. The duke, on his part, was no less embarrassed how he should receive the dethroned monarch. As he had ever borne a greater affection to the house of Lancaster than to that of York, nothing but political views had engaged him to contract an alliance with the latter; and he foresaw, that probably the revolution in England would now turn this alliance against him, and render the reigning family his implacable and jealous enemy. For this reason, when the first rumour of that event reached him, attended with the circumstance of Edward's death, he seemed rather pleased with the catastrophe; and it was no agreeable disappointment to find, that he must either undergo the burthen of supporting an exiled prince, or the dishonour of abandoning so near a relation. He began already to say, that his connexions were with the kingdom of England, not with the king; and it was indifferent to him, whether the name of Edward, or that of Henry, were

[x] Comines, liv. 3. chap. 5.

employed

employed in the articles of treaty. These sentiments were continually strengthened by the subsequent events. Vaucler, the deputy governor of Calais, though he had been confirmed in his command by Edward, and had even received a pension from the duke of Burgundy on account of his fidelity to the crown, no sooner saw his old master, Warwic, reinstated in authority, than he declared for him, and, with great demonstrations of zeal and attachment, put the whole garrison in his livery. And the intelligence, which the duke received every day from England, seemed to promise an entire and full settlement in the family of Lancaster.

CHAP.
XXII.
1470.

IMMEDIATELY after Edward's flight had left the kingdom at Warwic's disposal, that nobleman hastened to London; and taking Henry from his confinement in the Tower, into which he himself had been the chief cause of throwing him, he proclaimed him king with great solemnity. A parliament was summoned, in the name of that prince, to meet at Westminster; and as this assembly could pretend to no liberty, while surrounded by such enraged and insolent victors, governed by such an impetuous spirit as Warwic, their votes were entirely dictated by the ruling faction. The treaty with Margaret was here fully executed: Henry was recognized as lawful king; but his incapacity for government being avowed, the regency was entrusted to Warwic and Clarence till the majority of prince Edward; and in default of that prince's issue, Clarence was declared successor to the crown. The usual business also of reversals went on without opposition: Every statute, made during the reign of Edward, was repealed; that prince was declared to be an usurper; he and his adherents were attainted; and, in particular, Richard duke of Glocester, his younger brother: All the attainders of the Lancastrians, the dukes of Somerset and Exeter, the earls of Richmond, Pembroke,

Henry VI. restored.

CHAP.
XXII.

1470.

broke, Oxford, and Ormond, were reversed; and every one was restored, who had lost either honours or fortune, by his former adherence to the cause of Henry.

The ruling party were more sparing in their executions, than was usual after any revolution during those violent times. The only victim of distinction was John Tibetot, earl of Worcester. This accomplished person, born in an age and nation where the nobility valued themselves on ignorance as their privilege, and left learning to monks and schoolmasters, for whom indeed the spurious erudition that prevailed was best fitted, had been struck with the first rays of true science, which began to penetrate from the south, and had been zealous, by his exhortation and example, to propagate the love of letters among his unpolished countrymen. It is pretended, that knowledge had not produced, on this nobleman himself, the effect which so naturally attends it, of humanizing the temper, and softening the heart; and that he had enraged the Lancastrians against him, by the severities which he exercised upon them during the prevalence of his own party. He endeavoured to conceal himself after the flight of Edward; but was caught on the top of a tree in the forest of Weybridge, was conducted to London, tried before the earl of Oxford, condemned, and executed. All the other considerable Yorkists either fled beyond sea, or took shelter in sanctuaries; where the ecclesiastical privileges afforded them protection. In London alone, it is computed, that no less than 2000 persons saved themselves in this manner*; and, among the rest, Edward's queen, who was there delivered of a son, called by his father's name*.

Queen Margaret, the other rival queen, had not yet appeared in England; but, on receiving intelligence of

F Hall, fol. 210. Stowe, p. 422.   * Comines, liv. 3. chap. 7.
* Hall, fol. 210. Stowe, p. 483. Hollingshed, p. 677. Grafton, p. 690.

Warwic's success, was preparing with prince Edward for her journey. All the banished Lancastrians flocked to her; and, among the rest, the duke of Somerset, son of the duke beheaded after the battle of Hexham. This nobleman, who had long been regarded as the head of the party, had fled into the Low Countries on the discomfiture of his friends; and as he concealed his name and quality, he had there languished in extreme indigence. Philip de Comines tells us[b], that he himself saw him, as well as the duke of Exeter, in a condition no better than that of a common beggar; till being discovered by Philip duke of Burgundy, they had small pensions allotted them, and were living in silence and obscurity, when the success of their party called them from their retreat. But both Somerset and Margaret were detained by contrary winds from reaching England[c], till a new revolution in that kingdom, no less sudden and surprising than the former, threw them into greater misery than that from which they had just emerged.

Though the duke of Burgundy, by neglecting Edward, and paying court to the established government, had endeavoured to conciliate the friendship of the Lancastrians, he found that he had not succeeded to his wish; and the connexions between the king of France and the earl of Warwic still held him in great anxiety[d]. This nobleman, too hastily regarding Charles as a determined enemy, had sent over to Calais a body of 4000 men, who made inroads into the Low Countries[e]; and the duke of Burgundy saw himself in danger of being overwhelmed by the united arms of England and of France. He resolved therefore to grant some assistance to his brother-in-law; but in such a covert manner, as should

[b] Liv. 3. chap. 4. [c] Grafton, p. 692. Polyd. Virg. p. 511.
[d] Hall, fol. 205. [e] Comines, liv. 3. chap. 6.

CHAP. XXII.

1471.

give the least offence possible to the English government. He equipped four large vessels, in the name of some private merchants, at Terveer in Zealand; and causing fourteen ships to be secretly hired from the Easterlings, he delivered this small squadron to Edward, who, receiving also a sum of money from the duke, immediately set sail for England. No sooner was Charles informed of his departure, than he issued a proclamation inhibiting all his subjects from giving him countenance or assistance[f]; an artifice which could not deceive the earl of Warwic, but which might serve as a decent pretence, if that nobleman were so disposed, for maintaining friendship with the duke of Burgundy.

15th March. Edward IV. returns.

EDWARD, impatient to take revenge on his enemies, and to recover his lost authority, made an attempt to land with his forces, which exceeded not 2000 men, on the coast of Norfolk; but being there repulsed, he sailed northwards, and disembarked at Ravenspur in Yorkshire. Finding that the new magistrates, who had been appointed by the earl of Warwic, kept the people every where from joining him, he pretended, and even made oath, that he came not to challenge the crown, but only the inheritance of the house of York, which of right belonged to him; and that he did not intend to disturb the peace of the kingdom. His partizans every moment flocked to his standard: He was admitted into the city of York: And he was soon in such a situation, as gave him hopes of succeeding in all his claims and pretensions. The marquis of Montague commanded in the northern counties; but, from some mysterious reasons, which, as well as many other important transactions in that age, no historian has cleared up, he totally neglected the beginnings of an insurrection, which he ought to have esteemed so formidable. Warwic assembled an

[f] Comines, liv. 3. chap. 6.

army

army at Leicester, with an intention of meeting and of giving battle to the enemy; but Edward, by taking another road, passed him unmolested, and presented himself before the gates of London. Had he here been refused admittance, he was totally undone: But there were many reasons, which inclined the citizens to favour him. His numerous friends, issuing from their sanctuaries, were active in his cause; many rich merchants, who had formerly lent him money, saw no other chance for their payment but his restoration; the city-dames, who had been liberal of their favours to him, and who still retained an affection for this young and gallant prince, swayed their husbands and friends in his favour [g]; and, above all, the archbishop of York, Warwic's brother, to whom the care of the city was committed, had secretly, from unknown reasons, entered into a correspondence with him; and he facilitated Edward's admission into London. The most likely cause which can be assigned for those multiplied infidelities, even in the family of Nevil itself, is the spirit of faction, which, when it becomes inveterate, it is very difficult for any man entirely to shake off. The persons, who had long distinguished themselves in the York party, were unable to act with zeal and cordiality for the support of the Lancastrians; and they were inclined, by any prospect of favour or accommodation offered them by Edward, to return to their ancient connexions. However this may be, Edward's entrance into London, made him master not only of that rich and powerful city, but also of the person of Henry, who, destined to be the perpetual sport of fortune, thus fell again into the hands of his enemies [h].

It appears not that Warwic, during his short administration, which had continued only six months, had

[g] Comines, liv. 3, chap. 7.   [h] Grafton, p. 702.

been

been guilty of any unpopular act, or had anywise deserved to lose that general favour with which he had so lately overwhelmed Edward. But this prince, who was formerly on the defensive, was now the aggressor; and having overcome the difficulties which always attend the beginnings of an insurrection, possessed many advantages above his enemy: His partizans were actuated by that zeal and courage which the notion of an attack inspires; his opponents were intimidated for a like reason; every one who had been disappointed in the hopes which he had entertained from Warwic's elevation, either became a cool friend, or an open enemy to that nobleman; and each malcontent, from whatever cause, proved an accession to Edward's army. The king, therefore, found himself in a condition to face the earl of Warwic; who, being reinforced by his son-in-law, the duke of Clarence, and his brother the marquis of Montague, took post at Barnet, in the neighbourhood of London. The arrival of queen Margaret was every day expected, who would have drawn together all the genuine Lancastrians, and have brought a great accession to Warwic's forces: But this very consideration proved a motive to the earl rather to hurry on a decisive action, than to share the victory with rivals and ancient enemies, who, he foresaw, would, in case of success, claim the chief merit in the enterprize[1]. But while his jealousy was all directed towards that side, he overlooked the dangerous infidelity of friends, who lay the nearest to his bosom. His brother, Montague, who had lately temporized, seems now to have remained sincerely attached to the interests of his family: But his son-in-law, though bound to him by every tie of honour and gratitude, though he shared the power of the regency, though he had been invested by Warwic in all the honours and patrimony of the house of York, resolved to

[1] Comines, liv. 3. chap. 7.

fulfil

fulfil the secret engagements which he had formerly taken with his brother, and to support the interests of his own family: He deserted to the king in the night-time, and carried over a body of 12,000 men along with him [k]. Warwic was now too far advanced to retreat; and as he rejected with disdain all terms of peace offered him by Edward and Clarence, he was obliged to hazard a general engagement. The battle was fought with obstinacy on both sides: The two armies, in imitation of their leaders, displayed uncommon valour: And the victory remained long undecided between them. But an accident threw the balance to the side of the Yorkists. Edward's cognisance was a sun; that of Warwic a star with rays; and the mistiness of the morning rendering it difficult to distinguish them, the earl of Oxford, who fought on the side of the Lancastrians, was, by mistake, attacked by his friends and chaced off the field of battle [l]. Warwic, contrary to his more usual practice, engaged that day on foot, resolving to show his army that he meant to share every fortune with them; and he was slain in the thickest of the engagement [m]: His brother underwent the same fate: And as Edward had issued orders not to give any quarter, a great and undistinguished slaughter was made in the pursuit [n]. There fell about 1500 on the side of the victors.

THE same day on which this decisive battle was fought [o], queen Margaret and her son, now about eighteen years of age, and a young prince of great hopes, landed at Weymouth, supported by a small body of French forces. When this princess received intelligence of her husband's captivity, and of the defeat and death of the earl of Warwic, her courage, which had supported her under so many disas-

[k] Grafton, p. 700. Comines, liv. 3. chap. 7. Leland's Collect. vol. II. p. 505. [l] Habington. p. 449. [m] Comines, liv. 3. chap. 7. [n] Hall, fol. 218. [o] Leland's Collect, vol. II. p. 505.

trous events, here quite left her; and she immediately foresaw all the dismal consequences of this calamity. At first she took sanctuary in the abbey of Beaulieu*; but being encouraged by the appearance of Tudor, earl of Pembroke, and Courtney, earl of Devonshire, of the lords Wenloc and St. John, with other men of rank, who exhorted her still to hope for success, she resumed her former spirit, and determined to defend to the utmost the ruins of her fallen fortunes. She advanced through the counties of Devon, Somerset, and Glocester, encreasing her army on each day's march; but was at last overtaken by the rapid and expeditious Edward at Teukesbury, on the banks of the Severne. The Lancastrians were here totally defeated: The earl of Devonshire and lord Wenloc were killed in the field: The duke of Somerset, and about twenty other persons of distinction, having taken shelter in a church, were surrounded, dragged out, and immediately beheaded: About 3000 of their side fell in battle: And the army was entirely dispersed.

QUEEN Margaret and her son were taken prisoners, and brought to the king, who asked the prince, after an insulting manner, how he dared to invade his dominions? The young prince, more mindful of his high birth than of his present fortune, replied, that he came thither to claim his just inheritance. The ungenerous Edward, insensible to pity, struck him on the face with his gauntlet; and the dukes of Clarence and Glocester, Lord Hastings, and Sir Thomas Gray, taking the blow as a signal for farther violence, hurried the prince into the next apartment, and there dispatched him with their daggers*. Margaret was thrown into the Tower: King Henry expired in that confinement a few days after the battle of

*Hall, fol. 219. Habington, p. 451. Grafton, p. 706. Polyd. Virg. p. 516. *Holl. fol. 221. Habington, p. 453. Hollingshed, p. 683. Polyd. Virg. p. 530.

Teukesbury

EDWARD IV.

Teukesbury; but whether he died a natural or violent death, is uncertain. It is pretended, and was generally believed, that the duke of Glocester killed him with his own hands[f]: But the universal odium which that prince has incurred, inclined perhaps the nation to aggravate his crimes without any sufficient authority. It is certain, however, that Henry's death was sudden; and though he laboured under an ill state of health, this circumstance, joined to the general manners of the age, gave a natural ground of suspicion; which was rather encreased than diminished by the exposing of his body to public view. That precaution served only to recal many similar instances in the English history, and to suggest the comparison.

CHAP. XXII.

1471. Death of Henry VI.

ALL the hopes of the house of Lancaster seemed now to be utterly extinguished. Every legitimate prince of that family was dead: Almost every great leader of the party had perished in battle, or on the scaffold: The earl of Pembroke, who was levying forces in Wales, disbanded his army when he received intelligence of the battle of Teukesbury; and he fled into Britanny with his nephew, the young earl of Richmond[g]. The bastard of Falconberg, who had levied some forces, and had advanced to London during Edward's absence, was repulsed; his men deserted him; he was taken prisoner, and immediately executed[h]: And peace being now fully restored to the nation, a parliament was summoned, which ratified, as usual, all the acts of the victor, and recognized his legal authority.

6th Oct.

BUT this prince, who had been so firm, and active, and intrepid, during the course of adversity, was still unable to resist the allurements of a prosperous fortune; and he

[f] Comines, Hall. fol. 213. Grafton, p. 703. [g] Habington, p. 454. Polyd. Virg. p. 531. [h] Hollingshed, p. 689, 690, 693. Vid. Croyl. cont. p. 554.

wholly

CHAP.
XXII.
1472.

wholly devoted himself, as before, to pleasure and amusement, after he became entirely master of his kingdom, and had no longer any enemy who could give him anxiety or alarm. He recovered, however, by this gay and inoffensive course of life, and by his easy, familiar manners, that popularity which, it is natural to imagine, he had lost by the repeated cruelties exercised upon his enemies; and the example also of his jovial festivity served to abate the former acrimony of faction among his subjects, and to restore the social disposition which had been so long interrupted between the opposite parties. All men seemed to be fully satisfied with the present government; and the memory of past calamities served only to impress the people more strongly with a sense of their allegiance, and with the resolution of never incurring any more the hazard of renewing such direful scenes.

1474.

But while the king was thus indulging himself in pleasure, he was rouzed from his lethargy by a prospect of foreign conquests, which, it is probable, his desire of popularity, more than the spirit of ambition, had made him covet. Though he deemed himself little beholden to the duke of Burgundy for the reception which that prince had given him during his exile*, the political interests of their states maintained still a close connexion between them; and they agreed to unite their arms in making a powerful invasion on France. A league was formed, in which Edward stipulated to pass the seas with an army exceeding 10,000 men, and to invade the French territories: Charles promised to join him with all his forces: The king was to challenge the crown of France, and to obtain at least the provinces of Normandy and Guienne: The duke was to acquire Champaigne and some other territories, and to free all his dominions from the burthen

* Cominæs, liv. 3. chap. 7.

of homage to the crown of France: And neither party was to make peace without the consent of the other [w]. They were the more encouraged to hope for success from this league, as the count of St. Pol, constable of France, who was master of St. Quintin, and other towns on the Somme, had secretly promised to join them; and there were also hopes of engaging the duke of Britanny to enter into the confederacy.

THE prospect of a French war was always a sure means of making the parliament open their purses, as far as the habits of that age would permit. They voted the king a tenth of rents, or two shillings in the pound; which must have been very inaccurately levied, since it produced only 31,460 pounds; and they added to this supply a whole fifteenth, and three quarters of another [x]: But as the king deemed these sums still unequal to the undertaking, he attempted to levy money by way of *benevolence*; a kind of exaction, which, except during the reigns of Henry III. and Richard II., had not been much practised in former times, and which, though the consent of the parties was pretended to be gained, could not be deemed entirely voluntary [y]. The clauses, annexed to the parliamentary grant, show sufficiently the spirit of the nation in this respect. The money levied by the fifteenth was not to be put into the king's hands, but to be kept in religious houses; and if the expedition into France should not take place, it was immediately to be refunded to the people. After these grants, the parliament was dissolved, which had sitten near two years and a half, and had undergone several prorogations; a practice not very usual at that time in England.

[w] Rymer, vol. xi. p. 806, 807, 808, &c.
[x] Cotton, p. 696, 700. Hist. Croyl. cont. p. 558.
[y] Hall, fol. 226. Habington, p. 461. Grafton, p. 719. Fabian, fol. 226.

CHAP.
XXII.

1475.
Invasion of
France.

THE king passed over to Calais with an army of 1500 men at arms, and 15,000 archers, attended by all the chief nobility of England, who, prognosticating future successes from the past, were eager to appear on this great theatre of honour [y]. But all their sanguine hopes were damped, when they found, on entering the French territories, that neither did the constable open his gates to them, nor the duke of Burgundy bring them the smallest assistance. That prince, transported by his ardent temper, had carried all his armies to a great distance, and had employed them in wars on the frontiers of Germany, and against the duke of Lorrain: And though he came in person to Edward, and endeavoured to apologize for this breach of treaty, there was no prospect that they would be able this campaign to make a conjunction with the English. This circumstance gave great disgust to the king, and inclined him to hearken to those advances, which Lewis continually made him for an accommodation.

THAT monarch, more swayed by political views than by the point of honour, deemed no submissions too mean, which might free him from enemies, who had proved so formidable to his predecessors, and who, united to so many other enemies, might still shake the well-established government of France. It appears from Comines, that discipline was, at this time, very imperfect among the English; and that their civil wars, though long continued, yet, being always decided by hasty battles, had still left them ignorant of the improvements, which the military art was beginning to receive upon the continent [z]. But as Lewis was sensible, that the warlike genius of the

---

[y] Comines, liv. 4. chap. 5. This author says (chap. 12.) that the king artfully brought over some of the richest of his subjects, who, he knew, would be soon tired of the war, and would promote all proposals of peace, which, he foresaw, would be soon necessary.

[z] Comines, liv. 4. chap. 5.

people

people would soon render them excellent soldiers, he was far from despising them for their present want of experience; and he employed all his art to detach them from the alliance of Burgundy. When Edward sent him a herald to claim the crown of France, and to carry him a defiance in case of refusal, so far from answering to this bravado in like haughty terms, he replied with great temper, and even made the herald a considerable present [b]: He took afterwards an opportunity of sending a herald to the English camp; and having given him directions to apply to the lords Stanley and Howard, who, he heard, were friends to peace, he desired the good offices of these noblemen in promoting an accommodation with their master [c]. As Edward was now fallen into like dispositions, a truce was soon concluded on terms more advantageous than honourable to Lewis. He stipulated to pay Edward immediately 75,000 crowns, on condition that he should withdraw his army from France, and promised to pay him 50,000 crowns a year during their joint lives: It was added, that the dauphin, when of age, should marry Edward's eldest daughter [d]. In order to ratify this treaty, the two monarchs agreed to have a personal interview; and, for that purpose, suitable preparations were made at Pecquigni, near Amiens. A close rail was drawn across a bridge in that place, with no larger intervals than would allow the arm to pass; a precaution against a similar accident to that which befel the duke of Burgundy in his conference with the dauphin at Montereau. Edward and Lewis came to the opposite sides; conferred privately together; and having confirmed their friendship, and interchanged many mutual civilities, they soon after parted [e].

CHAP.
XXII.

1475.

29th Aug.

Peace of Pecquignol.

[b] Comines, liv. 4. chap. 5. Hall, fol. 227. chap. 7. [d] Rymer, vol. xii. p. 17. [e] Comines, liv. 4. [e] Comines, lib. 4. chap. 9.

CHAP. XXII.
1475.

Lewis was anxious not only to gain the king's friendship, but also that of the nation, and of all the considerable persons in the English court. He bestowed pensions, to the amount of 16,000 crowns a year, on several of the king's favourites; on lord Hastings two thousand crowns; on lord Howard and others in proportion; and these great ministers were not ashamed thus to receive wages from a foreign prince[f]. As the two armies, after the conclusion of the truce, remained some time in the neighbourhood of each other, the English were not only admitted freely into Amiens, where Lewis resided, but had also their charges defrayed, and had wine and victuals furnished them in every inn, without any payment's being demanded. They flocked thither in such multitudes, that once above nine thousand of them were in the town, and they might have made themselves masters of the king's person; but Lewis concluding, from their jovial and dissolute manner of living, that they had no bad intentions, was careful not to betray the least sign of fear or jealousy. And when Edward, informed of this disorder, desired him to shut the gates against him, he replied, that he would never agree to exclude the English from the place where he resided; but that Edward, if he pleased, might recal them, and place his own officers at the gates of Amiens to prevent their returning[g].

Lewis's desire of confirming a mutual amity with England engaged him even to make imprudent advances, which it cost him afterwards some pains to evade. In the conference at Pecquigni, he had said to Edward, that he wished to have a visit from him at Paris; that he would there endeavour to amuse him with the ladies; and that, in case any offences were then committed, he would assign him the cardinal of Bourbon for confessor, who, from fellow-feeling, would not be over and above severe in the

[f] Hall, fol. 235. [g] Cominæs, liv. 4. chap. 9. Hall, fol. 233.

penances

penances which he would enjoin. This hint made
deeper impression than Lewis intended. Lord Howard,
who accompanied him back to Amiens, told him, in confidence, that, if he were so disposed, it would not be impossible to persuade Edward to take a journey with him to
Paris, where they might make merry together. Lewis
pretended at first not to hear the offer; but, on Howard's
repeating it, he expressed his concern that his wars with
the duke of Burgundy would not permit him to attend
his royal guest, and do him the honours he intended.
"Edward," said he, privately to Comines, "is a very
"handsome and a very amorous prince: Some lady at
"Paris may like him as well as he shall do her; and may
"invite him to return in another manner. It is better
"that the sea be between us [b]."

This treaty did very little honour to either of these
monarchs: It discovered the imprudence of Edward, who
had taken his measures so ill with his allies as to be
obliged, after such an expensive armament, to return
without making any acquisitions adequate to it: It
showed the want of dignity in Lewis, who, rather than
run the hazard of a battle, agreed to subject his kingdom
to a tribute, and thus acknowledge the superiority of a
neighbouring prince, possessed of less power and territory
than himself. But, as Lewis made interest the sole test of
honour, he thought that all the advantages of the treaty
were on his side, and that he had over-reached Edward,
by sending him out of France on such easy terms. For
this reason he was very solicitous to conceal his triumph;
and he strictly enjoined his courtiers never to show
the English the least sign of mockery or derision. But
he did not himself very carefully observe so prudent
a rule: He could not forbear, one day, in the joy of his
heart, throwing out some raillery on the easy simplicity

[b] Comines, liv. iv. chap. 10. Habington, p. 459.

CHAP.
XXII.
1475.

of Edward and his council; when he perceived that he was overheard by a Gascon who had settled in England. He was immediately sensible of his indiscretion; sent a message to the gentleman; and offered him such advantages in his own country, as engaged him to remain in France. *It is but just,* said he, *that I pay the penalty of my talkativeness* [1].

THE most honourable part of Lewis's treaty with Edward was the stipulation for the liberty of queen Margaret, who, though after the death of her husband and son she could no longer be formidable to government, was still detained in custody by Edward. Lewis paid fifty thousand crowns for her ransom; and that princess, who had been so active on the stage of the world, and who had experienced such a variety of fortune, passed the remainder of her days in tranquillity and privacy, till the year 1482, when she died: An admirable princess, but more illustrious by her undaunted spirit in adversity, than by her moderation in prosperity. She seems neither to have enjoyed the virtues, nor been subject to the weaknesses, of her sex; and was as much tainted with the ferocity, as endowed with the courage, of that barbarous age in which she lived.

THOUGH Edward had so little reason to be satisfied with the conduct of the duke of Burgundy, he referred to that prince a power of acceding to the treaty of Pecquigni: But Charles, when the offer was made him, haughtily replied, that he was able to support himself without the assistance of England, and that he would make no peace with Lewis till three months after Edward's return into his own country. This prince possessed all the ambition and courage of a conqueror; but being defective in policy and prudence, qualities no less essential, he was unfortunate in all his enterprizes, and perished

[1] Comines, liv. III. chap. 10.

at last in battle against the Swifs[b]; a people whom he despised, and who, though brave and free, had hitherto been in a manner overlooked in the general system of Europe. This event, which happened in the year 1477, produced a great alteration in the views of all the princes, and was attended with consequences which were felt for many generations. Charles left only one daughter, Mary, by his first wife; and this princess being heir of his opulent and extensive dominions, was courted by all the potentates of Christendom, who contended for the possession of so rich a prize. Lewis, the head of her family, might, by a proper application, have obtained this match for the dauphin, and have thereby united to the crown of France all the provinces of the Low Countries, together with Burgundy, Artois, and Picardy; which would, at once, have rendered his kingdom an overmatch for all its neighbours. But a man wholly interested, is as rare as one entirely endowed with the opposite quality; and Lewis, though impregnable to all the sentiments of generosity and friendship, was, on this occasion, carried from the road of true policy by the passions of animosity and revenge. He had imbibed so deep a hatred to the house of Burgundy, that he rather chose to subdue the princess by arms, than unite her to his family by marriage: He conquered the dutchy of Burgundy and that part of Picardy, which had been ceded to Philip the Good by the treaty of Arras: But he thereby forced the states of the Netherlands to bestow their sovereign in marriage on Maximilian of Austria, son of the emperor Frederic, from whom they looked for protection in their present distresses: And by these means France lost the opportunity, which she never could recal, of making that important acquisition of power and territory.

[b] Comines, liv. v. chap. 1.

CHAP.
XXII.

1477.

During this interesting crisis, Edward was no less defective in policy, and was no less actuated by private passions, unworthy of a sovereign and a statesman. Jealousy of his brother, Clarence, had caused him to neglect the advances which were made of marrying that prince, now a widower, to the heiress of Burgundy [1]; and he sent her proposals of espousing Anthony earl of Rivers, brother to his queen, who still retained an entire ascendant over him. But the match was rejected with disdain [m]; and Edward, resenting this treatment of his brother-in-law, permitted France to proceed, without interruption, in her conquests over his defenceless ally. Any pretence sufficed him for abandoning himself entirely to indolence and pleasure, which were now become his ruling passions. The only object which divided his attention, was the improving of the public revenue, which had been dilapidated by the necessities or negligence of his predecessors; and some of his expedients for that purpose, though unknown to us, were deemed, during the time, oppressive to the people [n]. The detail of private wrongs naturally escapes the notice of history; but an act of tyranny, of which Edward was guilty in his own family, has been taken notice of by all writers, and has met with general and deserved censure.

Trial and execution of the duke of Clarence.

The duke of Clarence, by all his services in deserting Warwic, had never been able to regain the king's friendship, which he had forfeited by his former confederacy with that nobleman. He was still regarded, at court, as a man of a dangerous and a fickle character; and the imprudent openness and violence of his temper, though it rendered him much less dangerous, tended extremely to multiply his enemies, and to incense them against him. Among others, he had had the misfortune to give displea-

[1] Pol'yd Virg. Hall, fol. 240. Hollingshed, p. 703. Habington, p. 474. Grafton, p. 732. Hist. Croyl. cont. p. 559. [m] Hall, fol. 240. [n] Ibid. 241.

sure

sure to the queen herself, as well as to his brother the duke of Glocester, a prince of the deepest policy, of the most unrelenting ambition, and the least scrupulous in the means which he employed for the attainment of his ends. A combination between these potent adversaries being secretly formed against Clarence, it was determined to begin by attacking his friends; in hopes, that if he patiently endured this injury, his pusillanimity would dishonour him in the eyes of the public; if he made resistance, and expressed resentment, his passion would betray him into measures which might give them advantages against him. The king, hunting one day in the park of Thomas Burdet of Arrow, in Warwickshire, had killed a white buck, which was a great favourite of the owner; and Burdet, vexed at the loss, broke into a passion, and wished the horns of the deer in the belly of the person who had advised the king to commit that insult upon him. This natural expression of resentment, which would have been overlooked or forgotten, had it fallen from any other person, was rendered criminal and capital in that gentleman, by the friendship in which he had the misfortune to live with the duke of Clarence: He was tried for his life; the judges and jury were found servile enough to condemn him; and he was publicly beheaded at Tyburn for this pretended offence[*]. About the same time, one John Stacey, an ecclesiastic, much connected with the duke, as well as with Burdet, was exposed to a like iniquitous and barbarous prosecution. This clergyman, being more learned in mathematics and astronomy than was usual in that age, lay under the imputation of necromancy with the ignorant vulgar; and the court laid hold of this popular rumour to effect his destruction. He was brought to his trial for that imaginary crime; many of the greatest peers

[*] Habington, p. 475. Hollingshed, p. 703. Sir Thomas More in Kennet, p. 498.

countenanced the profecution by their prefence; he was condemned, put to the torture, and executed [p].

The duke of Clarence was alarmed when he found thefe acts of tyranny exercifed on all around him: He reflected on the fate of the good duke of Glocefter in the laft reign, who, after feeing the moft infamous pretences employed for the deftruction of his neareft connections, at laft fell himfelf a victim to the vengeance of his enemies. But Clarence, inftead of fecuring his own life againft the prefent danger by filence and referve, was open and loud in juftifying the innocence of his friends, and in exclaiming againft the iniquity of their profecutors. The king, highly offended with his freedom, or ufing that pretence againft him, committed him to the Tower [q], fummoned a parliament, and tried him for his life before the houfe of peers, the fupreme tribunal of the nation.

The duke was accufed of arraigning public juftice, by maintaining the innocence of men who had been condemned in courts of judicature; and of inveighing againft the iniquity of the king, who had given orders for their profecution [r]. Many rafh expreffions were imputed to him, and fome too reflecting on Edward's legitimacy; but he was not accufed of any overt act of treafon; and even the truth of thefe fpeeches may be doubted of, fince the liberty of judgment was taken from the court, by the king's appearing perfonally as his brother's accufer [s], and pleading the caufe againft him. But a fentence of condemnation, even when this extraordinary circumftance had not place, was a neceffary confequence, in thofe times, of any profecution by the court or the prevailing party; and the duke of Clarence was pronounced guilty by the peers. The houfe of commons

[p] Hift. Croyl. cont. p. 561.   [q] Ibid. p. 562.   [r] Stowe, p. 430.   [s] Hift. Croyl. cont. p. 562.

commons were no less slavish and unjust: They both petitioned for the execution of the duke, and afterwards passed a bill of attainder against him [1]. The measures of the parliament, during that age, furnish us with examples of a strange contrast of freedom and servility: They scruple to grant, and sometimes refuse, to the king the smallest supplies, the most necessary for the support of government, even the most necessary for the maintenance of wars, for which the nation, as well as the parliament itself, expressed great fondness: But they never scruple to concur in the most flagrant act of injustice or tyranny, which falls on any individual, however distinguished by birth or merit. These maxims, so ungenerous, so opposite to all principles of good government, so contrary to the practice of present parliaments, are very remarkable in all the transactions of the English history, for more than a century after the period in which we are now engaged:

THE only favour which the king granted his brother, after his condemnation, was to leave him the choice of his death; and he was privately drowned in a butt of malmesey in the Tower: A whimsical choice, which implies that he had an extraordinary passion for that liquor. The duke left two children by the elder daughter of the earl of Warwic; a son, created an earl by his grandfather's title, and a daughter, afterwards countess of Salisbury. Both this prince and princess were also unfortunate in their end, and died a violent death; a fate which, for many years, attended almost all the descendants of the royal blood in England. There prevails a report, that a chief source of the violent prosecution of the duke of Clarence, whose name was George, was a current prophecy, that the king's son should be murdered by one, the initial letter of whose name was G [2]. It

[1] Stowe, p. 430. Hist. Croyl. cont. p. 562.
[2] Hall, fol. 139. Hollingshed, p. 703. Grafton, p. 741. Polyd. Virg. p. 537. Sir Thomas More in Kennet, p. 497.

is not impossible but, in those ignorant times, such a silly reason might have some influence: But it is more probable that the whole story is the invention of a subsequent period, and founded on the murder of these children by the duke of Glocester. Comines remarks, that, at that time, the English never were without some superstitious prophecy or other, by which they accounted for every event.

All the glories of Edward's reign terminated with the civil wars, where his laurels too were extremely sullied with blood, violence, and cruelty. His spirit seems afterwards to have been sunk in indolence and pleasure, or his measures were frustrated by imprudence and the want of foresight. There was no object on which he was more intent than to have all his daughters settled by splendid marriages, though most of these princesses were yet in their infancy, and though the completion of his views, it was obvious, must depend on numberless accidents, which were impossible to be foreseen or prevented. His eldest daughter, Elizabeth, was contracted to the dauphin; his second, Cicely, to the eldest son of James III. king of Scotland; his third, Anne, to Philip, only son of Maximilian and the duchess of Burgundy; his fourth, Catharine, to John, son and heir to Ferdinand, king of Arragon, and Isabella, queen of Castile*. None of these projected marriages took place; and the king himself saw, in his life-time, the rupture of the first, that with the dauphin, for which he had always discovered a peculiar fondness. Lewis, who paid no regard to treaties or engagements, found his advantage in contracting the dauphin to the princess Margaret, daughter of Maximilian; and the king, notwithstanding his indolence, prepared to revenge the indignity. The French monarch, eminent for prudence, as well as perfidy, endeavoured to guard against the blow; and, by a proper distribution of

* Rymer, vol. xi. p. 130.

presents

presents in the court of Scotland, he incited James to make war upon England. This prince, who lived on bad terms with his own nobility, and whose force was very unequal to the enterprize, levied an army; but when he was ready to enter England, the barons, conspiring against his favourites, put them to death without trial; and the army presently disbanded. The duke of Glocester, attended by the duke of Albany, James's brother, who had been banished his country, entered Scotland at the head of an army, took Berwick, and obliged the Scots to accept of a peace, by which they resigned that fortress to Edward. This success emboldened the king to think more seriously of a French war; but while he was making preparations for that enterprize, he was seized with a distemper, of which he expired in the forty-second year of his age, and the twenty-third of his reign: A prince more splendid and showy, than either prudent or virtuous; brave, though cruel; addicted to pleasure, though capable of activity in great emergencies; and less fitted to prevent ills by wise precautions, than to remedy them, after they took place, by his vigour and enterprize. Besides five daughters, this king left two sons; Edward, prince of Wales, his successor, then in his thirteenth year, and Richard, duke of York, in his ninth.

CHAP. XXII.

1482.

9th April. Death and character of Edward IV.

CHAP. XXIII.

EDWARD V. and RICHARD III.

Edward V.——State of the court——The earl of Rivers arrested——Duke of Glocester protector——Execution of Lord Hastings——The protector aims at the crown——Assumes the crown——Murder of Edward V. and of the duke of York——Richard III.——Duke of Buckingham discontented——The earl of Richmond——Buckingham executed——Invasion by the earl of Richmond——Battle of Bosworth——Death and character of Richard III.

EDWARD V.

DURING the later years of Edward IV. the nation having, in a great measure, forgotten the bloody feuds between the two roses, and peaceably acquiescing in the established government, was agitated only by some court-intrigues, which, being restrained by the authority of the king, seemed nowise to endanger the public tranquillity. These intrigues arose from the perpetual rivalship between two parties; one consisting of the queen and her relations, particularly the earl of Rivers, her brother, and the marquis of Dorset, her son; the other composed of the ancient nobility, who envied the sudden growth and unlimited credit of that aspiring family[a]. At the head of this latter party was the duke of Buckingham, a man of very noble birth, of ample possessions,

---

[a] Sir Thomas More, p. 481.

possessions, of great alliances, of shining parts; who, though he had married the queen's sister, was too haughty to act in subserviency to her inclinations, and aimed rather at maintaining an independent influence and authority. Lord Hastings, the chamberlain, was another leader of the same party; and as this nobleman had, by his bravery and activity, as well as by his approved fidelity, acquired the confidence and favour of his master, he had been able, though with some difficulty, to support himself against the credit of the queen. The lords Howard and Stanley maintained a connection with these two noblemen, and brought a considerable accession of influence and reputation to their party. All the other barons, who had no particular dependance on the queen, adhered to the same interest; and the people in general, from their natural envy against the prevailing power, bore great favour to the cause of these noblemen.

But Edward knew that, though he himself had been able to overawe those rival factions, many disorders might arise from their contests during the minority of his son; and he therefore took care, in his last illness, to summon together several of the leaders on both sides, and, by composing their ancient quarrels, to provide, as far as possible, for the future tranquillity of the government. After expressing his intentions that his brother, the duke of Glocester, then absent in the north, should be entrusted with the regency, he recommended to them peace and unanimity during the tender years of his son; represented to them the dangers which must attend the continuance of their animosities; and engaged them to embrace each other with all the appearance of the most cordial reconciliation. But this temporary or feigned agreement lasted no longer than the king's life. He had no sooner expired, than the jealousies of the parties broke out afresh: And each of them applied, by separate mes-

sages,

sages, to the duke of Glocester, and endeavoured to acquire his favour and friendship.

THIS prince, during his brother's reign, had endeavoured to live on good terms with both parties; and his high birth, his extensive abilities, and his great services, had enabled him to support himself without falling into a dependance on either. But the new situation of affairs, when the supreme power was devolved upon him, immediately changed his measures; and he secretly determined to preserve no longer that neutrality which he had hitherto maintained. His exorbitant ambition, unrestrained by any principle either of justice or humanity, made him carry his views to the possession of the crown itself; and as this object could not be attained without the ruin of the queen and her family, he fell, without hesitation, into concert with the opposite party. But being sensible, that the most profound dissimulation was requisite for effecting his criminal purposes, he redoubled his professions of zeal and attachment to that princess; and he gained such credit with her, as to influence her conduct in a point, which, as it was of the utmost importance, was violently disputed between the opposite factions.

THE young king, at the time of his father's death, resided in the castle of Ludlow, on the borders of Wales; whither he had been sent, that the influence of his presence might overawe the Welsh, and restore the tranquillity of that country, which had been disturbed by some late commotions. His person was committed to the care of his uncle, the earl of Rivers, the most accomplished nobleman in England, who, having united an uncommon taste for literature[y] to great abilities in business, and valour in the field, was entitled, by his

---

[y] This nobleman first introduced the noble art of printing into England. Caxton was recommended by him to the patronage of Edward IV. See Catalogue of Royal and Noble Authors.

talents,

talents, still more than by nearness of blood, to direct the
education of the young monarch. The queen, anxious
to preserve that ascendant over her son, which she had
long maintained over her husband, wrote to the earl of
Rivers, that he should levy a body of forces, in order to
escort the king to London, to protect him during his coronation, and to keep him from falling into the hands of
their enemies. The opposite faction, sensible that Edward was now of an age when great advantages could be
made of his name and countenance, and was approaching to the age when he would be legally intitled to
exert in person his authority, foresaw, that the tendency
of this measure was to perpetuate their subjection under
their rivals; and they vehemently opposed a resolution,
which they represented as the signal for renewing a civil
war in the kingdom. Lord Hastings threatened to depart
instantly to his government of Calais [a]: The other nobles
seemed resolute to oppose force by force: And as the
duke of Glocester, on pretence of pacifying the quarrel,
had declared against all appearance of an armed power,
which might be dangerous, and was nowise necessary,
the queen, trusting to the sincerity of his friendship, and
overawed by so violent an opposition, recalled her orders
to her brother, and desired him to bring up no greater
retinue than should be necessary to support the state and
dignity of the young sovereign [b].

THE duke of Glocester, mean while, set out from
York, attended by a numerous train of the northern gentry.
When he reached Northampton, he was joined by the
duke of Buckingham, who was also attended by a splendid retinue; and as he heard that the king was hourly
expected on that road, he resolved to await his arrival, under colour of conducting him thence in person to London.
The earl of Rivers, apprehensive that the place would be

[a] Hist. Croyl. cont. p. 564, 565. [b] Sir T. More, p. 483.

too narrow to contain so many attendants, sent his pupil forward by another road to Stony-Stratford; and came himself to Northampton, in order to apologize for this measure, and to pay his respects to the duke of Glocester. He was received with the greatest appearance of cordiality: He passed the evening in an amicable manner with Glocester and Buckingham: He proceeded on the road with them next day to join the king: But as he was entering Stony-Stratford, he was arrested by orders from the duke of Glocester[b]: Sir Richard Gray, one of the queen's sons, was at the same time put under a guard, together with Sir Thomas Vaughan, who possessed a considerable office in the king's household; and all the prisoners were instantly conducted to Pomfret. Glocester approached the young prince with the greatest demonstrations of respect; and endeavoured to satisfy him with regard to the violence committed on his uncle and brother: But Edward, much attached to these near relations, by whom he had been tenderly educated, was not such a master of dissimulation as to conceal his displeasure[c].

The people, however, were extremely rejoiced at this revolution; and the duke was received in London with the loudest acclamations: But the queen no sooner received intelligence of her brother's imprisonment, than she foresaw, that Glocester's violence would not stop there, and that her own ruin, if not that of all her children, was finally determined. She therefore fled into the sanctuary of Westminster, attended by the marquis of Dorset; and she carried thither the five princesses, together with the duke of York[d]. She trusted, that the ecclesiastical privileges, which had formerly, during the total ruin of her husband and family, given her pro-

[b] Hist. Croyl. cont. p. 564, 565.   [c] Sir T. More, p. 484.
[d] Hist. Croyl. cont. p. 565.

tection

tection against the fury of the Lancastrian faction, would not now be violated by her brother-in-law, while her son was on the throne; and she resolved to await there the return of better fortune. But Glocester, anxious to have the duke of York in his power, proposed to take him by force from the sanctuary; and he represented to the privy-council, both the indignity put upon the government by the queen's ill-grounded apprehensions, and the necessity of the young prince's appearance at the ensuing coronation of his brother. It was farther urged, that ecclesiastical privileges were originally intended only to give protection to unhappy men, persecuted for their debts or crimes; and were entirely useless to a person, who, by reason of his tender age, could lie under the burden of neither, and who, for the same reason, was utterly incapable of claiming security from any sanctuary. But the two archbishops, cardinal Bourchier the primate, and Rotherham archbishop of York, protesting against the sacrilege of this measure; it was agreed, that they should first endeavour to bring the queen to compliance by persuasion, before any violence should be employed against her. These prelates were persons of known integrity and honour; and being themselves entirely persuaded of the duke's good intentions, they employed every argument, accompanied with earnest entreaties, exhortations, and assurances, to bring her over to the same opinion. She long continued obstinate, and insisted, that the duke of York, by living in the sanctuary, was not only secure himself, but gave security to the king, whose life no one would dare to attempt, while his successor and avenger remained in safety. But finding, that none supported her in these sentiments, and that force, in case of refusal, was threatened by the council, she at last complied, and produced her son to the two prelates. She was here on a sudden struck with a kind of presage of his future fate: She tenderly embraced

CHAP. XXIII.
1483.

Duke of Glocester protector.

braced him; she bedewed him with her tears; and bidding him an eternal adieu, delivered him, with many expressions of regret and reluctance, into their custody [e].

THE duke of Glocester, being the nearest male of the royal family capable of exercising the government, seemed intitled, by the customs of the realm, to the office of protector; and the council, not waiting for the consent of parliament, made no scruple of investing him with that high dignity [f]. The general prejudice, entertained by the nobility against the queen and her kindred, occasioned this precipitation and irregularity; and no one foresaw any danger to the succession, much less to the lives of the young princes, from a measure so obvious and so natural. Besides that the duke had hitherto been able to cover, by the most profound dissimulation, his fierce and savage nature; the numerous issue of Edward, together with the two children of Clarence, seemed to be an eternal obstacle to his ambition; and it appeared equally impracticable for him to destroy so many persons possessed of a preferable title, and imprudent to exclude them. But a man, who had abandoned all principles of honour and humanity, was soon carried by his predominant passion beyond the reach of fear or precaution; and Glocester, having so far succeeded in his views, no longer hesitated in removing the other obstructions which lay between him and the throne. The death of the earl of Rivers, and of the other prisoners detained in Pomfret, was first determined; and he easily obtained the consent of the duke of Buckingham, as well as of lord Hastings, to this violent and sanguinary measure. However easy it was, in those times, to procure a sentence against the most innocent person, it appeared still more easy to dispatch an enemy, without any trial or form of process; and orders were accordingly issued to Sir Richard Ratcliffe, a proper instrument in the

[e] Sir T. More, p. 491. [f] Hist. Croyl. cont. p. 566.

hands

hands of this tyrant, to cut off the heads of the prisoners. The protector then assailed the fidelity of Buckingham by all the arguments capable of swaying a vicious mind, which knew no motive of action but interest and ambition. He represented, that the execution of persons so nearly related to the king, whom that prince so openly professed to love, and whose fate he so much resented, would never pass unpunished; and all the actors in that scene were bound in prudence to prevent the effects of his future vengeance: That it would be impossible to keep the queen for ever at a distance from her son, and equally impossible to prevent her from instilling into his tender mind the thoughts of retaliating, by like executions, the sanguinary insults committed on her family: That the only method of obviating these mischiefs was to put the sceptre in the hands of a man, of whose friendship the duke might be assured, and whose years and experience taught him to pay respect to merit and to the rights of ancient nobility: And that the same necessity, which had carried them so far in resisting the usurpation of these intruders, must justify them in attempting farther innovations, and in making, by national consent, a new settlement of the succession. To these reasons, he added the offers of great private advantages to the duke of Buckingham; and he easily obtained from him a promise of supporting him in all his enterprizes.

THE duke of Glocester, knowing the importance of gaining lord Hastings, sounded at a distance his sentiments, by means of Catesby, a lawyer, who lived in great intimacy with that nobleman; but found him impregnable in his allegiance and fidelity to the children of Edward, who had ever honoured him with his friendship[s]. He saw, therefore, that there were no longer any measures

[s] Sir T. More, p. 495.

CHAP. XXIII.

1483. 13th June.

to be kept with him; and he determined to ruin utterly the man, whom he despaired of engaging to concur in his usurpation. On the very day when Rivers, Gray, and Vaughan were executed, or rather murdered, at Pomfret, by the advice of Hastings, the protector summoned a council in the Tower; whither that nobleman, suspecting no design against him, repaired without hesitation. The duke of Glocester was capable of committing the most bloody and treacherous murders with the utmost coolness and indifference. On taking his place at the council-table, he appeared in the easiest and most jovial humour imaginable. He seemed to indulge himself in familiar conversation with the counsellors, before they should enter on business; and having paid some compliments to Morton, bishop of Ely, on the good and early strawberries which he raised in his garden at Holborn, he begged the favour of having a dish of them, which that prelate immediately dispatched a servant to bring to him. The protector then left the council, as if called away by some other business; but soon after returning with an angry and inflamed countenance, he asked them, what punishment those deserved that had plotted against *his* life, who was so nearly related to the king, and was entrusted with the administration of government? Hastings replied, that they merited the punishment of traitors. *These traitors*, cried the protector, *are the sorceress, my brother's wife, and Jane Shore, his mistress, with others, their associates: See to what a condition they have reduced me by their incantations and witchcraft*: Upon which he laid bare his arm, all shrivelled and decayed. But the counsellors, who knew that this infirmity had attended him from his birth, looked on each other with amazement; and above all, lord Hastings, who, as he had, since Edward's death, engaged in an intrigue with Jane Shore[b], was naturally anxious con-

[b] See note [K] at the end of the volume.

cerning

EDWARD V.

cerning the iſſue of theſe extraordinary proceedings. Certainly, my lord, ſaid he, if they be guilty of theſe crimes, they deſerve the ſevereſt puniſhment. And do you reply to me, exclaimed the protector, with your ifs and your ands? You are the chief abettor of that witch, Shore: You are yourſelf a traitor: And I ſwear by St. Paul, that I will not dine before your head be brought me. He ſtruck the table with his hand: Armed men ruſhed in at the ſignal: The counſellors were thrown into the utmoſt conſternation: And one of the guards, as if by accident or miſtake, aimed a blow with a poll-ax at lord Stanley, who, aware of the danger, ſlunk under the table; and though he ſaved his life, received a ſevere wound in the head, in the protector's preſence. Haſtings was ſeized, was hurried away, and inſtantly beheaded on a timber-log, which lay in the court of the Tower[i]. Two hours after, a proclamation, well penned and fairly written, was read to the citizens of London, enumerating his offences, and apologizing to them, from the ſuddenneſs of the diſcovery, for the ſudden execution of that nobleman, who was very popular among them: But the ſaying of a merchant was much talked of on the occaſion, who remarked, that the proclamation was certainly drawn by the ſpirit of prophecy[k].

LORD Stanley, the archbiſhop of York, the biſhop of Ely, and other counſellors, were committed priſoners in different chambers of the Tower: And the protector, in order to carry on the farce of his accuſations, ordered the goods of Jane Shore to be ſeized; and he ſummoned her to anſwer before the council for ſorcery and witchcraft. But as no proofs, which could be received even in that ignorant age, were produced againſt her, he directed her to be tried in the ſpiritual court, for her adulteries and lewdneſs; and ſhe did penance in a white ſheet at St. Paul's,

CHAP. XXI.
1483.

Execution of lord Haſtings.

[i] Hiſt. Croyl. cont. p. 566.   [k] Sir T. More, p. 496.

CHAP.
XXIII.

1483.

before the whole people. This lady was born of reputable parents in London, was well educated, and married to a substantial citizen; but unhappily, views of interest, more than the maid's inclinations, had been consulted in the match, and her mind, though framed for virtue, had proved unable to resist the allurements of Edward, who solicited her favours. But while seduced from her duty by this gay and amorous monarch, she still made herself respectable by her other virtues; and the ascendant, which her charms and vivacity long maintained over him, was all employed in acts of beneficence and humanity. She was still forward to oppose calumny, to protect the oppressed, to relieve the indigent; and her good offices, the genuine dictates of her heart, never waited the solicitation of presents, or the hopes of reciprocal services. But she lived not only to feel the bitterness of shame imposed on her by this tyrant, but to experience, in old age and poverty, the ingratitude of those courtiers, who had long solicited her friendship, and been protected by her credit. No one, among the great multitudes whom she had obliged, had the humanity to bring her consolation or relief: She languished out her life in solitude and indigence: And amidst a court, inured to the most atrocious crimes, the frailties of this woman justified all violations of friendship towards her, and all neglect of former obligations.

The protector aims at the crown.

THESE acts of violence, exercised against all the nearest connexions of the late king, prognosticated the severest fate to his defenceless children; and after the murder of Hastings, the protector no longer made a secret of his intentions to usurp the crown. The licentious life of Edward, who was not restrained in his pleasures either by honour or prudence, afforded a pretence for declaring his marriage with the queen invalid, and all his posterity illegitimate. It was asserted, that, before espousing the lady Elizabeth

Elizabeth Gray, he had paid court to the lady Eleanor Talbot, daughter of the earl of Shrewsbury; and being repulsed by the virtue of that lady, he was obliged, ere he could gratify his desires, to consent to a private marriage, without any witnesses, by Stillington, bishop of Bath, who afterwards divulged the secret [1]. It was also maintained, that the act of attainder, passed against the duke of Clarence, had virtually incapacitated his children from succeeding to the crown; and these two families being set aside, the protector remained the only true and legitimate heir of the house of York. But as it would be difficult, if not impossible, to prove the preceding marriage of the late king; and as the rule, which excludes the heirs of an attainted blood from private successions, was never extended to the crown; the protector resolved to make use of another plea still more shameful and scandalous. His partizans were taught to maintain, that both Edward IV. and the duke of Clarence were illegitimate; that the duchess of York had received different lovers into her bed, who were the fathers of these children; that their resemblance to those gallants was a sufficient proof of their spurious birth; and that the duke of Glocester alone, of all her sons, appeared, by his features and countenance, to be the true offspring of the duke of York. Nothing can be imagined more impudent than this assertion, which threw so foul an imputation on his own mother, a princess of irreproachable virtue, and then alive; yet the place chosen for first promulgating it was the pulpit, before a large congregation, and in the protector's presence. Dr. Shaw was appointed to preach in St. Paul's; and having chosen this passage for his text, *Bastard slips shall not thrive*; he enlarged on all the topics which could discredit the birth of Edward IV. the duke of Clarence, and of all their children. He then broke

[1] Hist. Croyl. cont. p. 567. Comines. Sir Thomas More, p. 482.

out

out in a panegyric on the duke of Glocester; and exclaimed, "Behold this excellent prince, the express image "of his noble father, the genuine descendant of the "house of York; bearing, no less in the virtues of his "mind, than in the features of his countenance, the cha-"racter of the gallant Richard, once your hero and fa-"vourite: He alone is entitled to your allegiance: He "must deliver you from the dominion of all intruders: "He alone can restore the lost glory and honour of the "nation." It was previously concerted, that, as the doctor should pronounce these words, the duke of Glocester should enter the church; and it was expected that the audience would cry out, *God save King Richard!* which would immediately have been laid hold of as a popular consent, and interpreted to be the voice of the nation: But by a ridiculous mistake, worthy of the whole scene, the duke did not appear, till after this exclamation was already recited by the preacher. The doctor was therefore obliged to repeat his rhetorical figure out of its proper place: The audience, less from the absurd conduct of the discourse, than from their detestation of these proceedings, kept a profound silence: And the protector and his preacher were equally abashed at the ill success of their stratagem.

But the duke was too far advanced to recede from his criminal and ambitious purpose. A new expedient was tried to work on the people. The mayor, who was brother to Dr. Shaw, and entirely in the protector's interests, called an assembly of the citizens; where the duke of Buckingham, who possessed some talents for eloquence, harangued them on the protector's title to the crown, and displayed those numerous virtues, of which, he pretended, that prince was possessed. He next asked them, whether they would have the duke for king? and then stopped, in expectation of hearing the cry, *God save King Richard!*

He

He was surprized to observe them silent; and, turning about to the mayor, asked him the reason. The mayor replied, that perhaps they did not understand him. Buckingham then repeated his discourse with some variation; inforced the same topics, asked the same question, and was received with the same silence. "I now see the "cause," said the mayor; "the citizens are not accustomed to be harangued by any but their recorder; and "know not how to answer a person of your grace's "quality." The recorder, Fitz-Williams, was then commanded to repeat the substance of the duke's speech; but the man, who was averse to the office, took care, throughout his whole discourse, to have it understood that he spoke nothing of himself, and that he only conveyed to them the sense of the duke of Buckingham. Still the audience kept a profound silence: "This is wonderful "obstinacy," cried the duke: "Express your meaning, my "friends, one way or other: When we apply to you on "this occasion, it is merely from the regard which we "bear to you. The lords and commons have sufficient "authority, without your consent, to appoint a king: "But I require you here to declare, in plain terms, "whether or not you will have the duke of Glocester "for your sovereign?" After all these efforts, some of the meanest apprentices, incited by the protector's and Buckingham's servants, raised a feeble cry, *God save King Richard*[m]*!* The sentiments of the nation were now sufficiently declared: The voice of the people was the voice of God: And Buckingham, with the mayor, hastened to Baynard's castle, where the protector then resided, that they might make him a tender of the crown.

WHEN Richard was told that a great multitude was in the court, he refused to appear to them, and pretended to be apprehensive for his personal safety: A circumstance

[m] Sir Thomas More, p. 496.

CHAP. XXIII.
1483.

taken notice of by Buckingham, who observed to the citizens, that the prince was ignorant of the whole design. At last he was persuaded to step forth, but he still kept at some distance; and he asked the meaning of their intrusion and importunity. Buckingham told him that the nation was resolved to have him for king: The protector declared his purpose of maintaining his loyalty to the present sovereign, and exhorted them to adhere to the same resolution. He was told that the people had determined to have another prince; and if he rejected their unanimous voice, they must look out for one who would be more compliant. This argument was too powerful to be resisted: He was prevailed on to accept of the crown: And he thenceforth acted as legitimate and rightful sovereign.

The protector assumes the throne.

Murder of Edward V. and of the duke of York.

THIS ridiculous farce was soon after followed by a scene truly tragical: The murder of the two young princes. Richard gave orders to Sir Robert Brakenbury, constable of the Tower, to put his nephews to death; but this gentleman, who had sentiments of honour, refused to have any hand in the infamous office. The tyrant then sent for Sir James Tyrrel, who promised obedience; and he ordered Brakenbury to resign to this gentleman the keys and government of the Tower for one night. Tyrrel, chusing three associates, Slater, Dighton, and Forest, came in the night-time to the door of the chamber where the princes were lodged; and sending in the assassins, he bade them execute their commission, while he himself staid without. They found the young princes in bed, and fallen into a profound sleep. After suffocating them with the bolster and pillows, they shewed their naked bodies to Tyrrel, who ordered them to be buried at the foot of the stairs, deep in the ground, under a heap of stones[a]. These circumstances were all confessed by the actors in the following reign; and they were never

[a] Sir T. More, p. 501.

punished

punished for the crime: Probably, because Henry, whose maxims of government were extremely arbitrary, desired to establish it as a principle, that the commands of the reigning sovereign ought to justify every enormity in those who paid obedience to them. But there is one circumstance not so easy to be accounted for: It is pretended that Richard, displeased with the indecent manner of burying his nephews, whom he had murdered, gave his chaplain orders to dig up the bodies, and to inter them in consecrated ground; and, as the man died soon after, the place of their burial remained unknown, and the bodies could never be found by any search which Henry could make for them. Yet, in the reign of Charles II. when there was occasion to remove some stones, and to dig in the very spot which was mentioned as the place of their first interment, the bones of two persons were there found, which, by their size, exactly corresponded to the age of Edward and his brother: They were concluded, with certainty, to be the remains of those princes, and were interred under a marble monument, by orders of king Charles°. Perhaps Richard's chaplain had died before he found an opportunity of executing his master's commands; and the bodies being supposed to be already removed, a diligent search was not made for them by Henry in the place where they had been buried.

° Kennet, p. 551.

RICHARD III.

CHAP. XXIII.
1483.

THE first acts of Richard's administration were to bestow rewards on those who had assisted him in usurping the crown, and to gain, by favours, those who, he thought, were best able to support his future government. Thomas, lord Howard, was created duke of Norfolk; Sir Thomas Howard, his son, earl of Surry; lord Lovel, a viscount, by the same name; even lord Stanley was set at liberty, and made steward of the household. This nobleman had become obnoxious by his first opposition to Richard's views, and also by his marrying the countess dowager of Richmond, heir of the Somerset family; but, sensible of the necessity of submitting to the present government, he feigned such zeal for Richard's service, that he was received into favour, and even found means to be entrusted with the most important commands by that politic and jealous tyrant.

But the person who, both from the greatness of his services, and the power and splendor of his family, was best entitled to favours under the new government, was the duke of Buckingham; and Richard seemed determined to spare no pains or bounty in securing him to his interests. Buckingham was descended from a daughter of Thomas of Woodstock, duke of Glocester, uncle to Richard II. and by this pedigree, he not only was allied to the royal family, but had claims for dignities, as well as estates, of a very extensive nature. The duke of Glocester, and Henry earl of Derby, afterwards Henry IV. had married the two daughters and co-heirs of Bohun earl of Hereford, one of the greatest of the ancient barons, whose immense property came thus to be divided into two shares. One was inherited by the family of Buckingham;

# RICHARD III.

Buckingham; the other was united to the crown by the house of Lancaster, and, after the attainder of that royal line, was seized, as legally devolved to them, by the sovereigns of the house of York. The duke of Buckingham laid hold of the present opportunity, and claimed the restitution of that portion of the Hereford estate which had escheated to the crown, as well as of the great office of constable, which had long continued, by inheritance, in his ancestors of that family. Richard readily complied with these demands, which were probably the price stipulated to Buckingham for his assistance in promoting the usurpation. That nobleman was invested with the office of constable; he received a grant of the estate of Hereford [p], many other dignities and honours were conferred upon him; and the king thought himself sure of preserving the fidelity of a man, whose interests seemed so closely connected with those of the present government.

BUT it was impossible that friendship could long remain inviolate between two men of such corrupt minds as Richard and the duke of Buckingham. Historians ascribe their first rupture to the king's refusal of making restitution of the Hereford estate; but it is certain, from records, that he passed a grant for that purpose, and that the full demands of Buckingham were satisfied in this particular. Perhaps Richard was soon sensible of the danger which might ensue from conferring such an immense property on a man of so turbulent a disposition, and afterwards raised difficulties about the execution of his own grant: Perhaps he refused some other demands of Buckingham, whom he found it impossible to gratify for his past services: Perhaps he resolved, according to the usual maxim of politicians, to seize the first opportunity of ruining this powerful subject, who had been the principal instrument of his own elevation; and the discovery

CHAP. XXIII.
1483.

Duke of Buckingham discontented.

[p] Dugdale's Baron. vol. I. p. 168, 169.

CHAP. of this intention begat the first discontent in the duke of
XXIII. Buckingham. However this may be, it is certain that
1483. the duke, soon after Richard's accession, began to form a
conspiracy against the government, and attempted to
overthrow that usurpation which he himself had so zealously contributed to establish.

NEVER was there in any country an usurpation more
flagrant than that of Richard, or more repugnant to every
principle of justice and public interest. His claim was
entirely founded on impudent allegations, never attempted
to be proved, some of them incapable of proof, and all
of them implying scandalous reflections on his own family, and on the persons with whom he was the most
nearly connected. His title was never acknowledged by
any national assembly, scarcely even by the lowest populace to whom he appealed; and it had become prevalent,
merely for want of some person of distinction who might
stand forth against him, and give a voice to those sentiments of general detestation which arose in every bosom.
Were men disposed to pardon these violations of public
right, the sense of private and domestic duty, which is
not to be effaced in the most barbarous times, must have
begotten an abhorrence against him; and have represented
the murder of the young and innocent princes, his nephews, with whose protection he had been entrusted, in
the most odious colours imaginable. To endure such a
bloody usurper, seemed to draw disgrace upon the nation,
and to be attended with immediate danger to every individual who was distinguished by birth, merit, or services. Such was become the general voice of the people;
all parties were united in the same sentiments; and the
Lancastrians, so long oppressed, and, of late, so much
discredited, felt their blasted hopes again revive, and anxiously expected the consequences of these extraordinary
events. The duke of Buckingham, whose family had
been

RICHARD III.

been devoted to that interest, and who, by his mother, a daughter of Edmund duke of Somerset, was allied to the house of Lancaster, was easily induced to espouse the cause of this party, and to endeavour the restoring of it to its ancient superiority. Morton, bishop of Ely, a zealous Lancastrian, whom the king had imprisoned, and had afterwards committed to the custody of Buckingham, encouraged these sentiments; and, by his exhortations, the duke cast his eye towards the young earl of Richmond, as the only person who could free the nation from the tyranny of the present usurper[q].

CHAP. XXIII.
1483.

HENRY, earl of Richmond, was at this time detained in a kind of honourable custody by the duke of Britanny; and his descent, which seemed to give him some pretensions to the crown, had been a great object of jealousy both in the late and in the present reign. John, the first duke of Somerset, who was grandson of John of Gaunt by a spurious branch, but legitimated by act of parliament, had left only one daughter, Margaret; and his younger brother, Edmund, had succeeded him in his titles, and in a considerable part of his fortune. Margaret had espoused Edmund, earl of Richmond, half-brother of Henry VI. and son of Sir Owen Tudor and Catharine of France, relict of Henry V. and she bore him only one son, who received the name of Henry, and who, after his father's death, inherited the honours and fortune of Richmond. His mother, being a widow, had espoused, in second marriage, Sir Henry Stafford, uncle to Buckingham, and, after the death of that gentleman, had married lord Stanley; but had no children by either of these husbands; and her son, Henry, was thus, in the event of her death, the sole heir of all her fortunes. But this was not the most considerable advantage which he had reason to expect from her succession: He would represent

The earl of Richmond.

[q] Hist. Croyl. coar. p. 568.

the elder branch of the house of Somerset; he would inherit all the title of that family to the crown; and though its claim, while any legitimate branch subsisted of the house of Lancaster, had always been much disregarded, the zeal of faction, after the death of Henry VI. and the murder of prince Edward, immediately conferred a weight and consideration upon it.

EDWARD IV. finding that all the Lancastrians had turned their attention towards the young earl of Richmond, as the object of their hopes, thought him also worthy of his attention; and pursued him into his retreat in Britanny, whither his uncle, the earl of Pembroke, had carried him, after the battle of Teukesbury, so fatal to his party. He applied to Francis II. duke of Britanny, who was his ally, a weak but a good prince; and urged him to deliver up this fugitive, who might be the source of future disturbances in England: But the duke, averse to so dishonourable a proposal, would only consent, that, for the security of Edward, the young nobleman should be detained in custody; and he received an annual pension from England for the safe-keeping or the subsistence of his prisoner. But, towards the end of Edward's reign, when the kingdom was menaced with a war both from France and Scotland, the anxieties of the English court, with regard to Henry, were much encreased; and Edward made a new proposal to the duke, which covered, under the fairest appearances, the most bloody and treacherous intentions. He pretended that he was desirous of gaining his enemy, and of uniting him to his own family by a marriage with his daughter Elizabeth; and he solicited to have him sent over to England, in order to execute a scheme which would redound so much to his advantage. These pretences, seconded, as is supposed, by bribes to Peter Landais, a corrupt minister, by whom the duke was entirely governed, gained credit with the court of Britanny:

Henry

Henry was delivered into the hands of the English agents: He was ready to embark: When a suspicion of Edward's real design was suggested to the duke, who recalled his orders, and thus saved the unhappy youth from the imminent danger which hung over him.

THESE symptoms of continued jealousy in the reigning family of England, both seemed to give some authority to Henry's pretensions, and made him the object of general favour and compassion, on account of the dangers and persecutions to which he was exposed. The universal detestation of Richard's conduct turned still more the attention of the nation towards Henry; and as all the descendants of the house of York were either women or minors, he seemed to be the only person from whom the nation could expect the expulsion of the odious and bloody tyrant. But, notwithstanding these circumstances which were so favourable to him, Buckingham and the bishop of Ely well knew that there would still lie many obstacles in his way to the throne; and that, though the nation had been much divided between Henry VI. and the duke of York, while present possession and hereditary right stood in opposition to each other; yet, as soon as these titles were united in Edward IV. the bulk of the people had come over to the reigning family; and the Lancastrians had extremely decayed, both in numbers and in authority. It was therefore suggested by Morton, and readily assented to by the duke, that the only means of overturning the present usurpation, was to unite the opposite factions, by contracting a marriage between the earl of Richmond and the princess Elizabeth, eldest daughter of king Edward, and thereby blending together the opposite pretensions of their families, which had so long been the source of public disorders and convulsions. They were sensible that the people were extremely desirous of repose, after so many bloody and destructive commotions; that both Yorkists

CHAP. XXIII.
1483.

Yorkists and Lancastrians, who now lay equally under oppression, would embrace this scheme with ardour; and that the prospect of reconciling the two parties, which was in itself so desirable an end, would, when added to the general hatred against the present government, render their cause absolutely invincible. In consequence of these views, the prelate, by means of Reginald Bray, steward to the countess of Richmond, first opened the project of such an union to that lady; and the plan appeared so advantageous for her son, and, at the same time, so likely to succeed, that it admitted not of the least hesitation. Dr. Lewis, a Welsh physician, who had access to the queen-dowager in her sanctuary, carried the proposals to her; and found, that revenge for the murder of her brother and of her three sons, apprehensions for her surviving family, and indignation against her confinement, easily overcame all her prejudices against the house of Lancaster, and procured her approbation of a marriage to which the age and birth, as well as the present situation of the parties, seemed so naturally to invite them. She secretly borrowed a sum of money in the city, sent it over to the earl of Richmond, required his oath to celebrate the marriage as soon as he should arrive in England, advised him to levy as many foreign forces as possible, and promised to join him, on his first appearance, with all the friends and partizans of her family.

THE plan being thus laid upon the solid foundations of good sense and sound policy, it was secretly communicated to the principal persons of both parties in all the counties of England; and a wonderful alacrity appeared in every order of men to forward its success and completion. But it was impossible that so extensive a conspiracy could be conducted in so secret a manner as entirely to escape the jealous and vigilant eye of Richard; and he soon received intelligence that his enemies,

RICHARD III.

mies, headed by the duke of Buckingham, were forming some design against his authority. He immediately put himself in a posture of defence by levying troops in the North; and he summoned the duke to appear at court, in such terms as seemed to promise him a renewal of their former amity. But that nobleman, well acquainted with the barbarity and treachery of Richard, replied only by taking arms in Wales, and giving the signal to his accomplices for a general insurrection in all parts of England. But at that very time there happened to fall such heavy rains, so incessant and continued, as exceeded any known in the memory of man; and the Severne, with the other rivers in that neighbourhood, swelled to a height which rendered them impassable, and prevented Buckingham from marching into the heart of England to join his associates. The Welshmen, partly moved by superstition at this extraordinary event, partly distressed by famine in their camp, fell off from him; and Buckingham, finding himself deserted by his followers, put on a disguise, and took shelter in the house of Banister, an old servant of his family. But being detected in his retreat, he was brought to the king at Salisbury; and was instantly executed, according to the summary method practised in that age[f]. The other conspirators, who took arms in four different places, at Exeter, at Salisbury, at Newbury, and at Maidstone, hearing of the duke of Buckingham's misfortunes, despaired of success, and immediately dispersed themselves.

CHAP. XXIII.
1483.

October.

Buckingham executed.

The marquis of Dorset and the bishop of Ely made their escape beyond sea: Many others were equally fortunate: Several fell into Richard's hands, of whom he made some examples. His executions seem not to have been remarkably severe; though we are told of one gentleman,

[f] Hist. Croyl. cont. p. 568.

VOL. III. U William

CHAP.
XXIII.

1483.

William Colingbourne, who suffered under colour of this rebellion, but in reality for a distich of quibbling verses, which he had composed against Richard and his ministers'. The earl of Richmond, in concert with his friends, had set sail from St. Malo's, carrying on board a body of 5000 men, levied in foreign parts; but his fleet being at first driven back by a storm, he appeared not on the coast of England till after the dispersion of all his friends; and he found himself obliged to return to the court of Britanny.

1484.
7 jd ol Jan.

THE king, every where triumphant, and fortified by this unsuccessful attempt to dethrone him, ventured at last to summon a parliament; a measure which his crimes and flagrant usurpation had induced him hitherto to decline. Though it was natural that the parliament, in a contest of national parties, should always adhere to the victor, he seems to have apprehended, lest his title, founded on no principle, and supported by no party, might be rejected by that assembly. But his enemies being now at his feet, the parliament had no choice left but to recognize his authority, and acknowledge his right to the crown. His only son, Edward, then a youth of twelve years of age, was created prince of Wales: The duties of tonnage and poundage were granted to the king for life: And Richard, in order to reconcile the nation to his government, passed some popular laws, particularly one against the late practice of extorting money on pretence of benevolence.

ALL the other measures of the king tended to the same object. Sensible, that the only circumstance which could

'The lines were:
The Rat, the Cat, and Lovel that Dog,
Rule all England under the Hog.
Alluding to the names of Ratcliffe and Catesby; and to Richard's arms, which were a boar.

give

give him security, was to gain the confidence of the Yorkists, he paid court to the queen-dowager with such art and address, made such earnest protestations of his sincere good-will and friendship, that this princess, tired of confinement, and despairing of any success from her former projects, ventured to leave her sanctuary, and to put herself and her daughters into the hands of the tyrant. But he soon carried farther his views for the establishment of his throne. He had married Anne, the second daughter of the earl of Warwic, and widow of Edward prince of Wales, whom Richard himself had murdered; but this princess having born him but one son, who died about this time, he considered her as an invincible obstacle to the settlement of his fortune, and he was believed to have carried her off by poison; a crime for which the public could not be supposed to have any solid proof, but which the usual tenor of his conduct made it reasonable to suspect. He now thought it in his power to remove the chief perils which threatened his government. The earl of Richmond, he knew, could never be formidable but from his projected marriage with the princess Elizabeth, the true heir of the crown; and he therefore intended, by means of a papal dispensation, to espouse, himself, this princess, and thus to unite in his own family their contending titles. The queen-dowager, eager to recover her lost authority, neither scrupled this alliance, which was very unusual in England, and was regarded as incestuous; nor felt any horror at marrying her daughter to the murderer of her three sons and of her brother: She even joined so far her interests with those of the usurper, that she wrote to all her partizans, and, among the rest, to her son, the marquis of Dorset, desiring them to withdraw from the earl of Richmond; an injury which the earl could never afterwards forgive: The court of Rome was applied to for a dispensation:

CHAP.
XXIII.

1484

Richard thought that he could easily defend himself during the interval, till it arrived; and he had afterwards the agreeable prospect of a full and secure settlement. He flattered himself that the English nation, seeing all danger removed of a disputed succession, would then acquiesce under the dominion of a prince, who was of mature years, of great abilities, and of a genius qualified for government; and that they would forgive him all the crimes which he had committed, in paving his way to the throne.

But the crimes of Richard were so horrid and so shocking to humanity, that the natural sentiments of men, without any political or public views, were sufficient to render his government unstable; and every person of probity and honour was earnest to prevent the sceptre from being any longer polluted by that bloody and faithless hand which held it. All the exiles flocked to the earl of Richmond in Britanny, and exhorted him to hasten his attempt for a new invasion, and to prevent the marriage of the princess Elizabeth, which must prove fatal to all his hopes. The earl, sensible of the urgent necessity, but dreading the treachery of Peter Landais, who had entered into a negociation with Richard for betraying him, was obliged to attend only to his present safety; and he made his escape to the court of France. The ministers of Charles VIII. who had now succeeded to the throne after the death of his father Lewis, gave him countenance and protection; and being desirous of raising disturbance to Richard, they secretly encouraged the earl in the levies which he made for the support of his enterprize upon England. The earl of Oxford, whom Richard's suspicions had thrown into confinement, having made his escape, here joined Henry; and inflamed his ardour for the attempt, by the favourable accounts which he brought of the dispositions of the English

RICHARD III.

CHAP. XXIII.

tish nation, and their universal hatred of Richard's crimes and usurpation.

1485. Invasion by the earl of Richmond. 7th August.

THE earl of Richmond set sail from Harfleur in Normandy with a small army of about 2000 men; and after a navigation of six days, he arrived at Milford-haven in Wales, where he landed without opposition. He directed his course to that part of the kingdom, in hopes that the Welsh, who regarded him as their countryman, and who had been already prepossessed in favour of his cause by means of the duke of Buckingham, would join his standard, and enable him to make head against the established government. Richard, who knew not in what quarter he might expect the invader, had taken post at Nottingham, in the centre of the kingdom; and having given commissions to different persons in the several counties, whom he empowered to oppose his enemy, he purposed in person to fly, on the first alarm, to the place exposed to danger. Sir Rice ap Thomas and Sir Walter Herbert were entrusted with his authority in Wales; but the former immediately deserted to Henry; the second made but feeble opposition to him: And the earl, advancing towards Shrewsbury, received every day some reinforcement from his partizans. Sir Gilbert Talbot joined him with all the vassals and retainers of the family of Shrewsbury: Sir Thomas Bourchier, and Sir Walter Hungerford, brought their friends to share his fortunes; and the appearance of men of distinction in his camp made already his cause wear a favourable aspect.

BUT the danger, to which Richard was chiefly exposed, proceeded not so much from the zeal of his open enemies, as from the infidelity of his pretended friends. Scarce any nobleman of distinction was sincerely attached to his cause, except the duke of Norfolk; and all

CHAP. XXIII.

1485.

those who feigned the most loyalty, were only watching for an opportunity to betray and desert him. But the persons, of whom he entertained the greatest suspicion, were lord Stanley and his brother Sir William; whose connexions with the family of Richmond, notwithstanding their professions of attachment to his person, were never entirely forgotten or overlooked by him. When he empowered lord Stanley to levy forces, he still retained his eldest son, lord Strange, as a pledge for his fidelity; and that nobleman was, on this account, obliged to employ great caution and reserve in his proceedings. He raised a powerful body of his friends and retainers in Cheshire and Lancashire, but without openly declaring himself: And though Henry had received secret assurances of his friendly intentions, the armies on both sides knew not what to infer from his equivocal behaviour. The two rivals, at last, approached each other, at Bosworth, near Leicester; Henry, at the head of six thousand men, Richard with an army of above double the number; and a decisive action was every hour expected between them. Stanley, who commanded above seven thousand men, took care to post himself at Atherstone, not far from the hostile camps; and he made such a disposition as enabled him on occasion to join either party. Richard had too much sagacity not to discover his intentions from those movements; but he kept the secret from his own men for fear of discouraging them: He took not immediate revenge on Stanley's son, as some of his courtiers advised him; because he hoped that so valuable a pledge would induce the father to prolong still farther his ambiguous conduct: And he hastened to decide by arms the quarrel with his competitor; being certain, that a victory over the earl of Richmond would enable him to take ample revenge on all his enemies, open and concealed.

21st August. Battle of Bosworth.

THE

RICHARD III.

THE van of Richmond's army, consisting of archers, was commanded by the earl of Oxford: Sir Gilbert Talbot led the right wing; Sir John Savage the left: The earl himself, accompanied by his uncle, the earl of Pembroke, placed himself in the main body. Richard also took post in his main body, and entrusted the command of his van to the duke of Norfolk: As his wings were never engaged, we have not learned the names of the several commanders. Soon after the battle began, lord Stanley, whose conduct in this whole affair discovers great precaution and abilities, appeared in the field, and declared for the earl of Richmond. This measure, which was unexpected to the men, though not to their leaders, had a proportional effect on both armies: It inspired unusual courage into Henry's soldiers; it threw Richard's into dismay and confusion. The intrepid tyrant, sensible of his desperate situation, cast his eye around the field, and descrying his rival at no great distance, he drove against him with fury, in hopes that either Henry's death or his own would decide the victory between them. He killed with his own hands Sir William Brandon, standard-bearer to the earl: He dismounted Sir John Cheyney: He was now within reach of Richmond himself, who declined not the combat; when Sir William Stanley, breaking in with his troops, surrounded Richard, who, fighting bravely to the last moment, was overwhelmed by numbers, and perished by *Death*, a fate too mild and honourable for his multiplied and detestable enormities. His men every where fought for safety by flight.

THERE fell in this battle about four thousand of the vanquished; and among these the duke of Norfolk, lord Ferrers of Chartley, Sir Richard Ratcliffe, Sir Robert Piercy, and Sir Robert Brackenbury. The loss was inconsiderable on the side of the victors. Sir William Catesby, a great instrument of Richard's crimes, was taken,

CHAP. XXIII.

1485.

taken, and soon after beheaded, with some others, at Leicester. The body of Richard was found in the field, covered with dead enemies, and all besmeared with blood: It was thrown carelesly across a horse; was carried to Leicester amidst the shouts of the insulting spectators; and was interred in the Gray-Friars church of that place.

and character of Richard III.

THE historians who favour Richard (for even this tyrant has met with partizans among the later writers) maintain, that he was well qualified for government, had he legally obtained it; and that he committed no crimes but such as were necessary to procure him possession of the crown: But this is a poor apology, when it is confessed that he was ready to commit the most horrid crimes which appeared necessary for that purpose; and it is certain, that all his courage and capacity, qualities in which he really seems not to have been deficient, would never have made compensation to the people for the danger of the precedent, and for the contagious example of vice and murder, exalted upon the throne. This prince was of a small stature, humpbacked, and had a harsh disagreeable countenance; so that his body was in every particular no less deformed than his mind.

* * * * * *

THUS have we pursued the history of England through a series of many barbarous ages; till we have at last reached the dawn of civility and science, and have the prospect, both of greater certainty in our historical narrations, and of being able to present to the reader a spectacle more worthy of his attention. The want of certainty, however, and of circumstances, is not alike to be complained of throughout every period of this long narration. This Island possesses many ancient historians of good credit; as well as many historical monuments; and it is rare, that

that the annals of so uncultivated a people, as were the English as well as the other European nations, after the decline of Roman learning, have been transmitted to posterity so complete, and with so little mixture of falsehood and of fable. This advantage we owe entirely to the clergy of the church of Rome; who, founding their authority on their superior knowledge, preserved the precious literature of antiquity from a total extinction [1]; and, under shelter of their numerous privileges and immunities, acquired a security, by means of the superstition, which they would in vain have claimed from the justice and humanity of those turbulent and licentious ages. Nor is the spectacle altogether unentertaining and uninstructive which the history of those times presents to us. The view of human manners, in all their variety of appearances, is both profitable and agreeable; and if the aspect in some periods seem horrid and deformed, we may thence learn to cherish with the greater anxiety that science and civility which has so close a connexion with virtue and humanity, and which, as it is a sovereign antidote against superstition, is also the most effectual remedy against vice and disorders of every kind.

The rise, progress, perfection, and decline of art and science, are curious objects of contemplation, and intimately connected with a narration of civil transactions. The events of no particular period can be fully accounted for, but by considering the degrees of advancement which men have reached in those particulars.

Those who cast their eye on the general revolutions of society will find, that, as almost all improvements of the human mind had reached nearly to their state of perfection about the age of Augustus, there was a sensible de-

[1] See note [L] at the end of the volume.

CHAP.
XXIII.

cline from that point or period; and men thenceforth relapsed gradually into ignorance and barbarism. The unlimited extent of the Roman empire, and the consequent despotism of its monarchs, extinguished all emulation, debased the generous spirits of men, and depressed that noble flame by which all the refined arts must be cherished and enlivened. The military government, which soon succeeded, rendered even the lives and properties of men insecure and precarious; and proved destructive to those vulgar and more necessary arts of agriculture, manufactures, and commerce; and, in the end, to the military art and genius itself, by which alone the immense fabric of the empire could be supported. The irruption of the barbarous nations, which soon followed, overwhelmed all human knowledge, which was already far in its decline; and men sunk every age deeper into ignorance, stupidity, and superstition; till the light of ancient science and history had very nearly suffered a total extinction in all the European nations.

But there is a point of depression, as well as of exaltation, from which human affairs naturally return in a contrary direction, and beyond which they seldom pass either in their advancement or decline. The period in which the people of Christendom were the lowest sunk in ignorance, and consequently in disorders of every kind, may justly be fixed at the eleventh century, about the age of William the Conqueror; and from that æra, the sun of science, beginning to re-ascend, threw out many gleams of light, which preceded the full morning, when letters were revived in the fifteenth century. The Danes, and other northern people, who had so long infested all the coasts, and even the inland parts of Europe, by their depredations, having now learned the arts of tillage and agriculture, found a certain subsistence at home, and were no longer tempted to desert their industry,

dustry, in order to seek a precarious livelihood by rapine, and by the plunder of their neighbours. The feudal governments also, among the more southern nations, were reduced to a kind of system; and though that strange species of civil polity was ill fitted to ensure either liberty or tranquillity, it was preferable to the universal licence and disorder which had every where preceded it. But perhaps there was no event which tended farther to the improvement of the age, than one, which has not been much remarked, the accidental finding of a copy of Justinian's Pandects, about the year 1130, in the town of Amalfi in Italy.

The ecclesiastics, who had leisure, and some inclination to study, immediately adopted with zeal this excellent system of jurisprudence, and spread the knowledge of it throughout every part of Europe. Besides the intrinsic merit of the performance, it was recommended to them by its original connexion with the imperial city of Rome, which, being the seat of their religion, seemed to acquire a new lustre and authority, by the diffusion of its laws over the western world. In less than ten years after the discovery of the Pandects, Vacarius, under the protection of Theobald, archbishop of Canterbury, read public lectures of civil law in the university of Oxford; and the clergy every where, by their example as well as exhortation, were the means of diffusing the highest esteem for this new science. That order of men, having large possessions to defend, was, in a manner, necessitated to turn their studies towards the law; and their properties being often endangered by the violence of the princes and barons, it became their interest to enforce the observance of general and equitable rules, from which alone they could receive protection. As they possessed all the knowledge of the age, and were alone acquainted with the habits of thinking, the practice, as well as science

science of the law, fell mostly into their hands: And though the close connexion which, without any necessity, they formed between the canon and civil law, begat a jealousy in the laity of England, and prevented the Roman jurisprudence from becoming the municipal law of the country, as was the case in many states of Europe, a great part of it was secretly transferred into the practice of the courts of justice, and the imitation of their neighbours made the English gradually endeavour to raise their own law from its original state of rudeness and imperfection.

It is easy to see what advantages Europe must have reaped by its inheriting at once from the ancients so complete an art, which was also so necessary for giving security to all other arts, and which, by refining, and still more by bestowing, solidity on the judgment, served as a model to farther improvements. The sensible utility of the Roman law, both to public and private interest, recommended the study of it, at a time when the more exalted and speculative sciences carried no charms with them; and thus the last branch of ancient literature which remained uncorrupted, was happily the first transmitted to the modern world: For it is remarkable, that in the decline of Roman learning, when the philosophers were universally infected with superstition and sophistry, and the poets and historians with barbarism, the lawyers, who, in other countries, are seldom models of science or politeness, were yet able, by the constant study and close imitation of their predecessors, to maintain the same good sense in their decisions and reasonings, and the same purity in their language and expression.

What bestowed an additional merit on the civil law, was the extreme imperfection of that jurisprudence which preceded it among all the European nations, especially among the Saxons or ancient English. The absurdities which prevailed at that time in the administration

ministration of justice, may be conceived from the authentic monuments which remain of the ancient Saxon laws; where a pecuniary commutation was received for every crime, where stated prices were fixed for men's lives and members, where private revenges were authorised for all injuries, where the use of the ordeal, corsnet, and afterwards of the duel, was the received method of proof, and where the judges were rustic freeholders, assembled of a sudden, and deciding a cause from one debate or altercation of the parties. Such a state of society was very little advanced beyond the rude state of nature: Violence universally prevailed, instead of general and equitable maxims: The pretended liberty of the times was only an incapacity of submitting to government: And men, not protected by law in their lives and properties, sought shelter by their personal servitude and attachments under some powerful chieftain, or by voluntary combinations.

THE gradual progress of improvement raised the Europeans somewhat above this uncultivated state; and affairs, in this island particularly, took early a turn which was more favourable to justice and to liberty. Civil employments and occupations soon became honourable among the English: The situation of that people rendered not the perpetual attention to wars so necessary as among their neighbours, and all regard was not confined to the military profession: The gentry, and even the nobility, began to deem an acquaintance with the law a necessary part of education: They were less diverted, than afterwards, from studies of this kind by other sciences; and in the age of Henry VI. as we are told by Fortescue, there were in the inns of court about two thousand students, most of them men of honourable birth, who gave application to this branch of civil knowledge: A circumstance which proves that a considerable progress was already

CHAP.
XXIII.
already made in the science of government, and which prognosticated a still greater.

One chief advantage which resulted from the introduction and progress of the arts, was the introduction and progress of freedom; and this consequence affected men both in their *personal* and *civil* capacities.

If we consider the ancient state of Europe, we shall find that the far greater part of the society were every-where bereaved of their *personal* liberty, and lived entirely at the will of their masters. Every one that was not noble was a slave: The peasants were sold along with the land: The few inhabitants of cities were not in a better condition: Even the gentry themselves were subjected to a long train of subordination under the greater barons or chief vassals of the crown; who, though seemingly placed in a high state of splendor, yet, having but a slender protection from law, were exposed to every tempest of the state, and, by the precarious condition in which they lived, paid dearly for the power of oppressing and tyrannizing over their inferiors. The first incident which broke in upon this violent system of government was the practice, begun in Italy, and imitated in France, of erecting communities and corporations, endowed with privileges and a separate municipal government, which gave them protection against the tyranny of the barons, and which the prince himself deemed it prudent to respect*. The relaxation of the feudal tenures, and an

* There appear early symptoms of the jealousy entertained by the barons against the progress of the arts, as destructive of their licentious power. A law was enacted, 7 Henry IV. chap. 17. prohibiting any one who did not possess twenty-shillings a year in land from binding his sons apprentices to any trade. They found already that the cities began to drain the country of the labourers and husbandmen; and did not foresee how much the encrease of commerce would encrease the value of their estates. See further, Cotton, p. 179. The kings, to encourage the boroughs, granted them this privilege, that any villain who had lived a twelvemonth in any corporation, and had been of the guild, should be thenceforth regarded as free.

execution

execution somewhat stricter, of the public law, bestowed CHAP. XXIII. an independence on vassals, which was unknown to their forefathers. And even the peasants themselves, though later than other orders of the state, made their escape from those bonds of villenage or slavery in which they had formerly been retained.

It may appear strange, that the progress of the arts, which seems, among the Greeks and Romans, to have daily encreased the number of slaves, should, in later times, have proved so general a source of liberty; but this difference in the events proceeded from a great difference in the circumstances which attended those institutions. The ancient barons, obliged to maintain themselves continually in a military posture, and little emulous of elegance or splendor, employed not their villains as domestic servants, much less as manufacturers; but composed their retinue of freemen, whose military spirit rendered the chieftain formidable to his neighbours, and who were ready to attend him in every warlike enterprize. The villains were entirely occupied in the cultivation of their master's land, and paid their rents either in corn and cattle and other produce of the farm, or in servile offices, which they performed about the baron's family, and upon the farms which he retained in his own possession. In proportion as agriculture improved, and money encreased, it was found that these services, though extremely burdensome to the villain, were of little advantage to the master; and that the produce of a large estate could be much more conveniently disposed of by the peasants themselves who raised it, than by the landlord or his bailiff, who were formerly accustomed to receive it. A commutation was therefore made of rents for services, and of money-rents for those in kind; and as men, in a subsequent age, discovered that farms were better cultivated where the farmer enjoyed a security in
his

CHAP. XXIII. his possession, the practice of granting leases to the peasant began to prevail, which entirely broke the bonds of servitude, already much relaxed from the former practices. After this manner, villenage went gradually into disuse throughout the more civilized parts of Europe: The interest of the master, as well as that of the slave, concurred in this alteration. The latest laws, which we find in England for enforcing or regulating this species of servitude, were enacted in the reign of Henry VII. And though the ancient statutes on this subject remain still unrepealed by parliament, it appears that, before the end of Elizabeth, the distinction of villain and freeman was totally, though insensibly, abolished, and that no person remained in the state to whom the former laws could be applied.

THUS *personal* freedom became almost general in Europe; an advantage which paved the way for the encrease of *political* or *civil* liberty, and which, even where it was not attended with this salutary effect, served to give the members of the community some of the most considerable advantages of it.

THE constitution of the English government, ever since the invasion of this island by the Saxons, may boast of this pre-eminence, that in no age the will of the monarch was ever entirely absolute and uncontrouled: But in other respects the balance of power has extremely shifted among the several orders of the state; and this fabric has experienced the same mutability that has attended all human institutions.

THE ancient Saxons, like the other German nations, where each individual was enured to arms, and where the independence of men was secured by a great equality of possessions, seem to have admitted a considerable mixture of democracy into their form of government, and to have been one of the freest nations, of which there remains

RICHARD III.

remains any account in the records of history. After this tribe was settled in England, especially after the diffolution of the Heptarchy, the great extent of the kingdom produced a great inequality in property; and the balance seems to have inclined to the side of Aristocracy. The Norman conquest threw more authority into the hands of the sovereign, which, however, admitted of great controul; though derived less from the general forms of the constitution, which were inaccurate and irregular, than from the independent power enjoyed by each baron in his particular district or province. The establishment of the Great Charter exalted still higher the Aristocracy, imposed regular limits on royal power, and gradually introduced some mixture of Democracy into the constitution. But even during this period, from the accession of Edward I. to the death of Richard III. the condition of the commons was nowise eligible; a kind of Polish Aristocracy prevailed; and, though the kings were limited, the people were as yet far from being free. It required the authority almost absolute of the sovereigns, which took place in the subsequent period, to pull down those disorderly and licentious tyrants, who were equally averse from peace and from freedom, and to establish that regular execution of the laws, which, in a following age, enabled the people to erect a regular and equitable plan of liberty.

In each of these successive alterations, the only rule of government, which is intelligible or carries any authority with it, is the established practice of the age, and the maxims of administration which are at that time prevalent and universally assented to. Those who, from a pretended respect to antiquity, appeal, at every turn, to an original plan of the constitution, only cover their turbulent spirit and their private ambition under the appearance of venerable forms; and, whatever period they pitch

CHAP.
XXIII.
on for their model, they may still be carried back to a more ancient period, where they will find the measures of power entirely different, and where every circumstance, by reason of the greater barbarity of the times, will appear still less worthy of imitation. Above all, a civilized nation, like the English, who have happily established the most perfect and most accurate system of liberty that was ever found compatible with government, ought to be cautious in appealing to the practice of their ancestors, or regarding the maxims of uncultivated ages as certain rules for their present conduct. An acquaintance with the ancient periods of their government is chiefly *useful*, by instructing them to cherish their present constitution, from a comparison or contrast with the condition of those distant times. And it is also *curious*, by shewing them the remote, and commonly faint and disfigured originals of the most finished and most noble institutions, and by instructing them in the great mixture of accident, which commonly concurs with a small ingredient of wisdom and foresight, in erecting the complicated fabric of the most perfect government.

CHAP. XXIV.

HENRY VII.

Acceſſion of Henry VII.——His title to the crown ——King's prejudice againſt the houſe of York—— His joyful reception in London——His coronation ——Sweating ſickneſs——A parliament——Entail of the crown——King's marriage——An inſurrection——Diſcontents of the people——Lambert Simnel——Revolt of Ireland——Intrigues of the ducheſs of Burgundy——Lambert Simnel invades England——Battle of Stoke.

THE victory, which the earl of Richmond gained at Boſworth, was entirely deciſive; being attended, as well with the total rout and diſperſion of the royal army, as with the death of the king himſelf. Joy for this great ſucceſs ſuddenly prompted the ſoldiers, in the field of battle, to beſtow on their victorious general the appellation of king, which he had not hitherto aſſumed; and the acclamations of *Long live Henry the Seventh!* by a natural and unpremeditated movement, reſounded from all quarters. To beſtow ſome appearance of formality on this ſpecies of military election, Sir William Stanley brought a crown of ornament, which Richard wore in battle, and which had been found among the ſpoils; and he put it on the head of the victor. Henry himſelf remained not in ſuſpenſe; but immediately, without heſitation, accepted of the magnificent preſent which was tendered him. He was come to the criſis of his fortune; and being obliged ſuddenly to determine

CHAP. XXIV.
1485.
His title to the crown.

termine himself, amidst great difficulties which he must have frequently revolved in his mind, he chose that part which his ambition suggested to him, and to which he seemed to be invited by his present success.

THERE were many titles on which Henry could found his right to the crown; but no one of them free from great objections, if considered with respect either to justice or to policy.

DURING some years Henry had been regarded as heir to the house of Lancaster by the party attached to that family; but the title of the house of Lancaster itself was generally thought to be very ill-founded. Henry IV. who had first raised it to royal dignity, had never clearly defined the foundation of his claim; and while he plainly invaded the order of succession, he had not acknowledged the election of the people. The parliament, it is true, had often recognized the title of the Lancastrian princes; but these votes had little authority, being considered as instances of complaisance towards a family in possession of present power; And they had accordingly been often reversed during the late prevalence of the house of York. Prudent men also, who had been willing, for the sake of peace, to submit to any established authority, desired not to see the claims of that family revived; claims which must produce many convulsions at present, and which disjointed, for the future, the whole system of hereditary right. Besides, allowing the title of the house of Lancaster to be legal, Henry himself was not the true heir of that family; and nothing but the obstinacy natural to faction, which never, without reluctance, will submit to an antagonist, could have engaged the Lancastrians to adopt the earl of Richmond as their head. His mother, indeed, Margaret, countess of Richmond, was sole daughter and heir of the duke of Somerset, sprung from John of Gaunt, duke of Lancaster: But the descent of the Somerset line

was

was itself illegitimate and even adulterous. And though the duke of Lancaster had obtained the legitimation of his natural children by a patent from Richard II. confirmed in parliament; it might justly be doubted whether this deed could bestow any title to the crown; since in the patent itself all the privileges conferred by it are fully enumerated, and the succession to the kingdom is expressly excluded [v]. In all settlements of the crown, made during the reigns of the Lancastrian princes, the line of Somerset had been entirely overlooked; and it was not till the failure of the legitimate branch, that men had paid any attention to their claim. And, to add to the general dissatisfaction against Henry's title, his mother, from whom he derived all his right, was still alive; and evidently preceded him in the order of succession.

THE title of the house of York, both from the plain reason of the case, and from the late popular government of Edward IV. had universally obtained the preference in the sentiments of the people; and Henry might engraft his claim on the rights of that family, by his intended marriage with the princess Elizabeth, the heir of it; a marriage which he had solemnly promised to celebrate, and to the expectation of which he had chiefly owed all his past successes. But many reasons dissuaded Henry from adopting this expedient. Were he to receive the crown only in right of his consort, his power, he knew, would be very limited; and he must expect rather to enjoy the bare title of king by a sort of courtesy, than possess the real authority which belongs to it. Should the princess die before him without issue, he must descend from the throne, and give place to the next in succession: And even if his bed should be blest with offspring, it seemed dangerous to expect that filial piety in his children would prevail over the ambition of obtaining present

[v] Rymer, tom. vii. p. 849. Coke's Inst. 4 Inst. part 1. p. 37.

CHAP.
XXIV.

1485.

possession of regal power. An act of parliament, indeed, might easily be procured to settle the crown on him during life; but Henry knew how much superior the claim of succession by blood was to the authority of an assembly [x], which had always been overborne by violence in the shock of contending titles, and which had ever been more governed by the conjunctures of the times, than by any consideration derived from reason or public interest.

THERE was yet a third foundation on which Henry might rest his claim, the right of conquest, by his victory over Richard, the present possessor of the crown. But, besides that Richard himself was deemed no better than an usurper, the army, which fought against him, consisted chiefly of Englishmen; and a right of conquest over England could never be established by such a victory. Nothing also would give greater umbrage to the nation than a claim of this nature; which might be construed as an abolition of all their rights and privileges, and the establishment of absolute authority in the sovereign [y]. William himself, the Norman, though at the head of a powerful and victorious army of foreigners, had at first declined the invidious title of conqueror; and it was not till the full establishment of his authority, that he had ventured to advance so violent and destructive a pretension.

BUT Henry was sensible that there remained another foundation of power somewhat resembling the right of conquest, namely, present possession; and that this title, guarded by vigour and abilities, would be sufficient to secure perpetual possession of the throne. He had before him the example of Henry IV. who, supported by no better pretension, had subdued many insurrections, and had been able to transmit the crown peaceably to his posterity. He could perceive that this claim, which had been perpetuated through three generations of the family of Lancaster,

[x] Bacon in Kennett's complete History, p. 579.   [y] Bacon, p. 579.

might

might still have subsisted, notwithstanding the preferable title of the house of York; had not the sceptre devolved into the hands of Henry VI. which were too feeble to sustain it. Instructed by this recent experience, Henry was determined to put himself in possession of regal authority; and to show all opponents that nothing but force of arms, and a successful war, should be able to expel him. His claim as heir to the house of Lancaster he was resolved to advance; and never allowed to be discussed: And he hoped that this right, favoured by the partizans of that family, and seconded by present power, would secure him a perpetual and an independent authority.

These views of Henry are not exposed to much blame; because founded on good policy, and even on a species of necessity: But there entered into all his measures and counsels another motive, which admits not of the same apology. The violent contentions which, during so long a period, had been maintained between the rival families, and the many sanguinary revenges which they had alternately taken on each other, had inflamed the opposite factions to a high pitch of animosity. Henry himself, who had seen most of his near friends and relations perish in battle or by the executioner, and who had been exposed, in his own person, to many hardships and dangers, had imbibed a violent antipathy to the York party, which no time or experience were ever able to efface. Instead of embracing the present happy opportunity of abolishing these fatal distinctions, of uniting his title with that of his consort, and of bestowing favour indiscriminately on the friends of both families; he carried to the throne all the partialities which belong to the head of a faction, and even the passions which are carefully guarded against by every true politician in that situation. To exalt the Lancastrian party, to depress the adherents of the house of York, were still the favourite objects of his pursuit; and through the

CHAP.
XI.V.

1485.

the whole course of his reign, he never forgot these early prepossessions. Incapable, from his natural temper, of a more enlarged and more benevolent system of policy, he exposed himself to many present inconveniencies, by too anxiously guarding against that future possible event, which might disjoin his title from that of the princess whom he espoused. And while he treated the Yorkists as enemies, he soon rendered them such, and taught them to discuss that right to the crown, which he so carefully kept separate; and to perceive its weakness and invalidity.

To these passions of Henry, as well as to his suspicious politics, we are to ascribe the measures which he embraced two days after the battle of Bosworth. Edward Plantagenet, earl of Warwic, son of the duke of Clarence, was detained in a kind of confinement at Sherif-Hutton in Yorkshire, by the jealousy of his uncle Richard; whose title to the throne was inferior to that of the young prince. Warwic had now reason to expect better treatment, as he was no obstacle to the succession either of Henry or Elizabeth; and, from a youth of such tender years, no danger could reasonably be apprehended. But Sir Robert Willoughby was dispatched by Henry, with orders to take him from Sherif-Hutton, to convey him to the Tower, and to detain him in close custody[a]. The same messenger carried directions that the princess Elizabeth, who had been confined to the same place, should be conducted to London, in order to meet Henry, and there celebrate her nuptials.

HENRY himself set out for the capital, and advanced by slow journies. Not to rouse the jealousy of the people, he took care to avoid all appearance of military triumph; and so to restrain the insolence of victory, that every

[a] Bacon, p. 579. Polydore Virgil, p. 565.

thing

HENRY VII.

thing about him bore the appearance of an established monarch, making a peaceable progress through his dominions, rather than of a prince who had opened his way to the throne by force of arms. The acclamations of the people were every where loud, and no less sincere and hearty. Besides that a young and victorious prince, on his accession, was naturally the object of popularity; the nation promised themselves great felicity from the new scene which opened before them. During the course of near a whole century the kingdom had been laid waste by domestic wars and convulsions; and if at any time the noise of arms had ceased, the sound of faction and discontent still threatened new disorders. Henry, by his marriage with Elizabeth, seemed to ensure a union of the contending titles of the two families; and having prevailed over a hated tyrant, who had anew disjointed the succession even of the house of York, and had filled his own family with blood and murder, he was, every where, attended with the unfeigned favour of the people. Numerous and splendid troops of gentry and nobility accompanied his progress. The mayor and companies of London received him as he approached the city: The crowds of people and citizens were zealous in their expressions of satisfaction. But Henry, amidst this general effusion of joy, discovered still the stateliness and reserve of his temper, which made him scorn to court popularity: He entered London in a close chariot, and would not gratify the people with a sight of their new sovereign.

CHAP. XXIV.

1485.
His joyful reception in London.

But the king did not so much neglect the favour of the people, as to delay giving them assurances of his marriage with the princess Elizabeth, which he knew to be so passionately desired by the nation. On his leaving Britanny, he had artfully dropped some hints, that, if he should succeed in his enterprize, and obtain the crown of England, he would espouse Anne, the heir of that dutchy;

CHAP. XXIV.

1485.

His coronation.

Sweating sickness.

30th Oct.

dutchy; and the report of this engagement had already reached England, and had begotten anxiety in the people, and even in Elizabeth herself. Henry took care to dissipate these apprehensions, by solemnly renewing, before the council and principal nobility, the promise which he had already given to celebrate his nuptials with the English princess. But though bound by honour, as well as by interest, to complete this alliance, he was resolved to postpone it, till the ceremony of his own coronation should be finished, and till his title should be recognized by parliament. Still anxious to support his personal and hereditary right to the throne, he dreaded lest a preceding marriage with the princess should imply a participation of sovereignty in her, and raise doubts of his own title by the house of Lancaster.

THERE raged at that time in London, and other parts of the kingdom, a species of malady, unknown to any other age or nation, the Sweating sickness, which occasioned the sudden death of great multitudes; though it seemed not to be propagated by any contagious infection, but arose from the general disposition of the air and of the human body. In less than twenty-four hours the patient commonly died or recovered; but when the pestilence had exerted its fury for a few weeks, it was observed, either from alterations in the air, or from a more proper regimen, which had been discovered, to be considerably abated [a]. Preparations were then made for the ceremony of Henry's coronation. In order to heighten the splendor of that spectacle, he bestowed the rank of knight banneret on twelve persons; and he conferred peerages on three. Jasper earl of Pembroke, his uncle, was created duke of Bedford; Thomas lord Stanley, his father-in-law, earl of Derby; and Edward Courteney, earl of Devonshire. At the coronation likewise there appeared a

[a] Polydore Virgil, p. 567.

new

new institution, which the king had established for security as well as pomp, a band of fifty archers, who were termed yeomen of the guard. But lest the people should take umbrage at this unusual symptom of jealousy in the prince, as if it implied a personal diffidence of his subjects, he declared the institution to be perpetual. The ceremony of coronation was performed by cardinal Bourchier, archbishop of Canterbury.

CHAP. XXIV.

1485.

THE parliament being assembled at Westminster, the majority immediately appeared to be devoted partizans of Henry; all persons of another disposition, either declining to stand in those dangerous times, or being obliged to dissemble their principles and inclinations. The Lancastrian party had every where been successful in the elections; and even many had been returned, who, during the prevalence of the house of York, had been exposed to the rigour of law, and had been condemned by sentence of attainder and outlawry. Their right to take seats in the house being questioned, the case was referred to all the judges, who assembled in the Exchequer Chamber, in order to deliberate on so delicate a subject. The opinion delivered was prudent, and contained a just temperament between law and expediency [b]. The judges determined, that the members attainted should forbear taking their seat till an act were passed for the reversal of their attainder. There was no difficulty in obtaining this act; and in it were comprehended a hundred and seven persons of the king's party [c].

7th Nov. A parliament.

BUT a scruple was started of a nature still more important. The king himself had been attainted; and his right of succession to the crown might thence be exposed to some doubt. The judges extricated themselves from this dangerous question, by asserting it as a maxim; "That the crown takes away all defects, and stops in

[b] Bacon, p. 581. [c] Rot. Parl. : Hen. VII, n. 2, 3, 4— 15. 17. 26—65.

" blood ;

"blood; and that from the time the king assumed royal authority, the fountain was cleared, and all attainders and corruptions of blood discharged [d]." Besides that the case, from its urgent necessity, admitted of no deliberation; the judges probably thought, that no sentence of a court of judicature had authority sufficient to bar the right of succession; that the heir of the crown was commonly exposed to such jealousy as might often occasion stretches of law and justice against him; and that a prince might even be engaged in unjustifiable measures during his predecessor's reign, without meriting on that account to be excluded from the throne, which was his birthright.

With a parliament so obsequious, the king could not fail of obtaining whatever act of settlement he was pleased to require. He seems only to have entertained some doubt within himself on what claim he should found his pretensions. In his speech to the parliament he mentioned his just title by hereditary right: But left that title should not be esteemed sufficient, he subjoined his claim by the judgment of God, who had given him victory over his enemies. And again, lest this pretension should be interpreted as assuming a right of conquest, he ensured to his subjects the full enjoyment of their former properties and possessions.

Entail of the crown.

The entail of the crown was drawn according to the sense of the king, and probably in words dictated by him. He made no mention in it of the princess Elizabeth, nor of any branch of her family; but in other respects the act was compiled with sufficient reserve and moderation. He did not insist, that it should contain a declaration or recognition of his preceding right; as, on the other hand, he avoided the appearance of a new law or ordinance. He chose a middle course, which, as is

[d] Bacon, p. 581.

generally

generally unavoidable in such cases, was not entirely free from uncertainty and obscurity. It was voted, "That the inheritance of the crown should rest, remain, and abide in the king*;" but whether as rightful heir, or only as present possessor, was not determined. In like manner, Henry was contented that the succession should be secured to the heirs of his body; but he pretended not, in case of their failure, to exclude the house of York, or give the preference to that of Lancaster: He left that great point ambiguous for the present, and trusted that, if it should ever become requisite to determine it, future incidents would open the way for the decision.

But even after all these precautions, the king was so little satisfied with his own title, that, in the following year, he applied to papal authority for a confirmation of it; and as the court of Rome gladly laid hold of all opportunities, which the imprudence, weakness, or necessities of princes afforded it to extend its influence, Innocent VIII. the reigning pope, readily granted a bull, in whatever terms the king was pleased to desire. All Henry's titles, by succession, marriage, parliamentary choice, even conquest, are there enumerated; and to the whole the sanction of religion is added; excommunication is denounced against every one who should either disturb him in the present possession, or the heirs of his body in the future succession, of the crown; and from this penalty, no criminal, except in the article of death, could be absolved but by the pope himself, or his special commissioners. It is difficult to imagine, that the security, derived from this bull, could be a compensation for the defect which it betrayed in Henry's title, and for the danger of thus inviting the pope to interpose in these concerns.

* Bacon, p. 585.

CHAP.
XXIV.

1485.

It was natural, and even laudable in Henry to reverse the attainders which had passed against the partizans of the house of Lancaster: But the revenges, which he exercised against the adherents of the York family, to which he was so soon to be allied, cannot be considered in the same light. Yet the parliament, at his instigation, passed an act of attainder against the late king himself, against the duke of Norfolk, the earl of Surrey, viscount Lovel, the lords Zouche and Ferrars of Chartley, Sir Walter and Sir James Harrington, Sir William Berkeley, Sir Humphrey Stafford, Catesby, and about twenty other gentlemen, who had fought on Richard's side in the battle of Bosworth. How men could be guilty of treason, by supporting the king in possession against the earl of Richmond, who assumed not the title of king, it is not easy to conceive; and nothing but a servile complaisance in the parliament could have engaged them to make this stretch of justice. Nor was it a small mortification to the people in general, to find, that the king, prompted either by avarice or resentment, could, in the very beginning of his reign, so far violate the cordial union, which had previously been concerted between the parties, and to the expectation of which he had plainly owed his succession to the throne.

10th Dec.

The king, having gained so many points of consequence from the parliament, thought it not expedient to demand any supply from them, which the profound peace enjoyed by the nation, and the late forfeiture of Richard's adherents, seemed to render somewhat superfluous. The parliament, however, conferred on him during life the duty of tonnage and poundage, which had been enjoyed in the same manner by some of his immediate predecessors; and they added, before they broke up, other money bills of no great moment. The king, on his part, made returns of grace and favour to his people. He published lifhed his royal proclamation, offering pardon to all such as had taken arms, or formed any attempts against him; provided they submitted themselves to mercy by a certain day, and took the usual oath of fealty and allegiance. Upon this proclamation many came out of their sanctuaries; and the minds of men were every where much quieted. Henry chose to take wholly to himself the merit of an act of grace, so agreeable to the nation; rather than communicate it with the parliament (as was his first intention), by passing a bill to that purpose. The earl of Surrey, however, though he had submitted, and delivered himself into the king's hands, was sent prisoner to the Tower.

During this parliament, the king also bestowed favours and honours on some particular persons who were attached to him. Edward Stafford, eldest son of the duke of Buckingham, attainted in the late reign, was restored to the honours of his family, as well as to its fortune, which was very ample. This generosity, so unusual in Henry, was the effect of his gratitude to the memory of Buckingham, who had first concerted the plan of his elevation, and who by his own ruin had made way for that great event. Chandos of Britanny was created earl of Bath, Sir Giles Daubeny lord Daubeny, and Sir Robert Willoughby lord Broke. These were all the titles of nobility conferred by the king during this session of parliament [f].

But the ministers, whom Henry most trusted and favoured, were not chosen from among the nobility, or even from among the laity. John Morton, and Richard Fox, two clergymen, persons of industry, vigilance, and capacity, were the men to whom he chiefly confided his affairs and secret counsels. They had shared with him all his former dangers and distresses; and he now took

[f] Polydore Virgil, p. 566.

CHAP.
XXIV.

1485.

care to make them participate in his good fortune. They were both called to the privy council; Morton was restored to the bishopric of Ely, Fox was created bishop of Exeter. The former soon after, upon the death of Bourchier, was raised to the see of Canterbury. The latter was made privy seal; and successively, bishop of Bath and Wells, Durham and Winchester. For Henry, as lord Bacon observes, loved to employ and advance prelates; because, having rich bishoprics to bestow, it was easy for him to reward their services: And it was his maxim to raise them by slow steps, and make them first pass through the inferior sees[f]. He probably expected, that, as they were naturally more dependant on him than the nobility, who, during that age, enjoyed possessions and jurisdictions dangerous to royal authority; so the prospect of farther elevation would render them still more active in his service, and more obsequious to his commands.

1486.
18th Jan.

King's marriage.

In presenting the bill of tonnage and poundage, the parliament, anxious to preserve the legal, undisputed succession to the crown, had petitioned Henry, with demonstrations of the greatest zeal, to espouse the princess Elizabeth; but they covered their true reason under the dutiful pretence of their desire to have heirs of his body. He now thought in earnest of satisfying the minds of his people in that particular. His marriage was celebrated at London, and that with greater appearance of universal joy, than either his first entry or his coronation. Henry remarked with much displeasure this general favour borne to the house of York. The suspicions, which arose from it, not only disturbed his tranquillity during his whole reign; but bred disgust towards his consort herself, and poisoned all his domestic enjoyments. Though virtuous,

[f] Bacon, p. 582.

amiable,

HENRY VII.

amiable, and obsequious to the last degree, she never met with a proper return of affection, or even of complaisance from her husband; and the malignant ideas of faction still, in his sullen mind, prevailed over all the sentiments of conjugal tenderness.

CHAP. XXIV.
1486.

THE king had been carried along, with such a tide of success, ever since his arrival in England, that he thought nothing could withstand the fortune and authority which attended him. He now resolved to make a progress into the North, where the friends of the house of York, and even the partizans of Richard, were numerous; in hopes of curing, by his presence and conversation, the prejudices of the malcontents. When he arrived at Nottingham, he heard that viscount Lovel, with Sir Humphrey Stafford and Thomas, his brother, had secretly withdrawn themselves from their sanctuary at Colchester: But this news appeared not to him of such importance as to stop his journey; and he proceeded forward to York. He there heard, that the Staffords had levied an army, and were marching to besiege the city of Worcester: And that Lovel, at the head of three or four thousand men, was approaching to attack him in York. Henry was not dismayed with this intelligence. His active courage, full of resources, immediately prompted him to find the proper remedy. Though surrounded with enemies in these disaffected counties, he assembled a small body of troops in whom he could confide; and he put them under the command of the duke of Bedford. He joined to them all his own attendants; but he found that this hasty armament was more formidable by their spirit and their zealous attachment to him, than by the arms or military stores with which they were provided. He therefore gave Bedford orders not to approach the enemy; but previously to try every proper expedient to disperse them. Bedford published a general promise of pardon to the re-

An insurrection.

bels; which had a greater effect on their leader than on his followers. Lovel, who had undertaken an enterprize that exceeded his courage and capacity, was so terrified with the fear of desertion among his troops, that he suddenly withdrew himself; and, after lurking some time in Lancashire, he made his escape into Flanders, where he was protected by the dutchess of Burgundy. His army submitted to the king's clemency; and the other rebels, hearing of this success, raised the siege of Worcester, and dispersed themselves. The Staffords took sanctuary in the church of Colnham, a village near Abingdon; but as it was found that this church had not the privilege of giving protection to rebels, they were taken thence: The elder was executed at Tyburn; the younger, pleading that he had been misled by his brother, obtained a pardon[s].

20th Sept.

HENRY's joy for this success was followed, some time after, by the birth of a prince, to whom he gave the name of Arthur, in memory of the famous British king of that name, from whom, it was pretended, the family of Tudor derived its descent.

Discontents of the people.

THOUGH Henry had been able to defeat this hasty rebellion, raised by the relics of Richard's partizans, his government was become in general unpopular: The source of public discontent arose chiefly from his prejudices against the house of York, which was generally beloved by the nation, and which, for that very reason, became every day more the object of his hatred and jealousy. Not only a preference on all occasions, it was observed, was given to the Lancastrians; but many of the opposite party had been exposed to great severity, and had been bereaved of their fortunes by acts of attainder. A general resumption likewise had passed of all grants made by the princes of the house of York; and though

[s] Polydore Virgil, p. 569.

this

HENRY VII.

this rigour had been covered under the pretence that the revenue was become insufficient to support the dignity of the crown, and though the grants, during the later years of Henry VI. were resumed by the same law, yet the York party, as they were the principal sufferers by the resumption, though it chiefly levelled against them. The severity exercised against the earl of Warwic, begat compassion for youth and innocence, exposed to such oppression; and his confinement in the Tower, the very place where Edward's children had been murdered by their uncle, made the public expect a like catastrophe for him, and led them to make a comparison between Henry and that detested tyrant. And when it was remarked, that the queen herself met with harsh treatment, and even, after the birth of a son, was not admitted to the honour of a public coronation, Henry's prepossessions were then concluded to be inveterate, and men became equally obstinate in their disgust to his government. Nor was the manner and address of the king calculated to cure these prejudices contracted against his administration; but had, in every thing, a tendency to promote fear, or at best reverence, rather than goodwill and affection [b]. While the high idea entertained of his policy and vigour, retained the nobility and men of character in obedience, the effects of his unpopular government soon appeared, by incidents of an extraordinary nature.

CHAP. XXIV.
1486.

There lived in Oxford one Richard Simon, a priest, who possessed some subtlety, and still more enterprize and temerity. This man had entertained the design of disturbing Henry's government, by raising a pretender to his crown; and for that purpose, he cast his eyes on Lambert Simnel, a youth of fifteen years of age, who was son of a baker, and who, being endowed with under-

Lambert Simnel.

[b] Bacon, p. 585.

standing

CHAP.
XXIV.

1486.

standing above his years, and address above his condition, seemed well fitted to personate a prince of royal extraction. A report had been spread among the people, and received with great avidity, that Richard duke of York, second son of Edward IV. had, by a secret escape, saved himself from the cruelty of his uncle, and lay somewhere concealed in England. Simon, taking advantage of this rumour, had at first instructed his pupil to assume that name, which he found to be so fondly cherished by the public: But hearing afterwards a new report, that Warwic had made his escape from the Tower, and observing that this news was attended with no less general satisfaction, he changed the plan of his imposture, and made Simnel personate that unfortunate prince[1]. Though the youth was qualified by nature for the part which he was instructed to act; yet was it remarked, that he was better informed in circumstances relating to the royal family, particularly in the adventures of the earl of Warwic, than he could be supposed to have learned from one of Simon's condition: And it was thence conjectured, that persons of higher rank, partizans of the house of York, had laid the plan of this conspiracy, and had conveyed proper instructions to the actors. The queen-dowager herself was exposed to suspicion; and it was indeed the general opinion, however unlikely it might seem, that she had secretly given her consent to the imposture. This woman was of a very restless disposition. Finding that, instead of receiving the reward of her services, in contributing to Henry's elevation, she herself was fallen into absolute insignificance, her daughter treated with severity, and all her friends brought under subjection, she had conceived the most violent animosity against him, and had resolved to make him feel the effects of her resentment. She knew that the impostor, however successful,

[1] Polydore Virgil, p. 565, 570.

might

might easily at last be set aside; and if a way could be found at his risque to subvert the government, she hoped that a scene might be opened, which, though difficult at present exactly to foresee, would gratify her revenge, and be on the whole less irksome to her, than that slavery and contempt to which she was now reduced [k].

But whatever care Simon might take to convey instruction to his pupil Simnel, he was sensible, that the imposture would not bear a close inspection; and he was therefore determined to open the first public scene of it in Ireland. That island, which was zealously attached to the house of York, and bore an affectionate regard to the memory of Clarence, Warwic's father, who had been their lieutenant, was improvidently allowed by Henry to remain in the same condition in which he found it; and all the counsellors and officers, who had been appointed by his predecessors, still retained their authority. No sooner did Simnel present himself to Thomas Fitz-gerald, earl of Kildare, the deputy, and claim his protection as the unfortunate Warwic, than that credulous nobleman, not suspecting so bold an imposture, gave attention to him, and began to consult some persons of rank with regard to this extraordinary incident. These he found even more sanguine in their zeal and belief than himself: And in proportion as the story diffused itself among those of lower condition, it became the object of still greater passion and credulity, till the people in Dublin with one consent tendered their allegiance to Simnel, as to the true Plantagenet. Fond of a novelty, which flattered their natural propension, they overlooked the daughters of Edward IV. who stood before Warwic in the order of succession; they payed the pretended prince attendance as their sovereign, lodged him in the castle of Dublin, crowned him with a diadem taken from a statue of the virgin, and publicly

[k] Polydore Virgil, p. 570.

proclaimed

CHAP.
XXIV.
1486.

proclaimed him king, by the appellation of Edward VI, The whole island followed the example of the capital; and not a sword was any where drawn in Henry's quarrel.

WHEN this intelligence was conveyed to the king, it reduced him to some perplexity. Determined always to face his enemies in person, he yet scrupled at present to leave England, where, he suspected, the conspiracy was first framed, and where, he knew, many persons of condition, and the people in general, were much disposed to give it countenance. In order to discover the secret source of the contrivance, and take measures against this open revolt, he held frequent consultations with his ministers and counsellors, and laid plans for a vigorous defence of his authority, and the suppression of his enemies.

THE first event, which followed these deliberations, gave surprize to the public: It was the seizure of the queen-dowager, the forfeiture of all her lands and revenue, and the close confinement of her person in the nunnery of Bermondsey. This act of authority was covered with a very thin pretence. It was alleged that, notwithstanding the secret agreement to marry her daughter to Henry, she had yet yielded to the solicitations and menaces of Richard, and had delivered that princess and her sisters into the hands of the tyrant. This crime, which was now become obsolete, and might admit of alleviations, was therefore suspected not to be the real cause of the severity with which she was treated; and men believed that the king, unwilling to accuse so near a relation of a conspiracy against him, had cloaked his vengeance or precaution under colour of an offence known to the whole world[1]. They were afterwards the more confirmed in this suspicion, when they found, that the unfortunate queen, though she survived this disgrace several years,

[1] Bacon, p. 583. Polydore Virgil, p. 571.

was never treated with any more lenity, but was allowed to end her life in poverty, solitude, and confinement.

THE next measure of the king's was of a less exceptionable nature. He ordered that Warwic should be taken from the Tower, be led in procession through the streets of London, be conducted to St. Paul's, and there exposed to the view of the whole people. He even gave directions that some men of rank, attached to the house of York, and best acquainted with the person of this prince, should approach him, and converse with him: And he trusted that these, being convinced of the absurd imposture of Simnel, would put a stop to the credulity of the populace. The expedient had its effect in England: But in Ireland the people still persisted in their revolt, and zealously retorted on the king the reproach of propagating an imposture, and of having shewn a counterfeit Warwic to the public.

HENRY had soon reason to apprehend that the design against him was not laid on such flight foundations as the absurdity of the contrivance seemed to indicate. John, earl of Lincoln, son of John de la Pole, duke of Suffolk, and of Elizabeth, eldest sister to Edward IV. was engaged to take part in the conspiracy. This nobleman, who possessed capacity and courage, had entertained very aspiring views; and his ambition was encouraged by the known intentions of his uncle Richard, who had formed a design, in case he himself should die without issue, of declaring Lincoln successor to the crown. The king's jealousy against all eminent persons of the York party, and his rigour towards Warwic, had farther struck Lincoln with apprehensions, and made him resolve to seek for safety in the most dangerous counsels. Having fixed a secret correspondence with Sir Thomas Broughton, a man of great interest in Lancashire, he retired to Flanders, where Lovel had arrived a little before him; and he
lived,

CHAP.
XIV.

1486.

Intrigues of
the dutchess
of Burgundy

lived, during some time, in the court of his aunt the dutchess of Burgundy, by whom he had been invited over.

MARGARET, widow of Charles the Bold, duke of Burgundy, not having any children of her own, attached herself, with an entire friendship, to her daughter-in-law, married to Maximilian, archduke of Austria; and after the death of that princess, she persevered in her affection to Philip and Margaret, her children, and occupied herself in the care of their education and of their persons. By her virtuous conduct and demeanour, she had acquired great authority among the Flemings; and lived with much dignity, as well as œconomy, upon that ample dowry which she inherited from her husband. The resentments of this princess were no less warm than her friendships; and that spirit of faction, which it is so difficult for a social and sanguine temper to guard against, had taken strong possession of her heart, and entrenched somewhat on the probity which shone forth in the other parts of her character. Hearing of the malignant jealousy entertained by Henry against her family, and his oppression of all its partizans, she was moved with the highest indignation, and she determined to make him repent of that enmity to which so many of her friends, without any reason or necessity, had fallen victims. After consulting with Lincoln and Lovel, she hired a body of two thousand veteran Germans, under the command of Martin Swart, a brave and experienced officer [a]; and sent them over, together with these two noblemen, to join Simnel in Ireland. The countenance given by persons of such high rank, and the accession of this military force, much raised the courage of the Irish, and made them entertain the resolution of invading Eng-

1487.

Lambert Simnel invades England.

[a] Polyd. Virg. p. 570, 572.

land,

HENRY VII.

land, where they believed the spirit of disaffection as prevalent as it appeared to be in Ireland. The poverty also, under which they laboured, made it impossible for them to support any longer their new court and army, and inspired them with a strong desire of enriching themselves by plunder and preferment in England.

HENRY was not ignorant of these intentions of his enemies; and he prepared himself for defence. He ordered troops to be levied in different parts of the kingdom, and put them under the command of the duke of Bedford and earl of Oxford. He confined the marquis of Dorset, who, he suspected, would resent the injuries suffered by his mother the queen dowager: And, to gratify the people by an appearance of devotion, he made a pilgrimage to our lady of Walsingham, famous for miracles; and there offered up prayers for success, and for deliverance from his enemies.

BEING informed that Simnel was landed at Foudrey in Lancashire, he drew together his forces, and advanced towards the enemy as far as Coventry. The rebels had entertained hopes that the disaffected counties in the North would rise in their favour: But the people in general, averse to join Irish and German invaders, convinced of Lambert's imposture, and kept in awe by the king's reputation for success and conduct, either remained in tranquillity, or gave assistance to the royal army. The earl of Lincoln, therefore, who commanded the rebels, finding no hopes but in victory, was determined to bring the matter to a speedy decision; and the king, supported by the native courage of his temper, and emboldened by a great accession of volunteers, who had joined him under the earl of Shrewsbury and lord Strange, declined not the combat. The hostile armies met at Stoke, in the county of Nottingham, and fought a battle,

CHAP. XXIV.

1487.

6th June. Battle of Stoke.

CHAP. XXIV.
1487.

battle, which was bloody, and more obstinately disputed than could have been expected from the inequality of their force. All the leaders of the rebels were resolved to conquer or to perish; and they inspired their troops with like resolution. The Germans also, being veteran and experienced soldiers, kept the event long doubtful; and even the Irish, though ill-armed and almost defenceless, showed themselves not defective in spirit and bravery. The king's victory was purchased with loss, but was entirely decisive. Lincoln, Broughton, and Swart perished in the field of battle, with four thousand of their followers. As Lovel was never more heard of, he was believed to have undergone the same fate. Simnel, with his tutor, Simon, was taken prisoner. Simon, being a priest, was not tried at law, and was only committed to close custody: Simnel was too contemptible to be an object either of apprehension or resentment to Henry. He was pardoned, and made a scullion in the king's kitchen; whence he was afterwards advanced to the rank of a falconer [a].

HENRY had now leisure to revenge himself on his enemies. He made a progress into the northern parts, where he gave many proofs of his rigorous disposition. A strict enquiry was made after those who had assisted or favoured the rebels. The punishments were not all sanguinary: The king made his revenge subservient to his avarice. Heavy fines were levied upon the delinquents. The proceedings of the courts, and even the courts themselves, were arbitrary. Either the criminals were tried by commissioners appointed for the purpose, or they suffered punishment by sentence of a court-martial. And, as a rumour had prevailed before the battle of Stoke, that the rebels had gained the victory, that the royal army was cut in pieces, and that the king himself had escaped

[a] Bacon, p. 586. Pol. Virg. p. 574.

by flight, Henry was resolved to interpret the belief or propagation of this report as a mark of disaffection; and he punished many for that pretended crime. But such, in this age, was the situation of the English government, that the royal prerogative, which was but imperfectly restrained during the most peaceable periods, was sure, in tumultuous, or even suspicious times, which frequently recurred, to break all bounds of law, and to violate public liberty.

CHAP.
XXIV.

1487.

AFTER the king had gratified his rigour by the punishment of his enemies, he determined to give contentment to the people, in a point which, though a mere ceremony, was passionately desired by them. The queen had been married near two years, but had not yet been crowned; and this affectation of delay had given great discontent to the public, and had been one principal source of the disaffection which prevailed. The king, instructed by experience, now finished the ceremony of her coronation; and, to shew a disposition still more gracious, he restored to liberty the marquis of Dorset, who had been able to clear himself of all the suspicions entertained against him,

25th Nov.

CHAP. XXV.

State of foreign affairs——State of Scotland——of Spain——of the Low Countries——of France——of Britanny——French invasion of Britanny——French embassy to England——Dissimulation of the French court——An insurrection in the North——suppressed——King sends forces into Britanny——Annexation of Britanny to France——A parliament——War with France——Invasion of France——Peace with France——Perkin Warbec——His imposture——He is avowed by the dutchess of Burgundy——and by many of the English nobility——Trial and execution of Stanley——A parliament.

CHAP.
XXV.

1483.
State of foreign affairs.

THE king acquired great reputation throughout Europe by the vigorous and prosperous conduct of his domestic affairs: But as some incidents, about this time, invited him to look abroad, and exert himself in behalf of his allies, it will be necessary, in order to give a just account of his foreign measures, to explain the situation of the neighbouring kingdoms; beginning with Scotland, which lies most contiguous.

State of Scotland.

THE kingdom of Scotland had not yet attained that state which distinguishes a civilized monarchy, and which enables the government, by the force of its laws and institutions alone, without any extraordinary capacity in the sovereign, to maintain itself in order and tranquillity. James III. who now filled the throne, was a prince of little industry, and of a narrow genius; and

though

though it behoved him to yield the reins of government to his ministers, he had never been able to make any choice which could give contentment both to himself and to his people. When he bestowed his confidence on any of the principal nobility, he found that they exalted their own family to such a height as was dangerous to the prince, and gave umbrage to the state: When he conferred favour on any person of meaner birth, on whose submission he could more depend, the barons of his kingdom, enraged at the power of an upstart minion, proceeded to the utmost extremities against their sovereign. Had Henry entertained the ambition of conquests, a tempting opportunity now offered of reducing that kingdom to subjection; but as he was probably sensible that a warlike people, though they might be over-run by reason of their domestic divisions, could not be retained in obedience without a regular military force, which was then unknown in England, he rather intended the renewal of the peace with Scotland, and sent an embassy to James for that purpose. But the Scots, who never desired a durable peace with England, and who deemed their security to consist in constantly preserving themselves in a warlike posture, would not agree to more than a seven years truce, which was accordingly concluded [e].

THE European states on the continent were then hastening fast to the situation in which they have remained, without any material alteration, for near three centuries; and began to unite themselves into one extensive system of policy, which comprehended the chief powers of Christendom. Spain, which had hitherto been almost entirely occupied within herself, now became formidable by the union of Arragon and Castile in the persons of Ferdinand and Isabella, who, being princes of great

[e] Polyd. Virg. p. 575.

capacity,

CHAP. XXV.

1492.

capacity, employed their force in enterprizes the most advantageous to their combined monarchy. The conquest of Granada from the Moors was then undertaken, and brought near to a happy conclusion. And, in that expedition, the military genius of Spain was revived; honour and security were attained; and her princes, no longer kept in awe by a domestic enemy so dangerous, began to enter into all the transactions of Europe, and make a great figure in every war and negociation.

Of the Low Countries.

MAXIMILIAN, king of the Romans, son of the emperor Frederic, had, by his marriage with the heiress of Burgundy, acquired an interest in the Netherlands; and, though the death of his consort had weakened his connexions with that country, he still pretended to the government as tutor to his son Philip, and his authority had been acknowledged by Brabant, Holland, and several of the provinces. But as Flanders and Hainault still refused to submit to his regency, and even appointed other tutors to Philip, he had been engaged in long wars against that obstinate people, and never was able thoroughly to subdue their spirit. That he might free himself from the opposition of France, he had concluded a peace with Lewis XI. and had given his daughter, Margaret, then an infant, in marriage to the dauphin; together with Artois, Franche-Compté, and Charolois, as her dowry. But this alliance had not produced the desired effect. The dauphin succeeded to the crown of France by the appellation of Charles VIII.; but Maximilian still found the mutinies of the Flemings fomented by the intrigues of the court of France.

State of France.

FRANCE, during the two preceding reigns, had made a mighty encrease in power and greatness; and had not other states of Europe at the same time received an accession of force, it had been impossible to have retained her within her ancient boundaries. Most of the

great

great fiefs, Normandy, Champagne, Anjou, Dauphiny, Guienne, Provence, and Burgundy, had been united to the crown; the English had been expelled from all their conquests; the authority of the prince had been raised to such a height as enabled him to maintain law and order; a considerable military force was kept on foot, and the finances were able to support it. Lewis XI. indeed, from whom many of these advantages were derived, was dead, and had left his son, in early youth and ill educated, to sustain the weight of the monarchy: But, having entrusted the government to his daughter Anne, lady of Beaujeu, a woman of spirit and capacity, the French power suffered no check or decline. On the contrary, this princess formed the great project, which at last she happily effected, of uniting to the crown Britanny, the last and most independent fief of the monarchy.

CHAP.
XXV.
1452.

Francis II. duke of Britanny, conscious of his own incapacity for government, had resigned himself to the direction of Peter Landais, a man of mean birth, more remarkable for abilities than for virtue or integrity. The nobles of Britanny, displeased with the great advancement of this favourite, had even proceeded to disaffection against their sovereign; and, after many tumults and disorders, they at last united among themselves, and in a violent manner seized, tried, and put to death the obnoxious minister. Dreading the resentment of the prince for this invasion of his authority, many of them retired to France; others, for protection and safety, maintained a secret correspondence with the French ministry, who, observing the great dissentions among the Bretons, thought the opportunity favourable for invading the dutchy; and so much the rather, as they could cover their ambition under the specious pretence of providing for domestic security.

Of Britanny.

LEWIS,

CHAP. XXV.

1488.

LEWIS, duke of Orleans, first prince of the blood, and presumptive heir of the monarchy, had disputed the administration with the lady of Beaujeu; and though his pretensions had been rejected by the states, he still maintained cabals with many of the grandees, and laid schemes for subverting the authority of that princess. Finding his conspiracies detected, he took to arms, and fortified himself in Beaugenci; but as his revolt was precipitate, before his confederates were ready to join him, he had been obliged to submit, and to receive such conditions as the French ministry were pleased to impose upon him. Actuated, however, by his ambition, and even by his fears, he soon retired out of France, and took shelter with the duke of Britanny, who was desirous of strengthening himself against the designs of the lady of Beaujeu by the friendship and credit of the duke of Orleans. This latter prince also, perceiving the ascendant which he soon acquired over the duke of Britanny, had engaged many of his partizans to join him at that court, and had formed the design of aggrandizing himself by a marriage with Anne, the heir of that opulent dutchy.

French Invasion of Britanny.

THE barons of Britanny, who saw all favour engrossed by the duke of Orleans and his train, renewed a stricter correspondence with France, and even invited the French king to make an invasion on their country. Desirous, however, of preserving its independency, they had regulated the number of succours which France was to send them, and had stipulated that no fortified place in Britanny should remain in the possession of that monarchy: A vain precaution, where revolted subjects treat with a power so much superior! The French invaded Britanny with forces three times more numerous than those which they had promised to the barons; and, advancing into the heart of the country, laid siege to Ploermel. To oppose them, the duke raised a numerous, but ill-disciplined army,

army, which he put under the command of the duke of Orleans, the count of Dunois, and others of the French nobility. The army, discontented with his choice, and jealous of their confederates, soon disbanded, and left their prince with too small a force to keep the field against his invaders. He retired to Vannes; but being hotly pursued by the French, who had now made themselves masters of Ploermel, he escaped to Nantz; and the enemy, having previously taken and garrisoned Vannes, Dinant, and other places, laid close siege to that city. The barons of Britanny, finding their country menaced with total subjection, began gradually to withdraw from the French army, and to make peace with their sovereign.

This desertion, however, of the Bretons discouraged not the court of France from pursuing her favourite project of reducing Britanny to subjection. The situation of Europe appeared favourable to the execution of this design. Maximilian was indeed engaged in close alliance with the duke of Britanny, and had even opened a treaty for marrying his daughter; but he was on all occasions so indigent, and at that time so disquieted by the mutinies of the Flemings, that little effectual assistance could be expected from him. Ferdinand was entirely occupied in the conquest of Granada; and it was also known, that, if France would resign to him Roussillon and Cerdagne, to which he had pretensions, she could at any time engage him to abandon the interest of Britanny. England alone was both enabled by her power, and engaged by her interests, to support the independency of that dutchy; and the most dangerous opposition was therefore, by Anne of Beaujeu, expected from that quarter. In order to cover her real designs, no sooner was she informed of Henry's success against Simnel and his partizans, than she dispatched ambassadors to the court of London, and made professions of the greatest trust and confidence in that monarch.

CHAP.
XXV.

1488.
French embassy to England.

THE ambassadors, after congratulating Henry on his late victory, and communicating to him, in the most cordial manner, as to an intimate friend, some successes of their master against Maximilian, came in the progress of their discourse to mention the late transactions in Britanny. They told him that the duke having given protection to French fugitives and rebels, the king had been necessitated, contrary to his intention and inclination, to carry war into that dutchy: That the honour of the crown was interested not to suffer a vassal so far to forget his duty to his liege lord; nor was the security of the government less concerned to prevent the consequences of this dangerous temerity: That the fugitives were no mean or obscure persons; but, among others, the duke of Orleans, first prince of the blood, who, finding himself obnoxious to justice for treasonable practices in France, had fled into Britanny; where he still persevered in laying schemes of rebellion against his sovereign: That the war being thus, on the part of the French monarch, entirely defensive, it would immediately cease, when the duke of Britanny, by returning to his duty, should remove the causes of it: That their master was sensible of the obligations which the duke, in very critical times, had conferred on Henry; but it was known also, that, in times still more critical, he or his mercenary counsellors had deserted him, and put his life in the utmost hazard: That his sole refuge in these desperate extremities had been the court of France, which not only protected his person, but supplied him with men and money, with which, aided by his own valour and conduct, he had been enabled to mount the throne of England: That France, in this transaction, had, from friendship to Henry, acted contrary to what, in a narrow view, might be esteemed her own interest; since, instead of an odious tyrant, she had contributed to establish on a

rival

rival throne a prince endowed with such virtue and abilities: And that as both the justice of the cause, and the obligations conferred on Henry, thus preponderated on the side of France, she reasonably expected that, if the situation of his affairs did not permit him to give her assistance, he would at least preserve a neutrality between the contending parties [p].

THIS discourse of the French ambassadors was plausible; and to give it greater weight, they communicated to Henry, as in confidence, their master's intention, after he should have settled the differences with Britanny, to lead an army into Italy, and make good his pretensions to the kingdom of Naples: A project which, they knew, would give no umbrage to the court of England. But all these artifices were in vain employed against the penetration of the king. He clearly saw, that France had entertained the view of subduing Britanny; but he also perceived, that she would meet with great, and, as he thought, insuperable difficulties in the execution of her project. The native force of that dutchy, he knew, had always been considerable, and had often, without any foreign assistance, resisted the power of France; the natural temper of the French nation, he imagined, would make them easily abandon any enterprize which required perseverance; and as the heir of the crown was confederated with the duke of Britanny, the ministers would be still more remiss in prosecuting a scheme, which must draw on them his resentment and displeasure. Should even these internal obstructions be removed, Maximilian, whose enmity to France was well known, and who now paid his addresses to the heiress of Britanny, would be able to make a diversion on the side of Flanders; nor could it be expected that France, if she prosecuted such ambitious projects, would be allowed to remain in tranquillity by

[p] Bacon, p. 583.

Ferdinand

CHAP. XXV.
1488.

Ferdinand and Isabella. Above all, he thought the French court could never expect that England, so deeply interested to preserve the independency of Britanny, so able by her power and situation to give effectual and prompt assistance, would permit such an accession of force to her rival. He imagined, therefore, that the ministers of France, convinced of the impracticability of their scheme, would at last embrace pacific views, and would abandon an enterprize so obnoxious to all the potentates of Europe.

This reasoning of Henry was solid, and might justly engage him in dilatory and cautious measures: But there entered into his conduct another motive, which was apt to draw him beyond the just bounds, because founded on a ruling passion. His frugality, which by degrees degenerated into avarice, made him averse to all warlike enterprizes and distant expeditions, and engaged him previously to try the expedient of negociation. He dispatched Urswic, his almoner, a man of address and abilities, to make offer of his mediation to the contending parties: An offer which, he thought, if accepted by France, would soon lead to a composure of all differences; if refused or eluded, would at least discover the perseverance of that court in her ambitious projects. Urswic found the lady of Beaujeu, now dutchess of Bourbon, engaged in the siege of Nantz, and had the satisfaction to find that his master's offer of mediation was readily embraced, and with many expressions of confidence and moderation. That able princess concluded, that the duke of Orleans, who governed the court of Britanny, foreseeing that every accommodation must be made at his expence, would use all his interest to have Henry's proposal rejected; and would by that means make an apology for the French measures, and draw on the Bretons the reproach of obstinacy and injustice. The event justified her prudence. When the English

Dissimulation of the French court.

English ambassador made the same offer to the duke of Britanny, he received for answer, in the name of that prince, that having so long acted the part of protector and guardian to Henry, during his youth and adverse fortune, he had expected, from a monarch of such virtue, more effectual assistance in his present distresses, than a barren offer of mediation, which suspended not the progress of the French arms: That if Henry's gratitude were not sufficient to engage him in such a measure, his prudence, as king of England, should discover to him the pernicious consequences attending the conquest of Britanny, and its annexation to the crown of France: That that kingdom, already too powerful, would be enabled, by so great an accession of force, to display, to the ruin of England, that hostile disposition which had always subsisted between those rival nations: That Britanny, so useful an ally, which, by its situation, gave the English an entrance into the heart of France; being annexed to that kingdom, would be equally enabled, from its situation, to disturb, either by piracies or naval armaments, the commerce and peace of England: And that, if the duke rejected Henry's mediation, it proceeded neither from an inclination to a war, which he experienced to be ruinous to him, nor from a confidence in his own force, which he knew to be much inferior to that of the enemy; but, on the contrary, from a sense of his present necessities, which must engage the king to act the part of his confederate, not that of a mediator.

WHEN this answer was reported to the king, he abandoned not the plan which he had formed: He only concluded, that some more time was requisite to quell the obstinacy of the Bretons, and make them submit to reason. And when he learned that the people of Britanny, anxious for their duke's safety, had formed a tumultuary army of 60,000 men, and had obliged the French to raise the

CHAP. XXV.
1488.

siege of Nantz, he fortified himself the more in his opinion, that the court of France would at last be reduced, by multiplied obstacles and difficulties, to abandon the project of reducing Britanny to subjection. He continued therefore his scheme of negociation, and thereby exposed himself to be deceived by the artifices of the French ministry; who, still pretending pacific intentions, sent lord Bernard Daubigny, a Scotchman of quality, to London, and pressed Henry not to be discouraged in offering his mediation to the court of Britanny. The king, on his part, dispatched another embassy, consisting of Urswic, the abbot of Abingdon, and Sir Richard Tonstal, who carried new proposals for an amicable treaty. No effectual succours, meanwhile, were provided for the distressed Bretons. Lord Woodville, brother to the queen dowager, having asked leave to raise underhand a body of volunteers, and to transport them into Britanny, met with a refusal from the king, who was desirous of preserving the appearance of a strict neutrality. That nobleman, however, still persisted in his purpose. He went over to the Isle of Wight, of which he was governor; levied a body of 400 men; and having at last obtained, as is supposed, the secret permission of Henry, sailed with them to Britanny. This enterprize proved fatal to the leader, and brought small

28th July. relief to the unhappy duke. The Bretons rashly engaged in a general action with the French at St. Aubin, and were discomfited. Woodville and all the English were put to the sword; together with a body of Bretons, who had been accoutred in the garb of Englishmen, in order to strike a greater terror into the French, to whom the martial prowess of that nation was always formidable [q]. The duke of Orleans, the prince of Orange, and many other persons of rank, were taken prisoners: And the mi-

[q] Argentré Hist. de Bretagne, liv. xii.

litary force of Britanny was totally broken. The death
of the duke, which followed soon after, threw affairs into
still greater confusion, and seemed to threaten the state
with a final subjection.

CHAP.
XXV.

1485.
9th Sept.

Though the king did not prepare against these events,
so hurtful to the interests of England, with sufficient vigour and precaution, he had not altogether overlooked
them. Determined to maintain a pacific conduct, as far
as the situation of affairs would permit, he yet knew the
warlike temper of his subjects, and observed, that their
ancient and inveterate animosity to France was now
revived by the prospect of this great accession to her
power and grandeur. He resolved therefore to make advantage of this disposition, and draw some supplies from
the people, on pretence of giving assistance to the duke of
Britanny. He had summoned a parliament at Westminster [r]; and he soon persuaded them to grant him a considerable subsidy [s]. But this supply, though voted by parliament, involved the king in unexpected difficulties.
The counties of Durham and York, always discontented
with Henry's government, and farther provoked by the
late oppressions, under which they had laboured, after the
suppression of Simnel's rebellion, resisted the commissioners who were appointed to levy the tax. The commissioners, terrified with this appearance of sedition, made
application to the earl of Northumberland, and desired of
him advice and assistance in the execution of their office.
That nobleman thought the matter of importance enough
to consult the king; who, unwilling to yield to the humours of a discontented populace, and foreseeing the pernicious consequence of such a precedent, renewed his
orders for strictly levying the imposition. Northumber-

An insur-
rection in
the North.

[r] 9th November, 1487.   [s] Polydore Virgil. p. 579, says, that
this imposition was a capitation tax; the other historians say, it was a tax
of two shillings in the pound.

land

CHAP. XXV.
1489.

land summoned together the justices and chief freeholders, and delivered the king's commands in the most imperious terms, which, he thought, would enforce obedience, but which tended only to provoke the people, and make them believe him the adviser of those orders which he delivered to them[1]. They flew to arms, attacked Northumberland in his house, and put him to death. Having incurred such deep guilt, their mutinous humour prompted them to declare against the king himself; and being instigated by John Achamber, a seditious fellow of low birth, they chose Sir John Egremond their leader, and prepared themselves for a vigorous resistance. Henry was not dismayed with an insurrection so precipitate and ill-supported. He immediately levied a force, which he put under the command of the earl of Surrey, whom he had freed from confinement, and received into favour. His intention was to send down these troops, in order to check the progress of the rebels; while he himself should follow with a greater body, which would absolutely insure success. But Surrey thought himself strong enough to encounter alone a raw and unarmed multitude; and he succeeded in the attempt. The rebels were dissipated; John Achamber was taken prisoner, and afterwards executed with some of his accomplices; Sir John Egremund fled to the dutchess of Burgundy, who gave him protection; the greater number of the rebels received a pardon.

Suppressed.

HENRY had probably expected, when he obtained this grant from parliament, that he should be able to terminate the affair of Britanny by negociation, and that he might thereby fill his coffers with the money levied by the imposition. But as the distresses of the Bretons still multiplied, and became every day more urgent; he found himself under the necessity of taking more vigorous measures, in order to support them. On the death of

[1] Bacon. p. 595.

the duke, the French had revived some antiquated claims to the dominion of the dutchy; and as the duke of Orleans was now captive in France, their former pretence for hostilities could no longer serve as a cover to their ambition. The king resolved, therefore, to engage as auxiliary to Britanny; and to consult the interests, as well as desires of his people, by opposing himself to the progress of the French power. Besides entering into a league with Maximilian, and another with Ferdinand, which were distant resources, he levied a body of troops, to the number of 6000 men, with an intention of transporting them into Britanny. Still anxious, however, for the re-payment of his expences, he concluded a treaty with the young dutchess, by which she engaged to deliver into his hands two sea-port towns, there to remain till she should entirely refund the charges of the armament[s]. Though he engaged for the service of these troops during the space of ten months only, yet was the dutchess obliged, by the necessity of her affairs, to submit to such rigid conditions, imposed by an ally so much concerned in interest to protect her. The forces arrived under the command of lord Willoughby of Broke; and made the Bretons, during some time, masters of the field. The French retired into their garrisons; and expected, by dilatory measures, to waste the fire of the English, and disgust them with the enterprize. The scheme was well laid, and met with success. Lord Broke found such discord and confusion in the counsels of Britanny, that no measures could be concerted for any undertaking; no supply obtained; no provisions, carriages, artillery, or military stores procured. The whole court was rent into factions: No one minister had acquired the ascendant: And whatever project was formed by one, was sure to be traversed by another. The English, disconcerted in every

[s] Du Tillet, Recueil des Traités.

CHAP. XXV.

1489.

1490.

enterprize by these animosities and uncertain counsels, returned home as soon as the time of their service was elapsed; leaving only a small garrison in those towns which had been consigned into their hands. During their stay in Britanny, they had only contributed still farther to waste the country; and by their departure, they left it entirely at the mercy of the enemy. So feeble was the succour which Henry, in this important conjuncture, afforded his ally, whom the invasion of a foreign enemy, concurring with domestic dissentions, had reduced to the utmost distress.

The great object of the domestic dissentions in Britanny was the disposal of the young dutchess in marriage. The mareschal Rieux, favoured by Henry, seconded the suit of the lord d'Albret, who led some forces to her assistance. The chancellor Montauban, observing the aversion of the dutchess to this suitor, insisted that a petty prince, such as d'Albret, was unable to support Anne in her present extremities; and he recommended some more powerful alliance, particularly that of Maximilian, king of the Romans. This party at last prevailed; the marriage with Maximilian was celebrated by proxy; and the dutchess thenceforth assumed the title of Queen of the Romans. But this magnificent appellation was all she gained by her marriage. Maximilian, destitute of troops and money, and embarrassed with the continual revolts of the Flemings, could send no succour to his distressed consort; while d'Albret, enraged at the preference given to his rival, deserted her cause, and received the French into Nantz, the most important place in the dutchy, both for strength and riches.

The French court now began to change their scheme with regard to the subjection of Britanny. Charles had formerly been affianced to Margaret, daughter of Maximilian; who, though too young for the consummation of her

her marriage, had been sent to Paris to be educated, and at this time bore the title of Queen of France. Besides the rich dowry which she brought the king, she was, after her brother Philip, then in early youth, heir to all the dominions of the house of Burgundy; and seemed, in many respects, the most proper match that could be chosen for the young monarch. These circumstances had so blinded both Maximilian and Henry, that they never suspected any other intentions in the French court; nor were they able to discover that engagements, seemingly so advantageous, and so solemnly entered into, could be infringed and set aside. But Charles began to perceive that the conquest of Britanny, in opposition to the natives, and to all the great powers of Christendom, would prove a difficult enterprize; and that even if he should over-run the country, and make himself master of the fortresses, it would be impossible for him long to retain possession of them. The marriage alone of the dutchess could fully re-annex that fief to the crown; and the present and certain enjoyment of so considerable a territory seemed preferable to the prospect of inheriting the dominions of the house of Burgundy; a prospect which became every day more distant and precarious. Above all, the marriage of Maximilian and Anne appeared destructive to the grandeur, and even security, of the French monarchy; while that prince, possessing Flanders on the one hand, and Britanny on the other, might thus, from both quarters, make inroads into the heart of the country. The only remedy for these evils was therefore concluded to be the dissolution of the two marriages, which had been celebrated, but not consummated; and the espousal of the dutchess of Britanny by the king of France.

It was necessary that this expedient, which had not been foreseen by any court in Europe, and which they were all so much interested to oppose, should be kept a profound a profound secret, and should be discovered to the world only by the full execution of it. The measures of the French ministry in the conduct of this delicate enterprize were wise and political. While they pressed Britanny with all the rigours of war, they secretly gained the count of Dunois, who possessed great authority with the Bretons; and having also engaged in their interests the prince of Orange, cousin-german to the dutchess, they gave him his liberty, and sent him into Britanny. These partizans, supported by other emissaries of France, prepared the minds of men for the great revolution projected, and displayed, though still with many precautions, all the advantages of a union with the French monarchy. They represented to the barons of Britanny, that their country, harassed during so many years with perpetual war, had need of some repose, and of a solid and lasting peace with the only power that was formidable to them: That their alliance with Maximilian was not able to afford them even present protection; and, by closely uniting them to a power which was rival to the greatness of France, fixed them in perpetual enmity with that potent monarchy: That their vicinity exposed them first to the inroads of the enemy; and the happiest event which, in such a situation, could befal them, would be to attain a peace, though by a final subjection to France, and by the loss of that liberty transmitted to them from their ancestors: And that any other expedient, compatible with the honour of the state, and their duty to their sovereign, was preferable to a scene of such disorder and devastation.

These suggestions had influence with the Bretons: But the chief difficulty lay in surmounting the prejudices of the young dutchess herself. That princess had imbibed a strong prepossession against the French nation, particularly against Charles, the author of all the calamities which,

which, from her earliest infancy, had befallen her family. She had also fixed her affections on Maximilian; and as she now deemed him her husband, she could not, she thought, without incurring the greatest guilt, and violating the most solemn engagements, contract a marriage with any other person. In order to overcome her obstinacy, Charles gave the duke of Orleans his liberty, who, though formerly a suitor to the dutchess, was now contented to ingratiate himself with the king, by employing in his favour all the interest which he still possessed in Britanny. Mareschal Rieux and chancellor Montauban were reconciled by his mediation; and these rival ministers now concurred with the prince of Orange and the count of Dunois, in pressing the conclusion of a marriage with Charles. By their suggestion, Charles advanced with a powerful army, and invested Rennes, at that time the residence of the dutchess; who, assailed on all hands, and finding none to support her in her inflexibility, at last opened the gates of the city, and agreed to espouse the king of France. She was married at Langey in Touraine; conducted to St. Dennis, where she was crowned; thence made her entry into Paris, amidst the joyful acclamations of the people, who regarded this marriage as the most prosperous event that could have befallen the monarchy.

THE triumph and success of Charles was the most sensible mortification to the king of the Romans. He had lost a considerable territory, which he thought he had acquired, and an accomplished princess, whom he had espoused; he was affronted in the person of his daughter Margaret, who was sent back to him after she had been treated, during some years, as queen of France; he had reason to reproach himself with his own supine security, in neglecting the consummation of his marriage, which was easily practicable for him, and which would have rendered the tye indissoluble: These considerations

CHAP. XXV.

1490.

1491.

Annexation of Britanny to France.

derations threw him into the most violent rage, which he vented in very indecent expressions; and he threatened France with an invasion from the united arms of Austria, Spain, and England.

THE king of England had also just reason to reproach himself with misconduct in this important transaction; and though the affair had terminated in a manner which he could not precisely foresee, his negligence, in leaving his most useful ally so long exposed to the invasion of superior power, could not but appear, on reflection, the result of timid caution and narrow politics. As he valued himself on his extensive foresight and profound judgment, the ascendant acquired over him by a raw youth, such as Charles, could not but give him the highest displeasure, and prompt him to seek vengeance, after all remedy for his miscarriage was become absolutely impracticable. But he was farther actuated by avarice, a motive still more predominant with him than either pride or revenge; and he sought, even from his present disappointments, the gratification of this ruling passion. On pretence of a French war, he issued a commission for levying a *Benevolence* on his people[a]; a species of taxation which had been abolished by a recent law of Richard III. This violence (for such it really was) fell chiefly on the commercial part of the nation, who were possessed of the ready money. London alone contributed to the amount of near 10,000 pounds. Archbishop Morton, the chancellor, instructed the commissioners to employ a dilemma, in which every one might be comprehended: If the persons applied to lived frugally, they were told that their parsimony must necessarily have enriched them: If their method of living were splendid and hospitable, they were concluded to be

---

[a] Rymer, vol. xii. p. 446. Bacon says that the benevolence was levied with consent of parliament, which is a mistake.

opulent

opulent on account of their expences. This device was by some called chancellor Morton's fork, by others his crutch.

So little apprehensive was the king of a parliament on account of his levying this arbitrary imposition, that he soon after summoned that assembly to meet at Westminster; and he even expected to enrich himself farther by working on their passions and prejudices. He knew the displeasure which the English had conceived against France on account of the acquisition of Britanny; and he took care to insist on that topic, in the speech which he himself pronounced to the parliament. He told them that France, elated with her late successes, had even proceeded to a contempt of England, and had refused to pay the tribute which Lewis XI. had stipulated to Edward IV.: That it became so warlike a nation as the English to be roused by this indignity, and not to limit their pretensions merely to repelling the present injury: That, for his part, he was determined to lay claim to the crown itself of France, and to maintain by force of arms so just a title, transmitted to him by his gallant ancestors: That Crecy, Poictiers, and Azincour, were sufficient to instruct them in their superiority over the enemy; nor did he despair of adding new names to the glorious catalogue: That a king of France had been prisoner in London, and a king of England had been crowned at Paris; events which should animate them to an emulation of like glory with that which had been enjoyed by their forefathers: That the domestic dissentions of England had been the sole cause of her losing these foreign dominions; and her present internal union would be the effectual means of recovering them: That where such lasting honour was in view, and such an important acquisition, it became not brave men to repine at the advance of a little treasure: And that,

CHAP. XXV.
1491.

that, for his part, he was determined to make the war maintain itself; and hoped, by the invasion of so opulent a kingdom as France, to encreafe, rather than diminish, the riches of the nation [v].

NOTWITHSTANDING these magnificent vaunts of the king, all men of penetration concluded, from the personal character of the man, and still more from the situation of affairs, that he had no serious intention of pushing the war to such extremities as he pretended. France was not now in the same condition as when such successful inroads had been made upon her by former kings of England. The great fiefs were united to the crown; the princes of the blood were desirous of tranquillity; the nation abounded with able captains and veteran soldiers; and the general aspect of her affairs seemed rather to threaten her neighbours, than to promise them any considerable advantages against her. The levity and vain-glory of Maximilian were supported by his pompous titles; but were ill seconded by military power, and still less by any revenue proportioned to them. The politic Ferdinand, while he made a show of war, was actually negociating for peace; and, rather than expose himself to any hazard, would accept of very moderate concessions from France. Even England was not free from domestic discontents; and in Scotland, the death of Henry's friend and ally, James III. who had been murdered by his rebellious subjects, had made way for the succession of his son, James IV. who was devoted to the French interest, and would surely be alarmed at any important progress of the English arms. But all these obvious considerations had no influence on the parliament. Inflamed by the ideas of subduing France, and of enriching themselves by the spoils of that kingdom,

[v] Bacon, p. 601.

they

they gave into the snare prepared for them, and voted the supply which the king demanded. Two fifteenths were granted him; and the better to enable his vassals and nobility to attend him, an act was passed, empowering them to sell their estates, without paying any fines for alienation.

CHAP. XXV.
1491.

THE nobility were universally seized with a desire of military glory; and, having credulously swallowed all the boasts of the king, they dreamed of no less than carrying their triumphant banners to the gates of Paris, and putting the crown of France on the head of their sovereign. Many of them borrowed large sums, or sold off manors, that they might appear in the field with greater splendour, and lead out their followers in more complete order. The king crossed the sea, and arrived at Calais on the sixth of October, with an army of twenty-five thousand foot and sixteen hundred horse, which he put under the command of the duke of Bedford and the earl of Oxford: But as some inferred, from his opening the campaign in so late a season, that peace would soon be concluded between the crowns, he was desirous of suggesting a contrary inference. "He had come over," he said, "to make an entire conquest of France, which "was not the work of one summer. It was there"fore of no consequence at what season he began the in"vasion; especially as he had Calais ready for winter"quarters." As if he had seriously intended this enterprize, he instantly marched into the enemy's country, and laid siege to Bulloigne: But, notwithstanding this appearance of hostility, there had been secret advances made towards peace above three months before; and commissioners had been appointed to treat of the terms. The better to reconcile the minds of men to this unexpected measure, the king's ambassadors arrived in the

1492.

6th Oct. War with France.

Invasion of France.

VOL. III.   A a   camp

CHAP.
XXV.

1492.

camp from the Low Countries, and informed him that Maximilian was in no readiness to join him; nor was any affistance to be expected from that quarter. Soon after, meffengers came from Spain, and brought news of a peace concluded between that kingdom and France, in which Charles had made a ceffion of the counties of Rouffillon and Cerdagne to Ferdinand. Though thefe articles of intelligence were carefully difperfed throughout the army, the king was ftill apprehenfive left a fudden peace, after fuch magnificent promifes and high expectations, might expofe him to reproach. In order the more effectually to cover the intended meafures, he fecretly engaged the marquis of Dorfet, together with twenty-three perfons of diftinction, to prefent him a petition for agreeing to a treaty with France. The pretence was founded on the late feafon of the year, the difficulty of fupplying the army at Calais during winter, the obftacles which arofe in the fiege of Bulloigne, the defertion of thofe allies whofe affiftance had been moft relied on: Events which might, all of them, have been forefeen before the embarkation of the forces.

3d Nov.
Peace with
France.

In confequence of thefe preparatory fteps, the bifhop of Exeter and lord Daubeny were fent to confer at Eftaples with the marefchal de Cordes, and to put the laft hand to the treaty. A few days fufficed for that purpofe: The demands of Henry were wholly pecuniary; and the king of France, who deemed the peaceable poffeffion of Britanny an equivalent for any fum, and who was all on fire for his projected expedition into Italy, readily agreed to the propofals made him. He engaged to pay Henry 745,000 crowns, near 400,000 pounds fterling of our prefent money; partly as a reimburfement of the fums advanced to Britanny, partly as arrears of the penfion due to Edward IV. And he ftipulated a yearly penfion to Henry and his heirs of 25,000 crowns.

crowns. Thus the king, as remarked by his historian, made profit upon his subjects for the war; and upon his enemies for the peace [a]. And the people agreed that he had fulfilled his promise, when he said to the parliament that he would make the war maintain itself. Maximilian was, if he pleased, comprehended in Henry's treaty; but he disdained to be, in any respect, beholden to an ally, of whom, he thought, he had reason to complain: He made a separate peace with France; and obtained restitution of Artois, Franchecompté, and Charolois, which had been ceded as the dowry of his daughter, when she was affianced to the king of France.

THE peace concluded between England and France was the more likely to continue, because Charles, full of ambition and youthful hopes, bent all his attention to the side of Italy, and, soon after, undertook the conquest of Naples; an enterprize which Henry regarded with the greater indifference, as Naples lay remote from him, and France had never, in any age, been successful in that quarter. The king's authority was fully established at home; and every rebellion, which had been attempted against him, had hitherto tended only to confound his enemies, and consolidate his power and influence. His reputation for policy and conduct was daily augmenting; his treasures had encreased even from the most unfavourable events; the hopes of all pretenders to his throne were cut off, as well by his marriage as by the issue which it had brought him. In this prosperous situation the king had reason to flatter himself with the prospect of durable peace and tranquillity: But his inveterate and indefatigable enemies, whom he had wantonly provoked, raised him an adversary, who long kept him in inquietude, and sometimes even brought him into danger.

[a] Bacon, p. 605. Pol. Virg. p. 586.

CHAP.
XXV.

1492.

THE dutchess of Burgundy, full of resentment for the depression of her family and its partizans, rather irritated than discouraged by the ill success of her past enterprizes, was determined, at least, to disturb that government which she found it so difficult to subvert. By means of her emissaries she propagated a report that her nephew, Richard Plantagenet, duke of York, had escaped from the Tower when his elder brother was murdered, and that he still lay somewhere concealed: And, finding this rumour, however improbable, to be greedily received by the people, she had been looking out for some young man proper to personate that unfortunate prince.

Perkin Warbec.

THERE was one Osbec, or Warbec, a renegado Jew of Tournay, who had been carried by some business to London in the reign of Edward IV. and had there a son born to him. Having had opportunities of being known to the king, and obtaining his favour, he prevailed with that prince, whose manners were very affable, to stand godfather to his son, to whom he gave the name of Peter, corrupted, after the Flemish manner, into Peterkin, or Perkin. It was by some believed that Edward, among his amorous adventures, had a secret commerce with Warbec's wife; and people thence accounted for that resemblance which was afterwards remarked between young Perkin and that monarch [r]. Some years after the birth of this child, Warbec returned to Tournay; where Perkin, his son, did not long remain, but, by different accidents, was carried from place to place, and his birth and fortunes became thereby unknown, and difficult to be traced by the most diligent enquiry. The variety of his adventures had happily favoured the natural versatility and sagacity of his genius; and he seemed to be a youth perfectly fitted to act any part, or

[r] Bacon, p. 606.

assume

HENRY VII.

assume any character. In this light he had been represented to the dutchess of Burgundy, who, struck with the concurrence of so many circumstances suited to her purpose, desired to be made acquainted with the man on whom she already began to ground her hopes of success. She found him to exceed her most sanguine expectations; so comely did he appear in his person, so graceful in his air, so courtly in his address, so full of docility and good sense in his behaviour and conversation. The lessons, necessary to be taught him, in order to his personating the duke of York, were soon learned by a youth of such quick apprehension; but as the season seemed not then favourable for his enterprize, Margaret, in order the better to conceal him, sent him, under the care of lady Brampton, into Portugal, where he remained a year, unknown to all the world.

CHAP. XXV.
1492.

His impos-
ture.

THE war, which was then ready to break out between France and England, seemed to afford a proper opportunity for the discovery of this new phænomenon; and Ireland, which still retained its attachments to the house of York, was chosen as the proper place for his first appearance [z]. He landed at Corke; and immediately assuming the name of Richard Plantagenet, drew to him partizans among that credulous people. He wrote letters to the earls of Desmond and Kildare, inviting them to join his party: He dispersed, every where, the strange intelligence of his escape from the cruelty of his uncle Richard: And men, fond of every thing new and wonderful, began to make him the general subject of their discourse, and even the object of their favour.

THE news soon reached France; and Charles, prompted by the secret solicitations of the dutchess of Burgundy, and the intrigues of one Frion, a secretary of Henry's,

[z] Polyd. Virg. p. 589.

A a 3   who

CHAP.
XXV.

1492.

who had deserted his service, sent Perkin an invitation to repair to him at Paris. He received him with all the marks of regard due to the duke of York; settled on him a handsome pension, assigned him magnificent lodgings, and, in order to provide at once for his dignity and security, gave him a guard for his person, of which lord Congresal accepted the office of captain. The French courtiers readily embraced a fiction which their sovereign thought it his interest to adopt: Perkin, both by his deportment and personal qualities, supported the prepossession which was spread abroad of his royal pedigree: And the whole kingdom was full of the accomplishments, as well as the singular adventures and misfortunes of the young Plantagenet. Wonders of this nature are commonly augmented at a distance. From France, the admiration and credulity diffused themselves into England: Sir George Nevil, Sir John Taylor, and above a hundred gentlemen more, came to Paris, in order to offer their services to the supposed duke of York, and to share his fortunes: And the impostor had now the appearance of a court attending him, and began to entertain hopes of final success in his undertakings.

He is avowed by the dutchess of Burgundy.

WHEN peace was concluded between France and England at Estaples, Henry applied to have Perkin put into his hands; but Charles, resolute not to betray a young man, of whatever birth, whom he had invited into his kingdom, would agree only to dismiss him. The pretended Richard retired to the dutchess of Burgundy, and craving her protection and assistance, offered to lay before her all the proofs of that birth to which he laid claim. The princess affected ignorance of his pretensions; even put on the appearance of distrust; and having, as she said, been already deceived by Simnel, she was determined never again to be seduced by any impostor. She desired before all the world to be instructed in his reasons for

assuming

assuming the name which he bore; seemed to examine every circumstance with the most scrupulous nicety; put many particular questions to him; affected astonishment at his answers; and at last, after long and severe scrutiny, burst out into joy and admiration at his wonderful deliverance, embraced him as her nephew, the true image of Edward, the sole heir of the Plantagenets, and the legitimate successor to the English throne. She immediately assigned him an equipage suited to his pretended birth; appointed him a guard of thirty halberdiers; engaged every one to pay court to him; and, on all occasions, honoured him with the appellation of the *White Rose of England*. The Flemings, moved by the authority which Margaret, both from her rank and personal character, enjoyed among them, readily adopted the fiction of Perkin's royal descent: No surmise of his true birth was as yet heard of: Little contradiction was made to the prevailing opinion: And the English, from their great communication with the Low Countries, were every day more and more prepossessed in favour of the impostor.

It was not the populace, alone, of England that gave credit to Perkin's pretensions. Men of the highest birth and quality, disgusted at Henry's government, by which they found the nobility depressed, began to turn their eyes towards the new claimant; and some of them even entered into a correspondence with him. Lord Fitzwater, Sir Simon Mountfort, Sir Thomas Thwaites, betrayed their inclination towards him: Sir William Stanley, himself, lord chamberlain, who had been so active in raising Henry to the throne, moved either by blind credulity or a restless ambition, entertained the project of a revolt in favour of his enemy [a]. Sir Robert Clifford and William Barley were still more open in their measures: They went over to Flanders, were introduced by

[a] Bacon, p. 608.

CHAP. XXV.

1493.

the dutchefs of Burgundy to the acquaintance of Perkin, and made him a tender of their fervices. Clifford wrote back to England, that he knew perfectly the perfon of Richard duke of York, that this young man was undoubtedly that prince himfelf, and that no circumftance of his ftory was expofed to the leaft difficulty. Such pofitive intelligence, conveyed by a perfon of rank and character, was fufficient, with many, to put the matter beyond queftion, and excited the attention and wonder even of the moft indifferent. The whole nation was held in fufpence; a regular confpiracy was formed againft the king's authority; and a correfpondence fettled between the malcontents in Flanders and thofe in England.

The king was informed of all thefe particulars; but, agreeably to his character, which was both cautious and refolute, he proceeded deliberately, though fteadily, in counter-working the projects of his enemies. His firft object was to afcertain the death of the real duke of York; and to confirm the opinion that had always prevailed with regard to that event. Five perfons had been employed by Richard in the murder of his nephews, or could give evidence with regard to it; Sir James Tirrel, to whom he had committed the government of the Tower for that purpofe, and who had feen the dead princes; Forreft, Dighton, and Slater, who perpetrated the crime; and the prieft, who buried the bodies. Tirrel and Dighton alone were alive, and they agreed in the fame ftory; but, as the prieft was dead, and as the bodies were fuppofed to have been removed, by Richard's orders, from the place where they were firft interred, and could not now be found, it was not in Henry's power to put the fact, fo much as he wifhed, beyond all doubt and controverfy.

He met at firft with more difficulty, but was, in the end, more fuccefsful, in detecting who this wonderful perfon was that thus boldly advanced pretenfions to his crown.

crown. He dispersed his spies all over Flanders and England; he engaged many to pretend that they had embraced Perkin's party; he directed them to insinuate themselves into the confidence of the young man's friends; in proportion as they conveyed intelligence of any conspirator, he bribed his retainers, his domestic servants, nay sometimes his confessor, and by these means traced up some other confederate; Clifford himself he engaged, by the hope of rewards and pardon, to betray the secrets committed to him; the more trust he gave to any of his spies, the higher resentment did he feign against them; some of them he even caused to be publicly anathematized, in order the better to procure them the confidence of his enemies: And in the issue, the whole plan of the conspiracy was clearly laid before him; and the pedigree, adventures, life, and conversation of the pretended duke of York. This latter part of the story was immediately published for the satisfaction of the nation: The conspirators he reserved for a slower and surer vengeance.

MEANWHILE, he remonstrated with the archduke, Philip, on account of the countenance and protection which was afforded in his dominions to so infamous an impostor; contrary to treaties subsisting between the sovereigns, and to the mutual amity which had so long been maintained by the subjects of both states. Margaret had interest enough to get his application rejected; on pretence that Philip had no authority over the demesnes of the dutchess dowager. And the king, in resentment of this injury, cut off all commerce with the Low-Countries, banished the Flemings, and recalled his own subjects from these provinces. Philip retaliated by like edicts; but Henry knew, that so mutinous a people as the Flemings would not long bear, in compliance with the

CHAP. XXV.
1494.

the humours of their prince, to be deprived of the beneficial branch of commerce which they carried on with England.

He had it in his power to inflict more effectual punishment on his domestic enemies; and when his projects were sufficiently matured, he failed not to make them feel the effects of his resentment. Almost in the same instant, he arrested Fitzwater, Mountfort, and Thwaites, together with William Daubeney, Robert Ratcliff, Thomas Cressenor, and Thomas Astwood. All these were arraigned, convicted, and condemned for high treason, in adhering and promising aid to Perkin. Mountfort, Ratcliff, and Daubeney, were immediately executed: Fitzwater was sent over to Calais, and detained in custody; but being detected in practising on his keeper for an escape, he soon after underwent the same fate. The rest were pardoned, together with William Worseley, dean of St. Paul's, and some others, who had been accused and examined, but not brought to public trial [b].

GREATER and more solemn preparations were deemed requisite for the trial of Stanley, lord chamberlain, whose authority in the nation, whose domestic connexions with the king as well as his former services, seemed to secure him against any accusation or punishment. Clifford was directed to come over privately to England, and to throw himself at the king's feet, while he sat in council; craving pardon for past offences, and offering to atone for them by any services which should be required of him. Henry then told him, that the best proof he could give of penitence, and the only service he could now render him, was the full confession of his guilt, and the discovery of all his accomplices, however distinguished by rank or character. Encouraged by this exhortation, Clifford accused Stanley, then present, as his chief abettor; and of-

[b] Polydore Virgil, p. 592.

fered

fered to lay before the council the full proof of his guilt. Stanley himself could not discover more surprize than was affected by Henry on the occasion. He received the intelligence as absolutely false and incredible; that a man, to whom he was in a great measure beholden for his crown, and even for his life; a man, to whom, by every honour and favour, he had endeavoured to express his gratitude; whose brother, the earl of Derby, was his own father-in-law; to whom he had even committed the trust of his person, by creating him lord chamberlain: That this man, enjoying his full confidence and affection, not actuated by any motive of discontent or apprehension, should engage in a conspiracy against him. Clifford was therefore exhorted to weigh well the consequences of his accusation; but as he persisted in the same positive asseverations, Stanley was committed to custody, and was soon after examined before the council[c]. He denied not the guilt imputed to him by Clifford; he did not even endeavour much to extenuate it; whether he thought that a frank and open confession would serve as an atonement, or trusted to his present connexions, and his former services, for pardon and security. But princes are often apt to regard great services as a ground of jealousy, especially if accompanied with a craving and restless disposition, in the person who has performed them. The general discontent also, and mutinous humour of the people, seemed to require some great example of severity. And as Stanley was one of the most opulent subjects in the kingdom, being possessed of above three thousand pounds a-year in land, and forty thousand marks in plate and money, besides other property of great value, the prospect of so rich a forfeiture was deemed no small motive for Henry's proceeding to extremities against him. After six weeks delay, which was interposed, in order to shew that the

[c] Bacon, p. 611. Polyd. Virg. p. 593.

king was restrained by doubts and scruples; the prisoner was brought to his trial, condemned, and presently after beheaded. Historians are not agreed with regard to the crime which was proved against him. The general report is, that he should have said in confidence to Clifford, that, if he were sure the young man, who appeared in Flanders, was really son to king Edward, he never would bear arms against him. The sentiment might disgust Henry, as implying a preference of the house of York to that of Lancaster; but could scarcely be the ground, even in those arbitrary times, of a sentence of high treason against Stanley. It is more probable, therefore, as is asserted by some historians, that he had expressly engaged to assist Perkin, and had actually sent him some supply of money.

The fate of Stanley made great impression on the kingdom, and struck all the partizans of Perkin with the deepest dismay. From Clifford's desertion, they found that all their secrets were betrayed; and as it appeared, that Stanley, while he seemed to live in the greatest confidence with the king, had been continually surrounded by spies, who reported and registered every action in which he was engaged, nay, every word which fell from him, a general distrust took place, and all mutual confidence was destroyed, even among intimate friends and acquaintance. The jealous and severe temper of the king, together with his great reputation for sagacity and penetration, kept men in awe, and quelled not only the movements of sedition, but the very murmurs of faction. Libels, however, creeped out against Henry's person and administration; and being greedily propagated by every secret art, shewed that there still remained among the people a considerable root of discontent, which wanted only a proper opportunity to discover itself.

But

BUT Henry continued more intent on encreasing the terrors of his people, than on gaining their affections. Trusting to the great success which attended him in all his enterprizes, he gave every day, more and more, a loose to his rapacious temper, and employed the arts of perverted law and justice, in order to exact fines and compositions from his people. Sir William Capel, alderman of London, was condemned on some penal statutes to pay the sum of 2743 pounds, and was obliged to compound for sixteen hundred and fifteen. This was the first noted case of the kind; but it became a precedent, which prepared the way for many others. The management, indeed, of these arts of chicanery, was the great secret of the king's administration. While he depressed the nobility, he exalted and honoured and caressed the lawyers; and by that means both bestowed authority on the laws, and was enabled, whenever he pleased, to pervert them to his own advantage. His government was oppressive; but it was so much the less burthensome, as, by his extending royal authority, and curbing the nobles, he became in reality the sole oppressor in his kingdom.

CHAP. XXV.

1495.

As Perkin found, that the king's authority daily gained ground among the people, and that his own pretensions were becoming obsolete, he resolved to attempt something, which might revive the hopes and expectations of his partizans. Having collected a band of outlaws, pirates, robbers, and necessitous persons of all nations, to the number of 600 men, he put to sea, with a resolution of making a descent in England, and of exciting the common people to arms, since all his correspondence with the nobility was cut off by Henry's vigilance and severity. Information being brought him, that the king had made a progress to the north, he cast anchor on the coast of Kent, and sent some of his retainers ashore, who invited the country to join him. The gentlemen of Kent assembled

assembled some troops to oppose him; but they purposed to do more essential service than by repelling the invasion: They carried the semblance of friendship to Perkin, and invited him to come, himself, ashore, in order to take the command over them. But the wary youth, observing that they had more order and regularity in their movements than could be supposed in new levied forces, who had taken arms against established authority, refused to entrust himself into their hands; and the Kentish troops, despairing of success in their stratagem, fell upon such of his retainers, as were already landed; and besides some whom they slew, they took a hundred and fifty prisoners. These were tried and condemned; and all of them executed, by orders from the king, who was resolved to use no lenity towards men of such desperate fortunes[c].

A parliament.

This year a parliament was summoned in England, and another in Ireland; and some remarkable laws were passed in both countries. The English parliament enacted, that no person, who should by arms or otherwise assist the king for the time being, should ever afterwards, either by course of law or act of parliament, be attainted for such an instance of obedience. This statute might be exposed to some censure, as favourable to usurpers; were there any precise rule, which always, even during the most factious times, could determine the true successor, and render every one inexcusable who did not submit to him. But as the titles of princes are then the great subject of dispute, and each party pleads topics in its own favour, it seems but equitable to secure those who act in support of public tranquillity, an object at all times of undoubted benefit and importance. Henry, conscious of his disputed title, promoted this law, in order to secure his partizans against all events; but as he had himself observ-

[c] Polydore Virgil, p. 595.

ed a contrary practice with regard to Richard's adherents, he had reason to apprehend, that, during the violence which usually ensues on public convulsions, his example, rather than his law, would, in case of a new revolution, be followed by his enemies. And the attempt to bind the legislature itself, by prescribing rules to future parliaments, was contradictory to the plainest principles of political government.

This parliament also passed an act, impowering the king to levy, by course of law, all the sums which any person had agreed to pay by way of benevolence: A statute, by which that arbitrary method of taxation was indirectly authorized and justified.

The king's authority appeared equally prevalent and uncontrolled in Ireland. Sir Edward Poynings had been sent over to that country, with an intention of quelling the partizans of the house of York, and of reducing the natives to subjection. He was not supported by forces sufficient for that enterprize: The Irish, by flying into their woods, and morasses, and mountains, for some time eluded his efforts: But Poynings summoned a parliament at Dublin, where he was more successful. He passed that memorable statute, which still bears his name, and which establishes the authority of the English government in Ireland. By this statute, all the former laws of England were made to be of force in Ireland; and no bill can be introduced into the Irish parliament, unless it previously receive the sanction of the council of England. This latter clause seems calculated for ensuring the dominion of the English; but was really granted at the desire of the Irish commons, who intended, by that means, to secure themselves from the tyranny of their lords, particularly of such lieutenants or deputies as were of Irish birth[a].

[a] Sir John Davies, p. 235.

CHAP.
XXV.

1495.

WHILE Henry's authority was thus established throughout his dominions, and general tranquillity prevailed, the whole continent was thrown into combustion by the French invasion of Italy, and by the rapid success which attended Charles in that rash and ill-concerted enterprize. The Italians, who had entirely lost the use of arms, and who, in the midst of continual wars, had become every day more unwarlike, were astonished to meet an enemy, that made the field of battle not a pompous tournament, but a scene of blood, and fought, at the hazard of their own lives, the death of their enemy. Their effeminate troops were dispersed every where on the approach of the French army: Their best fortified cities opened their gates: Kingdoms and states were in an instant overturned: And through the whole length of Italy, which the French penetrated without resistance, they seemed rather to be taking quarters in their own country, than making conquests over an enemy. The maxims, which the Italians, during that age, followed in negociations, were as ill calculated to support their states, as the habits to which they were addicted in war: A treacherous, deceitful, and inconsistent system of politics prevailed; and even those small remains of fidelity and honour, which were preserved in the councils of the other European princes, were ridiculed in Italy as proofs of ignorance and rusticity. Ludovico, duke of Milan, who invited the French to invade Naples, had never desired or expected their success; and was the first that felt terror from the prosperous issue of those projects, which he himself had concerted. By his intrigues, a league was formed among several potentates to oppose the progress of Charles's conquests, and secure their own independency. This league was composed of Ludovico himself, the pope, Maximilian king of the Romans, Ferdinand of Spain, and the republic of Venice. Henry too entered into the confederacy;

racy; but was not put to any expence or trouble in consequence of his engagements. The king of France, terrified by so powerful a combination, retired from Naples with the greater part of his army; and returned to France. The forces which he left in his new conquest were, partly by the revolt of the inhabitants, partly by the invasion of the Spaniards, soon after subdued; and the whole kingdom of Naples suddenly returned to its allegiance under Ferdinand, son to Alphonso, who had been suddenly expelled by the irruption of the French. Ferdinand died soon after; and left his uncle, Frederic, in full possession of the throne.

CHAP. XXVI.

Perkin retires to Scotland——Insurrection in the west ——Battle of Blackheath——Truce with Scotland ——Perkin taken prisoner——Perkin executed ——The earl of Warwic executed——Marriage of prince Arthur with Catharine of Arragon—— His death——Marriage of the princess Margaret with the king of Scotland——Oppressions of the people——A parliament——Arrival of the king of Castile——Intrigues of the earl of Suffolk—— Sickness of the king——His death——and character——His laws.

CHAP. XXVI.
1495.

AFTER Perkin was repulsed from the coast of Kent, he retired into Flanders; but as he found it impossible to procure subsistence for himself and his followers, while he remained in tranquillity, he soon after made an attempt upon Ireland, which had always appeared forward to join every invader of Henry's authority. But Poynings had now put the affairs of that island in so good a posture, that Perkin met with little success; and, being tired of the savage life which he was obliged to lead, while skulking among the wild Irish, he bent his course towards Scotland, and presented himself to James IV. who then governed that kingdom. He had been previously recommended to this prince by the king of France, who was disgusted at Henry for entering into the general league against him; and this recommendation was even seconded by Maximilian, who, though one of the confederates, was also displeased with the king, on account of of his prohibiting in England all commerce with the Low Countries. The countenance given to Perkin by these princes procured him a favourable reception with the king of Scotland, who assured him, that, whatever he were, he never should repent putting himself in his hands [f]: The insinuating address and plausible behaviour of the youth himself, seem even to have gained him credit and authority. James, whom years had not yet taught distrust or caution, was seduced to believe the story of Perkin's birth and adventures; and he carried his confidence so far as to give him in marriage the lady Catherine Gordon, daughter of the earl of Huntley, and related to himself; a young lady too, eminent for virtue as well as beauty.

CHAP. XXVI.

1495. Perkin retire to Scotland.

THERE subsisted at that time a great jealousy between the courts of England and Scotland; and James was probably the more forward on that account to adopt any fiction, which, he thought, might reduce his enemy to distress or difficulty. He suddenly resolved to make an inroad into England, attended by some of the borderers; and he carried Perkin along with him, in hopes that the appearance of the pretended prince might raise an insurrection in the northern counties. Perkin himself dispersed a manifesto, in which he set forth his own story, and craved the assistance of all his subjects in expelling the usurper, whose tyranny and mal-administration, whose depression of the nobility by the elevation of mean persons, whose oppression of the people by multiplied impositions and vexations, had justly, he said, rendered him odious to all men. But Perkin's pretensions, attended with repeated disappointments, were now become stale in the eyes even of the populace; and the hostile dispositions, which subsisted between the kingdoms rendered a

1496.

[f] Bacon, p. 615. Polydore Virgil, p. 596, 597.

CHAP. XXVI.
1496.

prince, supported by the Scots, but an unwelcome present to the English nation. The ravages also committed by the borderers, accustomed to licence and disorder, struck a terror into all men; and made the people prepare rather for repelling the invaders than for joining them. Perkin, that he might support his pretensions to royal birth, feigned great compassion for the misery of his plundered subjects; and publicly remonstrated with his ally against the depredations exercised by the Scottish army [s]: But James told him, that he doubted his concern was employed only in behalf of an enemy, and that he was anxious to preserve what never should belong to him. That prince now began to perceive that his attempt would be fruitless; and hearing of an army which was on its march to attack him, he thought proper to retreat into his own country.

THE king discovered little anxiety to procure either reparation or vengeance for this insult committed on him by the Scottish nation: His chief concern was to draw advantage from it, by the pretence which it might afford him to levy impositions on his own subjects. He summoned a parliament, to whom he made bitter complaints against the irruption of the Scots, the absurd imposture countenanced by that nation, the cruel devastations committed in the northern counties, and the multiplied insults thus offered both to the king and kingdom of England. The parliament made the expected return to this discourse, by granting a subsidy to the amount of 120,000 pounds, together with two fifteenths. After making this grant, they were dismissed.

1497.

THE vote of parliament for imposing the tax was without much difficulty procured by the authority of Henry; but he found it not so easy to levy the money upon his subjects. The people, who were acquainted

[s] Polydore Virgil, p. 592.

with

with the immense treasures which he had amassed, could ill brook the new impositions raised on every flight occasion; and it is probable, that the flaw, which was universally known to be in his title, made his reign the more subject to insurrections and rebellions. When the subsidy began to be levied in Cornwal, the inhabitants, numerous and poor, robust and courageous, murmured against a tax, occasioned by a sudden inroad of the Scots, from which they esteemed themselves entirely secure, and which had usually been repelled by the force of the northern counties. Their ill-humour was farther incited by one Michael Joseph, a farrier of Bodmin, a notable prating fellow, who, by thrusting himself forward on every occasion, and being loudest in every complaint against the government, had acquired an authority among those rude people. Thomas Flammoc too, a lawyer, who had become the oracle of the neighbourhood, encouraged the sedition, by informing them that the tax, though imposed by parliament, was entirely illegal; that the northern nobility were bound, by their tenures, to defend the nation against the Scots; and that if these new impositions were tamely submitted to, the avarice of Henry and of his ministers would soon render the burden intolerable to the nation. The Cornish, he said, must deliver to the king a petition, seconded by such a force as would give it authority; and, in order to procure the concurrence of the rest of the kingdom, care must be taken, by their orderly deportment, to shew that they had nothing in view but the public good, and the redress of all those grievances under which the people had so long laboured.

CHAP. XXVI.
1497.
Insurrection in the West.

ENCOURAGED by these speeches, the multitude flocked together, and armed themselves with axes, bills, bows, and such weapons as country people are usually possessed of. Flammoc and Joseph were chosen their leaders. They soon conducted the Cornish through the county of Devon.

CHAP. XXVI.

1197.

Devon, and reached that of Somerset. At Taunton the rebels killed, in their fury, an officious and eager commissioner of the subsidy, whom they called the provost of Perin. When they reached Wells, they were joined by lord Audley, a nobleman of an ancient family, popular in his deportment, but vain, ambitious, and restless in his temper. He had from the beginning maintained a secret correspondence with the first movers of the insurrection; and was now joyfully received by them as their leader. Proud of the countenance given them by so considerable a nobleman, they continued their march; breathing destruction to the king's ministers and favourites, particularly to Morton, now a cardinal, and Sir Reginald Bray, who were deemed the most active instruments in all his oppressions. Notwithstanding their rage against the administration, they carefully followed the directions given them by their leaders; and as they met with no resistance, they committed, during their march, no violence or disorder.

THE rebels had been told by Flammoc, that the inhabitants of Kent, as they had ever, during all ages, remained unsubdued, and had even maintained their independence during the Norman conquest, would surely embrace their party, and declare themselves for a cause, which was no other than that of public good and general liberty. But the Kentish people had very lately distinguished themselves by repelling Perkin's invasion; and as they had received from the king many gracious acknowledgments for this service, their affections were, by that means, much conciliated to his government. It was easy, therefore, for the earl of Kent, lord Abergavenny, and lord Cobham, who possessed great authority in those parts, to retain the people in obedience; and the Cornish rebels, though they pitched their camp near Eltham, at the very gates of London, and invited all the people to

join

join them, got reinforcement from no quarter. There wanted not discontents every where, but no one would take part in so rash and ill-concerted an enterprize; and besides, the situation in which the king's affairs then stood, discouraged even the boldest and most daring.

CHAP.
XXVI.
1497.

HENRY, in order to oppose the Scots, had already levied an army, which he put under the command of lord Daubeney, the chamberlain; and as soon as he heard of the Cornish insurrection, he ordered it to march southwards, and suppress the rebels. Not to leave the northern frontier defenceless, he dispatched thither the earl of Surrey, who assembled the forces on the borders, and made head against the enemy. Henry found here the concurrence of the three most fatal incidents that can befal a monarchy; a foreign enemy, a domestic rebellion, and a pretender to his crown; but he enjoyed great resources in his army and treasure, and still more, in the intrepidity and courage of his own temper. He did not, however, immediately give full scope to his military spirit. On other occasions, he had always hastened to a decision; and it was a usual saying with him, *that he desired but to see his rebels:* But as the Cornish mutineers behaved in an inoffensive manner, and committed no spoil on the country; as they received no accession of force on their march or in their encampment; and as such hasty and popular tumults might be expected to diminish every moment by delay; he took post in London, and assiduously prepared the means of ensuring victory.

AFTER all his forces were collected, he divided them into three bodies, and marched out to assail the enemy. The first body, commanded by the earl of Oxford, and under him by the earls of Essex and Suffolk, were appointed to place themselves behind the hill on which the rebels were encamped: The second and most considerable, Henry put under the command of lord Daubeney,

Battle of Blackheath.

CHAP. XXVI.

1497.

June 22d.

and ordered him to attack the enemy in front, and bring on the action. The third, he kept as a body of reserve about his own person, and took post in St. George's fields; where he secured the city, and could easily, as occasion served, either restore the fight, or finish the victory. To put the enemy off their guard, he had spread a report that he was not to attack them till some days after; and, the better to confirm them in this opinion, he began not the action till near the evening. Daubeney beat a detachment of the rebels from Deptford bridge; and before the main body could be in order to receive him, he had gained the ascent of the hill, and placed himself in array before them. They were formidable from their numbers, being sixteen thousand strong, and were not defective in valour; but being tumultuary troops, ill armed, and not provided with cavalry or artillery, they were but an unequal match for the king's forces. Daubeney began the attack with courage, and even with a contempt of the enemy, which had almost proved fatal to him. He rushed into the midst of them, and was taken prisoner; but soon after was released by his own troops. After some resistance, the rebels were broken, and put to flight[b], Lord Audley, Flammoc, and Joseph, their leaders, were taken, and all three executed. The latter seemed even to exult in his end, and boasted, with a preposterous ambition, that he should make a figure in history. The rebels, being surrounded on every side by the king's troops, were almost all made prisoners, and immediately dismissed without farther punishment: Whether that Henry was satisfied with the victims who had fallen in the field, and who amounted to near two thousand, or that he pitied the ignorance and simplicity of the multitude, or favoured them on account of their inoffensive behaviour, or was pleased that they had never,

[b] Polydore Virgil, p. 601.

during

during their infurrection, difputed his title, and had fhewn no attachment to the houfe of York, the higheft crime, of which, in his eyes, they could have been guilty.

THE Scottifh king was not idle during thefe commotions in England. He levied a confiderable army, and fat down before the caftle of Norham in Northumberland; but found that place, by the precaution of Fox, bifhop of Durham, fo well provided both with men and ammunition, that he made little or no progrefs in the fiege. Hearing that the earl of Surrey had collected fome forces, and was advancing upon him, he retreated into his own country, and left the frontiers expofed to the inroads of the Englifh general, who befieged and took Aiton, a fmall caftle lying a few miles beyond Berwic. Thefe unfuccefsful or frivolous attempts on both fides prognofticated a fpeedy end to the war; and Henry, notwithftanding his fuperior force, was no lefs defirous than James of terminating the differences between the nations. Not to depart, however, from his dignity, by making the firft advances, he employed in this friendly office Peter Hialas, a man of addrefs and learning, who had come to him as ambaffador from Ferdinand and Ifabella, and who was charged with a commiffion of negociating the marriage of the infanta Catherine, their daughter, with Arthur prince of Wales [1].

HIALAS took a journey northwards, and offered his mediation between James and Henry, as minifter of a prince who was in alliance with both potentates. Commiffioners were foon appointed to meet, and confer on terms of accommodation. The firft demand of the Englifh was, that Perkin fhould be put into their hands: James replied, that he himfelf was no judge of the young man's pretenfions, but having received him as a fuppli-

[1] Polydore Virgil, p. 603.

cant,

cent, and promised him protection, he was determined not to betray a man who had trusted to his good faith and his generosity. The next demand of the English met with no better reception: They required reparation for the ravages committed by the late inroads into England: The Scottish commissioners replied, that the spoils were like water spilt upon the ground, which could never be recovered, and that Henry's subjects were better able to bear the loss, than their master's to repair it. Henry's commissioners next proposed, that the two kings should have an interview at Newcastle, in order to adjust all differences; but James said, that he meant to treat of a peace, not to go a begging for it. Lest the conferences should break off altogether without effect, a truce was concluded for some months; and James, perceiving that, while Perkin remained in Scotland, he himself never should enjoy a solid peace with Henry, privately desired him to depart the kingdom.

Access was now barred Perkin into the Low Countries, his usual retreat in all his disappointments. The Flemish merchants, who severely felt the loss resulting from the interruption of commerce with England, had made such interest in the archduke's council, that commissioners were sent to London, in order to treat of an accommodation. The Flemish court agreed, that all English rebels should be excluded the Low Countries; and in this prohibition the demesnes of the dutchess-dowager were expresly comprehended. When this principal article was agreed to, all the other terms were easily adjusted. A treaty of commerce was finished, which was favourable to the Flemings, and to which they long gave the appellation of *Intercursus magnus*, the great treaty. And when the English merchants returned to their usual abode at Antwerp, they were publicly received, as in procession, with joy and festivity.

PERKIN

PERKIN was a Fleming by descent, though born in England; and it might therefore be doubted, whether he were included in the treaty between the two nations: But as he must dismiss all his English retainers if he took shelter in the Low Countries, and as he was sure of a cold reception, if not bad usage, among people who were determined to keep on terms of friendship with the court of England; he thought fit rather to hide himself, during some time, in the wilds and fastnesses of Ireland. Impatient, however, of a retreat, which was both disagreeable and dangerous, he held consultations with his followers, Herne, Skelton, and Astley, three broken tradesmen: By their advice, he resolved to try the affections of the Cornish, whose mutinous disposition, notwithstanding the king's lenity, still subsisted, after the suppression of their rebellion. No sooner did he appear at Bodmin in Cornwal, than the populace, to the number of three thousand, flocked to his standard; and Perkin, elated with this appearance of success, took on him, for the first time, the appellation of Richard IV. king of England. Not to suffer the expectations of his followers to languish, he presented himself before Exeter; and, by many fair promises, invited that city to join him. Finding that the inhabitants shut their gates against him, he laid siege to the place; but being unprovided with artillery, ammunition, and every thing requisite for the attempt, he made no progress in his undertaking. Messengers were sent to the king, informing him of this insurrection: The citizens of Exeter, meanwhile, were determined to hold out to the last extremity, in expectation of receiving succour from the well-known vigilance of that monarch.

WHEN Henry was informed that Perkin was landed in England, he expressed great joy, and prepared himself with alacrity to attack him, in hopes of being able, at length, to put a period to pretensions which had so long given

CHAP. XXVI.

1497.

CHAP.
XXVI.

1497.

given him vexation and inquietude. All the courtiers, sensible that their activity on this occasion would be the most acceptable service which they could render the king, displayed their zeal for the enterprize, and forwarded his preparations. The lords Daubeney and Broke, with Sir Rice ap Thomas, hastened forward with a small body of troops to the relief of Exeter. The earl of Devonshire, and the most considerable gentlemen in the county of that name, took arms of their own accord, and marched to join the king's generals. The duke of Buckingham put himself at the head of a troop, consisting of young nobility and gentry, who served as volunteers, and who longed for an opportunity of displaying their courage and their loyalty. The king himself prepared to follow with a considerable army; and thus all England seemed united against a pretender who had at first engaged their attention, and divided their affections.

PERKIN, informed of these great preparations, immediately raised the siege of Exeter, and retired to Taunton. Though his followers now amounted to the number of near seven thousand, and seemed still resolute to maintain his cause, he himself despaired of success, and secretly withdrew to the sanctuary of Beaulieu in the new forest. The Cornish rebels submitted to the king's mercy, and found that it was not yet exhausted in their behalf. Except a few persons of desperate fortunes who were executed, and some others who were severely fined, all the rest were dismissed with impunity. Lady Catherine Gordon, wife to Perkin, fell into the hands of the victor, and was treated with a generosity which does him honour. He soothed her mind with many marks of regard, placed her in a reputable station about the queen, and assigned her a pension, which she enjoyed even under his successor.

HENRY

Henry deliberated what course to take with Perkin himself. Some counselled him to make the privileges of the church yield to reasons of state, to take him by violence from the sanctuary, to inflict on him the punishment due to his temerity, and thus at once to put an end to an imposture which had long disturbed the government, and which the credulity of the people, and the artifices of malcontents, were still capable of reviving. But the king deemed not the matter of such importance as to merit so violent a remedy. He employed some persons to deal with Perkin, and persuade him, under promise of pardon, to deliver himself into the king's hands [1]. The king conducted him, in a species of mock triumph, to London. As Perkin passed along the road, and through the streets of the city, men of all ranks flocked about him, and the populace treated with the highest derision his fallen fortunes. They seemed desirous of revenging themselves, by their insults, for the shame which their former belief of his impostures had thrown upon them. Though the eyes of the nation were generally opened with regard to Perkin's real parentage, Henry required of him a confession of his life and adventures; and he ordered the account of the whole to be dispersed, soon after, for the satisfaction of the public. But as his regard to decency made him entirely suppress the share which the dutchess of Burgundy had had in contriving and conducting the imposture, the people, who knew that she had been the chief instrument in the whole affair, were inclined, on account of the silence on that head, to pay the less credit to the authenticity of the narrative.

Perkin taken prisoner.

But Perkin, though his life was granted him, was still detained in custody; and keepers were appointed to guard

1499.

[1] Polydore Virgil, p. 606.

CHAP.
XXVI.

1499.

guard him. Impatient of confinement, he broke from his keepers, and flying to the sanctuary of Shyne, put himself into the hands of the prior of that monastery. The prior had obtained great credit by his character of sanctity; and he prevailed on the king again to grant a pardon to Perkin. But in order to reduce him to still greater contempt, he was set in the stocks at Westminster and Cheapside, and obliged in both places to read aloud to the people the confession which had formerly been published in his name. He was then confined to the Tower, where his habits of restless intrigue and enterprize followed him. He insinuated himself into the intimacy of four servants of Sir John Digby, lieutenant of the Tower; and, by their means, opened a correspondence with the earl of Warwic, who was confined in the same prison. This unfortunate prince, who had from his earliest youth been shut up from the commerce of men, and who was ignorant even of the most common affairs of life, had fallen into a simplicity which made him susceptible of any impression. The continued dread also of the more violent effects of Henry's tyranny, joined to the natural love of liberty, engaged him to embrace a project for his escape, by the murder of the lieutenant; and Perkin offered to conduct the whole enterprize. The conspiracy escaped not the king's vigilance: It was even very generally believed that the scheme had been laid by himself, in order to draw Warwic and Perkin into the snare: But the subsequent execution of two of Digby's servants for the contrivance, seems to clear the king of that imputation, which was indeed founded more on the general idea entertained of his character, than on any positive evidence.

PERKIN, by this new attempt, after so many enormities, had rendered himself totally unworthy of mercy; and he was accordingly arraigned, condemned, and soon after

HENRY VII.

after hanged at Tyburn, persisting still in the confession of his imposture[m]. It happened about that very time, that one Wilford, a cordwainer's son, encouraged by the surprising credit given to other impostures, had undertaken to personate the earl of Warwic; and a priest had even ventured from the pulpit to recommend his cause to the people, who seemed still to retain a propensity to adopt it. This incident served Henry as a pretence for his severity towards that prince. He was brought to trial, and accused not of contriving his escape (for as he was committed for no crime, the desire of liberty must have been regarded as natural and innocent), but of forming designs to disturb the government, and raise an insurrection among the people. Warwic confessed the indictment, was condemned, and the sentence was executed upon him.

CHAP. XXVI.

1499. Perkin executed.

The earl of Warwic executed, 28 Nov.

THIS violent act of tyranny, the great blemish of Henry's reign, by which he destroyed the last remaining male of the line of Plantagenet, begat great discontent among the people, who saw an unhappy prince, that had long been denied all the privileges of his high birth, even been cut off from the common benefits of nature, now at last deprived of life itself, merely for attempting to shake off that oppression under which he laboured. In vain did Henry endeavour to alleviate the odium of this guilt, by sharing it with his ally, Ferdinand of Arragon, who, he said, had scrupled to give his daughter Catherine in marriage to Arthur, while any male descendant of the house of York remained. Men, on the contrary, felt higher indignation at seeing a young prince sacrificed, not to law and justice, but to the jealous politics of two subtle and crafty tyrants.

BUT though these discontents festered in the minds of men, they were so checked by Henry's watchful policy

[m] See note [M] at the end of the volume.

and

CHAP.
XXIV.

1499.

and ready severity; that they seemed not to weaken his government; and foreign princes, deeming his throne now entirely secure, paid him rather the greater deference and attention. The archduke Philip, in particular, desired an interview with him; and Henry, who had passed over to Calais, agreed to meet him in St. Peter's church near that city. The archduke, on his approaching the king, made haste to alight, and offered to hold Henry's stirrup; a mark of condescension which that prince would not admit of. He called the king *father, patron, protector*; and, by his whole behaviour, expressed a strong desire of conciliating the friendship of England. The duke of Orleans had succeeded to the crown of France by the appellation of Lewis XII. and having carried his arms into Italy, and subdued the dutchy of Milan, his progress begat jealousy in Maximillian, Philip's father, as well as in Ferdinand, his father-in-law. By the counsel, therefore, of these monarchs, the young prince endeavoured by every art to acquire the amity of Henry, whom they regarded as the chief counterpoise to the greatness of France. No particular plan, however, of alliance seems to have been concerted between these two princes in their interview: All passed in general professions of affection and regard; at least, in remote projects of a closer union, by the future intermarriages of their children, who were then in a state of infancy.

1500.

THE pope too, Alexander VI. neglected not the friendship of a monarch whose reputation was spread over Europe. He sent a nuntio into England, who exhorted the king to take part in the great alliance projected for the recovery of the Holy Land, and to lead in person his forces against the infidels. The general frenzy for crusades was now entirely exhausted in Europe; but
it

it was still thought a necessary piece of decency to pretend zeal for those pious enterprizes. Henry regretted to the nuncio, the distance of his situation, which rendered it inconvenient for him to expose his person in defence of the Christian cause. He promised, however, his utmost assistance by aids and contributions; and rather than the pope should go alone to the holy wars, unaccompanied by any monarch, he even promised to overlook all other considerations, and to attend him in person. He only required as a necessary condition, that all differences should previously be adjusted among Christian princes, and that some sea-port towns in Italy should be consigned to him for his retreat and security. It was easy to conclude, that Henry had determined not to intermeddle in any war against the Turk: But as a great name, without any real assistance, is sometimes of service, the knights of Rhodes, who were at that time esteemed the bulwark of Christendom, chose the king protector of their order.

CHAP.
XXVI.

1500.

But the prince, whose alliance Henry valued the most, was Ferdinand of Arragon, whose vigorous and steady policy, always attended with success, had rendered him, in many respects, the most considerable monarch in Europe. There was also a remarkable similarity of character between these two princes: Both were full of craft, intrigue, and design; and though a resemblance of this nature be a slender foundation for confidence and amity, where the interests of the parties in the least interfere; such was the situation of Henry and Ferdinand, that no jealousy ever on any occasion arose between them. The king had now the satisfaction of completing a marriage, which had been projected and negociated during the course of seven years, between Arthur prince of Wales, and the Infanta Catherine, fourth daughter of Ferdinand and Isabella; he near sixteen years

1501.
Marriage of prince Arthur with Catherine of Arragon. 10th Nov.

CHAP. XXVI.

1502.
2d April.
His death.

of age, she eighteen. But this marriage proved in the issue unprosperous. The young prince, a few months after, sickened and died, much regretted by the nation. Henry, desirous to continue his alliance with Spain, and also unwilling to restore Catherine's dowry, which was two hundred thousand ducats, obliged his second son, Henry, whom he created prince of Wales, to be contracted to the Infanta. The prince made all the opposition, of which a youth of twelve years of age was capable; but as the king persisted in his resolution, the espousals were at length, by means of the pope's dispensation, contracted between the parties: An event, which was afterwards attended with the most important consequences.

Marriage of the princess Margaret with the King of Scotland.

The same year, another marriage was celebrated, which was also, in the next age, productive of great events: The marriage of Margaret, the king's elder daughter, with James king of Scotland. This alliance had been negociated during three years, though interrupted by several broils; and Henry hoped, from the completion of it, to remove all source of discord with that neighbouring kingdom, by whose animosity England had so often been infested. When this marriage was deliberated on in the English council, some objected, that England might, by means of that alliance, fall under the dominion of Scotland. "No;" replied Henry, "Scot-
"land, in that event, will only become an accession to
"England." Amidst these prosperous incidents, the king met with a domestic calamity, which made not such impression on him as it merited: His queen died in childbed; and the infant did not long survive her. This princess was deservedly a favourite of the nation; and the general affection for her encreased, on account of the harsh treatment which, it was thought, she met with from her consort.

1503.
11th Feb.

THE

THE situation of the king's affairs, both at home and abroad, was now, in every respect, very fortunate. All the efforts of the European princes, both in war and negociation, were turned to the side of Italy; and the various events which there arose, made Henry's alliance be courted by every party, yet interested him so little as never to touch him with concern or anxiety. His close connexions with Spain and Scotland ensured his tranquillity; and his continued successes over domestic enemies, owing to the prudence and vigour of his conduct, had reduced the people to entire submission and obedience. Uncontrouled, therefore, by apprehension or opposition of any kind, he gave full scope to his natural propensity; and avarice, which had ever been his ruling passion, being encreased by age, and encouraged by absolute authority, broke all restraints of shame or justice. He had found two ministers, Empson and Dudley, perfectly qualified to second his rapacious and tyrannical inclinations, and to prey upon his defenceless people. These instruments of oppression were both lawyers, the first of mean birth, of brutal manners, of an unrelenting temper; the second better born, better educated, and better bred, but equally unjust, severe and inflexible. By their knowledge in law, these men were qualified to pervert the forms of justice to the oppression of the innocent; and the formidable authority of the king supported them in all their iniquities.

It was their usual practice at first to observe so far the appearance of law as to give indictments to those whom they intended to oppress: Upon which the persons were committed to prison, but never brought to trial; and were at length obliged, in order to recover their liberty, to pay heavy fines and ransoms, which were called mitigations and compositions. By degrees, the very appearance of law was neglected: The two ministers sent forth their precepts

CHAP.
XXVI.

1503.

precepts to attach men, and summon them before themselves and some others, at their private houses, in a court of commission, where, in a summary manner, without trial or jury, arbitrary decrees were issued, both in pleas of the crown, and controversies between private parties. Juries themselves, when summoned, proved but small security to the subject; being brow-beaten by these oppressors; nay, fined, imprisoned, and punished, if they gave sentence against the inclination of the ministers. The whole system of the feudal law, which still prevailed, was turned into a scheme of oppression. Even the king's wards, after they came of age, were not suffered to enter into possession of their lands without paying exorbitant fines. Men were also harassed with informations of intrusion upon scarce colourable titles. When an outlawry in a personal action was issued against any man, he was not allowed to purchase his charter of pardon, except on the payment of a great sum; and if he refused the composition required of him, the strict law, which, in such cases, allows forfeiture of goods, was rigorously insisted on. Nay, without any colour of law, the half of men's lands and rents were seized during two years, as a penalty in case of outlawry. But the chief means of oppression, employed by these ministers, were the penal statutes, which, without consideration of rank, quality, or services, were rigidly put in execution against all men: Spies, informers, and inquisitors were rewarded and encouraged in every quarter of the kingdom: And no difference was made whether the statute were beneficial or hurtful, recent or obsolete, possible or impossible to be executed. The sole end of the king and his ministers was to amass money, and bring every one under the lash of their authority [n].

[n] Bacon, p. 629, 630. Hollingshed, p. 504. Polyd. Virg. p. 613. 615.

THROUGH

HENRY VII.

THROUGH the prevalence of such an arbitrary and iniquitous administration, the English, it may safely be affirmed, were considerable losers by their ancient privileges, which secured them from all taxations, except such as were imposed by their own consent in parliament. Had the king been impowered to levy general taxes at pleasure, he would naturally have abstained from these oppressive expedients, which destroyed all security in private property, and begat an universal diffidence throughout the nation. In vain did the people look for protection from the parliament, which was pretty frequently summoned during this reign. That assembly was so overawed, that, at this very time, during the greatest rage of Henry's oppressions, the commons chose Dudley their speaker, the very man who was the chief instrument of his iniquities. And though the king was known to be immensely opulent, and had no pretence of wars or expensive enterprizes of any kind, they granted him the subsidy which he demanded. But so insatiable was his avarice, that next year he levied a new benevolence, and renewed that arbitrary and oppressive method of taxation. By all these arts of accumulation, joined to a rigid frugality in his expence, he so filled his coffers, that he is said to have possessed in ready money the sum of 1,800,000 pounds: A treasure almost incredible, if we consider the scarcity of money in those times [o].

BUT while Henry was enriching himself by the spoils of his oppressed people, there happened an event abroad, which engaged his attention, and was even the object of

---

[o] Silver was, during this reign, at 37 shillings and sixpence a pound, which makes Henry's treasure near three millions of our present money. Besides many commodities have become above thrice as dear by the increase of gold and silver in Europe. And what is a circumstance of still greater weight, all other states were then very poor in comparison of what they are at present. These circumstances make Henry's treasure appear very great; and may lead us to conceive the oppressions of his government.

CHAP. XXVI.
1505.

his anxiety and concern. Isabella, queen of Castile, died about this time; and it was foreseen, that by this incident the fortunes of Ferdinand, her husband, would be much affected. The king was not only attentive to the fate of his ally, and watchful lest the general system of Europe should be affected by so important an event: He also considered the similarity of his own situation with that of Ferdinand, and regarded the issue of these transactions as a precedent for himself. Joan, the daughter of Ferdinand by Isabella, was married to the archduke Philip, and being, in right of her mother, heir of Castile, seemed entitled to dispute with Ferdinand the present possession of that kingdom. Henry knew, that notwithstanding his own pretensions by the house of Lancaster, the greater part of the nation was convinced of the superiority of his wife's title; and he dreaded lest the prince of Wales, who was daily advancing towards manhood, might be tempted by ambition to lay immediate claim to the crown. By his perpetual attention to depress the partizans of the York family, he had more closely united them into one party, and encreased their desire of shaking off that yoke under which they had so long laboured, and of taking every advantage, which his oppressive government should give his enemies against him. And as he possessed no independent force like Ferdinand, and governed a kingdom more turbulent and unruly, which he himself, by his narrow politics, had confirmed in factious prejudices; he apprehended that his situation would prove in the issue still more precarious.

NOTHING at first could turn out more contrary to the king's wishes than the transactions in Spain. Ferdinand, as well as Henry, had become very unpopular, and from a like cause, his former exactions and impositions; and the states of Castile discovered an evident resolution of preferring the title of Philip and Joan. In order

HENRY VII.

order to take advantage of these favourable dispositions, the archduke, now king of Castile, attended by his consort, embarked for Spain during the winter season; but meeting with a violent tempest in the channel, was obliged to take shelter in the harbour of Weymouth. Sir John Trenchard, a gentleman of authority in the county of Dorset, hearing of a fleet upon the coast, had assembled some forces; and being joined by Sir John Cary, who was also at the head of an armed body, he came to that town. Finding that Philip, in order to relieve his sickness and fatigue, was already come ashore, he invited him to his house; and immediately dispatched a messenger, to inform the court of this important incident. The king sent in all haste the earl of Arundel to compliment Philip on his arrival in England, and to inform him, that he intended to pay him a visit in person, and to give him a suitable reception in his dominions. Philip knew, that he could not now depart without the king's consent; and therefore, for the sake of dispatch, he resolved to anticipate his visit, and to have an interview with him at Windsor. Henry received him with all the magnificence possible, and with all the seeming cordiality; but he resolved, notwithstanding, to draw some advantage from this involuntary visit, paid him by his royal guest.

CHAP. XXVI.

1506.

Arrival of the king of Castile.

EDMOND de la Pole, earl of Suffolk, nephew to Edward IV. and brother to the earl of Lincoln, slain in the battle of Stoke, had some years before killed a man in a sudden fit of passion, and had been obliged to apply to the king for a remission of the crime. The king had granted his request; but being little indulgent to all persons connected with the house of York, he obliged him to appear openly in court and plead his pardon. Suffolk, more resenting the affront than grateful for the favour, had fled into Flanders, and taken shelter with his aunt, the

Intrigues of the earl of Suffolk.

dutchess

dutchess of Burgundy: But being promised forgiveness by the king, he returned to England, and obtained a new pardon. Actuated, however, by the natural inquietude of his temper, and uneasy from debts which he had contracted by his great expence at prince Arthur's wedding, he again made an elopement into Flanders. The king, well acquainted with the general discontent which prevailed against his administration, neglected not this incident, which might become of importance; and he employed his usual artifices to elude the efforts of his enemies. He directed Sir Robert Curson, governor of the castle of Hammes, to desert his charge, and to insinuate himself into the confidence of Suffolk, by making him a tender of his services. Upon information secretly conveyed by Curson, the king seized William Courtney, eldest son to the earl of Devonshire, and married to the lady Catherine, sister of the queen; William de la Pole, brother to the earl of Suffolk; Sir James Tirrel, and Sir James Windham, with some persons of inferior quality; and he committed them to custody. Lord Abergavenny and Sir Thomas Green were also apprehended; but were soon after released from their confinement. William de la Pole was long detained in prison; Courtney was attainted, and though not executed, he recovered not his liberty during the king's life-time. But Henry's chief severity fell upon Sir James Windham, and Sir James Tirrel, who were brought to their trial, condemned, and executed: The fate of the latter gave general satisfaction, on account of his participation in the murder of the young princes, sons of Edward IV. Notwithstanding these discoveries and executions, Curson was still able to maintain his credit with the earl of Suffolk: Henry, in order to remove all suspicion, had ordered him to be excommunicated, together with Suffolk himself, for his pretended rebellion. But after that traitor had performed all the services expected from him, he suddenly deserted the earl,

and

and came over to England, where the king received him with unusual marks of favour and confidence. Suffolk, astonished at this instance of perfidy, finding that even the dutchess of Burgundy, tired with so many fruitless attempts, had become indifferent to his cause, fled secretly into France, thence into Germany, and returned, at last, into the Low-Countries; where he was protected, though not countenanced, by Philip, then in close alliance with the king.

HENRY neglected not the present opportunity of complaining to his guest of the reception which Suffolk had met with in his dominions. "I really thought," replied the king of Castile, "that your greatness and felicity "had set you far above apprehensions from any person "of so little consequence: But, to give you satisfaction, "I shall banish him my state." "I expect that you "will carry your complaisance farther," said the king; "I desire to have Suffolk put into my hands, where alone "I can depend upon his submission and obedience." "That measure," said Philip, "will reflect dishonour "upon you as well as myself. You will be thought to "have treated me as a prisoner." "Then the matter is "at an end," replied the king, "for I will take that "dishonour upon me; and so your honour is saved[p]." The king of Castile found himself under a necessity of complying; but he first exacted Henry's promise that he would spare Suffolk's life. That nobleman was invited over to England by Philip; as if the king would grant him a pardon, on the intercession of his friend and ally. Upon his appearance he was committed to the Tower; and the king of Castile, having fully satisfied Henry, as well by this concession as by signing a treaty of commerce between England and Castile, which was advantageous to the former kingdom[q], was at last allowed to depart,

[p] Bacon, p. 633.   [q] Rymer, vol. xiii. p. 148.

after

CHAP.
XXVI.

1507.

1508.

Sickness of the king.

after a stay of three months. He landed in Spain, was joyfully received by the Castilians, and put in possession of the throne. He died soon after; and Joan, his widow, falling into deep melancholy, Ferdinand was again enabled to re-instate himself in authority, and to govern, till the day of his death, the whole Spanish monarchy.

THE king survived these transactions two years; but nothing memorable occurs in the remaining part of his reign, except his affiancing his second daughter, Mary, to the young archduke, Charles, son of Philip of Castile. He entertained also some intentions of marriage for himself, first with the queen-dowager of Naples, relict of Ferdinand; afterwards with the dutchess dowager of Savoy, daughter of Maximilian, and sister of Philip. But the decline of his health put an end to all such thoughts; and he began to cast his eye towards that future existence, which the iniquities and severities of his reign rendered a very dismal prospect to him. To allay the terrors under which he laboured, he endeavoured, by distributing alms, and founding religious houses, to make atonement for his crimes, and to purchase, by the sacrifice of part of his ill-gotten treasures, a reconciliation with his offended Maker. Remorse even seized him, at intervals, for the abuse of his authority by Empson and Dudley; but not sufficient to make him stop the rapacious hand of those oppressors. Sir William Capel was again fined two thousand pounds, under some frivolous pretence, and was committed to the Tower, for daring to murmur against the iniquity. Harris, an alderman of London, was indicted, and died of vexation before his trial came to an issue. Sir Laurence Ailmer, who had been mayor, and his two sheriffs, were condemned in heavy fines, and sent to prison till they made payment. The king gave countenance to all these oppressions; till death, by its nearer approaches,

HENRY VII.

approaches, impreſſed new terrors upon him; and he then ordered, by a general clauſe in his will, that reſtitution ſhould be made to all thoſe whom he had injured. He died of a conſumption, at his favourite palace of Richmond, after a reign of twenty-three years and eight months, and in the fifty-ſecond year of his age[r].

CHAP. XXVI.

1509. His death, 22d April.

THE reign of Henry VII. was, in the main, fortunate for his people at home, and honourable abroad. He put an end to the civil wars with which the nation had long been haraſſed, he maintained peace and order in the ſtate, he depreſſed the former exorbitant power of the nobility, and, together with the friendſhip of ſome foreign princes, he acquired the conſideration and regard of all. He loved peace without fearing war; though agitated with continual ſuſpicions of his ſervants and miniſters, he diſcovered no timidity, either in the conduct of his affairs, or in the day of battle; and, though often ſevere in his puniſhments, he was commonly leſs actuated by revenge than by maxims of policy. The ſervices which he rendered the people were derived from his views of private advantage, rather than the motives of public ſpirit; and where he deviated from intereſted regards, it was unknown to himſelf, and ever from the malignant prejudices of faction, or the mean projects of avarice; not from the ſallies of paſſion, or allurements of pleaſure; ſtill leſs from the benign motives of friendſhip and generoſity. His capacity was excellent, but ſomewhat contracted by the narrowneſs of his heart; he poſſeſſed inſinuation and addreſs, but never employed theſe talents, except where ſome great point of intereſt was to be gained; and, while he neglected to conciliate the affections of his people, he often felt the danger of reſting his authority on their fear and reverence alone. He was always extremely attentive to his affairs; but poſſeſſed not the faculty of ſeeing far into futurity; and

and character.

[r] Dugd. Baronage, II. p. 237.

was

CHAP. XXVI.

1509.

was more expert at providing a remedy for his mistakes, than judicious in avoiding them. Avarice was, on the whole, his ruling passion*; and he remains an instance, almost singular, of a man placed in a high station, and possessed of talents for great affairs, in whom that passion predominated above ambition. Even among private persons, avarice is commonly nothing but a species of ambition, and is chiefly incited by the prospect of that regard, distinction, and consideration, which attend on riches.

THE power of the kings of England had always been somewhat irregular or discretionary; but was scarcely ever so absolute during any former reign, at least after the establishment of the Great Charter, as during that of Henry. Besides the advantages derived from the personal character of the man, full of vigour, industry, and severity, deliberate in all projects, steady in every purpose, and attended with caution, as well as good fortune, in every enterprize; he came to the throne after long and bloody civil wars, which had destroyed all the great nobility, who alone could resist the encroachments of his authority: The people were tired with discord and intestine convulsions, and willing to submit to usurpations, and even to injuries, rather than plunge themselves anew into like miseries: The fruitless efforts made against him, served always, as is usual, to confirm his authority: As he ruled by a faction, and the lesser faction, all those on whom he conferred offices, sensible that they owed every thing to his protection, were willing to support his power, though at

* As a proof of Henry's attention to the smallest profits, Bacon tells us, that he had seen a book of accompts kept by Empson, and subscribed, in almost every leaf, by the king's own hand. Among other articles was the following: "Item, Received of such a one five marks for a pardon, which, if it do not pass, the money to be repayed, or the party otherwise satisfied." Opposite to the memorandum the king had writ with his own hand, "otherwise satisfied." Bacon, p. 630.

the expence of justice and national privileges. These seem the chief causes which at this time bestowed on the crown so considerable an addition of prerogative, and rendered the present reign a kind of epoch in the English constitution.

CHAP.
XXVI.

1509.

THIS prince, though he exalted his prerogative above law, is celebrated by his historian for many good laws which he made be enacted for the government of his subjects. Several considerable regulations, indeed, are found among the statutes of this reign, both with regard to the police of the kingdom, and its commerce: But the former are generally contrived with much better judgment than the latter. The more simple ideas of order and equity are sufficient to guide a legislator in every thing that regards the internal administration of justice: But the principles of commerce are much more complicated, and require long experience and deep reflection to be well understood in any state. The real consequence of a law or practice is there often contrary to first appearances. No wonder that, during the reign of Henry VII. these matters were frequently mistaken; and it may safely be affirmed that, even in the age of lord Bacon, very imperfect and erroneous ideas were formed on that subject.

His laws.

EARLY in Henry's reign, the authority of the Star Chamber, which was before founded on common law, and ancient practice, was, in some cases, confirmed by act of parliament[t]: Lord Bacon extols the utility of this court; but men began, even during the age of that historian, to feel that so arbitrary a jurisdiction was incompatible with liberty; and, in proportion as the spirit of independence still rose higher in the nation, the aversion to it en-

[t] See note [N] at the end of the volume.

creased,

creased, till it was entirely abolished by act of parliament in the reign of Charles I. a little before the commencement of the civil wars.

Laws were passed in this reign, ordaining the king's suit for murder to be carried on within a year and day[a]. Formerly, it did not usually commence till after; and as the friends of the person murdered often, in the interval, compounded matters with the criminal, the crime frequently passed unpunished. Suits were given to the poor *in forma pauperis*, as it is called: That is, without paying dues for the writs, or any fees to the council[v]: A good law at all times, especially in that age, when the people laboured under the oppression of the great; but a law difficult to be carried into execution. A law was made against carrying off any woman by force[x]. The benefit of clergy was abridged[y]; and the criminal, on the first offence, was ordered to be burned in the hand with a letter, denoting his crime; after which he was punished capitally for any new offence. Sheriffs were no longer allowed to fine any person, without previously summoning him before their court[z]. It is strange that such a practice should ever have prevailed. Attaint of juries was granted in cases which exceeded forty pounds value[a]: A law which has an appearance of equity, but which was afterwards found inconvenient. Actions popular were not allowed to be eluded by fraud or covin. If any servant of the king's conspired against the life of the steward, treasurer, or comptroller of the king's household, this design, though not followed by any overt act, was made liable to the punishment of felony[b]. This statute was enacted for the security of archbishop

[a] 3 H. 7. cap. 1.
[y] 4 H. 7. cap. 13.
[z] 19 H. 7. cap. 6.
[v] 11 H. 7. cap. 12.
[x] 11 H. 7. cap. 15.
[b] 3 H. 7. cap. 13.
[a] 3 H. 7. cap. 2.
[a] Ibid. cap. 24.

Morton,

CHAP. XXVI.

1509.

Morton, who found himself exposed to the enmity of great numbers.

There scarcely passed any session during this reign without some statute against engaging retainers, and giving them badges or liveries[c]; a practice by which they were, in a manner, inlisted under some great lord, and were kept in readiness to assist him in all wars, insurrections, riots, violences, and even in bearing evidence for him in courts of justice[d]. This disorder, which had prevailed during many reigns, when the law could give little protection to the subject, was then deeply rooted in England; and it required all the vigilance and rigour of Henry to extirpate it. There is a story of his severity against this abuse; and it seems to merit praise, though it is commonly cited as an instance of his avarice and rapacity. The earl of Oxford, his favourite general, in whom he always placed great and deserved confidence, having splendidly entertained him at his castle of Heningham, was desirous of making a parade of his magnificence at the departure of his royal guest; and ordered all his retainers, with their liveries and badges, to be drawn up in two lines, that their appearance might be the more gallant and splendid. "My lord," said the king, "I have heard much of your hospitality; but "the truth far exceeds the report. These handsome "gentlemen and yeomen, whom I see on both sides of "me, are, no doubt, your menial servants." The earl smiled, and confessed that his fortune was too narrow for such magnificence. "They are most of them," subjoined he, "my retainers, who are come to do me "service at this time, when they know I am honoured "with your majesty's presence." The king started a little, and said, "By my faith, my lord, I thank you

[c] 3 H. 7. cap. 1. & 12.   11 H. 7. cap. 3.   19 H. 7. cap. 24.
[d] 3 H. 7. cap. 12.   11 H. 7. cap. 25.

"for

CHAP.
XXVI.

1509.

"for your good cheer, but I must not allow my laws to be broken in my sight. My attorney must speak with you." Oxford is said to have paid no less than fifteen thousand marks, as a composition for his offence.

THE encrease of the arts, more effectually than all the severities of law, put an end to this pernicious practice. The nobility, instead of vying with each other in the number and boldness of their retainers, acquired, by degrees, a more civilized species of emulation, and endeavoured to excel in the splendour and elegance of their equipage, houses, and tables. The common people, no longer maintained in vicious idleness by their superiors, were obliged to learn some calling or industry, and became useful both to themselves and to others. And it must be acknowledged, in spite of those who declaim so violently against refinement in the arts, or what they are pleased to call luxury, that as much as an industrious tradesman is both a better man and a better citizen than one of those idle retainers who formerly depended on the great families; so much is the life of a modern nobleman more laudable than that of an ancient baron [e].

BUT the most important law, in its consequences, which was enacted during the reign of Henry, was that by which the nobility and gentry acquired a power of breaking the ancient entails, and of alienating their estates [f]. By means of this law, joined to the beginning luxury and refinements of the age, the great fortunes of the barons were gradually dissipated, and the property of the commons encreased in England. It is probable that Henry foresaw and intended this consequence; because

[e] See note [O] at the end of the volume.

[f] 4 H. 7. cap. 24. The practice of breaking entails by means of a fine and recovery was introduced in the reign of Edward the IVth: But it was not, properly speaking, law, till the statute of Henry the VIIth; which, by correcting some abuses that attended that practice, gave indirectly a sanction to it.

HENRY VII.

the constant scheme of his policy consisted in depressing the great, and exalting churchmen, lawyers, and men of new families, who were more dependant on him.

CHAP. XXVI.
1509.

THIS king's love of money naturally led him to encourage commerce, which encreased his customs; but, if we may judge by most of the laws enacted during his reign, trade and industry were rather hurt than promoted by the care and attention given to them. Severe laws were made against taking interest for money, which was then denominated usury [f]. Even the profits of exchange were prohibited, as favouring of usury [h], which the superstition of the age zealously proscribed. All evasive contracts, by which profits could be made from the loan of money, were also carefully guarded against [i]. It is needless to observe how unreasonable and iniquitous these laws, how impossible to be executed, and how hurtful to trade, if they could take place. We may observe, however, to the praise of this king, that sometimes, in order to promote commerce, he lent to merchants sums of money without interest, when he knew that their stock was not sufficient for those enterprizes which they had in view [k].

LAWS were made against the exportation of money, plate, or bullion [l]: A precaution, which serves to no other purpose than to make more be exported. But so far was the anxiety on this head carried, that merchants alien, who imported commodities into the kingdom, were obliged to invest, in English commodities, all the money acquired by their sales, in order to prevent their conveying it away in a clandestine manner [m].

IT was prohibited to export horses; as if that exportation did not encourage the breed, and render them more plentiful in the kingdom [n]. In order to promote archery,

[f] 3 H. 7. cap. 5. [h] Ibid. cap. 6. [i] 7 H. 7. cap. 8.
[k] Polyd. Virg. [l] 4 H. 7. cap. 23. [m] 3 H. 7. cap. 8.
[n] 11 H. 7. cap 13.

VOL. III. D d

no bows were to be sold at a higher price than six shillings and four-pence, reducing money to the denomination of our time. The only effect of this regulation must be, either that the people would be supplied with bad bows, or none at all. Prices were also affixed to woollen cloth, to caps and hats: And the wages of labourers were regulated by law. It is evident, that these matters ought always to be left free, and be entrusted to the common course of business and commerce. To some it may appear surprising, that the price of a yard of scarlet cloth should be limited to six and twenty shillings, money of our age; that of a yard of coloured cloth to eighteen; higher prices than these commodities bear at present; and that the wages of a tradesman, such as a mason, bricklayer, tyler, &c. should be regulated at near ten-pence a-day; which is not much inferior to the present wages given in some parts of England. Labour and commodities have certainly risen since the discovery of the West-Indies; but not so much in every particular as is generally imagined. The greater industry of the present times has encreased the number of tradesmen and labourers, so as to keep wages nearer a par than could be expected from the great encrease of gold and silver. And the additional art employed in the finer manufactures has even made some of these commodities fall below their former value. Not to mention, that merchants and dealers, being contented with less profit than formerly, afford the goods cheaper to their customers. It appears by a statute of this reign, that goods bought for sixteen pence would sometimes be sold by the merchants for three shillings. The commodities whose price has chiefly risen, are butchers meat, fowl, and fish (especially the latter), which cannot be much augmented in quantity by

HENRY VII.

the encreafe of art and induftry. The profeffion which then abounded moft, and was fometimes embraced by perfons of the loweft rank, was the church: By a claufe of a ftatute, all clerks or ftudents of the univerfity were forbidden to beg, without a permiffion from the vice-chancellor [t].

ONE great caufe of the low ftate of induftry during this period, was the reftraints put upon it; and the parliament, or rather the king (for he was the prime mover in every thing), enlarged a little fome of thefe limitations, but not to the degree that was requifite. A law had been enacted during the reign of Henry IV. [u], that no man could bind his fon or daughter to an apprenticefhip, unlefs he were poffeffed of twenty fhillings a-year in land; and Henry VII. becaufe the decay of manufactures was complained of in Norwich from the want of hands, exempted that city from the penalties of the law [w]. Afterwards the whole county of Norfolk obtained a like exemption with regard to fome branches of the woollen manufacture [x]. Thefe abfurd limitations proceeded from a defire of promoting hufbandry, which, however, is never more effectually encouraged than by the encreafe of manufactures. For a like reafon, the law enacted againft inclofures, and for the keeping up of farm-houfes [y], fcarcely deferves the high praifes beftowed on it by lord Bacon. If hufbandmen underftand agriculture, and have a ready vent for their commodities, we need not dread a diminution of the people employed in the country. All methods of fupporting populoufnefs, except by the intereft of the proprietors, are violent and ineffectual. During a century and a half after this period, there was a frequent renewal of laws and edicts againft depopulation; whence we may infer, that none of them were ever

---

[t] 11 H. 7. cap. 22. [u] 7 H. 7. cap. 17. [w] 11 H. 7. cap. 11. [x] 12 H. 7. cap. 1. [y] 4 H. 7. cap. 19.

executed,

CHAP. XXVI.

1509.

executed. The natural course of improvement at last provided a remedy.

ONE check to industry in England was the erecting of corporations; an abuse which is not yet entirely corrected. A law was enacted, that corporations should not pass any by-laws without the consent of three of the chief officers of state [e]. They were prohibited from imposing tolls at their gates [a]. The cities of Glocester and Worcester had even imposed tolls on the Severne, which were abolished [b].

THERE is a law of this reign [c], containing a preamble, by which it appears, that the company of merchant adventurers in London had, by their own authority, debarred all the other merchants of the kingdom from trading to the great marts in the Low Countries, unless each trader previously paid them the sum of near seventy pounds. It is surprising that such a by-law (if it deserve the name) could ever be carried into execution, and that the authority of parliament should be requisite to abrogate it.

IT was during this reign, on the second of August 1492, a little before sun-set, that Christopher Columbus, a Genoese, set out from Spain on his memorable voyage for the discovery of the western world; and, a few years after, Vasquez de Gama, a Portuguese, passed the Cape of Good Hope, and opened a new passage to the East Indies. These great events were attended with important consequences to all the nations of Europe, even to such as were not immediately concerned in those naval enterprizes. The enlargement of commerce and navigation encreased industry and the arts every where: The nobles dissipated their fortunes in expensive pleasures:

[e] 19 H. 7. cap. 7. [a] Ibid. cap. 8. [b] Ibid. cap. 18.
[c] 12 H. 7. cap. 6.

Men

Men of an inferior rank both acquired a share in the landed property, and created to themselves a considerable property of a new kind, in stock, commodities, art, credit, and correspondence. In some nations the privileges of the commons encreased by this encrease of property: In most nations, the kings, finding arms to be dropped by the barons, who could no longer endure their former rude manner of life, established standing armies, and subdued the liberties of their kingdoms: But in all places, the condition of the people, from the depression of the petty tyrants by whom they had formerly been oppressed, rather than governed, received great improvement; and they acquired, if not entire liberty, at least the most considerable advantages of it. And as the general course of events thus tended to depress the nobles and exalt the people, Henry VII. who also embraced that system of policy, has acquired more praise than his institutions, strictly speaking, seem of themselves to deserve, on account of any profound wisdom attending them.

It was by accident only that the king had not a considerable share in those great naval discoveries by which the present age was so much distinguished. Columbus, after meeting with many repulses from the courts of Portugal and Spain, sent his brother, Bartholomew, to London, in order to explain his projects to Henry, and crave his protection for the execution of them. The king invited him over to England; but his brother being taken by pirates, was detained in his voyage; and Columbus, meanwhile, having obtained the countenance of Isabella, was supplied with a small fleet, and happily executed his enterprize. Henry was not discouraged by this disappointment: He fitted out Sebastian Cabot, a Venetian, settled in Bristol; and sent him westwards, in 1498, in search of new countries. Cabot discovered the main land

CHAP. XXVI.

1509.

of America towards the sixtieth degree of northern latitude: He sailed southwards along the coast, and discovered Newfoundland, and other countries; but returned to England without making any conquest or settlement. Elliot, and other merchants in Bristol, made a like attempt in 1502[d]. The king expended fourteen thousand pounds in building one ship, called the *Great Harry*[e]. She was, properly speaking, the first ship in the English navy. Before this period, when the prince wanted a fleet, he had no other expedient than hiring or pressing ships from the merchants.

But though this improvement of navigation, and the discovery of both the Indies, was the most memorable incident that happened during this or any other period, it was not the only great event by which the age was distinguished. In 1453, Constantinople was taken by the Turks; and the Greeks, among whom some remains of learning were still preserved, being scattered by these barbarians, took shelter in Italy, and imported, together with their admirable language, a tincture of their science, and of their refined taste in poetry and eloquence. About the same time, the purity of the Latin tongue was revived, the study of antiquity became fashionable, and the esteem for literature gradually propagated itself throughout every nation in Europe. The art of printing, invented about that time, extremely facilitated the progress of all these improvements: The invention of gunpowder changed the whole art of war; Mighty innovations were soon after made in religion, such as not only affected those states that embraced them, but even those that adhered to the ancient faith and worship: And thus a general revolution was made in human affairs throughout this part of the world; and men gradually attained that situation, with regard to commerce, arts, science, government,

[d] Rymer, vol. viii. p. 17.   [e] Stowe, p. 484.

police,

police, and cultivation, in which they have ever since persevered. Here, therefore, commences the useful, as well as the more agreeable part of modern annals; certainty has place in all the considerable, and even most of the minute parts of historical narration; a great variety of events, preserved by printing, give the author the power of selecting, as well as adorning the facts which he relates; and as each incident has a reference to our present manners and situation, instructive lessons occur every moment during the course of the narration. Whoever carries his anxious researches into preceding periods, is moved by a curiosity, liberal indeed and commendable; not by any necessity for acquiring knowledge of public affairs, or the arts of civil government.

CHAP. XXVII.

HENRY VIII.

Popularity of the new king — His ministers — Punishment of Empson and Dudley — King's marriage — Foreign affairs — Julius II. — League of Cambray — War with France — Expedition to Fontarabia — Deceit of Ferdinand — Return of the English — Leo X. — A parliament — War with Scotland — Wolsey minister — His character — Invasion of France — Battle of Guinegate — Battle of Flouden — Peace with France.

CHAP. XXVII.
1509.

Popularity of the new king.

THE death of Henry VII. had been attended with as open and visible a joy among the people as decency would permit; and the accession and coronation of his son, Henry VIII. spread universally a declared and unfeigned satisfaction. Instead of a monarch jealous, severe, and avaricious, who, in proportion as he advanced in years, was sinking still deeper in those unpopular vices, a young prince of eighteen had succeeded to the throne, who, even in the eyes of men of sense, gave promising hopes of his future conduct, much more in those of the people, always enchanted with novelty, youth, and royal dignity. The beauty and vigour of his person, accompanied with dexterity in every manly exercise, was farther adorned with a blooming and ruddy countenance, with a lively air, with the appearance of spirit and activity in all his demeanour [f]. His father,

[f] T. Mori Lucubr. p. 182.

HENRY VIII.

in order to remove him from the knowledge of public business, had hitherto occupied him entirely in the pursuits of literature; and the proficiency which he made, gave no bad prognostic of his parts and capacity [r]. Even the vices of vehemence, ardour, and impatience, to which he was subject, and which afterwards degenerated into tyranny, were considered only as faults incident to unguarded youth, which would be corrected, when time had brought him to greater moderation and maturity. And as the contending titles of York and Lancaster were now at last fully united in his person, men justly expected from a prince, obnoxious to no party, that impartiality of administration, which had long been unknown in England.

These favourable prepossessions of the public were encouraged by the measures which Henry embraced in the commencement of his reign. His grandmother, the countess of Richmond and Derby, was still alive; and as she was a woman much celebrated for prudence and virtue, he wisely shewed great deference to her opinion in the establishment of his new council. The members were, Warham, archbishop of Canterbury and chancellor; the earl of Shrewsbury, steward; lord Herbert, chamberlain; Sir Thomas Lovel, master of the wards and constable of the Tower; Sir Edward Poynings, comptroller; Sir Henry Marney, afterwards lord Marney; Sir Thomas Darcy, afterwards lord Darcy; Thomas Ruthal, doctor of laws; and Sir Henry Wyat [b]. These men had long been accustomed to business under the late king, and were the least unpopular of all the ministers employed by that monarch.

His ministers.

But the chief competitors for favour and authority under the new king, were the earl of Surrey, treasurer,

[r] Father Paul, lib. 1. p. 799.   [b] Herbert, Stowe, p. 486. Hollingshed.

and

and Fox, bishop of Winchester, secretary and privy seal. This prelate, who enjoyed great credit during all the former reign, had acquired such habits of caution and frugality as he could not easily lay aside; and he still opposed, by his remonstrances, those schemes of dissipation and expence, which the youth and passions of Henry rendered agreeable to him. But Surrey was a more dexterous courtier; and, though few had borne a greater share in the frugal politics of the late king, he knew how to conform himself to the humour of his new master; and no one was so forward in promoting that liberality, pleasure, and magnificence, which began to prevail under the young monarch[i]. By this policy he ingratiated himself with Henry; he made advantage, as well as the other courtiers, of the lavish disposition of his master; and he engaged him in such a course of play and idleness as rendered him negligent of affairs, and willing to entrust the government of the state entirely into the hands of his ministers. The great treasures amassed by the late king, were gradually dissipated in the giddy expences of Henry. One party of pleasure succeeded to another: Tilts, tournaments, and carousals were exhibited with all the magnificence of the age: And as the present tranquillity of the public permitted the court to indulge itself in every amusement, serious business was but little attended to. Or if the king intermitted the course of his festivity, he chiefly employed himself in an application to music and literature, which were his favourite pursuits, and which were well adapted to his genius. He had made such proficiency in the former art, as even to compose some pieces of church-music which were sung in his chapel[k]. He was initiated in the elegant learning of the ancients. And, though he was so unfortunate as to be seduced into a study of the

[i] Lord Herbert.   [k] Ibid.

barren

barren controversies of the Schools, which were then fashionable, and had chosen Thomas Aquinas for his favourite author, he still discovered a capacity fitted for more useful and entertaining knowledge.

THE frank and careless humour of the king, as it led him to dissipate the treasures amassed by his father, rendered him negligent in protecting the instruments whom that prince had employed in his extortions. A proclamation being issued to encourage complaints, the rage of the people was let loose on all informers, who had so long exercised an unbounded tyranny over the nation[1]: They were thrown into prison, condemned to the pillory, and most of them lost their lives by the violence of the populace. Empson and Dudley, who were most exposed to public hatred, were immediately summoned before the council, in order to answer for their conduct, which had rendered them so obnoxious. Empson made a shrewd apology for himself, as well as for his associate. He told the council, that, so far from his being justly exposed to censure for his past conduct, his enemies themselves grounded their clamour on actions which seemed rather to merit reward and approbation: That a strict execution of law was the crime of which he and Dudley were accused; though that law had been established by general consent, and though they had acted in obedience to the king, to whom the administration of justice was entrusted by the constitution: That it belonged not to them, who were instruments in the hands of supreme power, to determine what laws were recent or obsolete, expedient or hurtful; since they were all alike valid, so long as they remained unrepealed by the legislature: That it was natural for a licentious populace to murmur against the restraints of authority; but all wise states had ever made their glory consist in the just distribution of re-

[1] Herbert, Stowe, p. 486. Hollingshed, p. 799. Polyd. Virg. lib. xxviii.

wards and punishments, and had annexed the former to the observance and enforcement of the laws, the latter to their violation and infraction: And that a sudden overthrow of all government might be expected, where the judges were committed to the mercy of the criminals, the rulers to that of the subjects [m].

NOTWITHSTANDING this defence, Empson and Dudley were sent to the Tower; and soon after brought to their trial. The strict execution of laws, however obsolete, could never be imputed to them as a crime in a court of judicature; and it is likely that, even where they had exercised arbitrary power, the king, as they had acted by the secret commands of his father, was not willing that their conduct should undergo too severe a scrutiny. In order, therefore, to gratify the people with the punishment of these obnoxious ministers, crimes very improbable, or indeed absolutely impossible, were charged upon them; that they had entered into a conspiracy against the sovereign, and had intended, on the death of the late king, to have seized by force the administration of government. The jury were so far moved by popular prejudices, joined to court influence, as to give a verdict against them; which was afterwards confirmed by a bill of attainder in parliament [n], and, at the earnest desire of the people, was executed by warrant from the king. Thus, in those arbitrary times, justice was equally violated, whether the king sought power and riches, or courted popularity.

[m] Herbert, Hollingshed, p. 804.
[n] This parliament met on the 21st January 1510. A law was there enacted, in order to prevent some abuses which had prevailed during the late reign. The forfeiture upon the penal statutes was reduced to the term of three years. Costs and damages were given against informers upon acquittal of the accused: More severe punishments were enacted against perjury: The false informations procured by Empson and Dudley were declared null and invalid. Traverses were allowed; and the time of tendering them enlarged. 1 H. V. c. 8, 10, 11, 12.

HENRY,

HENRY, while he punished the instruments of past tyranny, had yet such deference to former engagements as to deliberate, immediately after his accession, concerning the celebration of his marriage with the infanta Catherine, to whom he had been affianced during his father's lifetime. Her former marriage with his brother, and the inequality of their years, were the chief objections urged against his espousing her: But on the other hand, the advantages of her known virtue, modesty, and sweetness of disposition were insisted on; the affection which she bore to the king; the large dowry to which she was entitled as princess of Wales; the interest of cementing a close alliance with Spain; the necessity of finding some confederate to counterbalance the power of France; the expediency of fulfilling the engagements of the late king: When these considerations were weighed, they determined the council, though contrary to the opinion of the primate, to give Henry their advice for celebrating the marriage. The countess of Richmond, who had concurred in the same sentiments with the council, died soon after the marriage of her grandson.

THE popularity of Henry's government, his undisputed title, his extensive authority, his large treasures, the tranquillity of his subjects, were circumstances which rendered his domestic administration easy and prosperous: The situation of foreign affairs was no less happy and desirable. Italy continued still, as during the late reign, to be the centre of all the wars and negociations of the European princes; and Henry's alliance was courted by all parties; at the same time, that he was not engaged by any immediate interest or necessity to take part with any. Lewis XII. of France, after his conquest of Milan, was the only great prince that possessed any territory

CHAP.
XXVII.

1509.

tory in Italy; and could he have remained in tranquillity, he was enabled by his situation to prescribe laws to all the Italian princes and republics, and to hold the balance among them. But the desire of making a conquest of Naples, to which he had the same title or pretensions with his predecessor, still engaged him in new enterprizes; and as he foresaw opposition from Ferdinand, who was connected both by treaties and affinity with Frederic of Naples, he endeavoured, by the offers of interest, to which the ears of that monarch were ever open, to engage him in an opposite confederacy. He settled with him a plan for the partition of the kingdom of Naples, and the expulsion of Frederic: A plan which the politicians of that age regarded as the most egregious imprudence in the French monarch, and the greatest perfidy in the Spanish. Frederic, supported only by subjects, who were either discontented with his government, or indifferent about his fortunes, was unable to resist so powerful a confederacy, and was deprived of his dominions: but he had the satisfaction to see Naples immediately prove the source of contention among his enemies. Ferdinand gave secret orders to his general, Gonsalvo, whom the Spaniards honour with the appellation of the *great captain*, to attack the armies of France, and make himself master of all the dominions of Naples. Gonsalvo prevailed in every enterprize, defeated the French in two pitched battles, and ensured to his prince the entire possession of that kingdom. Lewis, unable to procure redress by force of arms, was obliged to enter into a fruitless negociation with Ferdinand for the recovery of his share of the partition; and all Italy, during some time, was held in suspence between these two powerful monarchs.

There has scarcely been any period, when the balance of power was better secured in Europe, and seemed
more

more able to maintain itself without any anxious concern or attention of the princes. Several great monarchies were established; and no one so far surpassed the rest as to give any foundation, or even pretence, for jealousy. England was united in domestic peace, and by its situation happily secured from the invasion of foreigners. The coalition of the several kingdoms of Spain had formed one powerful monarchy, which Ferdinand administered with arts, fraudulent indeed and deceitful, but full of vigour and ability. Lewis XII. a gallant and generous prince, had, by espousing Anne of Britanny, widow to his predecessor, preserved the union with that principality, on which the safety of his kingdom so much depended. Maximilian, the emperor, besides the hereditary dominions of the Austrian family, maintained authority in the empire, and, notwithstanding the levity of his character, was able to unite the German princes in any great plan of interest, at least of defence. Charles, prince of Castile, grandson to Maximilian and Ferdinand, had already succeeded to the rich dominions of the house of Burgundy; and being as yet in early youth, the government was entrusted to Margaret of Savoy, his aunt, a princess endowed with signal prudence and virtue. The internal force of these several powerful states, by balancing each other, might long have maintained general tranquillity, had not the active and enterprising genius of Julius II. an ambitious pontiff, first excited the flames of war and discord among them. By his intrigues, a league had been formed at Cambray*, between himself, Maximilian, Lewis, and Ferdinand; and the object of this great confederacy was to overwhelm, by their united arms, the commonwealth of Venice. Henry, without any motive from interest or passion, allowed his name to be inserted in the confederacy. This

CHAP.
XXVII.

1509.

Julius II.

League of Cambray.

* In 1508.

oppressive

oppressive and iniquitous league was but too successful against the republic.

The great force and secure situation of the considerable monarchies prevented any one from aspiring to any conquest of moment; and though this consideration could not maintain general peace, or remedy the natural inquietude of men, it rendered the princes of this age more disposed to desert engagements, and change their alliances, in which they were retained by humour and caprice, rather than by any natural or durable interest. Julius had no sooner humbled the Venetian republic, than he was inspired with a nobler ambition, that of expelling all foreigners from Italy, or, to speak in the stile affected by the Italians of that age, the freeing of that country entirely from the dominion of Barbarians [p]. He was determined to make the tempest fall first upon Lewis; and, in order to pave the way for this great enterprize, he at once sought for a ground of quarrel with the monarch, and courted the alliance of other princes. He declared war against the duke of Ferrara, the confederate of Lewis. He solicited the favour of England, by sending Henry a sacred rose, perfumed with musk and anointed with chrism [q]. He engaged in his interests Bambridge, archbishop of York, and Henry's ambassador at Rome, whom he soon after created a cardinal. He drew over Ferdinand to his party, though that monarch, at first, made no declaration of his intentions. And what he chiefly valued, he formed a treaty with the Swiss cantons, who, enraged by some neglects put upon them by Lewis, accompanied with contumelious expressions, had quitted the alliance of France, and waited for an opportunity of revenging themselves on that nation.

While the French monarch repelled the attacks of his enemies, he thought it also requisite to make an attempt

[p] Guicciard. lib. ix. [q] Spelman, Concil. vol. II. p. 725.

tempt on the pope himself, and to despoil him as much as possible, of that sacred character which chiefly rendered him formidable. He engaged some cardinals, disgusted with the violence of Julius, to desert him; and by their authority, he was determined, in conjunction with Maximilian, who still adhered to his alliance, to call a general council, which might reform the church, and check the exorbitancies of the Roman pontiff. A council was summoned at Pisa, which from the beginning bore a very inauspicious aspect, and promised little success to its adherents. Except a few French bishops, who unwillingly obeyed their king's commands in attending the council, all the other prelates kept aloof from an assembly, which they regarded as the offspring of faction, intrigue, and worldly politics. Even Pisa, the place of their residence, showed them signs of contempt; which engaged them to transfer their session to Milan, a city under the dominion of the French monarch. Notwithstanding this advantage, they did not experience much more respectful treatment from the inhabitants of Milan; and found it necessary to make another remove to Lyons[q]. Lewis himself fortified these violent prejudices in favour of papal authority, by the symptoms which he discovered, of regard, deference, and submission to Julius, whom he always spared, even when fortune had thrown into his hands the most inviting opportunities of humbling him. And as it was known, that his consort, who had great influence over him, was extremely disquieted in mind on account of his dissentions with the holy father, all men prognosticated to Julius final success in this unequal contest.

THE enterprizing pontiff knew his advantages, and availed himself of them with the utmost temerity and insolence. So much had he neglected his sacerdotal cha-

[q] Guicciardini, lib. 10.

CHAP. XXVII.

1511.

racter, that he acted in person at the siege of Mirandola, visited the trenches, saw some of his attendants killed by his side, and, like a young soldier, cheerfully bore all the rigours of winter and a severe season, in pursuit of military glory[e]: Yet was he still able to throw, even on his most moderate opponents, the charge of impiety and prophaneness. He summoned a council at the Lateran: He put Pisa under an interdict, and all the places which gave shelter to the schismatical council: He excommunicated the cardinals and prelates who attended it: He even pointed his spiritual thunder against the princes who adhered to it: He freed their subjects from all oaths of allegiance, and gave their dominions to every one who could take possession of them.

FERDINAND of Arragon, who had acquired the sirname of Catholic, regarded the cause of the pope and of religion only as a cover to his ambition and selfish politics: Henry, naturally sincere and sanguine in his temper, and the more so on account of his youth and inexperience, was moved with a hearty desire of protecting the pope from the oppression to which he believed him exposed from the ambitious enterprizes of Lewis. Hopes had been given him by Julius, that the title of *Most Christian King*, which had hitherto been annexed to the crown of France, and which was regarded as its most precious ornament, should, in reward of his services, be transferred to that of England[f]. Impatient also of acquiring that distinction in Europe to which his power and opulence entitled him, he could not long remain neuter amidst the noise of arms; and the natural enmity of the English against France, as well as their ancient claims upon that kingdom, led Henry to join that alliance, which the pope, Spain, and Venice had formed

1512.

[e] Guicciardini, lib. 9. [f] Guicciard. lib. 11. P. Daniel, vol. ii. p. 1893. Herbert. Hollingshed, p. 831.

against

HENRY VIII.

against the French monarch. A herald was sent to Paris, to exhort Lewis not to wage impious war against the sovereign pontiff; and when he returned without success, another was sent to demand the ancient patrimonial provinces, Anjou, Maine, Guienne, and Normandy. This message was understood to be a declaration of war; and a parliament being summoned, readily granted supplies for a purpose so much favoured by the English nation[1].

BUONAVISO, an agent of the pope's at London, had been corrupted by the court of France, and had previously revealed to Lewis all the measures which Henry was concerting against him. But this infidelity did the king inconsiderable prejudice, in comparison of the treachery, which he experienced from the selfish purposes of the ally, on whom he chiefly relied for assistance. Ferdinand, his father-in-law, had so long persevered in a course of crooked politics, that he began even to value himself on his dexterity in fraud and artifice; and he made a boast of those shameful successes. Being told one day, that Lewis, a prince of a very different character, had complained of his having once cheated him: "He lies, the drunkard!" said he, "I have cheated him above twenty times." This prince considered his close connexions with Henry, only as the means which enabled him the better to take advantage of his want of experience. He advised him not to invade France by the way of Calais, where he himself should not have it in his power to assist him: He exhorted him rather to send forces to Fontarabia, whence he could easily make a conquest of Guienne, a province, in which, it was imagined, the English had still some adherents. He promised to assist this conquest by the junction of a Spanish army. And so forward did he seem to promote the interests of his son-in-law, that he even sent

CHAP. XXVII.
1512.
War with France. 4th Feb.

Expedition to Fontarabia.

[1] Herbert. Hollingshed, p. 811.

vessels

CHAP. XXVII.
1512.

vessels to England, in order to transport over the forces which Henry had levied for that purpose. The marquis of Dorset commanded this armament, which consisted of ten thousand men, mostly infantry; lord Howard, son of the earl of Surrey, lord Broke, lord Ferrars, and many others of the young gentry and nobility, accompanied him in this service. All were on fire to distinguish themselves by military atchievements, and to make a conquest of importance for their master. The secret purpose of Ferdinand, in this unexampled generosity, was suspected by no body.

THE small kingdom of Navarre lies on the frontiers between France and Spain; and as John d'Albret, the sovereign, was connected by friendship and alliance with Lewis, the opportunity seemed favourable to Ferdinand, while the English forces were conjoined with his own, and while all adherents to the council of Pisa lay under the sentence of excommunication, to put himself in possession of these dominions. No sooner, therefore, was Dorset landed in Guipiscoa, than the Spanish monarch declared his readiness to join him with his forces, to make with united arms an invasion of France, and to form the siege of Bayonne, which opened the way into Guienne[a]: But he remarked to the English general how dangerous it might prove to leave behind them the kingdom of Navarre, which, being in close alliance with France, could easily give admittance to the enemy, and cut off all communication between Spain and the combined armies. To provide against so dangerous an event, he required, that John should stipulate a neutrality in the present war; and when that prince expressed his willingness to enter into any engagement for that purpose, he also required, that security should be given for the strict observance of it. John having likewise agreed to this condition, Ferdinand demanded,

[a] Herbert. Hollingshed, p. 813.

HENRY VIII.

demanded, that he should deliver into his hands six of the most considerable places of his dominions, together with his eldest son as a hostage. These were not terms to be proposed to a sovereign; and as the Spanish monarch expected a refusal, he gave immediate orders to the duke of Alva, his general, to make an invasion on Navarre, and to reduce that kingdom. Alva soon made himself master of all the smaller towns; and being ready to form the siege of Pampeluna, the capital, he summoned the marquis of Dorset to join him with the English army, and concert together all their operations.

CHAP. XXVII.
1512.

DORSET began to suspect, that the interests of his master were very little regarded in all these transactions; and having no orders to invade the kingdom of Navarre, or make war any where but in France, he refused to take any part in the enterprize. He remained therefore in his quarters at Fontarabia; but so subtile was the contrivance of Ferdinand, that, even while the English army lay in that situation, it was almost equally serviceable to his purpose, as if it had acted in conjunction with his own. It kept the French army in awe, and prevented it from advancing to succour the kingdom of Navarre; so that Alva, having full leisure to conduct the siege, made himself master of Pampeluna, and obliged John to seek for shelter in France. The Spanish general applied again to Dorset, and proposed to conduct with united counsels the operations of the *holy league,* so it was called, against Lewis: But as he still declined forming the siege of Bayonne, and rather insisted on the invasion of the principality of Bearne, a part of the king of Navarre's dominions, which lies on the French side of the Pyrenees, Dorset, justly suspicious of his sinister intentions, represented, that, without new orders from his master, he could not concur in such an undertaking. In order to

Deceit of Ferdinand.

E e 3
procure

CHAP.
XXVII.

1512.

procure thefe orders, Ferdinand difpatched Martin de Ampios to London; and perfuaded Henry, that, by the refractory and fcrupulous humour of the Englifh general, the moft favourable opportunities were loft, and that it was neceffary he fhould, on all occafions, act in concert with the Spanifh commander, who was beft acquainted with the fituation of the country, and the reafons of every operation. But before orders to this purpofe reached Spain, Dorfet had become extremely impatient; and obferving that his farther ftay ferved not to promote the main undertaking, and that his army was daily perifhing by want and ficknefs, he demanded fhipping from Ferdinand to transfport them back into England. Ferdinand, who was bound by treaty to furnifh him with this fupply, whenever demanded, was at length, after many delays, obliged to yield to his opportunity; and Dorfet, embarking his troops, prepared himfelf for the voyage. Meanwhile, the meffenger arrived with orders from Henry, that the troops fhould remain in Spain; but the foldiers were fo difcontented with the treatment which they had met with, that they mutinied, and obliged their commanders to fet fail for England. Henry was much difpleafed with the ill fuccefs of this enterprize; and it was with difficulty that Dorfet, by explaining the fraudulent conduct of Ferdinand, was at laft able to appeafe him.

Return of the Englifh.

THERE happened this fummer an action at fea, which brought not any more decifive advantage to the Englifh. Sir Thomas Knevet, mafter of horfe, was fent to the coaft of Britanny with a fleet of forty-five fail; and he carried with him Sir Charles Brandon, Sir John Carew, and many other young courtiers, who longed for an opportunity of difplaying their valour. After they had committed fome depredations, a French fleet of thirty-nine fail iffued from Breft, under the command of Primauget,

8
and

and began an engagement with the English. Fire seized the ship of Primauget, who, finding his destruction inevitable, bore down upon the vessel of the English admiral, and grappling with her, resolved to make her share his fate. Both fleets stood some time in suspence, as spectators of this dreadful engagement; and all men saw with horror the flames which consumed both vessels, and heard the cries of fury and despair, which came from the miserable combatants. At last, the French vessel blew up; and at the same time destroyed the English[n]. The rest of the French fleet made their escape into different harbours.

THE war, which England waged against France, though it brought no advantage to the former kingdom, was of great prejudice to the latter; and by obliging Lewis to withdraw his forces for the defence of his own dominions, lost him that superiority, which his arms, in the beginning of the campaign, had attained in Italy. Gaston de Foix, his nephew, a young hero, had been entrusted with the command of the French forces; and in a few months performed such feats of military art and prowess, as were sufficient to render illustrious the life of the oldest captain[r]. His career finished with the great battle of Ravenna, which, after the most obstinate conflict, he gained over the Spanish and papal armies. He perished the very moment his victory was complete; and with him perished the fortune of the French arms in Italy. The Swiss, who had rendered themselves extremely formidable by their bands of disciplined infantry, invaded the Milanese with a numerous army, and raised up that inconstant people to a revolt against the dominion of France. Genoa followed the example of the dutchy; and thus Lewis, in a few weeks, entirely

[n] Polydore Virgil, lib. 27. Stowe, p. 490. Lanquet's Epitome of chronicles, fol. 273. [r] Guicciard. lib. 10.

CHAP.
XXVII.
1513.

lost his Italian conquests, except some garrisons; and Maximilian Sforza, the son of Ludovic, was reinstated in possession of Milan.

Julius discovered extreme joy on the discomfiture of the French; and the more so, as he had been beholden for it to the Swiss, a people whose councils, he hoped, he should always be able to influence and govern. The pontiff survived this success a very little time; and in his place was chosen John de Medicis, who took the appellation of Leo X. and proved one of the most illustrious princes that ever sat on the papal throne. Humane, beneficent, generous, affable; the patron of every art, and friend of every virtue [a]; he had a soul no less capable of forming great designs than his predecessor, but was more gentle, pliant, and artful in employing means for the execution of them. The sole defect, indeed, of his character was too great finesse and artifice; a fault which, both as a priest and an Italian, it was difficult for him to avoid. By the negociations of Leo, the emperor Maximilian was detached from the French interest; and Henry, notwithstanding his disappointments in the former campaign, was still encouraged to prosecute his warlike measures against Lewis.

21st Feb.
Leo X.

A parliament.

Henry had summoned a new session of parliament [c], and obtained a supply for his enterprize. It was a poll-tax, and imposed different sums, according to the station and riches of the person. A duke payed ten marks, an earl five pounds, a baron four pounds, a knight four marks; every man valued at eight hundred pounds in goods, four marks. An imposition was also granted of two fifteenths and four tenths [b]. By these supplies, joined to the treasure which had been left by his father, and which was not yet entirely dissipated, he was enabled to levy a great

[a] Father Paul, lib. 1. [c] 4th November, 1512.
[b] Stowe.

army,

HENRY VIII.

army, and render himself formidable to his enemy. The English are said to have been much encouraged in this enterprize, by the arrival of a vessel in the Thames under the papal banner. It carried presents of wine and hams to the king, and the more eminent courtiers; and such fond devotion was at that time entertained towards the court of Rome, that these trivial presents were every where received with the greatest triumph and exultation.

CHAP.
XXVII.

1513.

IN order to prevent all disturbances from Scotland, while Henry's arms should be employed on the continent, Dr. West, dean of Windsor, was dispatched on an embassy to James, the king's brother-in-law; and instructions were given him to accommodate all differences between the kingdoms, as well as to discover the intentions of the court of Scotland [c]. Some complaints had already been made on both sides. One Barton, a Scotchman, having suffered injuries from the Portugueze, for which he could obtain no redress, had procured letters of marque against that nation; but he had no sooner put to sea, than he was guilty of the grossest abuses, committed depredations upon the English, and much infested the narrow seas [d]. Lord Howard and Sir Edward Howard, admirals, and sons of the earl of Surrey, sailing out against him, fought him in a desperate action, where the pirate was killed; and they brought his ships into the Thames. As Henry refused all satisfaction for this act of justice, some of the borderers, who wanted but a pretence for depredations, entered England under the command of lord Hume, warden of the marches, and committed great ravages on that kingdom. Notwithstanding these mutual grounds of dissatisfaction, matters might easily have been accommo-

[c] Polydore Virgil, lib. 27. p. 811. [d] Stowe, p. 489. Hollingshed,

dated,

dated, had it not been for Henry's intended invasion of France, which rouzed the jealousy of the Scottish nation[*]. The ancient league, which subsisted between France and Scotland, was conceived to be the strongest band of connexion; and the Scots universally believed, that, were it not for the countenance which they received from this foreign alliance, they had never been able so long to maintain their independence against a people so much superior. James was farther incited to take part in the quarrel by the invitations of Anne, queen of France, whose knight he had ever in all tournaments professed himself, and who summoned him, according to the ideas of romantic gallantry, prevalent in that age, to take the field in her defence, and prove himself her true and valorous champion. The remonstrances of his consort and of his wisest counsellors were in vain opposed to the martial ardour of this prince. He first sent a squadron of ships to the assistance of France; the only fleet which Scotland seems ever to have possessed. And though he still made professions of maintaining a neutrality, the English ambassador easily foresaw, that a war would in the end prove inevitable; and he gave warning of the danger to his master, who sent the earl of Surrey to put the borders in a posture of defence, and to resist the expected invasion of the enemy.

Henry, all on fire for military fame, was little discouraged by this appearance of a diversion from the north; and so much the less, as he flattered himself with the assistance of all the considerable potentates of Europe in his invasion of France. The pope still continued to thunder out his excommunications against Lewis, and all the adherents of the schismatical council: The Swiss cantons made professions of violent animosity against France;

[*] Buchanan, lib. 13. Drummond in the life of James IV.

HENRY VIII.

France: The ambassadors of Ferdinand and Maximilian had signed with those of Henry a treaty of alliance against that power, and had stipulated the time and place of their intended invasion: And though Ferdinand disavowed his ambassador, and even signed a truce for a twelvemonth with the common enemy; Henry was not yet fully convinced of his selfish and sinister intentions, and still hoped for his concurrence after the expiration of that term. He had now got a minister who complied with all his inclinations, and flattered him in every scheme to which his sanguine and impetuous temper was inclined.

CHAP. XXVII.

1513.

THOMAS WOLSEY, dean of Lincoln, and almoner to the king, surpassed in favour all his ministers, and was fast advancing towards that unrivalled grandeur which he afterwards attained. This man was son of a butcher at Ipswich; but having got a learned education, and being endowed with an excellent capacity, he was admitted into the marquis of Dorset's family as tutor to that nobleman's children, and soon gained the friendship and countenance of his patron [f]. He was recommended to be chaplain to Henry VII. and being employed by that monarch in a secret negociation, which regarded his intended marriage with Margaret of Savoy, Maximilian's daughter, he acquitted himself to the king's satisfaction, and obtained the praise both of diligence and dexterity in his conduct [g]. That prince, having given him a commission to Maximilian, who at that time resided in Brussels, was surprized, in less than three days after, to see Wolsey present himself before him; and supposing that he had protracted his departure, he began to reprove him for the dilatory execution of his orders. Wolsey informed him, that

Wolsey minister.

[f] Stowe, p. 997. [g] Cavendish. Fiddes's life of Wolsey. Stowe.

he had just returned from Brussels, and had successfully fulfilled all his majesty's commands. "But on second thoughts," said the king, "I found that somewhat was omitted in your orders; and have sent a messenger after you, with fuller instructions." "I met the messenger," replied Wolsey, "on my return: But as I had reflected on that omission, I ventured of myself to execute what, I knew, must be your majesty's intentions." The death of Henry, soon after this incident, retarded the advancement of Wolsey, and prevented his reaping any advantage from the good opinion which that monarch had entertained of him: But thenceforwards he was looked on at court as a rising man; and Fox, bishop of Winchester, cast his eye upon him as one who might be serviceable to him in his present situation[b]. This prelate, observing that the earl of Surrey had totally eclipsed him in favour, resolved to introduce Wolsey to the young prince's familiarity, and hoped that he might rival Surrey in his insinuating arts, and yet be contented to act in the cabinet a part subordinate to Fox himself, who had promoted him. In a little time, Wolsey gained so much on the king, that he supplanted both Surrey in his favour, and Fox in his trust and confidence. Being admitted to Henry's parties of pleasure, he took the lead in every jovial conversation, and promoted all that frolic and entertainment which he found suitable to the age and inclination of the young monarch. Neither his own years, which were near forty, nor his character of a clergyman, were any restraint upon him, or engaged him to check, by any useless severity, the gaiety, in which Henry, who had small propension to debauchery, passed his careless hours. Dur-

---

[b] Antiq. Brit. Eccles. p. 309. Polydore Virgil, lib. 27.

ing the intervals of amusement he introduced business, and insinuated those maxims of conduct which he was desirous his master should adopt. He observed to him, that, while he entrusted his affairs into the hands of his father's counsellors, he had the advantage indeed of employing men of wisdom and experience, but men who owed not their promotion to his favour, and who scarcely thought themselves accountable to him for the exercise of their authority: That by the factions, and cabals, and jealousies, which had long prevailed among them, they more obstructed the advancement of his affairs, than they promoted it by the knowledge which age and practice had conferred upon them : That while he thought proper to pass his time in those pleasures, to which his age and royal fortune invited him, and in those studies, which would in time enable him to sway the sceptre with absolute authority, his best system of government would be to entrust his authority into the hands of some one person, who was the creature of his will, and who could entertain no view but that of promoting his service : And that if this minister had also the same relish for pleasure with himself, and the same taste for science, he could more easily, at intervals, account to him for his whole conduct, and introduce his master gradually into the knowledge of public business; and thus, without tedious constraint or application, initiate him in the science of government [1].

HENRY entered into all the views of Wolsey; and finding no one so capable of executing this plan of administration as the person who proposed it, he soon advanced his favourite, from being the companion of his pleasures, to be a member of his council; and from be-

[1] Cavendish, p. 12. Stowe, p. 490.

ing a member of his council, to be his sole and absolute minister. By this rapid advancement and uncontrouled authority, the character and genius of Wolsey had full opportunity to display itself. Insatiable in his acquisitions, but still more magnificent in his expence: Of extensive capacity, but still more unbounded enterprize: Ambitious of power, but still more desirous of glory: Insinuating, engaging, persuasive; and, by turns, lofty, elevated, commanding: Haughty to his equals, but affable to his dependants; oppressive to the people, but liberal to his friends; more generous than grateful; less moved by injuries than by contempt; he was framed to take the ascendant in every intercourse with others, but exerted this superiority of *nature* with such ostentation as exposed him to envy, and made every one willing to recal the original inferiority, or rather meanness of his *fortune*.

THE branch of administration in which Henry most exerted himself, while he gave his entire confidence to Wolsey, was the military, which, as it suited the natural gallantry and bravery of his temper, as well as the ardour of his youth, was the principal object of his attention. Finding that Lewis had made great preparations both by sea and land to resist him, he was no less careful to levy a formidable army, and equip a considerable fleet for the invasion of France. The command of the fleet was entrusted to Sir Edward Howard; who, after scouring the channel for some time, presented himself before Brest, where the French navy then lay; and he challenged them to a combat. The French admiral, who expected from the Mediterranean a reinforcement of some gallies under the command of Prejeant de Bidoux, kept within the harbour, and saw with patience the English burn and destroy the country in the neighbourhood. At last Prejeant arrived with six gallies, and put into

into Conquet, a place within a few leagues of Brest; where he secured himself behind some batteries, which he had planted on rocks, that lay on each side of him. Howard was, notwithstanding, determined to make an attack upon him; and as he had but two gallies, he took himself the command of one, and gave the other to lord Ferrars. He was followed by some row-barges and some crayers under the command of Sir Thomas Cheyney, Sir William Sidney, and other officers of distinction. He immediately fastened on Prejeant's ship, and leaped on board of her, attended by one Carroz, a Spanish cavalier, and seventeen Englishmen. The cable, meanwhile, which fastened his ship to that of the enemy, being cut, the admiral was thus left in the hands of the French; and as he still continued the combat with great gallantry, he was pushed overboard by their pikes [k]. Lord Ferrars, seeing the admiral's galley fall off, followed with the other small vessels; and the whole fleet was so discouraged by the loss of their commander, that they retired from before Brest [l]. The French navy came out of harbour; and even ventured to invade the coast of Sussex. They were repulsed, and Prejeant, their commander, lost an eye by the shot of an arrow. Lord Howard, brother to the deceased admiral, succeeded to the command of the English fleet; and little memorable passed at sea during this summer.

GREAT preparations had been making at land, during the whole winter, for an invasion on France by the way

[k] It was a maxim of Howard's, that no admiral was good for any thing, that was not brave even to a degree of madness. As the sea-service requires much less plan and contrivance and capacity than the land, this maxim has great plausibility and appearance of truth: Though the fate of Howard himself may serve as a proof, that even there courage ought to be tempered with discretion.
[l] Stowe, p. 491. Herbert, Hollingshed, p. 816.

CHAP. XXVII.
1513.

of Calais; but the summer was well advanced before every thing was in sufficient readiness for the intended enterprize. The long peace which the kingdom had enjoyed, had somewhat unfitted the English for military expeditions; and the great change, which had lately been introduced in the art of war, had rendered it still more difficult to enure them to the use of the weapons now employed in action. The Swiss, and after them the Spaniards, had shown the advantage of a stable infantry, who fought with pike and sword, and were able to repulse even the heavy-armed cavalry, in which the great force of the armies formerly consisted. The practice of fire-arms was become common; though the caliver, which was the weapon now in use, was so inconvenient, and attended with so many disadvantages, that it had not entirely discredited the bow, a weapon in which the English excelled all European nations. A considerable part of the forces, which Henry levied for the invasion of France, consisted of archers; and as soon as affairs were in readiness, the vanguard of the army, amounting to 8000 men, under the command of the earl of Shrewsbury, sailed over to Calais. Shrewsbury was accompanied by the earl of Derby, the lords Fitzwater, Hastings, Cobham, and Sir Rice ap Thomas, captain of the light horse. Another body of 6000 men soon after followed under the command of lord Herbert, the chamberlain, attended by the earls of Northumberland and Kent, the lords Audley and Delawar, together with Carew, Curson, and other gentlemen.

THE king himself prepared to follow with the main body and rear of the army; and he appointed the queen regent of the kingdom during his absence. That he might secure her administration from all disturbance, he

ordered

CHAP. XXVII.

1513.

ordered Edmond de la Pole, earl of Suffolk, to be beheaded in the Tower, the nobleman who had been attainted and imprisoned during the late reign. Henry was led to commit this act of violence by the dying commands, as is imagined, of his father, who told him, that he never would be free from danger, while a man of so turbulent a disposition as Suffolk was alive. And as Richard de la Pole, brother of Suffolk, had accepted of a command in the French service, and foolishly attempted to revive the York faction, and to instigate them against the present government, he probably, by that means, drew more suddenly the king's vengeance on this unhappy nobleman.

At last Henry, attended by the duke of Buckingham, and many others of the nobility, arrived at Calais, and entered upon his French expedition, from which he fondly expected so much success and glory [a]. Of all those allies, on whose assistance he relied, the Swiss alone fully performed their engagements. Being put in motion by a sum of money sent them by Henry, and incited by their victories obtained in Italy, and by their animosity against France, they were preparing to enter that kingdom with an army of twenty-five thousand men; and no equal force could be opposed to their incursion. Maximilian had received an advance of 120,000 crowns from Henry, and had promised to reinforce the Swiss with 8000 men; but failed in his engagements. That he might make atonement to the king, he himself appeared in the Low Countries, and joined the English army with some German and Flemish soldiers, who were useful in giving an example of discipline to Henry's new levied forces. Observing the disposition of the English monarch to be more bent on glory than on interest, he inlisted himself in his service, wore the cross of St. George, and received pay,

30th June.

Invasion of France.

[a] Polydore Virgil, lib. 27. Belcarius, lib. 14.

a hundred

a hundred crowns a day, as one of his subjects and captains. But while he exhibited this extraordinary spectacle, of an emperor of Germany serving under a king of England, he was treated with the highest respect by Henry, and really directed all the operations of the English army.

BEFORE the arrival of Henry and Maximilian in the camp, the earl of Shrewsbury and lord Herbert had formed the siege of Terouane, a town situated on the frontiers of Picardy; and they began to attack the place with vigour. Teligni and Crequi commanded in the town, and had a garrison not exceeding two thousand men; yet made they such stout resistance as protracted the siege a month; and they at last found themselves more in danger from want of provisions and ammunition, than from the assaults of the besiegers. Having conveyed intelligence of their situation to Lewis, who had advanced to Amiens with his army, that prince gave orders to throw relief into the place. Fontrailles appeared at the head of 800 horsemen, each of whom carried a sack of gunpowder behind him, and two quarters of bacon. With this small force he made a sudden and unexpected irruption into the English camp, and, surmounting all resistance, advanced to the fossee of the town, where each horseman threw down his burden. They immediately returned at the gallop, and were so fortunate as again to break through the English, and to suffer little or no loss in this dangerous attempt [a].

BUT the English had, soon after, full revenge for the insult. Henry had received intelligence of the approach of the French horse, who had advanced to protect another incursion of Fontrailles; and he ordered some troops to pass the Lis, in order to oppose them. The cavalry of France, though they consisted chiefly of gentlemen who

[a] Hist. de Chev. Bayard, chap. 57. Memoires de Bellai.

had

had behaved with great gallantry in many desperate actions in Italy, were, on sight of the enemy, seized with so unaccountable a panic, that they immediately took to flight, and were pursued by the English. The duke of Longueville, who commanded the French, Bussi d'Amboise, Clermont, Imbercourt, the chevalier Bayard, and many other officers of distinction, were made prisoners[*]. This action, or rather rout, is sometimes called the battle of Guinegate, from the place where it was fought; but more commonly the *Battle of Spurs*, because the French, that day, made more use of their spurs than of their swords or military weapons.

AFTER so considerable an advantage, the king, who was at the head of a complete army of above 50,000 men, might have made incursions to the gates of Paris, and spread confusion and desolation every where. It gave Lewis great joy, when he heard that the English, instead of pushing their victory, and attacking the dismayed troops of France, returned to the siege of so inconsiderable a place as Terouane. The governors were obliged, soon after, to capitulate; and Henry found his acquisition of so little moment, though gained at the expence of some blood, and what, in his present circumstances, was more important, of much valuable time, that he immediately demolished the fortifications. The anxieties of the French were again revived with regard to the motions of the English. The Swiss, at the same time, had entered Burgundy with a formidable army, and laid siege to Dijon, which was in no condition to resist them. Ferdinand himself, though he had made a truce with Lewis, seemed disposed to lay hold of every advantage which fortune should present to him. Scarcely ever was the French monarchy in greater danger, or less in a condition to de-

[*] Memoires de Bellai, liv. 1. Polydore Virgil, liv. 27. Hollingshed, p. 812. Herbert.

send itself against those powerful armies, which on every side assailed or threatened it. Even many of the inhabitants of Paris, who believed themselves exposed to the rapacity and violence of the enemy, began to dislodge, without knowing what place could afford them greater security.

But Lewis was extricated from his present difficulties by the manifold blunders of his enemies. The Swiss allowed themselves to be seduced into a negociation by Tremoille, governor of Burgundy; and, without making enquiry whether that nobleman had any powers to treat, they accepted of the conditions which he offered them. Tremoille, who knew that he should be disavowed by his master, stipulated whatever they were pleased to demand; and thought himself happy, at the expence of some payments and very large promises, to get rid of so formidable an enemy [p].

The measures of Henry showed equal ignorance in the art of war with that of the Swiss in negociation. Tournay was a great and rich city, which, though it lay within the frontiers of Flanders, belonged to France, and afforded the troops of that kingdom a passage into the heart of the Netherlands. Maximilian, who was desirous of freeing his grandson from so troublesome a neighbour, advised Henry to lay siege to the place; and the English monarch, not considering that such an acquisition nowise advanced his conquests in France, was so imprudent as to follow this interested counsel. The city of Tournay, by its ancient charters, being exempted from the burden of a garrison, the burghers, against the remonstrance of their sovereign, strenuously insisted on maintaining this dangerous privilege; and they engaged, by themselves, to make a vigorous defence against the enemy [q]. Their courage failed them when matters

[p] Memoires du mareschal de Fleuranges, Ballarin, lib. 14.
[q] Memoires de Fleuranges.

came to trial; and, after a few days siege, the place was surrendered to the English. The bishop of Tournay was lately dead; and, as a new bishop was already elected by the chapter, but not installed in his office, the king bestowed the administration of the see on his favourite, Wolsey, and put him in immediate possession of the revenues, which were considerable[f]. Hearing of the retreat of the Swiss, and observing the season to be far advanced, he thought proper to return to England; and he carried the greater part of his army with him. Success had attended him in every enterprize; and his youthful mind was much elated with this seeming prosperity; but all men of judgment, comparing the advantages of his situation with his progress, his expence with his acquisitions, were convinced that this campaign, so much vaunted, was, in reality, both ruinous and inglorious to him[g].

THE success which, during this summer, had attended Henry's arms in the North, was much more decisive. The king of Scotland had assembled the whole force of his kingdom; and, having passed the Tweed with a brave, though a tumultuary army of above 50,000 men, he ravaged those parts of Northumberland which lay nearest that river, and he employed himself in taking the castles of Norham, Etal, Werke, Ford, and other places of small importance. Lady Ford, being taken prisoner in her castle, was presented to James, and so gained on the affections of the prince, that he wasted, in pleasure, the critical time which, during the absence of his enemy, he should have employed in pushing his conquests. His troops, lying in a barren country, where they soon consumed all the provisions, began to be pinched with hunger; and, as the authority of the prince was feeble, and military discipline, during that age, extremely relaxed, many of them had stolen from the camp, and retired

[f] Strype's Memorials, vol. i. p. 5, 6.   [g] Goistuin'nt. homewards.

CHAP. XXVII.

1513.

homewards. Meanwhile the earl of Surrey, having collected a force of 26,000 men, of which 5000 had been sent over from the king's army in France, marched to the defence of the country, and approached the Scots, who lay on some high ground near the hills of Cheviot. The river Till ran between the armies, and prevented an engagement: Surrey, therefore, sent a herald to the Scottish camp, challenging the enemy to descend into the plain of Milfield, which lay towards the south; and there, appointing a day for the combat, to try their valour on equal ground. As he received no satisfactory answer, he made a feint of marching towards Berwic; as if he intended to enter Scotland, to lay waste the borders, and cut off the provisions of the enemy. The Scottish army, in order to prevent his purpose, put themselves in motion; and, having set fire to the huts in which they had quartered, they descended from the hills. Surrey, taking advantage of the smoke, which was blown towards him, and which concealed his movements, passed the Till with his artillery and vanguard at the bridge of Twisel, and sent the rest of his army to seek a ford higher up the river.

9th Sep.

Battle of Flowden.

An engagement was now become inevitable, and both sides prepared for it with tranquillity and order[1]. The English divided their army into two lines: Lord Howard led the main body of the first line, Sir Edmond Howard the right wing, Sir Marmaduke Constable the left. The earl of Surrey, himself, commanded the main body of the second line, lord Dacres the right wing, Sir Edward Stanley the left. The front of the Scots presented three divisions to the enemy: The middle was led by the king himself: The right by the earl of Huntley, assisted by lord Hume: The left by the earls of Lenox and Argyle.

[1] Buchanan, lib. 13. Drummond. Herbert. Polydore Virgil, lib. 27. Stowe, p. 493. Paulus Jovius.

A fourth

A fourth division, under the earl of Bothwel, made a body of reserve. Huntley began the battle; and, after a sharp conflict, put to flight the left wing of the English, and chaced them off the field: But, on returning from the pursuit, he found the whole Scottish army in great disorder. The division under Lenox and Argyle, elated with the success of the other wing, had broken their ranks, and, notwithstanding the remonstrances and entreaties of La Motte, the French ambassador, had rushed headlong upon the enemy. Not only Sir Edmond Howard, at the head of his division, received them with great valour; but Dacres, who commanded in the second line, wheeling about during the action, fell upon their rear, and put them to the sword without resistance. The division under James, and that under Bothwel, animated by the valour of their leaders, still made head against the English, and, throwing themselves into a circle, protracted the action, till night separated the combatants. The victory seemed yet undecided, and the numbers that fell on each side were nearly equal, amounting to above 5000 men: But the morning discovered where the advantage lay. The English had lost only persons of small note; but the flower of the Scottish nobility had fallen in battle, and their king himself, after the most diligent enquiry, could no where be found. In searching the field, the English met with a dead body which resembled him, and was arrayed in a similar habit; and they put it in a leaden coffin, and sent it to London. During some time it was kept unburied; because James died under sentence of excommunication, on account of his confederacy with France, and his opposition to the holy see [u]: But, upon Henry's application, who pretended that this prince had, in the instant before his death, discovered signs of repentance, absolution was given him,

---

[u] Buchanan, lib. 13. Herbert.

CHAP.
XXVII.

1513.

and his body was interred. The Scots, however, still asserted that it was not James's body which was found on the field of battle, but that of one Elphinston, who had been arrayed in arms resembling their king's, in order to divide the attention of the English, and share the danger with his master. It was believed that James had been seen crossing the Tweed at Kelso; and some imagined that he had been killed by the vassals of lord Hume, whom that nobleman had instigated to commit so enormous a crime. But the populace entertained the opinion that he was still alive, and, having secretly gone in pilgrimage to the holy land, would soon return and take possession of the throne. This fond conceit was long entertained among the Scots.

1514.

THE king of Scotland and most of his chief nobles being slain in the field of Flouden, so this battle was called, an inviting opportunity was offered to Henry of gaining advantages over that kingdom, perhaps of reducing it to subjection. But he discovered, on this occasion, a mind truly great and generous. When the queen of Scotland, Margaret, who was created regent during the infancy of her son, applied for peace, he readily granted it; and took compassion of the helpless condition of his sister and nephew. The earl of Surrey, who had gained him so great a victory, was restored to the title of duke of Norfolk, which had been forfeited by his father for engaging on the side of Richard III. Lord Howard was honoured with the title of earl of Surrey. Sir Charles Brandon, the king's favourite, whom he had before created viscount Lisle, was now raised to the dignity of duke of Suffolk. Wolsey, who was both his favourite and his minister, was created bishop of Lincoln. Lord Herbert obtained the title of earl of Worcester. Sir Edward Stanley that of lord Monteagle.

THOUGH

HENRY VIII.

CHAP.
XXVII.

1514.

THOUGH peace with Scotland gave Henry security on that side, and enabled him to prosecute, in tranquillity, his enterprize against France, some other incidents had happened, which more than counterbalanced this fortunate event, and served to open his eyes with regard to the rashness of an undertaking into which his youth and high fortune had betrayed him.

LEWIS, fully sensible of the dangerous situation to which his kingdom had been reduced during the former campaign, was resolved, by every expedient, to prevent the return of like perils, and to break the confederacy of his enemies. The pope was nowise disposed to push the French to extremity; and, provided they did not return to take possession of Milan, his interests rather led him to preserve the balance among the contending parties. He accepted, therefore, of Lewis's offer to renounce the council of Lyons; and he took off the excommunication which his predecessor and himself had fulminated against that king and his kingdom. Ferdinand was now fast declining in years; and as he entertained no farther ambition than that of keeping possession of Navarre, which he had subdued by his arms and policy, he readily hearkened to the proposals of Lewis for prolonging the truce another year; and he even shewed an inclination of forming a more intimate connexion with that monarch. Lewis had dropped hints of his intention to marry his second daughter, Renée, either to Charles, prince of Spain, or his brother, Ferdinand, both of them grandsons of the Spanish monarch; and he declared his resolution of bestowing on her, as her portion, his claim to the dutchy of Milan. Ferdinand not only embraced these proposals with joy; but also engaged the emperor, Maximilian, in the same views, and procured his accession to a treaty, which opened so inviting a prospect of aggrandizing their common grandchildren.

WHEN

CHAP.
XXVII.

1514.

WHEN Henry was informed of Ferdinand's renewal of the truce with Lewis, he fell into a violent rage, and loudly complained, that his father-in-law had first, by high promises and professions, engaged him in enmity with France, and afterwards, without giving him the least warning, had now again sacrificed his interests to his own selfish purposes, and had left him exposed alone to all the danger and expence of the war. In proportion to his easy credulity, and his unsuspecting reliance on Ferdinand, was the vehemence with which he exclaimed against the treatment which he met with; and he threatened revenge for this egregious treachery and breach of faith [v]. But he lost all patience when informed of the other negociation by which Maximilian was also seduced from his alliance, and in which proposals had been agreed to, for the marriage of the prince of Spain with the daughter of France. Charles, during the lifetime of the late king, had been affianced to Mary, Henry's younger sister; and, as the prince now approached the age of puberty, the king had expected the immediate completion of the marriage, and the honourable settlement of a sister, for whom he had entertained a tender affection. Such a complication, therefore, of injuries gave him the highest displeasure, and inspired him with a desire of expressing his disdain towards those who had imposed on his youth and inexperience, and had abused his too great facility.

THE duke of Longueville, who had been made prisoner at the battle of Guinegate, and who was still detained in England, was ready to take advantage of all these dispositions of Henry, in order to procure a peace, and even an alliance, which he knew to be passionately desired by his master. He represented to the king that Anne, queen of France, being lately dead, a door was

[v] Petrus de Argensia, Epist. 545, 548.

thereby opened for an affinity which might tend to the advantage of both kingdoms, and which would serve to terminate honourably all the differences between them: That she had left Lewis no male children; and as he had ever entertained a strong desire of having heirs to the crown, no marriage seemed more suitable to him than that with the princess of England, whose youth and beauty afforded the most flattering hopes in that particular: That, though the marriage of a princess of sixteen with a king of fifty-three might seem unsuitable, yet the other advantages, attending the alliance, were more than a sufficient compensation for this inequality: And that Henry, in loosening his connexions with Spain, from which he had never reaped any advantage, would contract a close affinity with Lewis, a prince who, through his whole life, had invariably maintained the character of probity and honour.

CHAP.
XXVII.

1514.

As Henry seemed to hearken to this discourse with willing ears, Longueville informed his master of the probability, which he discovered, of bringing the matter to a happy conclusion; and he received full powers for negociating the treaty. The articles were easily adjusted between the monarchs. Lewis agreed that Tournay should remain in the hands of the English; that Richard de la Pole should be banished to Metz, there to live on a pension assigned him by Lewis; that Henry should receive payment of a million of crowns, being the arrears due by treaty to his father and himself; and that the princess Mary should bring four hundred thousand crowns as her portion, and enjoy as large a jointure as any queen of France, even the former, who was heiress of Britanny. The two princes also agreed on the succours with which they should mutually supply each other, in case either of them were attacked by an enemy [s].

Peace with France.
7th August.

[s] Du Tillet.

In consequence of this treaty, Mary was sent over to France with a splendid retinue, and Lewis met her at Abbeville, where the espousals were celebrated. He was enchanted with the beauty, grace, and numerous accomplishments of the young princess; and, being naturally of an amorous disposition, which his advanced age had not entirely cooled, he was seduced into such a course of gaiety and pleasure, as proved very unsuitable to his declining state of health [r]. He died in less than three months after the marriage, to the extreme regret of the French nation, who, sensible of his tender concern for their welfare, gave him, with one voice, the honourable appellation of *father of his people*.

FRANCIS, duke of Angouleme, a youth of one and twenty, who had married Lewis's elder daughter, succeeded him on the throne; and, by his activity, valour, generosity, and other virtues, gave prognostics of a happy and glorious reign. This young monarch had been extremely struck with the charms of the English princess; and, even during his predecessor's life-time, had payed her such assiduous court, as made some of his friends apprehend that he had entertained views of gallantry towards her. But being warned that, by indulging this passion, he might probably exclude himself from the throne, he forbore all farther addresses; and even watched the young dowager with a very careful eye during the first months of her widowhood. Charles Brandon, duke of Suffolk, was, at that time, in the court of France, the most comely personage of his time, and the most accomplished in all the exercises which were then thought to befit a courtier and a soldier. He was Henry's chief favourite; and that monarch had even once entertained thoughts of marrying him to his sister, and had given indulgence to the mutual passion which took place between

[r] Brantome Eloge de Lewis XII.

tween them. The queen afked Suffo'k, whether he had now the courage, without farther reflection, to efpoufe her? And fhe told him, that her brother would more eafily forgive him for not afking his confent, than for acting contrary to his orders. Suffolk declined not fo inviting an offer; and their nuptials were fecretly celebrated at Paris. Francis, who was pleafed with this marriage, as it prevented Henry from forming any powerful alliance by means of his fifter [a], interpofed his good offices in appeafing him: And even Wolfey, having entertained no jealoufy of Suffolk, who was content to participate in the king's pleafures, and had no ambition to engage in public bufinefs, was active in reconciling the king to his fifter and brother-in-law; and he obtained them permiffion to return to England.

[a] Petrus de Angleria, Epift. 544.

NOTES
TO THE
THIRD VOLUME.

NOTE [A], p. 4.

IN the fifth year of the king *the commons complained of the government about the king's person, his court, the exceffive number of his servants, of the abufes in the Chancery, King's Bench, Common Pleas, Exchequer, and of grievous oppreffions in the country, by the great multitudes of maintainers of quarrels* (men linked in confederacies together), *who behaved themfelves like kings in the country, fo as there was very little law or right, and of other things which, they faid, were the caufe of the late commotions under Wat Tyler.* Parl. Hift. vol. i. p. 365. This irregular government, which no king and no houfe of commons had been able to remedy, was the fource of the licentioufnefs of the great, and turbulency of the people, as well as tyranny of the princes.. If fubjects would enjoy liberty, and kings fecurity, the laws muft be executed.

In the ninth of this reign the commons alfo difcovered an accuracy and a jealoufy of liberty which we fhould little expect in thofe rude times. " It was agreed by parliament," fays Cotton, p. 309, " that the fubfidy of wools, wool fells, " and fkins, granted to the king until the time of Midfummer " then enfuing, fhould ceafe from the fame time unto the feaft " of St. Peter *ad vincula*; for that thereby the king fhould be " interrupted for claiming fuch grant as due." See alfo Cotton, p. 198.

NOTE [B], p. 16.

KNYGHTON, p. 2715, &c. The fame author, p. 2680, tells us, that the king, in return to the meffage, faid, that he would not, for their defire, remove the meaneft fcullion

from

from his kitchen. This author also tells us, that the king said to the commissioners, when they harangued him, that he saw his subjects were rebellious, and his best way would be to call in the king of France to his aid. But it is plain that all these speeches were either intended by Knyghton merely as an ornament to his history, or are false. For (1) when the five lords accuse the king's ministers in the next parliament, and impute to them every rash action of the king, they speak nothing of these replies which are so obnoxious, were so recent, and are pretended to have been so public. (2) The king, so far from having any connexions, at that time, with France, was threatened with a dangerous invasion from that kingdom. This story seems to have been taken from the reproaches afterwards thrown out against him, and to have been transferred by the historians to this time, to which they cannot be applied.

NOTE [C], p. 21.

WE must except the 12th article, which accuses Brembre of having cut off the heads of twenty-two prisoners, confined for felony or debt, without warrant or process of law. But, as it is not conceivable what interest Brembre could have to treat these felons and debtors in such a manner, we may presume that the fact is either false, or misrepresented. It was in these mens power to say any thing against the persons accused: No defence or apology was admitted: All was lawless will and pleasure.

They are also accused of designs to murder the lords: But these accusations either are general, or destroy one another. Sometimes, as in article 15th, they intend to murder them by means of the mayor and city of London: Sometimes, as in article 28th, by trial and false inquests: Sometimes, as in article 28th, by means of the king of France, who was to receive Calais for his pains.

NOTE [D], p. 23.

IN general, the parliament in those days never paid a proper regard to Edward's statute of treasons, though one of the most advantageous laws for the subject that has ever been enacted.

enacted. In the 17th of the king, *the dukes of Lancaster and Gloceſter complain to Richard, that Sir Thomas Talbot, with others of his adherents, conſpired the death of the ſaid dukes in divers parts of Cheſhire, as the ſame was confeſſed and well known; and praying that the parliament may judge of the fault.* Whereupon the king and the lords in the parliament judged the ſame fact to be open and high treaſon: And hereupon they award two writs, the one to the ſheriff of York, and the other to the ſheriffs of Derby, to take the body of the ſaid Sir Thomas, returnable in the King's Bench in the month of Eaſter then enſuing. And open proclamation was made in Weſtminſter hall, that upon the ſheriff's return, and at the next coming in of the ſaid Sir Thomas, the ſaid Thomas ſhould be convicted of treaſon, and incur the loſs and pain of the ſame: And all ſuch as ſhould receive him, after the proclamation, ſhould incur the ſame loſs and pain. Cotton, p. 354. It is to be obſerved, that this extraordinary judgment was paſſed in a time of tranquillity. Though the ſtatute itſelf, of Edward III. reſerves a power to the parliament to declare any new ſpecies of treaſon, it is not to be ſuppoſed that this power was reſerved to the houſe of lords alone, or that men were to be judged by a law *ex poſt facto*. At leaſt, if ſuch be the meaning of the clauſe, it may be affirmed, that men were, at that time, very ignorant of the firſt principles of law and juſtice.

NOTE [E], p. 30.

IN the preceding parliament, the commons had ſhewn a diſpoſition very complaiſant to the king; yet there happened an incident in their proceedings which is curious, and ſhews us the ſtate of the houſe during that period. The members were either country gentlemen or merchants, who were aſſembled for a few days, and were entirely unacquainted with buſineſs; ſo that it was eaſy to lead them aſtray, and draw them into votes and reſolutions very different from their intention. Some petitions, concerning the ſtate of the nation, were voted; in which, among other things, the houſe recommended frugality to the king; and, for that purpoſe, deſired that the court ſhould not be ſo much frequented, as formerly, by *biſhops* and *ladies*. The king was diſpleaſed with this

NOTE [G], p. 52.

THE following passage in Cotton's Abridgment, p. 196. shows a strange prejudice against the church and churchmen. *The commons afterwards coming into the parliament, and making their protestation, showed, that for want of good redress about the king's person, in his household, in all his courts, touching maintainers in every county, and purveyors, the commons were daily pilled, and nothing defended against the enemy, and that it should shortly deprive the king, and undo the state. Wherefore, in the same government, they entirely require redress. Whereupon the king appointed sundry bishops, lords, and nobles, to sit in privycouncil about these matters: Who, since that they must begin at the head, and go at the request of the commons, they, in the presence of the king, charged his confessor not to come into the court but upon the four principal festivals.* We should little expect that a popish privy-council, in order to preserve the king's morals, should order his confessor to be kept at a distance from him. This incident happened in the minority of Richard. As the popes had, for a long time, resided at Avignon, and the majority of the sacred college were Frenchmen, this circumstance naturally encreased the aversion of the nation to the papal power: But the prejudice against the English clergy cannot be accounted for from that cause.

NOTE [H], p. 223.

THAT we may judge how arbitrary a court that of the constable of England was, we may peruse the patent granted to the earl of Rivers in this reign, as it is to be found in Spellman's Glossary in verb. *Constabularius*: as also, more fully in Rymer, vol. xi. p. 581. Here is a clause of it: *Et ulterius de uberiori gratia nostra eidem comiti de Rivers plenam potestatem damus ad cognoscendum & procedendum, in omnibus & singulis causis et negotiis, de et super crimine læsæ majestatis seu super occasione cæterisque causis, quibuscunque per præfatum comitem de Rivers, ut constabularium Angliæ —— quæ in curia constabularii Angliæ ab antiquo viz. tempore dicti domini Gulielmi conquestoris, seu aliquo tempore citra tractari, audiri, examinari, aut decidi consueverant, aut jure debuerant, aut debent, cognoscanque et negotia prædicta cum omnibus et singulis emergentibus, in-*

sidentibus & commexis, audiendum, examinandum, et fine debito terminandum, etiam summarie et de plano, sine strepitu et figura justitiæ, sola facti veritate inspecta, ac etiam manu regia, si opportunum visum fuerit eidem comiti de Rivers, vices nostras, appellatione remota. The office of constable was perpetual in the monarchy; its jurisdiction was not limited to times of war, as appears from this patent, and as we learn from Spellman: Yet its authority was in direct contradiction to *Magna Charta*; and it is evident that no *regular* liberty could subsist with it. It involved a full dictatorial power, continually subsisting in the state. The only check on the crown, besides the want of force to support all its prerogatives, was, that the office of constable was commonly either hereditary or during life; and the person invested with it was, for that reason, not so proper an instrument of arbitrary power in the king. Accordingly the office was suppressed by Henry VIII. the most arbitrary of all the English princes. The practice, however, of exercising martial law, still subsisted; and was not abolished till the petition of Right under Charles I. This was the epoch of true liberty, confirmed by the Restoration, and enlarged and secured by the Revolution.

NOTE [I], p. 234.

WE shall give an instance: Almost all the historians, even Comines, and the continuator of the annals of Croyland, assert that Edward was, about this time, taken prisoner by Clarence and Warwic, and was committed to the custody of the archbishop of York, brother to the earl; but being allowed to take the diversion of hunting by this prelate, he made his escape, and afterwards chaced the rebels out of the kingdom. But that all the story is false, appears from Rymer, where we find, that the king, throughout all this period, continually exercised his authority, and never was interrupted in his government. On the 7th of March 14–0, he gives a commission of array to Clarence, whom he then imagined a good subject; and, on the 23d of the same month, we find him issuing an order for apprehending him. Besides, in the king's manifesto against the duke and earl (Claus. 10. Edward IV, m. 7, 8.),

ln. 7, 8.), where he enumerates all their treasons, he mentions
no such fact: He does not so much as accuse them of exciting
young Welles's rebellion: He only says, that they exhorted
him to continue in his rebellion. We may judge how smaller
facts will be misrepresented by historians, who can in the
most material transactions mistake so grosly. There may
even some doubt arise with regard to the proposal of marriage made to Bona of Savoy; though almost all the historians
concur in it, and the fact be very likely in itself: For there
are no traces in Rymer of any such embassy of Warwic's to
France. The chief certainty in this and the preceding reign
arises either from public records, or from the notice taken of
certain passages by the French historians. On the contrary,
for some centuries after the conquest, the French history is
not complete without the assistance of English authors. We
may conjecture, that the reason of the scarcity of historians
during this period, was the destruction of the convents, which
ensued so soon after: Copies of the more recent historians not
being yet sufficiently dispersed, these histories have perished.

NOTE [K], p. 274.

SIR Thomas More, who has been followed, or rather tran-
scribed, by all the historians of this short reign, says,
that Jane Shore had fallen into connections with lord Hastings;
and this account agrees best with the course of the events:
But, in a proclamation of Richard's, to be found in Rymer,
vol. xii. p. 204. the marquis of Dorset is reproached with
these connections. This reproach, however, might have been
invented by Richard, or founded only on popular rumour;
and is not sufficient to overbalance the authority of Sir Thomas More. The proclamation is remarkable for the hypo-
critical purity of manners affected by Richard: This bloody
and treacherous tyrant upbraids the marquis and others with
their gallantries and intrigues as the most terrible enormities.

NOTE [L], p. 297.

EVERY one that has perused the ancient monkish writers
knows, that however barbarous their own style, they are
full of allusions to the Latin classics, especially the poets.

There

There seems also, in those middle ages, to have remained many ancient books, that are now loft. Malmesbury, who flourished in the reign of Henry I. and king Stephen, quotes Livy's description of Cæsar's paſſage over the Rubicon. Fitz-Stephen, who lived in the reign of Henry II. alludes to a paſſage in the larger hiſtory of Salluſt. In the collection of letters, which paſſes under the name of Thomas à Becket, we ſee how familiar all the ancient hiſtory and ancient books were to the more ingenious and more dignified churchmen of that time, and conſequently how much that order of men muſt have ſurpaſſed all the other members of the ſociety. That prelate and his friends call each other Philoſophers in all the courſe of their correſpondence, and conſider the reſt of the world as ſunk in total ignorance and barbariſm.

NOTE [M], p. 383.

STOWE, Baker, Speed, Biondi, Hollingſhed, Bacon. Some late writers, particularly Mr. Carte, have doubted whether Perkin were an impoſtor, and have even aſſerted him to be the true Plantagenet. But, to refute this opinion, we need only reflect on the following particulars: (1) Though the circumſtances of the wars between the two roſes be, in general, involved in great obſcurity, yet is there a moſt luminous ray thrown on all the tranſactions during the uſurpation of Richard, and the murder of the two young princes, by the narrative of Sir Thomas More, whoſe ſingular magnanimity, probity, and judgment, make him an evidence beyond all exception! No hiſtorian, either of ancient or modern times, can poſſibly have more weight: He may alſo be juſtly eſteemed a contemporary with regard to the murder of the two princes: For, though he was but five years of age when that event happened, he lived, and was educated, among the chief actors during the period of Richard: And it is plain, from his narrative itſelf, which is often extremely circumſtantial, that he had the particulars from the eye-witneſſes themſelves: His authority, therefore, is irrefiſible; and ſufficient to overbalance a hundred little doubts and ſcruples and objections. For, in reality, his narrative is liable to no ſolid objection,

nor

NOTES TO THE THIRD VOLUME.

nor is there any mistake detected in it. He says, indeed, that the protector's partizans, particularly Dr. Shaw, spread abroad rumours of Edward IV.'s pre-contract with Elizabeth Lucy; whereas it now appears, from record, that the parliament afterwards declared the king's children illegitimate, on pretence of his pre-contract with lady Eleanor Talbot. But it must be remarked, that neither of these pre-contracts was ever so much as attempted to be proved: And why might not the protector's flatterers and partizans have made use sometimes of one false rumour, sometimes of another? Sir Thomas More mentions the one rumour as well as the other, and treats them both lightly, as they deserved. It is also thought incredible, by Mr. Carte, that Dr. Shaw should have been encouraged by Richard to calumniate openly his mother the dutchess of York, with whom that prince lived in good terms. But, if there be any difficulty in this supposition, we need only suppose that Dr. Shaw might have concerted, in general, his sermon with the protector or his ministers, and yet have chosen himself the particular topics, and chosen them very foolishly. This appears, indeed, to have been the case, by the disgrace into which he fell afterwards, and by the protector's neglect of him. (2) If Sir Thomas's quality of contemporary be disputed with regard to the duke of Glocester's protectorate, it cannot possibly be disputed with regard to Perkin's imposture: He was then a man, and had a full opportunity of knowing and examining and judging of the truth. In asserting that the duke of York was murdered by his uncle, he certainly asserts, in the most express terms, that Perkin, who personated him, was an impostor. (3) There is another great genius who has carefully treated this point of history; so great a genius as to be esteemed, with justice, one of the chief ornaments of the nation, and, indeed, one of the most sublime writers that any age or nation has produced. It is lord Bacon I mean, who has related, at full length, and without the least doubt or hesitation, all the impostures of Perkin Warbec. If it be objected, that lord Bacon was no contemporary, and that we have the same materials as he upon which to form our judgment; it must be

remarked

remarked, that lord Bacon plainly composed his elaborate and exact history from many records and papers which are now lost, and that, consequently, he is always to be cited as an original historian. It were very strange, if Mr. Carte's opinion were just, that, among all the papers which lord Bacon perused, he never found any reason to suspect Perkin to be the true Plantagenet. There was, at that time, no interest in defaming Richard III. Bacon, besides, is a very unbiassed historian, nowise partial to Henry: We know the detail of that prince's oppressive government from him alone. It may only be thought, that, in summing up his character, he has laid the colours of blame more faintly than the very facts he mentions seem to require. Let me remark, in passing, as a singularity, how much English history has been beholden to four great men who have possessed the highest dignity in the law, More, Bacon, Clarendon, and Whitlocke. (4) But if contemporary evidence be so much sought after, there may, in this case, be produced the strongest and most undeniable in the world. The queen-dowager, her son the marquis of Dorset, a man of excellent understanding, Sir Edward Woodville, her brother, Sir Thomas St. Leger, who had married the king's sister, Sir John Bourchier, Sir Robert Willoughby, Sir Giles Daubeney, Sir Thomas Arundel, the Courtneys, the Cheyneys, the Talbots, the Stanleys, and in a word, all the partizans of the house of York, that is, the men of chief dignity in the nation; all these great persons were so assured of the murder of the two princes, that they applied to the earl of Richmond, the mortal enemy of their party and family; they projected to set him on the throne, which must have been utter ruin to them if the princes were alive; and they stipulated to marry him to the princess Elizabeth, as heir to the crown, who, in that case, was no heir at all. Had each of those persons written the memoirs of his own times, would he not have said, that Richard murdered his nephews? Or would their pen be a better declaration, than their actions, of their real sentiments? (5) But we have another contemporary authority still better than even these great persons, so much interested to know the truth: It is that of Richard himself:

self: He projected to marry his niece, a very unusual alliance in England, in order to unite her title with his own. He knew, therefore, her title to be good: For as to the declaration of her illegitimacy, as it went upon no proof, or even pretence of proof, it was always regarded with the utmost contempt by the nation, and was considered as one of those parliamentary transactions, so frequent in that period, which were scandalous in themselves, and had no manner of authority. It was even so much despised as not to be reversed by parliament, after Henry and Elizabeth were on the throne. (6) We have also, as contemporary evidence, the universal established opinion of the age, both abroad and at home. This point was regarded as so uncontroverted, that when Richard notified his accession to the court of France, that court was struck with horror at his abominable parricide, in murdering both his nephews, as Philip de Comines tells us; and this sentiment went to such an unusual height, that, as we learn from the same author, the court would not make the least reply to him. (7) The same reasons, which convinced that age of the parricide, still subsist, and ought to carry the most undoubted evidence to us; namely, the very circumstance of the sudden disappearance of the princes from the Tower, and their appearance no where else. Every one said, *they have not escaped from their uncle, for he makes no search after them: He has not conveyed them elsewhere: For it is his business to declare so, in order to remove the imputation of murder from himself. He never would needlessly subject himself to the infamy and danger of being esteemed a parricide, without acquiring the security attending that crime. They were in his custody: He is answerable for them: If he gives no account of them, as he has a plain interest in their death, he must, by every rule of common sense, be regarded as the murderer.* His flagrant usurpation, as well as his other treacherous and cruel actions, makes no better be expected from him. He could not say, with Cain, that he was not his nephews' keeper. This reasoning, which was irrefragable, at the very first, became every day stronger, from Richard's continued silence, and the general and total ignorance of the place of these princes' abode. Richard's reign lasted about two years beyond this period; and surely he could not have

found

found a better expedient for disappointing the earl of Richmond's projects, as well as justifying his own character, than the producing of his nephews. (8) If it were necessary, amidst this blaze of evidence, to produce proofs, which, in any other case, would have been regarded as considerable, and would have carried great validity with them, I might mention Dighton and Tyrrel's account of the murder. This last gentleman especially was not likely to subject himself to the reproach of so great a crime, by an imposture, which, it appears, did not acquire him the favour of Henry. (9) The duke of York, being a boy of nine years of age, could not have made his escape without the assistance of some elder persons. Would it not have been their chief concern instantly to convey intelligence of so great an event to his mother, the queen-dowager, to his aunt, the dutchess of Burgundy, and to the other friends of the family? The dutchess protected Simnel; a project which, had it been successful, must have ended in the crowning of Warwic, and the exclusion of the duke of York! This, among many other proofs, evinces that she was ignorant of the escape of that prince, which is impossible had it been real. (10) The total silence with regard to the persons who aided him in his escape, as also with regard to the place of his abode during more than eight years, is a sufficient proof of the imposture. (11) Perkin's own account of his escape is incredible and absurd. He said that murderers were employed by his uncle to kill him and his brother: They perpetrated the crime against his brother; but took compassion on him, and allowed him to escape. This account is contained in all the historians of that age. (12) Perkin himself made a full confession of his imposture no less than three times; once when he surrendered himself prisoner, a second time when he was set in the stocks at Cheapside and Westminster, and a third time, which carries undoubted evidence, at the foot of the gibbet on which he was hanged. Not the least surmise that the confession had ever been procured by torture; And surely, the last time he had nothing farther to fear. (13) Had not Henry been assured that Perkin was a ridiculous impostor, disavowed by the whole nation, he never would have allowed him to live an hour after he came

into

NOTES TO THE THIRD VOLUME.

into his power; much less would he have twice pardoned him. His treatment of the innocent earl of Warwic, who in reality had no title to the crown, is a sufficient confirmation of this reasoning. (14) We know with certainty whence the whole imposture came, namely, from the intrigues of the dutchess of Burgundy: She had before acknowledged and supported Lambert Simnel, an avowed impostor. It is remarkable, that Mr. Carte, in order to preserve the weight of the dutchess's testimony in favour of Perkin, suppresses entirely this material fact: A strong effect of party prejudices, and this author's desire of blackening Henry VII. whose hereditary title to the crown was defective. (15) There never was, at that time, any evidence or shadow of evidence produced, of Perkin's identity with Richard Plantagenet. Richard had disappeared when near nine years of age, and Perkin did not appear till he was a man. Could any one, from his aspect, pretend then to be sure of the identity? He had got some stories concerning Richard's childhood, and the court of England: But all that it was necessary for a boy of nine to remark or remember, was easily suggested to him by the dutchess of Burgundy, or Frion, Henry's secretary, or by any body that had ever lived at court. It is true, many persons of note were at first deceived; but the discontents against Henry's government, and the general enthusiasm for the house of York, account sufficiently for this temporary delusion. Every body's eyes were opened long before Perkin's death. (16) The circumstance of finding the two dead bodies in the reign of Charles II. is not surely indifferent. They were found in the very place which More, Bacon, and other ancient authors had assigned as the place of interment of the young princes: The bones corresponded, by their size, to the age of the princes: The secret and irregular place of their interment, not being in holy ground, proves that the boys had been secretly murdered: And in the Tower, no boys but those who are very nearly related to the crown can be exposed to a violent death: If we compare all these circumstances, we shall find that the inference is just and strong, that they were the bodies of Edward the Vth and his brother; the very inference that was drawn at the time of the discovery.

Since

NOTES TO THE THIRD VOLUME.

Since the publication of this History, Mr. Walpole has published his Historic Doubts concerning Richard III. Nothing can be a stronger proof how ingenious and agreeable that gentleman's pen is, than his being able to make an enquiry concerning a remote point of English history, an object of general conversation. The foregoing note has been enlarged on account of that performance.

NOTE [N], p. 397.

ROT. Parl. 3 H. VII. n. 17. The preamble is remarkable, and shows the state of the nation at that time. " The king, our sovereign lord, remembereth how, by our " unlawful maintainances, giving of liveries, signs and to- " kens, retainders by indentures, promises, oaths, writings, " and other embraceries of his subjects, untrue demeanings " of sheriffs in making pannels, and untrue returns by taking " money, by juries, &c. the policy of this nation is most sub- " dued." It must indeed be confessed, that such a state of the country required great discretionary power in the sovereign; nor will the same maxims of government suit such a rude people, that may be proper in a more advanced stage of society. The establishment of the Star-chamber, or the enlargement of its power in the reign of Henry VII. might have been as wife as the abolition of it in that of Charles I.

NOTE [O], p. 400.

THE duke of Northumberland has lately printed a household book of an old earl of that family, who lived at this time: The author has been favoured with the perusal of it; and it contains many curious particulars, which mark the manners and way of living in that rude, not to say barbarous, age; as well as the prices of commodities. I have extracted a few of them from that piece, which gives a true picture of ancient manners, and is one of the most singular monuments that English antiquity affords us: For we may be confident, however rude the strokes, that no Baron's family was on a nobler or more splendid footing. The family consists of 166 persons, masters and servants: Fifty-seven strangers are reckoned upon every day: On the whole 223. Two-pence halfpenny are supposed to be the daily expence of each for meat,

meat, drink, and firing. This would make a groat of our present money: Supposing provisions between three and four times cheaper, it would be equivalent to fourteen-pence: No great sum for a nobleman's house-keeping; especially confidering, that the chief expence of a family, at that time, confifted in meat and drink: For the sum allotted by the earl for his whole annual expence is 1118 pounds seventeen fhillings and eight-pence; meat, drink, and firing coft 796 pounds eleven fhillings and two-pence, more than two thirds of the whole: In a modern family it is not above a third, p. 157, 158, 159. The whole expence of the earl's family is managed with an exactnefs that is very rigid, and, if we make no allowance for ancient manners, fuch as may feem to border on an extreme; infomuch, that the number of pieces which muft be cut out of every quarter of beef, mutton, pork, veal, nay ftock-fifh and falmon, are determined, and muft be entered and accounted for by the different clerks appointed for that purpofe: If a fervant be abfent a day, his mefs is ftruck off: If he go on my lord's bufinefs, board wages is allowed him, eight-pence a day for his journey in winter, five-pence in fummer: When he ftays in any place, two-pence a day are allowed him, befide the maintenance of his horfe. Somewhat above a quarter of wheat is allowed for every mouth throughout the year; and the wheat is eftimated at five fhillings and eight-pence a quarter. Two hundred and fifty quarters of malt are allowed, at four fhillings a quarter: Two hogfheads are to be made of a quarter; which amounts to about a bottle and a third of beer a day to each perfon, p. 4. and the beer will not be very ftrong. One hundred and nine fat beeves are to be bought at Allhallow-tide, at thirteen fhillings and four-pence a piece: And twenty-four lean beeves to be bought at St. Helens at eight fhillings a piece: Thefe are to be put into the paftures to feed; and are to ferve from Midfummer to Michaelmas; which is confequently the only time that the family eats frefh beef: During all the reft of the year they live on falted meat, p. 5. One hundred and fixty gallons of muftard are allowed in a year; which feems indeed requifite for the falt beef, p. 18. Six hundred and forty-feven fheep are allowed, at twenty pence a

piece;

piece; and these seem also to be all eat salted, except between Lammas and Michaelmas, p. 5. Only twenty-five hogs are allowed at two shillings a piece; twenty eight veals at twenty-pence; forty lambs at ten-pence or a shilling, p. 7. These seem to be reserved for my lord's table, or that of the upper servants, called the knights'-table. The other servants, as they eat salted meat almost through the whole year, and with few or no vegetables, had a very bad and unhealthy diet: So that there cannot be any thing more erroneous than the magnificent ideas formed of *the Roast Beef of Old England*. We must entertain as mean an idea of its cleanliness: Only seventy ells of linen at eight-pence an ell are annually allowed for this great family: No sheets were used: This linen was made into eight table-cloths for my lord's table; and one table-cloth for the knights, p. 16. This last, I suppose, was washed only once a month. Only forty shillings are allowed for washing throughout the whole year; and most of it seems expended on the linen belonging to the chapel. The drinking, however, was tolerable, namely, ten tuns and two hogsheads of Gascogny wine, at the rate of four pounds thirteen shillings and four-pence a ton, p. 6. Only ninety-one dozen of candles for the whole year, p. 14. The family rose at six in the morning, dined at ten, and supped at four in the afternoon: The gates were all shut at nine, and no farther ingress or egress permitted, p. 314. 318. My lord and lady have set on their table, for breakfast at seven o'clock in the morning, a quart of beer, as much wine; two pieces of salt fish, six red-herrings, four white ones, or a dish of sprats. In flesh days half a chyne of mutton, or a chyne of beef boiled, p. 73. 75. Mass is ordered to be said at six o'clock, in order, says the household-book, that all my lord's servants may rise early, p. 170. Only twenty-four fires are allowed, beside the kitchen and hall, and most of these have only a peck of coals a day allowed them, p. 99. After Lady-day, no fires permitted in the rooms, except half-fires in my lord's and lady's, and lord Piercy's and the nursery, p. 101. It is to be observed that my lord kept house in Yorkshire, where there is certainly much cold weather after Lady-day. Eighty chalders of coals at four shillings and two-pence a chalder, suffices throughout the whole year; and

and because coal will not burn without wood, says the household book, sixty-four loads of great wood are also allowed, at twelve-pence a load, p. 12. This is a proof that grates were not then used. Here is an article. *It is devised that from henceforth no capons to be bought but only for my lord's own mess, and that the said capons shall be bought for two-pence a piece, lean, and fed in the poultry; and master chamberlain and the stewards be fed with capons, if there be strangers sitting with them*, p. 102. Pigs are to be bought at three-pence or a groat a piece: Geese at the same price: Chickens at a halfpenny: Hens at two-pence, and only for the abovementioned tables. Here is another article. *Item, It is thought good that no plovers be bought at no season but only in Christmas and principal feasts, and my lord to be served therewith, and his board-end, and none other, and to be bought for a penny a piece, or a penny halfpenny at most*, p. 103. Woodcocks are to be bought at the same price. Partridges at two-pence, p. 104, 105. Pheasants a shilling; peacocks the same, p. 106. My lord keeps only twenty-seven horses in his stable at his own charge: His upper servants have allowance for maintaining their own horses, p. 126. These horses are, six gentle horses as they are called, at hay and hard meat throughout the whole year, four palfreys, three hobbies and nags, three sumpter horses, six horses for those servants to whom my lord furnishes a horse, two sumpter horses more, and three mill horses, two for carrying the corn, and one for grinding it; whence we may infer, that mills, either water or wind-mills, were then unknown, at least very rare: Besides these, there are seven great trotting horses for the chariot or waggon. He allows a peck of oats a day, besides loaves made of beans, for his principal horses; the oats at twenty pence, the beans at two shillings a quarter. The load of hay is at two shillings and eight-pence. When my lord is on a journey, he carries thirty-six horsemen along with him; together with bed and other accommodation, p. 157. The inns, it seems, could afford nothing tolerable. My lord passes the year in three country-seats, all in Yorkshire, Wrysel, Leckenfield, and Topclyffe; but he has furniture only for one: He carries every thing along with him, beds, tables, chairs, kitchen utensils, all which, we may conclude, were so coarse, that

they

NOTES TO THE THIRD VOLUME.

they could not be spoilt by the carriage: Yet seventeen carts and one waggon suffices for the whole, p. 391. One cart suffices for all his kitchen utensils, cooks beds, &c. p. 388. One remarkable circumstance is, that he has eleven priests in his house, besides seventeen persons, chanters, musicians, &c. belonging to his chapel: Yet he has only two cooks for a family of 223 persons, p. 315*. Their meals were certainly dressed in the slovenly manner of a ship's company. It is amusing to observe the pompous and even royal style assumed by this Tartar chief: He does not give any orders, though only for the right making of mustard, but it is introduced with this preamble, *It seemeth good to us and our council*. If we consider the magnificent and elegant manner in which the Venetian and other Italian noblemen then lived, with the progress made by the Italians in literature and the fine arts, we shall not wonder that they considered the ultramountaine nations as barbarous. The Flemish also seem to have much excelled the English and even the French. Yet the earl is sometimes not deficient in generosity; He pays, for instance, an annual pension of a groat a year to my lady of Walsingham, for her interest in Heaven; the same sum to the holy blood at Hales, p. 337. No mention is any where made of plate; but only of the hiring of pewter vessels. The servants seem all to have bought their own cloaths from their wages.

* In another place mention is made of four cooks, p. 388. But I suppose that the two servants, called, in p. 315, groom of the larder and child of the scullery, are, in p. 388, comprehended in the number of cooks.

END OF THE THIRD VOLUME.

www.ingramcontent.com/pod-product-compliance
Lightning Source LLC
Chambersburg PA
CBHW022105300426
44117CB00007B/595